Modern Perspectives on Entrepreneurship

Modern Perspectives on Entrepreneurship

Andrew E. Burke

Senate Hall Academic Publishing

Dublin

Published by Senate Hall Academic Publishing Ltd.

ISBN: 978-0-9546673-1-3

Modern Perspectives on Entrepreneurship

CONTENTS

Managing Growth

Entrepreneurial Finance

Technology and Entrepreneurship

Public Policy

Modern Perspectives on Entrepreneurship: Introduction

Andrew Burke
Cranfield University School of Management

Introduction

The aim of this book is to provide a compilation of the latest thinking on entrepreneurship by some of the leading international researchers in university business schools and departments of economics. It is primarily intended as either a partner book for the vast number of entrepreneurship textbooks which despite their titles are usually focused on aspects of small business management rather than the entrepreneurial process *per se*. This book is intended to bring the entrepreneurial dimension. It is also intended as a stand alone book for entrepreneurs, policy makers, lecturers, students and researchers who value a single accessible book which provides a series of articles containing surveys and perspectives on the latest advances in entrepreneurial thought.

Entrepreneurship has developed enormously as a field of research over the last 20 years but much of this advance in knowledge has yet to permeate its way into university entrepreneurship education programmes; particularly MBA courses. While most university textbooks and courses dealing with entrepreneurship provide a good foundation in terms of some of the fundamentals of small business management, few address the more challenging complexities of entrepreneurship. It is true to say that most business start-ups are not very entrepreneurial and involve mainly imitative low growth potential businesses, and for students who aspire to launch such ventures a small business management course which largely ignores the complexities of entrepreneurship may be entirely satisfactory. But the converse is not true. High risk/growth potential new ventures require a much more deep and analytically rigorous toolkit. Trying to serve this market with a traditional generic small business management course risks leaving students both unprepared and unaware of the real challenges associated with entrepreneurial ventures.

The *International Journal of Entrepreneurship Education (IJEE)* was established to fill this gap. The Journal acts as a medium between the pure research journals (which rightly produce narrowly focused research papers) and the textbook market. It encourages the leading entrepreneurship analysts to provide surveys and perspectives on advances in entrepreneurial thought in their area. Therefore, it provides a rapid and rigorous means of disseminating the latest research to lecturers, students and practitioners in an accessible and contextualized manner. It also provides an outlet for peer reviewed case studies which provide insights into the entrepreneurial process within firms and markets.

Since its foundation in 2002 the IJEE has been able to publish articles which provide the entrepreneurial dimension to small business management. The IJEE has led to the establishment of similar education journals in fields such as finance, strategy, leadership and business ethics.

This edited volume provides a selection of articles drawn from these journals. It is not the 'best of' or a 'greatest hits' compilation but rather an attempt to cover a wide remit of topics that are relevant to modern entrepreneurs. These include areas such as building a strategy under uncertainty, finance gaps, venture capital, network externalities, business shakeouts, dynamic minimum efficient scale, over optimism among entrepreneurs, asymmetric information, university spin out ventures to name just a few issues dealt with in the book. However, in order to put these and other contributions in context we first provide an overview of some of the core concerns for modern entrepreneurial new ventures. In figure 1 opposite a framework is provided to assist with the evaluation of an entrepreneurial venture and to develop a strategy. The term viability is used to refer to a firm's potential to create sustainable profits. The aim of figure 1 is to break down the various determinants of new venture viability into their component parts. In so doing, it is apparent that an assessment of a firm's viability also forms the basic structure (although not necessarily the content) of most university entrepreneurship courses. Moreover, figure 1 provides a framework with which to assess new venture viability by highlighting the various components that determine new venture viability. Thus, it can be used as an analytic guide to this end. The purpose is not just to undertake the relatively easy task of identifying problems or flaws in the venture but importantly to challenge the user to be entrepreneurial and try to enhance/alter the strategy of the venture so that it has a better chance of being viable.

The flow of figure 1 is from top to bottom. In order to use it effectively we need to put ourselves in the position of an entrepreneur who is developing an idea for a new venture. This allows us to analyse the venture from both a critical and creative perspective – identifying risks and problems but also attempting to develop a strategy which maximises the performance of the venture given these challenges. So starting at the top of the diagram, let us suppose that we have an idea for a business venture and we want to assess its viability. We need to investigate the idea from a long term perspective in order to see how far into the future it is likely to generate sustainable profits. Thus, we need to think beyond a quick short term snapshot of the market as it stands today which may indeed show a market gap but which has not yet factored in likely imitation and entry by other innovative firms. As we know from research, entrepreneurial markets are characterised by turbulence with firm entry and exit as well as changes in the distribution of market share across businesses. Very few markets remain static and hence snapshots of the market at one point in time are not likely to provide an accurate picture of the market for very long. Thus, we aim to form an assessment of how a market will develop basing our judgement on the best available information and the most appropriate analytical techniques which can give an insight into the dynamics of the market.

Figure 1: A framework to assess venture viability and develop an entrepreneurial strategic vision

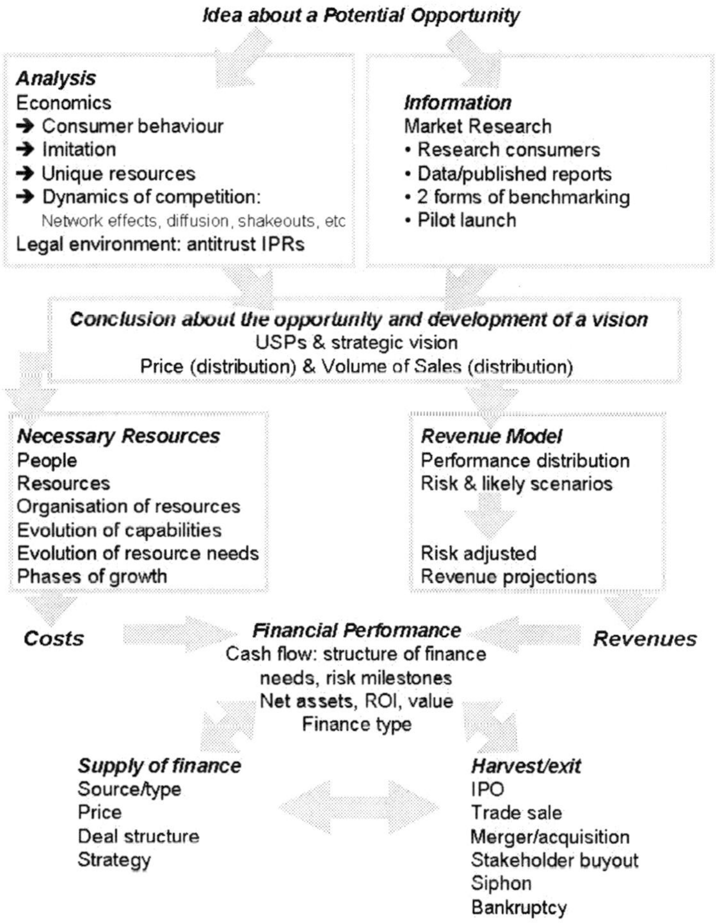

Idea about a Potential Opportunity

Analysis
Economics
➔ Consumer behaviour
➔ Imitation
➔ Unique resources
➔ Dynamics of competition:
Network effects, diffusion, shakeouts, etc
Legal environment: antitrust IPRs

Information
Market Research
• Research consumers
• Data/published reports
• 2 forms of benchmarking
• Pilot launch

Conclusion about the opportunity and development of a vision
USPs & strategic vision
Price (distribution) & Volume of Sales (distribution)

Necessary Resources
People
Resources
Organisation of resources
Evolution of capabilities
Evolution of resource needs
Phases of growth

Revenue Model
Performance distribution
Risk & likely scenarios
Risk adjusted
Revenue projections

Costs

Financial Performance
Cash flow: structure of finance needs, risk milestones
Net assets, ROI, value
Finance type

Revenues

Supply of finance
Source/type
Price
Deal structure
Strategy

Harvest/exit
IPO
Trade sale
Merger/acquisition
Stakeholder buyout
Siphon
Bankruptcy

Thus, the first part of figure 1 recommends two tasks. The first is to do some research to acquire more detailed information about the business idea. We need to find out if it has already been done and if there is still room for another provider in the market. Perhaps we can find a market or geographic niche where the idea has not been tried. If the idea has already been tried in some form we need to know how well it has fared. If we are prospective entrepreneurs, we can use the experience (observe the history) of these other firms to gauge likely prices and sales volumes. We can also use them to ascertain which features of the product or service are really generating sales i.e. the unique selling points (USPs). But an entrepreneurial idea will usually entail some differences and hence it makes sense for us to talk to target consumers in order to assess their likely response to our unique product offering. Even if there is not going to be much difference between our new venture and incumbents we still need to know if consumers would view us as the same. Alternatively if we are copying an idea but bringing it to a new region then we need to ascertain whether these consumers will react in the same way as those in the core market areas of incumbent firms. Overall, good market information is necessary in order to expose our idea to an element of reality. We can use this information to get an idea of which USPs we will need in order to be able to deliver as well as getting an assessment of feasible prices and sales volumes. In addition, we may want to pilot our product or service by trying to sell it on a small scale to a segment of the market. This works particularly well when it is possible to pitch for sales without having to incur the full costs of supplying sales or indeed scaling up the firm to a full trading size. Thus, for example, making a sales pitch to a few corporations by demonstrating a single prototype of the product, or attempting to sell tickets in advance of providing the service (e.g. holiday, concert, or training programme). The key benefit of piloting a product/ service is that we get real market feedback without incurring the full risks of the venture. The information generated allows us to more accurately assess potential, innovate further before marketing the product to the full market and perhaps get cheaper finance if the pilot consumer response is positive; thereby reducing the market and technology risks associated with the venture.

But we know that market demands don't remain fixed, firms will react to our market entry and if there is money to be made with our idea then other people will be seeking to exploit it too. Thus, we need to superimpose a layer of analysis onto the information we have gathered above in order to gain an understanding of how the competitive process will work. So we have to work out the economics of the market. This will, of course, tell us the extent to which firms compete on prices and USPs. But we need to know the extent to which these change over time. Therefore, we must assess the dynamics of the market. This involves looking at entry and exit of new firms and also assessing how market share changes. It also means looking at product entry and exit as well as changes in product market share. A highly dynamic market may reduce the length of time over which we can expect to make sustainable profits with our idea and require us to assess whether our venture will be able to undertake additional rounds of innovation in the future in order to keep pace with the evolution of the market.

At this point we are in a position to determine the revenue projections having identified likely prices and sales volumes (revenues = prices multiplied by unit sales volumes). But it also puts us in a position to consider the range of variation which these sales forecasts might be subject. By putting the market information and analysis together we get a view of the dynamic environment in which the firm is likely to enter. This also signals a range of possible scenarios relating to situations in which the firm might find itself e.g. rapid market acceptance and growth, or consumer disinterest, or stiff competition, or encountering unexpected entrants etc. Each of these scenarios will reflect different revenue projections. In turn, they can be used to form the basis of a sensitivity or scenario analysis as part of a risk assessment exercise. This is represented by the middle right hand panel of figure 1.

However, the analysis of the opportunity is not only about deriving revenue projections. It is also aimed to give a realistic assessment of the USPs which will define successful firms in the market. The key challenge for the lead entrepreneurs is to then choose and manage the resources which will most effectively deliver these USPs. Again the information and analysis of the market makes a key contribution here. It should provide a more rich and deep understanding of the market environment and hence start to indicate likely evolutionary performance and strategic paths which the venture might follow. Therefore, at this point the lead entrepreneurs start to move from a basic idea about a product for a market gap to having a distinct vision of the likely future development path of the venture. They can now start to visualise the venture in more detail and consider how it is likely to evolve and respond to situations. Thus, movement from an idea which may start embedded in vagueness and generalities begins to evolve to a strategic vision where detail and specifics play a major role in defining the resources that will be needed to exploit the opportunity. Thus, this detail alongside the identification of feasible pricing and USPs defines how the company will be run.

This is represented in the left hand middle panel of figure 1 which outlines all the resources which the firm needs to harness in order to realise its vision and supply the market gap. These then define the costs that will form part of the financial analysis. A clear vision of the evolution of the venture plays a key role in being able to be specific about which resources are going to be required and when they will be needed. Thus, they will encompass changes in the management, organizational structure and operations of the venture as it develops/grows. Thus, month by month costs can be identified in order to arrive at a clear indication of financial outgoings. As with the case of the revenues, being aware of likely scenarios (e.g. the need to offer more to consumers in order to compete with competitors, or losing a key supplier etc) allows these to be represented in separate spreadsheets so that a risk/sensitivity analyses can be carried out which mirror likely real situations rather than simple 'finger flicks' adjusting revenues and costs in a spreadsheet by fixed percentages.

At this point we can now move to the lower part of figure 1 where we combine the revenue and cost projections in the various scenarios in order to arrive at cash flow and a profit and loss account. The cash flow defines the financial needs of the venture, namely to ensure that the firm can ensure a positive cash flow. The various scenarios define variations in cash flow and hence start to indicate likely contingency needs in terms of financing. The cash flow also gives an indication regarding the feasibility of loan finance. Specifically, the extent to which a term loan can be repaid out of anticipated future positive cash flow – again bearing in mind likely scenarios and worst case scenarios in particular.

The revenue and cost data allow us to value the business using present discounted value of free cash flows. They also allow us to create profit and loss accounts and hence value the business using earnings multiples. These values can then be used to price equity finance in terms of percentage ownership offered for each $1 invested in the firm. The scenario analysis can also draw attention to opportunities to stage finance around key points in time – usually relating to key performance milestones and/or expenditure clusters. Correspondingly, they allow us to identify risk milestones and hence to gauge the cost of equity finance at various stages of the venture's development. Thus, the financial performance of the company not only provides useful information for the lead entrepreneurs in terms of assessing the viability of the venture but also indicates how much and what type of finance is feasible for the venture. Once we know what type of finance is available we can identify the various exit strategies that must be put in place in order to ensure that financiers can acquire an adequate return on their finance given the risks. In the case of loan finance, this involves defining the date interest payments will occur and the time of repayment of the principle. In the case of equity finance, it involves being able to deliver a tangible exit for investors which is usually in the form of a trade sale, financial market flotation or management buy out/in. These considerations form the lower panel of figure 1.

In its entirety, figure 1 comprises a whole range of activities and judgemental decisions which constitute successful entrepreneurship i.e. viable venturing. It has a logical flow which indicates that it makes sense to start by analysing the business opportunity and then to move on to consider how to manage and ultimately finance a new business venture. If one is to effectively use the framework then it demands the user to be an analytic jack of all trades. The framework requires expertise in multiple disciplines including economics, strategy and marketing in the top panel to organisational behaviour, psychology and operations management in the left hand middle panel, through to finance and accounting in the lower panel. However, it demands even more than this as the framework operates like a circulatory system where the different parts interact with one another. Therefore, for example, in a new entrepreneurial market with network externalities it requires the user to have sufficient competence in economics in order to identify likely market evolution paths and then use this to formulate a strategy. These in turn feed into the identification of scenarios with associated assumptions regarding prices and sales volumes which must be then imbedded in financial analysis. Furthermore, the approach requires different methodological approaches within each discipline encompassing both qualitative and quantitative, theoretical and empirical analytical techniques.

Any rigorous analysis must be grounded in theory and it is necessary to quantify its implications. However, an overemphasis of quantification often hides important dynamics which are aggregated out of the picture through the tendency for data to be based on totals. The implications of all of this for entrepreneurship education are stark. We cannot hide within our favoured discipline or methodological approach as doing so will cause us to neglect key components of the framework. It will cause us to undertake incomplete analysis and strategy development of an entrepreneurial idea. As a result, we will pretend or perhaps unwittingly lead students to believe that if an area of concern for a new venture falls outside of the area of expertise being emphasised on the course that then it does not matter. Since most university academics or adjunct professors are specialists by nature, the framework highlights a need for lecturers/professors to have a wide knowledge of disciplines and methodologies outside of the core expertise (derived from their doctorate/research and career history). It is fairly obvious that a good entrepreneurship department in a university should have expertise across disciplines and methodologies but this does not compensate for the need for these educators to be able to converse, interact and analyse across these boundaries. Right from the earliest days of entrepreneurial thought entrepreneurs have been dubbed as 'jacks of all trades' and the lessons we now impart is that entrepreneurship education needs to be able to deliver expertise in all of these trades in order to produce well rounded, competent and realistic entrepreneurs.

The chapters in this volume reflect this diversity and contain articles in disciplines as diverse as economics, strategy, finance and organisational behaviour. They also reflect a wide remit of methodological approaches including theory, case studies, econometrics and statistical analysis. The articles are written to communicate with readers who intend to use them in this cross discipline/methodological manner but do not seek to dumb down or oversimplify entrepreneurship. Of course, they are accessible as they need to be from a student's perspective, but they seek to inspire the reader to rise to the analytical challenge rather than pander to the lazy who require often trite and inevitably simplistic, unrealistic explanations of entrepreneurial performance.

The chapters in the book are broadly organised to reflect the flow and methodological approach outlined in figure 1 (the last two topics relate to articles that involve the entire framework). They cover a number of broad areas including the emergence of entrepreneurial economies, entrepreneurial markets, strategies for new ventures, managing growing ventures, finance for new and fast growth businesses, university spin out ventures and public policy impact on entrepreneurship. The topic areas and articles within them do not cover every aspect one would like but reflect progress so far in terms of the peer reviewed articles/cases published in the *International Journal of Entrepreneurship Education* and related education journals. Over time as these journals develop the plan is to update this volume in order to accommodate these new publications. However, sufficient progress has been made so far to prompt the launch of this book. In part, it is intended as an accompanying book for the many entrepreneurship textbooks which adequately cover small business management and business planning but lack modern analysis of entrepreneurship. Likewise, the cumulative insights and perspectives offered by the leading international researchers of entrepreneurship who comprise the authorship of this book deserve to be published in a stand alone compilation for use by entrepreneurs, students, researchers, lecturers, consultants and those engaged in public policy in order to have an accessible update on modern analysis of entrepreneurship.

1. The Types and Contextual Fit of Entrepreneurial Processes

Per Davidsson
Brisbane Graduate School of Business at Queensland University of Technology, and the Jönköping International Business School

Abstract. This article argues that unlike the early research findings on individual and environmental characteristics that are conducive of entrepreneurship, the more recent research on entrepreneurship as behaviors in the process of new venture creation holds great promise for educational purposes. Therefore, the purpose of the article is to integrate and expand on some key insights from recent conceptual and empirical work on the entrepreneurial process. While entrepreneurial phenomena are too heterogeneous for recipes on 'one best way' to be developed it is possible to gain systematic knowledge about the fit between the key elements involved in any process of new venture creation. Consequently, this article discusses under what conditions which type of process is more commendable. A model is developed depicting how characteristics of the individual(s), the venture idea and the environment interact with the type of entrepreneurial process in determining the outcomes of that process.

Keywords: process, discovery, exploitation, business planning, effectuation, uncertainty, contingency.

1. The Need For a Process Perspective on Entrepreneurship for Entrepreneurship Education

Early entrepreneurship research devoted almost all its attention to *the entrepreneur*. The implicit or explicit assumption underlying this research was that the explanation for entrepreneurial behavior and success was to be found in the unique characteristics of the individuals who undertook such endeavors (Brockhaus, 1982; Carland, Hoy, & Carland, 1988; Delmar, 2000; Stanworth, Blythe, Granger, & Stanworth, 1989). This line of research, had it been successful, held little promise for entrepreneurship education. The best one could hope for was perhaps a selection mechanism for advising students: "You're the right stuff; good for you!" vs. "Sorry, I think you should try some other career instead."

However, while some valid generalizations can be made concerning the average psychological and socio-demographic characteristics of business founders compared to other groups, the main take away from this research is that on the whole, business founders seem to be as heterogeneous as any other group of people. It is not possible to profile the "typical" entrepreneur. No psychological or sociological characteristics have been found, which predict with high accuracy that someone will become an entrepreneur or excel at entrepreneurship. Likewise, no such characteristics have been distilled that definitely exclude people from a successful entrepreneurial career. For two different reasons this is actually a very

This article was originally published in the International Journal of Entrepreneurship Education 2(4): pp. 407-430.

positive result for entrepreneurship education. First, the fact that entrepreneurial tendencies are not inborn suggests that the idea of trying to teach entrepreneurship is not futile. Second, it is of direct inspirational value in the entrepreneurship education context to be able to say that the research-based evidence suggests that faced with an opportunity that suits them, and in interaction with other people with complementary skills, most people would be able to pursue a successful career as entrepreneurs.

Partly as a reaction to the disappointingly weak results in individual-level research, researchers in the 1990's increasingly turned "from traits to rates" (Aldrich & Wiedenmayer, 1993). That is, the reasons for differences in entrepreneurial activity on aggregate levels were sought among the structural and cultural characteristics of nations, regions, industries, science parks, or organizations (Acs & Audretsch, 1990; Acs, Carlsson, & Karlsson, 1999; Braunerhjelm, Carlsson, Cetindamar, & Johansson, 2000; Davidsson & Henreksson, 2002; Reynolds, Bygrave, & Autio, 2003; Reynolds, Storey, & Westhead, 1994; Stevenson, 1984; Stevenson & Jarillo, 1990; Zahra, 1993; Zahra, 1993). This approach has been relatively more successful. For example, when researchers in six European countries and the US set out to study what regional characteristics lead to higher frequencies of new business start-ups, it was found that around 70 percent of the regional variation in start-up rates could be explained by a few structural factors (Reynolds et al, 1994)

This type of knowledge may be very valuable for policy-making purposes or – as regards the corporate entrepreneurship literature – for managers of large, established firms. However, these insights are of relatively limited value for giving advice to students or other people who are about to set up their own businesses, and who want to do so where they happen to live, whatever the general attractiveness of that place might be. For example, learning that Jukkasjärvi (a small and remote community up in the far north of Sweden) is a very unfavorable place for entrepreneurship would not have provided Yngve Bergkvist with the inspiration or knowledge necessary to create the highly successful *Ice Hotel* (see www.icehotel.com), which is an excellent example of turning the existing environmental conditions, whatever they may be, into advantages. Neither would attempting to establish the Ice Hotel in Silicon Valley or some other entrepreneurship hot spot be a very bright idea.

Thus, what aspiring entrepreneurs need to learn is not so much what kind of person they ought to be, because that does not seem to be critically important in itself and could not easily be changed even if it were. Neither are they much helped by knowledge about what kind of environments are conducive of business start-ups in general, because in most cases people choose the place they live in for other reasons and because these generally favorably conditions may be totally irrelevant for the particular kind of business a particular aspiring entrepreneur is considering. A much more fruitful line of research for education purposes concerns *how* to do it, i.e., entrepreneurial behavior (Gartner, 1988). Further, a new business does not go from non-existence to existence in one step, as the result of a single behavior. Rather, entrepreneurship involves a number of behaviors entrepreneurs have to perform sequentially over time. This calls for a *process* view of entrepreneurship.

The purpose of this article is to highlight and discuss some key insights from recent conceptual and empirical work on the entrepreneurial process. After first defining the key term "entrepreneurship", the next subsection will deepen the conceptualization of the entrepreneurial process and its two sub-processes, *discovery* and *exploitation*. The then following section will deal with two previously suggested categorizations of different types of processes, namely Bhave's (1994) distinction between internally and externally triggered processes and Sarasvathy's (2001) contrasting of causation vs. effectuation. It seems indisputable that these different types of processes are descriptively valid, i.e., real world entrepreneurs actually use them. For the purpose of entrepreneurial education, however, we need normatively valid results. The empirical co-existence of different process types makes it a plausible assumption that their applicability is contingent on the context. While no systematic "acid test" of the relative performance of the processes discussed by Bhave and Sarasvathy has been made, it is possible to use theoretical deduction and various empirical results to arrive at conclusions about under what conditions which type of process is more commendable. Therefore, the second half of this article will develop a model of how characteristics of the individual(s), the venture idea and the environment interact with the type of entrepreneurial process in determining the outcomes of the process.

2. Entrepreneurship and Entrepreneurial Process Defined

As different researchers and other authors who write on this topic tend to assign many different meanings to the term "entrepreneurship", let us first make clear that it is here defined as *the creation of economic activity that is new to the market* (see Davidsson, 2003, 2004, for an elaborate background on entrepreneurship definitions and rationales for this particular one). This includes the launching of product, service or business model innovations, but also imitative entry, i.e., the appearance of a new competitor, as this also gives buyers new choice alternatives and hence pose a threat to incumbent firms. This entrepreneurship concept thus includes all independent business start-ups, imitative as well as innovative. The definition includes more, namely established firms' introduction of product and service innovations, as well as their expansion into new markets. Although "independent" as well as "corporate" entrepreneurship are acknowledged, relatively more weight will in the exposition below be given to entrepreneurship understood as the start-up of new, independent businesses.

By *entrepreneurial process* is meant all cognitive and behavioral steps from the initial conception of a rough business idea, or first behavior towards the realization of a new business activity, until the process is either terminated or has lead to an up and running business venture with regular sales. Due to the extreme variability across cases a more precise definition of the start- and end-points than this is arguably not possible (cf. Klofsten, 1994; Shaver, Carter, Gartner, & Reynolds, 2001) and for our current purposes it is hardly necessary. To give an idea of what specific steps may be involved Table A1 (appendix) displays 48 steps regarding 23 different "gestation behaviors" included in the *Panel Study on Entrepreneurial Dynamics* (Davidsson & Honig, 2003; Gartner & Carter, 2003; Gartner, Shaver, Carter, & Reynolds, 2004).

Although it may not always be possible to uniquely attribute each step in Table A1 to either of the two, it is conceptually useful to further subdivide the entrepreneurial process into two interrelated sub-processes, discovery and exploitation (Shane & Venkataraman, 2000). *Discovery* refers to the conceptual side of venture development, from an initial idea to a fully developed business concept where many specific aspects of the operation are worked out in great detail. While the term "discovery" may seem to suggest that latent business concepts somehow exist "out there", ready to be discovered, this is not the view purported here. Thus, the term includes not only what is elsewhere called "idea generation", "opportunity identification" and "opportunity detection", but also "opportunity formation", "opportunity development" and "opportunity refinement" (Bhave, 1994; de Koning, 1999, 2003; Gaglio, 1997). Importantly, discovery is in itself a *process* – the venture idea is usually *not* formed as a complete and unchangeable entity at a sudden flash of insight (Davidsson, Hunter, & Klofsten, 2004; de Koning, 1999; Hmieleski & Ensley, 2004). Some key elements of the discovery process are:

- Ideas about *value creation*, i.e., how and for whom value is to be created in terms of product, market, production and organization (cf. Alvarez & Barney, 2004; Klofsten, 1994).

- Ideas about *value appropriation,* i.e., how a significant share of the created value is to be appropriated by the emerging firm rather than by customers, competitors or the Government (Amit & Zott, 2001; de Koning, 1999; McGrath, 2002).

- The development of *commitment* to and identification with the start-up on the part of key actors (Klofsten, 1994).

- Activities such as planning, making projections, and the gathering and analysis of information, to the extent these activities concern the development and evaluation of ideas rather than their (attempted) realization.

Exploitation refers to the action side of venture development. It is in the present context a neutral term, denoting the decision to act upon a perceived opportunity, and the behaviors that are undertaken to achieve its realization. The negative connotations the term "exploitation" has in some other contexts do not apply here. Exploitation thus simply means the attempted realization, or implementation, of ideas. Like discovery, exploitation is a process that may or may not lead to the attainment of profit or other goals. The following categorizations represent a way of trying to make abstracted sense of the many specific behaviors undertaken in the exploitation process (cf. Delmar & Shane, 2004; Sarasvathy, 1999; Shane & Eckhardt, 2003; Van de Ven, 1996):

- Efforts to *legitimize* the start-up, e.g., creating a legal entity; obtaining permits and licenses; developing a prototype of the product, and developing trustful relations with various stakeholders.

- Efforts to *acquire resources,* such as knowledge, financial capital, intellectual property, and various inputs.

- Efforts to *combine and coordinate* these resources through the creation of a functioning organization.

- Efforts to *generate demand* through marketing and contacts with prospective customers.

While all of the above are important, it may be argued that for the long term success of an independent start-up the most critical aspect of the exploitation process is to obtain resources and resource combinations that are *valuable, rare* and *imperfectly imitable* (Barney, 1997), thus providing some "isolating mechanism" (Rumelt, 1984).

It is tempting to think of the entrepreneurial process as linear: first you discover and then you exploit your discovery (cf. Shane, 2003; Shane & Eckhardt, 2003). However, the empirical evidence suggests that the processes of discovery and exploitation are interrelated and that the behaviors in Table A1 can be undertaken in almost any sequence, including having sales before thinking about starting a business (Carter, Gartner, & Reynolds, 1996; Gartner & Carter, 2003). The questions then are: is it possible to bring some order to this mess, i.e., can we identify a limited number of "typical" start-up processes? If so, under what conditions are different process types relatively more suitable? These are the questions to be dealt with in the remainder of this manuscript.

3. Types of Entrepreneurial Processes

Based on close-up study of 27 start-up processes, Bhave (1994) suggested they could be categorized into two main types depending on which came first: the wish to start a business, or the specific business idea that was being pursued. This is illustrated in Figure 1.

Figure 1: Bhave's Two Types of Entrepreneurial Processes (First Stages)

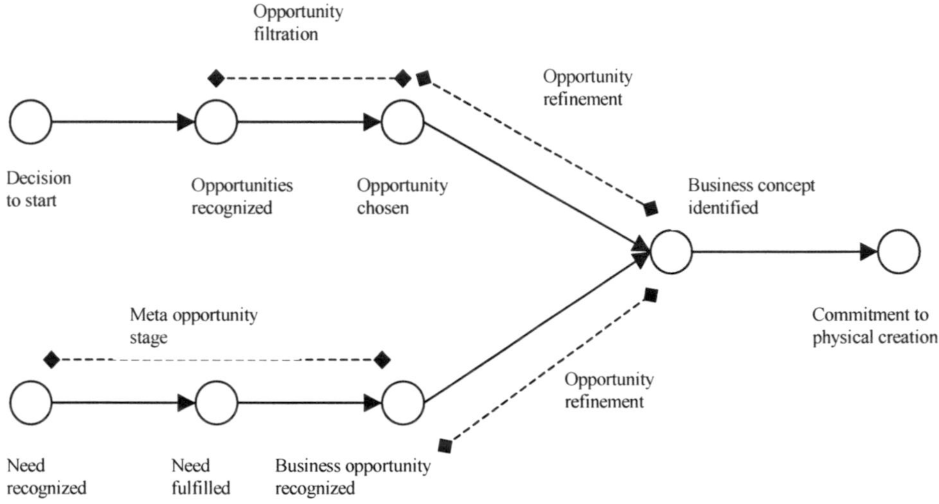

The first type, which Bhave calls "externally stimulated", is the more textbook-like process. It starts with a decision or desire to start a new business. The entrepreneur(s) therefore actively searches for business opportunities. Typically several different preliminary ideas are considered and evaluated ("opportunity filtration") before one is chosen. This preliminary idea is then elaborated and adapted. Finally, a relatively complete business idea that is judged viable has been developed by the entrepreneur, who then commits to "going for it".

The other type of process is less textbook-like, but probably about as common as the first. In this case, the individual has initially no particular intention to start a business. Instead, entrepreneurs involved in this type of process experience a problem related to their work, hobbies, or perhaps in their role as consumers. If they find a solution to the problem they may learn that others also have the same problem, and are willing to pay to get it fixed. Bhave exemplifies how one of the entrepreneurs in his sample started a violin repair business:

> I couldn't find anyone I had enough faith in to repair violins I was playing, so I started repairing myself, and the word got out that I would do that. So I started doing that. After a while it got to be a burden to do it for free, and I started charging people for it. (Bhave, 1994, p. 230)

At some point people involved in this type of process realize that their skill is a business opportunity ("business opportunity identified"), and if demand is high enough they are forced to make a conscious decision whether to "go for it" or not. It is tempting to believe that the latter type of process is typical for part-time or single-person businesses only. This is not the case. For example, Carin Lindahl, the inventor of the sports bra, was a workout and jogging freak in her upper teens. Slender but bosomy, she experienced that no bra on the market provided effective enough support for her breasts when working out. Neither were taping or bandaging convenient and effective solutions to the problem. When she several years later found the solution – a fabric that expanded in one direction while being completely stiff in the other – she sewed herself a couple of sports bras. Seeing the interest other women showed in her bra, and being unable to convince anyone to produce such bras, she decided to found her own firm. Although much larger competitors have captured most of the world market after Carin proved its existence, she still runs *Stay In Place* as a healthy small business, holding a significant share of the Swedish market for sports bras and related products (Davidsson, 2000). Many other firms providing sports- and hobby-related products and services are founded in the same manner.

A more spectacular success story exemplifying an internally stimulated process is the Swedish software company *Hogia AB* (Hogsved, 1996). The origin of this business was that Bert-Inge Hogsved helped his wife, who was a chartered accountant, with some computer programming for a very early PC so that she could get rid of some of the most tedious and repetitive parts of her job. Predictably, some of her colleagues got the word and wanted the same solution. From this humble beginning, Hogia has grown with the computer software market and through related diversification to become a medium- to large-sized business group and one of the most significant players on the Swedish software market.

Figure 1 actually captures only the first part of Bhave's model, which he calls the opportunity stage, similar to what has above been denoted the discovery process. This is followed by *the technology setup & organization stage,* and the *exchange stage.* As these latter stages involve the tangible actions needed for the creation of an organization, a production technology, a product (if that is what the firm is selling) as well as customer contacts and first sales, they coincide with what has above been called the *exploitation process.* Although Bhave calls the different parts of his models "stages" – as if they followed after one another – he is careful to point out that the customer contacts provide feedback that makes the entrepreneur(s) reconsider and adapt the business concept (strategic feedback) as well as the specific ways in which it is being realized (operational feedback).

Thus, there is interplay between discovery and exploitation; in part they evolve in parallel rather than sequentially. According to Bhave's (1994) conceptualization, then, we can distinguish between two types of process. The most important difference between them is that the externally stimulated process begins with a decision to start, and involves the consideration of several different business ideas. The internally stimulated process starts with the recognition and solution of a self-experienced problem, which proves to be the potential basis for a business. In the latter stages the two types of process converge. Both involve further refinement of the original idea to a more fully-fledged business concept, commitment to actually realizing this idea, and the carrying out of this realization. Bhave (1994) does not discuss differences between the two types of process in the latter stages.

Sarasvathy (2001) suggests another – although partly overlapping – division into two types of process. Again, the first variety – the *causation* process – is the more textbook-like of the two. A process that follows the causation logic takes a particular effect (or goal) as given and focuses on selecting the best means to achieve that effect. By contrast, a process that follows the alternative *effectuation* logic takes a set of means as given and focuses on selection between possible effects that can be achieved with these means. Sarasvathy illustrates the difference with two approaches to cooking dinner. If you follow the causation logic, you start by deciding on the menu, which determines what ingredients have to be obtained, and how they should be prepared and combined. If you follow the effectuation logic, you take the ingredients that happen to be available as given, and create whatever menu these ingredients can be used for.

In a business context, the causation model is compatible with the analysis-planning-implementation-control sequence that is implicitly or explicitly professed in most normative accounts of business processes. When applying this type of process, the entrepreneur would first carefully analyze the market and decide on a well-defined business concept. This business concept would then be implemented according to the plan, which is later on followed-up. Deviations between plan and outcome would typically lead to corrective action.

According to Sarasvathy's empirical research on successful entrepreneurs, the above does not adequately describe how they actually behave (Sarasvathy, 1999). Instead of starting from an analysis of the entire potential market, the entrepreneurs typically started out at their home turf by looking at what skills, resources and contacts they had (i.e., Who am I? What do I know? Whom do I know?). Rather than first developing a complete concept, which was then implemented according to plan, the process was typically much more iterative and interactive, and could take off in any new direction as a result of early feedback from customers. That is, their behavior was typically more in line with the inherently iterative and interactive effectuation model. This model is characterized by the following four principles:

1. Focus on affordable loss rather than expected returns. It is more important to limit the damage if unsuccessful, than to get the highest possible return if successful.

2. Strategic alliances rather than competitive analysis. Rather than thinking "Who do I have to beat?" the entrepreneur thinks, "With whom do I have to ally in order to be able to take this business one step further?"

3. Exploitation of contingencies rather than preexisting knowledge. The entrepreneur is sensitive to what comes up along the road, and prepared to turn these contingencies into business strengths.

4. Control of an unpredictable future, rather than prediction of an uncertain one. Causation logic assumes one can predict the future; effectuation logic suggests that if one can create the future one does not have to predict it.

Sarasvathy (2001) gives additional vivid illustration of the two processes with the hypothetical example of a start-up of an Indian fast food restaurant, *Curry in a Hurry.* In the causation model, this start up would begin with careful, formal (and costly) market research concerning in what city and location the restaurant (likely to be regarded the first in a chain) should be established, what type of customers should be targeted, as well as choices of menu, opening hours, décor, etc. All this analysis would lead to a careful plan to guide the launch and further operation, which would then be implemented. An effectuation version of the same start-up would begin, for example, with a person with an interest and skill in cooking Indian food. In order to make a living, this person may start a simple catering operation by talking her way into the lunchrooms of employers of her friends and family. If this start seems promising, it may then develop to a somewhat larger and more structured catering operation supplemented with an Indian fast food corner in rented space at some other, established restaurant. In the next step, a first own restaurant may be established, which then evolves into a chain, probably with the second and third units run by relatives or friends in the cities they happen to live. Importantly, however, the business may also take off in other directions. In Sarasvathy's own words:

> [A]fter a few weeks of trying to build the lunch business she might discover that the people who said they enjoyed her food did not really enjoy it so much as they did her quirky personality and conversation, particularly her rather unusual life perceptions. Our imaginary entrepreneur might now decide to give up the lunch business and start writing a book, going on the lecture circuit and eventually building a business in the motivational consulting industry! (Sarasvathy, 2001, p. 247)

Sarasvathy also describes several other directions this start-up could slide into. The point is that the original idea does not imply any one single strategic alternative. If whatever happens along the route suggests the given means can be used more effectively by pursuing some other (related) idea, the entrepreneur will and should do so.

4. Is There a "Best Process"?

It should be pointed out that the two pairs of contrasted process types above probably represent endpoints on continua. Most start-up processes in the real world are likely to fall somewhere in-between and display a mix of behaviors across the prototypical ideals. Further, the contrasted types of process reflect a tension between the *planned, analytical and linear* on the on hand, and the *emergent, creative and iterative* on the other. This leads to the question: Is one type of process generally recommendable over the other(s)?

Neither Bhave's nor Sarasvathy's process types have so far been put to an acid test as regards the outcomes they lead to, so any evidence on the matter is tentative and/or indirect at best. Bhave (1994) does not speculate about the relative merits of the two processes he identifies. However, it may be argued that Bhave's "internally stimulated" process has two distinctive disadvantages, namely questionable commitment to entrepreneurship on the part of the individual, and consideration of but one business opportunity rather than choosing the most promising out of several. These may or may not be outweighed by the advantage that there is by definition a strong link between the business concept and the specific skills and interests of the entrepreneur(s). Other research has indicated that this fit between person and idea (or "opportunity") is very important (Shane, 2000). Another advantage is that there is proof of at least some level of demand. In fact, it is in these cases proven demand that makes the entrepreneurs see their "private" problem solutions as business opportunities. Third, because these processes start on a small scale, they typically do not end with a very big crash in those cases when they eventually turn out not to be viable.

Sarasvathy (2001) is careful to point out that the effectuation process, while more descriptively valid in many cases, is not necessarily more normatively valid. That is, the effectuation model may sometimes describe better what entrepreneurs do, but this does not prove that they are right in doing so. They might have been more successful with a different approach. However, the fact that the effectuation model is derived on the behavior of highly successful entrepreneurs indicates it has some normative merit. As Sarasvathy's conceptualization overlaps with Bhave's the specific potential advantages are largely the same as those just described: fit with person, proven demand (before big investments), and limited damages if the effort fails.

The systematic empirical evidence that is available does not present a direct test of the process types described above, but it does cast light on planned, analytical and linear vs. emergent, creative and iterative. Delmar and Shane (2003b) interviewed 17 Swedish "expert entrepreneurs" about what they thought was the proper sequencing of start-up activities. The resulting "average" sequence is displayed below.

1. To write a business plan
2. To gather information about customers
3. To talk to customers
4. To project financial statements
5. To establish legal entity
6. To obtain permits and licenses (sig. diff. from 1)
7. To secure intellectual property (ditto 1, 5)
8. To seek financing (ditto 1, 3, 4, 5)
9. To initiate marketing (ditto 1-5)
10. To acquire inputs (ditto 1-5)

While the differences are small for the first five behaviors, we can at least conclude that the experts hold that planning should be done before the five activities at the bottom of the list. Overall, the sequencing seems more in line with a planned, analytical and linear process than with the alternative. Further, when testing the sequencing suggested by the experts on the data from the Swedish version of the *Panel Study on Entrepreneurial Dynamics,* Delmar and Shane (2003b) could confirm that start-ups that adhered to this pattern were more likely to be successful. Based on a slightly different analysis of the same data the same authors have suggested that early planning specifically increases the probability of success (Delmar & Shane, 2003a).

Further support for a systematic rather than emergent approach can be found in research focusing specifically on the discovery process. Fiet and Migliore (2001) established that students following a systematic search strategy within a consideration set made more and better discoveries than those who merely tried to stay alert to business opportunities. In the context of internal venturing in young, owner-managed firms, Chandler, Dahlqvist, and Davidsson (2003) found that initiatives discovered through proactive search were implemented more rapidly than those discovered through reactive search or fortuitous discovery.

After 18 months there was no significant difference in survival, but initiatives discovered through proactive search had achieved significantly higher levels of sales and returns than the other two groups.

However, although Delmar and Shane's is arguable the most comprehensive effort to date to test the sequencing of the process on a representative sample their research is not without limitations. Their sample of experts was very limited and so is therefore the generalizability of their favored sequence. Feedback loops and later adaptations of earlier behaviors cannot be captured by the design they used. In addition, their sample of start-ups was dominated by imitative rather than innovative ventures (Samuelsson, 2001, 2004), presumably involving less environmental uncertainty. Further, Delmar and Shane's research suggests that advance planning is beneficial, but this does not necessarily mean that sticking to the plan is a good strategy. The business plan has several potential roles or uses:

1. It can be an *analysis tool* used to internally go through the strengths and weaknesses of the venture as well as the threats and opportunities potential customers, competitors and other environmental conditions present.

2. It can be a *communication tool* that explains the logic and goals of the business to other parties, such as banks, venture capital firms, and government agencies that issue required licenses and permits.

3. Writing a plan may increase the entrepreneur(s) own *commitment* to the realization of the project (Cialdini, 1988).

4. Finally, the plan can be used as a blueprint; as a detailed *guide to action.* First you plan; then you do what the plan says.

Delmar and Shane (2004) associate the positive effect they found in their research mainly with the second point, arguing that the existence of a written business plan increases the legitimacy of the new venture in the eyes of others. The plan may make it easier to get customers and investors to accept the business concept – although it may have to undergo radical changes after their initial acceptance. In the light of Bhave's (1994) and Sarasvathy's (1999; 2001) research, the questionable part of the planning emphasis is (blind) use of the plan as guide to action.

Further, based on data very similar to those used by Delmar and Shane, other researchers have arrived at conclusions more skeptic towards the value of extensive early planning (Carter et al., 1996; Honig & Karlsson, 2004; Samuelsson, 2004). Carter et al (1996) interpret their results as suggesting that for success in entrepreneurial endeavors one should engage in tangible and visible start-up behaviors that prove to others as well as to the entrepreneur that s/he is serious about the start-up. They do not see planning as one of those behaviors.

In summary, there seems to be advantages and disadvantages associated with all the process types we have discussed so far. Whether the advantages outweigh the disadvantages or not is likely to depend on the fit between the type of process and the other key factors – the individual(s) and the environment (as discussed above) as well as the characteristics of the business idea ("opportunity"). This brings us to the next section.

5. The Entrepreneurial Process as a Matching Problem

The model in Figure 2 aims at putting the entrepreneurial process into context, and to illustrate how the different components of entrepreneurship – individual(s), environment, idea, and process – interact in determining the performance of entrepreneurial ventures. A main point in the model is that there is no direct effect of process (type) on performance. Instead, it is assumed that the relative success of a particular process approach is contingent upon its fit with characteristics of the individual(s), the venture idea (or "opportunity") and the environment. However, if "it depends" were all we could say not much would have been achieved. Fortunately, logic and empirical bits and pieces from different types of research arguable allow us to reach much farther than that.

Figure 2: How the Components of Entrepreneurship Fit Together

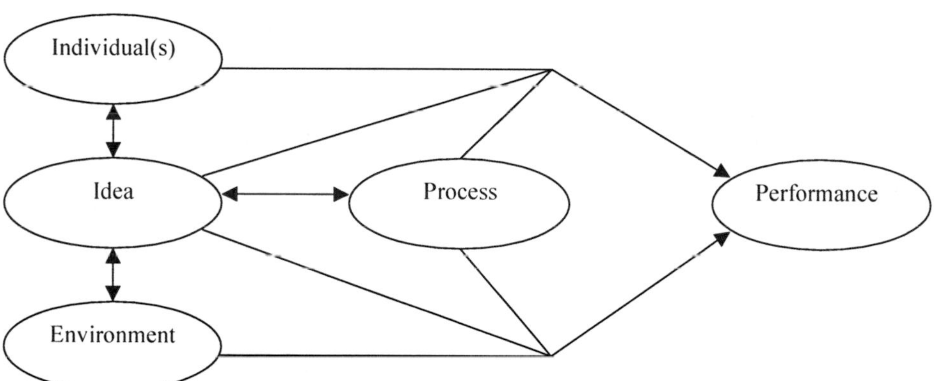

As regards *Individual(s) * Idea * Process* the literature strongly suggests that prospective entrepreneurs look not for business opportunities with maximum commercial potential for any entrepreneur, but for ideas where they can leverage their own unique interests and skills. This has been pointed out by influential authors who base their conclusions mainly on close-up familiarity with entrepreneurship practice (Vesper, 1991; Timmons, 1999) and recurs in systematic empirical research. Shane (2000) compellingly demonstrated that different ventures based on the same basic innovation had vastly different commercial potential – but also that on the basis of prior knowledge each team possessed an ability to discover and/or exploit their particular idea but none of the others. Bhave's (1994) "internally stimulated" process and Sarasvathy's (2001) "effectuation" both emphasize or imply fit between person and idea. While in many cases ideas leading to such processes were more or less stumbled over there is no strong empirical basis in the literature for suggesting that systematic search would not be possible, i.e., as regards fortuitous discovery one should not equate empirical ubiquity with normative validity. We noted above that Fiet's research (Fiet, 2002; Fiet & Migliore, 2001) showed more success for those who searched systematically within their idiosyncratic "consideration sets" (or "opportunity spaces"). Somewhat egocentric systematic search, then, seems to be the general recommendation that emerges from the literature as far as discovery goes (cf. Chandler et al, 2003; Dahlqvist et al, 2004).

When it comes to the exploitation process additional considerations complicate the picture. Gustafsson (2004), who derived her hypotheses from progress made within cognitive psychology, did not consider process explicitly in her design, but she tested one important aspect of how individual differences, namely expert vs. novice status, interacts with characteristics of the venture idea. Theory suggests – and Gustafsson's results largely confirm – that expert entrepreneurs will be able to alternate between analytical, heuristics-based and intuitive modes of decision making depending on the inherent degree of uncertainty of the task. Because experts display this type of behavior it is also assumed that this pattern of adaptations leads to better results. That part of the theory, however, has not been thoroughly tested in a systematic fashion.

It is here useful to think of low uncertainty ideas as what Sarasvathy, Dew, Velamuri, and Venkataraman (2003) call "opportunity recognition" – a situation where both supply and demand are essentially known; for example an imitative start-up or the opening of yet another outlet in a franchising chain. The other extreme is exemplified by what Sarasvathy et al (2003) call "opportunity creation" – potential breakthrough ideas for which neither supply nor demand are essentially known. Samuelsson (2001; 2004) has clearly established that the process and its success factors are different for innovative and imitative venture ideas, respectively. Gustafsson's (2004) theory and results suggest an expert entrepreneur would rely on analysis in the low uncertainty type of situation. In the high uncertainty situation the expert would rely on intuitive decision making, presumably implying less of a planned and linear process, because there is not enough reliable information to analyze. This makes sense because under conditions of high uncertainty, the fundamental problem with a planning approach is that there may be many things that cannot be planned in advance as a desk assignment. The most important parts of the analysis may not be possible to carry out until one has received feedback from customers, and potential competitors' possible countermoves may make retaining flexibility more important than collecting and analyzing all available information in advance.

To complete the picture we should note that in medium uncertainty situations the expert may prefer a heuristics-based mode of making decisions. Further, it should be noted that "intuition" here does not imply some mystical, inborn quality but is based on the experts' experience, although the experts themselves may not be able to account for exactly on what basis they arrive at their decisions.

Characteristic for novices is that they are not able to discriminate between situations and therefore apply the same analytical or heuristics-based approach regardless of the degree of uncertainty involved. One conclusion that emerges from this is that expert entrepreneurs can engage themselves in any type of venture idea and rely on their ability to adapt the way the approach its realization to what the situation calls for. As regards novices one could of course try to teach them to adapt their behavior in a similar way. The problem is that they do not have the experience it takes to make sound, intuitive decisions. Therefore the inescapable conclusion seems to be that novices should go for low uncertainty ideas and implement them in a planned and orderly fashion, so as to make use of the analytical approach that is within reach for them. This means avoiding attempts to succeed with radically innovative ideas until they have gained more experience as entrepreneurs. If, however, that is the nature of the idea they are considering the advice would be to seek the alliance of more experienced partners and let them navigate through the process in the hope of getting a substantial fraction of a success rather than sole ownership of a failure.

Disregarding individual differences for a moment there are additional *Idea * Process* interactions, based on logical reasoning, which deserve some discussion. For example, the more the idea's implementation requires heavy investments to create the very first saleable unit, the less it lends itself to iterative and flexible process. Arguably, this is even more the case if the unit value to the customer is low; if it is very high a prospective customer can be brought in as partner and co-finance the project. For example, while a company like *Starbuck's* can grow organically from very humble beginnings it would not have been possible to start *USA Today* or *Federal Express* as a small business in one city. Sarasvathy's (2001) effectuation strategy is arguable most likely to be successful when short series are economical and value per unit is low. In such situations both producers and customers can afford to experiment without much risk, and that makes it easier for a new actor to get established without much fanfare. When short series are economical while unit value is high a low key, incremental strategy may be difficult to implement successfully because the customer may not want to take the risk of dealing with a small, unknown seller. In addition, if the high unit value also means high margins the incrementally acting start-up may easily be outrun by slower starters that take bolder action. In other words the liabilities of newness and smallness (Aldrich & Auster, 1986) hit harder when the venture idea has these characteristics.

Turning now to the environment we noted early in this article that the idea of the *Ice Hotel* would be unlikely to emerge, and almost certain not to be successfully implemented, in environments characterized by high general levels of entrepreneurial activity and by what is generally thought of as a favorable climate. This demonstrates an *Environment * Idea* interaction that is important to consider both for individual entrepreneurs and for, e.g., policy makers and others engaged in issues of regional development. The importance of fit between idea and individual(s) has been emphasized above, and fit between characteristics of venture ideas and the unique resources of the firm is a central theme in Resource-based Theory (Barney, 1991; Wernerfelt, 1984, 1995). By essentially the same logic, regional development efforts ought to be directed towards identifying and utilizing the region's unique resources.

Our main focus here, however, is on the *Environment * Process* interaction. In line with the uncertainty arguments put forward above it may be assumed that causation processes, planning, and the early carving out of a narrowly defined business idea are relatively less commendable practices in dynamic and uncertain environments. In line with this reasoning, praise of improvisation, learning-by-doing, etc., is frequent in the literatures on dynamic capabilities and organizational learning (see Zahra, Sapienza, & Davidsson, forthcoming). A recent example of research within the entrepreneurship domain, which strongly supports the notion that more dynamic environments require incremental and flexible approaches to the process is a study by Hmieleski and Ensley (2004). In fact, their study can be said to capture the entire *Individual * Idea * Environment * Process* package, as they include degree of change of the venture idea (idea/process), proclivity for improvisation (individual/process) and environmental dynamism as their predictors of new venture performance. For our current purposes the most important aspects of their results are the following. First, they found that under conditions of high environmental dynamism a high degree of change of the original business idea lead to performance advantages in terms of sales revenue and growth. Second, proclivity for improvisation likewise led to superior performance under high environmental dynamism. Third, under conditions of low dynamism there was no or negative payoff to improvisation and degree of change of the business idea. Again, then, we find support for the non-existence of a generally preferable approach to the entrepreneurial process, and support for the notion that what really matters is the matching of the process to the characteristics of the idea, the environment and the individual(s).

6. Conclusion

This article has argued that entrepreneurship consists of an array of decisions and actions, and therefore is best conceived of as a behavioral *process* that unfolds over time. Such a perspective is particularly useful for educational purposes. The process can be further subdivided into *discovery* – the idea development – and *exploitation – the* actual behaviors undertaken in order to realize the idea. Importantly, these two sub-processes are best conceived of not as sequential, but parallel and interrelated. The discovery and exploitation processes feed back on one another.

Contrasting pairs of entrepreneurial processes have been discussed above: Bhave's (1994) internally vs. externally stimulated processes and Sarasvathy's (2001) causation and effectuation processes. It is on the basis of current, research-based knowledge not possible to say that one type of process is generally superior to any other. However, it definitely seems to be the case that rationalistic and linear process descriptions often do not match well with what practicing entrepreneurs actually do. There are also indications that they may sometimes be wise in deviating from such models. The most important issues appear to be the *fit* between the process and the other key elements of entrepreneurship: the individual(s), the environment, and the idea. It is reasonable to believe that the higher the degree of uncertainty inherent in the process, the more important it is to take small, trial steps forward at as small a cost as possible, and to remain open to reconsidering the business idea and the way to implement it until a concept that truly works has been found.

For entrepreneurship education the obvious implication of the themes discussed in this article is caution against singular focus on one winning recipe. While the above analysis suggests recommending students to search systematically for ideas related to their prior knowledge, experience and interests is sound advice, no equally general advice can be given as regards the approach to exploitation of ideas. Given the ubiquity of analytical and rationalistic business planning approaches to the teaching of entrepreneurship it is particularly important to emphasize that the entrepreneurial process implied by such an approach is unlikely to be the most successful way to exploit venture ideas with high inherent uncertainty, or to exercise entrepreneurship in highly dynamic environments. Emphasis on the business plan as a blueprint to action is especially questionable; its importance as a communication tool is much less questioned in the literature, if at all.

However, a systematic and planned approach may fit well with the low uncertainty ideas that suit relatively inexperienced prospective entrepreneurs better as first attempts to set up a new economic activity on one's own initiative. Therefore, it is equally important to point out that a singular focus on flexible and improvised ways to implement highly uncertain venture ideas is no more commendable as a general recipe. This may be particularly important to bear in mind when the audience is made up of undergraduate students. In short, what the literature suggest needs to be transferred to students is not a single recipe, but an ability to evaluate venture ideas and environments in order to assess whether systematic and planned process applies, or a more iterative and flexible approach is called for.

For future research the implication is that the design should be more sophisticated than assuming direct, additive and universal effects across heterogeneous samples of ventures. Instead, the design should either explicitly focus on interactions between key variables with respect to outcomes, or concentrate on relatively narrow empirical contexts (e.g., more homogeneous samples of ventures) and restrict the generalizations to that specific type of context. An inspiring example of the former strategy is the Hmieleski and Ensley (2004) study referred to above. As regards the latter strategy the study by Baum and Locke (2004) is an excellent role model.

References:

Acs, Z. J., & Audretsch, D. B. (1990), *Innovation and Small Firms*. Cambridge, MA: MIT Press.

Acs, Z. J., Carlsson, B., & Karlsson, C. (Eds.) (1999), *Entrepreneurship, Small and Medium-sized Enterprises and the Macroeconomy*. Cambridge: Cambridge University Press.

Aldrich, H. E., & Auster, E. R. (1986), "Even dwarfs started small: Liabilities of age and size and their strategic implications", *Research in Organizational Behavior, 8*, 165-198.

Aldrich, H. E., & Wiedenmayer, G. (1993), "From traits to rates: an ecological perspective on organizational foundings". In J. Katz & R. Brockhaus (Eds.), *Advances in Entrepreneurship, Firm Emergence, and Growth* (Vol. 1, pp. 145-196.). Greenwich, CT: JAI Press.

Alvarez, S. A., & Barney, J. B. (2004), "Organizing rent generation and appropriation: Toward a theory of the entrepreneurial firm", *Journal of Business Venturing,* 19(5), 621-636.

Amit, R., & Zott, C. (2001), "Value drivers in e-business", *Strategic Management Journal,* 22, 493-520.

Barney, J. B. (1991), "Firm resources and sustained competitive advantage", *Journal of Management, 17*(1), 99-120.

Barney, J. B. (1997). *Gaining and Sustaining Competitive Advantage*, Menlo Park, CA.: Addison Wesley.

Baum, J. R., & Locke, E. A. (2004), "The relationship of entrepreneurial traits, skill, and motivation to subsequent venture growth", *Journal of Applied Psychology,* 89(4), 587-598

Bhave, M. P. (1994), "A process model of entrepreneurial venture creation", *Journal of Business Venturing,* 9, 223-242.

Braunerhjelm, P., Carlsson, B., Cetindamar, D., & Johansson, D. (2000), "The old and the new: The evolution of polymer and biomedical clusters in Ohio and Sweden", *Journal of Evolutionary Economics,* 10(5), 471-488.

Brockhaus, R. H. (1982), "The psychology of the entrepreneur". In C. A. Kent, D. L. Sexton & K. H. Vesper (Eds.), *Encyclopedia of Entrepreneurship* (pp. 39-71). Englewood Cliffs, NJ: Prentice Hall.

Carland, J. H., Hoy, F., & Carland, J. A. C. (1988), ""Who is an entrepreneur?" is a question worth asking", *American Journal of Small Business,* (Spring, 1988), 33-39.

Carter, N. M., Gartner, W. B., & Reynolds, P. D. (1996), "Exploring start-up event sequences", *Journal of Business Venturing,* 11, 151-166.

Chandler, G. N., Dahlqvist, J., & Davidsson, P. (2003), "Opportunity recognition processes: A taxonomic classification and outcome implications", *Academy of Management Meeting.* Seattle.

Cialdini, R. B. (1988), *Influence: Science & Practice,* Harper Collins Publishers.

Davidsson, P. (2000), "Three cases in opportunity assessment: the Sports Bra, the Solar Mower, and A Decent Cup of Coffee (mimeo)", Brisbane: Queensland University of Technology.

Davidsson, P. (2003), "The domain of entrepreneurship research: Some suggestions". In J. Katz & D. Shepherd (Eds.), *Advances in Entrepreneurship, Firm Emergence and Growth. Cognitive Approaches to Entrepreneurship Research,* (Vol. 6, pp. 315-372), Oxford, UK: Elsevier/JAI Press.

Davidsson, P. (2004), *Researching Entrepreneurship.* New York: Springer.

Davidsson, P., & Henreksson, M. (2002), "Institutional determinants of the prevalence of start-ups and high-growth firms: Evidence from Sweden", *Small Business Economics, 19*(2), 81-104.

Davidsson, P., & Honig, B. (2003), "The role of social and human capital among nascent entrepreneurs", *Journal of Business Venturing,* 18(3), 301-331.

Davidsson, P., Hunter, E., & Klofsten, M. (2004), "The discovery process: External influences on refinement of the venture idea". In W. D. Bygrave et. al (Ed.), *Frontiers of Entreprenurship Research 2004*, Wellesley, MA: Babson College.

de Koning, A. (1999), *Conceptualising Opportunity Formation as a Socio-Cognitive Process*, Doctoral dissertation, Fontainbleau, France: INSEAD.

de Koning, A. (2003), "Opportunity development: a socio-cognitive perspective". In J. Katz & D. Shepherd (Eds.), *Advances in Entrepreneurship, Firm Emergence and Growth. Cognitive Approaches to Entrepreneurship Research,*Vol. 6, pp. 265-314, Oxford, UK: Elsevier/JAI Press.

Delmar, F. (2000), "The psychology of the entrepreneur". In S. Carter & D. Jones-Evans (Eds.), *Enterprise & Small Business: Principles, Practice and Polic,.* (pp. 132-154), Harlow: Financial Times.

Delmar, F., & Shane, S. (2003a), "Does business planning facilitate the development of new ventures?" *Strategic Management Journal,* 24, 1165-1185.

Delmar, F., & Shane, S. (2003b), "Does the order of organizing activities matter for new venture performance?" In P. D. Reynolds et al (Ed.), *Frontiers of Entrepreneurship 2003*, Wellesley, MA.: Babson College.

Delmar, F., & Shane, S. (2004), "Legitimating first: Organizing activities and the survival of new ventures", *Journal of Business Venturing,* 19, 385-410.

Fiet, J. O. (2002), *The Search for Entrepreneurial Discoveries*, Westport, CT.: Quorum Books.

Fiet, J. O., & Migliore, P. J. (2001), "The testing of a model of entrepreneurial discovery by aspiring entrepreneurs". In W. D. Bygrave, E. Autio, C. G. Brush, P. Davidsson, P. G. Green, P. D. Reynolds & H. J. Sapienza (Eds.), *Frontiers of Entrepreneurship Research 2001* (pp. 1-12). Wellesley, MA.

Gaglio, C. M. (1997), "Opportunity identification: Review, critique and suggested research directions". In J. Katz & J. Brockhaus (Eds.), *Advances in Entrepreneurship, Firm Emergence, and Growth,* (Vol. 3, pp. 139-202), Greenwich, CT: JAI Press.

Gartner, W. B. (1988), ""Who is an Entrepreneur?" is the wrong question", *American Small Business Journal,* (Spring), 11-31.

Gartner, W. B., & Carter, N. (2003), "Entrepreneurial behavior and firm organising processes". In Z. J. Acs & D. B. Audretsch (Eds.), *Handbook of Entrepreneurship Research*, Dordrecht, NL: Kluwer.

Gartner, W. B., Shaver, K. G., Carter, N. M., & Reynolds, P. D. (2004), *Handbook of Entrepreneurial Dynamics: The Process of Business Creation*, Thousand Oaks, CA: Sage.

Gustafsson, V. (2004), *Entrepreneurial Decision-Making*, Doctoral dissertation, Jönköping: Jönköping International Business School.

Hmieleski, K. M., & Ensley, M. D. (2004), "An investigation of improvisation as a strategy for exploiting dynamic opportunities". In W. D. Bygrave et al. (Ed.), *Frontiers of Entrepreneurship 2004.* Wellesley, MA: Babson College.

Hogsved, B.-I. (1996), *Klyv företagen! Hogias tillväxtmodell (Split the companies! Hogia's growth model)*, Falun: Ekerlids Förlag.

Honig, B., & Karlsson, T. (2004), "Institutional forces and the written business plan", *Journal of Management,* 30(1), 29-48.

Klofsten, M. (1994), "Technology-based firms: critical aspects of their early development", *Journal of Enterprising Culture,* 2(1), 535-557.

McGrath, R. G. (2002), "Entrepreneurship, small firms and wealth creation: a framework using real options reasoning". In A. Pettigrew, H. Thomas & R. Whittington (Eds.), *Handbook of Strategy and Management* (pp. 299-325). London: Sage.

Reynolds, P. D., Bygrave, W. D., & Autio, E. (2003), *GEM 2003 Global Report*, Kansas, MO: Kauffman Foundation.

Reynolds, P. D., Storey, D. J., & Westhead, P. (1994), "Cross-national comparisons of the variation in new firm formation rates", *Regional Studies*, 28(4), 443-456.

Rumelt, R. (1984), "Toward a strategic theory of the firm". In R. Lamb (Ed.), *Competitive Strategic Management*. Upper Saddle River, NJ: Prentice Hall.

Samuelsson, M. (2001), "Modelling the nascent venture opportunity exploitation process across time". In W. D. Bygrave, E. Autio, C. G. Brush, P. Davidsson, P. G. Green, P. D. Reynolds & H. J. Sapienza (Eds.), *Frontiers of Entrepreneurship Research 2001* (pp. 66-79), Wellesley, MA.

Samuelsson, M. (2004), *Creating New Ventures: A Longitudinal Investigation of the Nascent Venturing Process*, Doctoral dissertation, Jönköping: Jönköping International Business School.

Sarasvathy, S. (1999), "Decision making in the absence of markets: An empirically grounded model of entrepreneurial expertise", School of Business: University of Washington.

Sarasvathy, S. (2001), "Causation and effectuation: towards a theoretical shift from economic inevitability to entrepreneurial contingency", *Academy of Management Review*, 26(2), 243-288.

Sarasvathy, S., Dew, N., Velamuri, R., & Venkataraman, S. (2003), "Three views of entrepreneurial opportunity". In Z. J. Acs & D. B. Audretsch (Eds.), *Handbook of Entrepreneurship Research*. Dordrecht, NL: Kluwer.

Shane, S. (2000), "Prior knowledge and the discovery of entrepreneurial opportunities", *Organization Science*, 11(4), 448-469.

Shane, S. (2003), *A General Theory of Entrepreneurship: The Individual-Opportunity Nexus*, Cheltenham, UK: Edward Elgar.

Shane, S., & Eckhardt, J. (2003), "The individual-opportunity nexus". In Z. J. Acs & D. B. Audretsch (Eds.), *Handbook of Entrepreneurship Research* (pp. 161-194). Dordrecht, NL: Kluwer.

Shane, S., & Venkataraman, S. (2000), "The promise of entrepreneurship as a field of research", *Academy of Management Review*, 25(1), 217-226.

Shaver, K. G., Carter, N. M., Gartner, W. B., & Reynolds, P. D. (2001), "Who is a nascent entrepreneur? Decision rules for identifying and selecting entrepreneurs in the panel study of entrepreneurial dynamics (PSED) [summary]". In W. D. Bygrave, E. Autio, C. G. Brush, P. Davidsson, P. G. Green, P. D. Reynolds & H. J. Sapienza (Eds.), *Frontiers of Entrepreneurship Research 2001* (pp. 122), Wellesley, MA: Babson College.

Stanworth, J., Blythe, S., Granger, B., & Stanworth, C. (1989), "Who becomes an entrepreneur?" *International Small Business Journal*, 8, 11-22.

Stevenson, H. H. (1984), "A perspective of entrepreneurship". In H. H. Stevenson, M. J. Roberts & H. Grousebeck (Eds.), *New Business Venture and the Entrepreneur*, Boston, MA: Harvard Business School.

Stevenson, H. H., & Jarillo, J. C. (1990), "A paradigm of entrepreneurship: Entrepreneurial management", *Strategic Management Journal*, 11, 17-27.

Timmons, J. (1999), *New Venture Creation: Entrepreneurship for the 21st Century*, Boston: Irwin/ McGraw-Hill.

Van de Ven, A. H. (1996), "The business creation journey in different organizational settings", Symposium paper presented at the Academy of Management Meeting, Cincinatti, August 1996.

Wernerfelt, B. (1984), "A resource based view of the firm", *Strategic Management Journal*, 5, 171-180.

Wernerfelt, B. (1995), "The resource-based view of the firm: Ten years after", *Strategic Management Journal*, 16, 171-174.

Vesper, K. H. (1991), "New venture ideas: Do not overlook the experience factor". In W. A. Sahlman & H. H. Stevenson (Eds.), *The Entrepreneurial Venture* (pp. 73-80), Boston: Harvard Business School.

Zahra, S. A. (1993), "A conceptual model of entrepreneurship as firm behavior: A critique and extension", *Entrepreneurship Theory and Practice*, 16(Summer), 5-21.

Zahra, S. A. (1993), "Environment, corporate entrepreneurship, and financial performance: A taxonomic approach", *Journal of Business Venturing*, *8*, 319-340.

Zahra, S. A., Sapienza, H. J., & Davidsson, P. (forthcoming), "Entrepreneurship and the creation of dynamic capabilities", *Journal of Management*.

Table A1: 23 Gestation Behaviors and 48 Gestation Sequence Questions

Gestation Activity	*Question*
1 Business Plan	Have you prepared a business plan?
1 Business Plan	Is your plan written, (includes informally for internal use)?
1 Business Plan	Is your plan written formally for external use?
2 Development of product/service	At what stage of development is the product or service that will be provided to the customers?
3 Development of product/service	Idea or concept
3 Development of product/service	Initial development
3 Development of product/service	Tested on customers
3 Development of product/service	Ready for sale or delivery
4 Marketing	Have you started any marketing or promotional efforts?
4 Patent/copyright	Have you applied for a patent, copyright, or trademark?
4 Patent/copyright	Has the patent, copyright, or trademark been granted?
5 Raw material	Have you purchased any raw materials, inventory, supplies, or components?
6 Equipment	Have you purchased, leased, or rented any major items like equipment, facilities or property?
7 Gathering information	Have you gathered any information to estimate potential sales or revenues, such as sales forecasts or information on competition, customers, and pricing?
7 Gathering information	Have you discussed the company's product or service with any potential customers yet?
8 Finance	Have you asked others or financial institutions for funds?
8 Finance	Has this activity been completed (successfully or not)?
8 Finance	Have you developed projected financial statements such as income and cash flow statements, break-even analysis?
9 Saved money	Have you saved money in order to start this business?
10 Credit with supplier	Have you established credit with a supplier?
11 Household help	Have you arranged childcare or household help to allow yourself time to work on the business?
12 Team organized	Have you organized a team who start the business together?
13 Workforce	Are you presently devoting full time to the business, 35 or more hours per week?
13 Workforce	Do you have any part time employees working for the new company?
13 Workforce	How many employees are working full time for the new company? One?
13 Workforce	How many employees are working full time for the new company? Two?
13 Workforce	How many employees are working full time for the new company? Three or more?
14 Non-owners hired	Have you hired any employees or managers for pay, those that would not share ownership?
15 Education	Have you taken any classes or workshops on starting a business?
15 Education	How many classes or workshops have you taken part in? One only
15 Education	How many classes or workshops have you taken part in? Two only
15 Education	How many classes or workshops have you taken part in? Three or more
16 Contact information	Does the company have its own phone number?
16 Contact information	Does the company have its own mail address?
16 Contact information	Does anyone in the team have a mobile mainly used for the bus?
16 Contact information	Does the company have its own visiting address?
16 Contact information	Does the company have its own fax number?
16 Contact information	Is there an e-mail or internet address for this new business?

Table A1: (continued)

16 Contact information	Has a web page or homepage been established for this business?
17 Support agency contact	Have you contacted any support agency about this start-up?
18Gestation Marketing	Have you started any marketing or promotional efforts?
18 Gestation income	Do the monthly expenses include owner/manager salary in the computation of monthly expenses?
19 Obtained licenses	Has the new business obtained any business licenses or operating permits from any local, county, or state government agencies?
20 Legal form	Has the new business paid any federal social security taxes?
21 Legal form	Has the company received a company tax certificate?
22 Start-up benefits	Have you applied for start-up benefits? (cf. U.K. 'enterprise allowance scheme')
22 Start-up benefits	Has the application (the answer) regarding start up benefits been completed?
23 Tax certificate	Has the new business received a company tax certificate?

2. A Model of the Entrepreneurial Economy

David Audretsch[1]

Indiana University and Max Planck Institute for Research into Economic Systems (Entrepreneurship, Growth and Public Policy Group)

Roy Thurik

Erasmus University and Max Planck Institute for Research into Economic Systems (Entrepreneurship, Growth and Public Policy Group)

Abstract: The present paper deals with the distinction between the models of the managed and entrepreneurial economies. It explains why the model of the entrepreneurial economy may be a better frame of reference than the model of the managed economy in the contemporary, developed economies. This is done by contrasting the most fundamental elements of the managed economy model with those of the entrepreneurial economy model. Building upon Audretsch and Thurik (2000 and 2001), Audretsch, Thurik, Verheul and Wennekers (2002) and Thurik and Verheul (2003), fourteen dimensions are identified as the basis for comparing models of the entrepreneurial and the managed economy.

Keywords: entrepreneurship, innovation, knowledge economy and globalization.

1. Introduction

Robert Solow (1956) was awarded a Nobel Prize for identifying the sources of growth – the factors of capital and labor. These were factors best utilized in large scale production. Throughout the first three-quarters of the last century, the increasing level of transaction costs (Coase, 1937) incurred in large-scale production dictated increasing firm size over time. Certainly, statistical evidence points towards an increasing presence and role of large enterprises in the economy in this period (Caves, 1982; Teece, 1993; Brock and Evans, 1989). This development towards large-scale activity was visible, not just in one country, but in most of the OECD countries. In this same period, the importance of entrepreneurship and small business seemed to be fading. Although it was recognized that the small business sector was in need of protection for both social and political reasons, there were few that made this case on the grounds of economic efficiency.

Romer (1986), Lucas (1988 and 1993) and Krugman (1991) discovered that the traditional production factors of labor and capital are not sufficient in

1. The present paper benefited from a visit by Roy Thurik to Bloomington in the framework of the BRIDGE (Bloomington Rotterdam International Doctoral and Graduate) program in April 2003. Comments by Andrew Burke, Ingrid Verheul and two anonymous referees are gratefully acknowledged.

This article was originally published in the International Journal of Entrepreneurship Education 2(2): 143-166.

explaining growth and that knowledge instead has become the vital factor in endogenous growth models. Knowledge has typically been measured in terms of R&D, human capital and patented inventions (Audretsch and Thurik, 2000 and 2001). Many scholars have predicted that the emergence of knowledge as an important determinant of growth and competitiveness in global markets would render new and small firms even more futile. Conventional wisdom would have predicted increased globalization to present an even more hostile environment to small business (Vernon, 1970). Caves argued that the additional costs of knowledge activity that would be incurred by small businesses in a global economy "*constitute an important reason for expecting that foreign investment will be mainly an activity of large firms*" (Caves, 1982, p. 53). As Chandler (1990, p. 78) concluded: "*to compete globally you have to be big*". Furthermore, Gomes-Casseres (1997, p. 33) observed that "*students of international business have traditionally believed that success in foreign markets required large size*". In a world that became dominated by exporting giant firms, global markets, global products, global players became the focus of interest. Small firms were thought to be at a disadvantage vis-à-vis larger firms because of the fixed costs of learning about foreign environments, communicating at long distances, and negotiating with national governments.

Despite these counteracting forces, entrepreneurship has emerged as the engine of economic and social development throughout the world.[2] The role of entrepreneurship has changed dramatically, fundamentally shifting between what Audretsch and Thurik (2001) introduced as the model of the managed economy and that of the entrepreneurial economy. In particular, Audretsch and Thurik (2001) argue that the model of the managed economy is the political, social and economic response to an economy dictated by the forces of large-scale production, reflecting the predominance of the production factors of capital and (unskilled) labor as the sources of competitive advantage. By contrast, the model of the entrepreneurial economy is the political, social and economic response to an economy dictated not just by the dominance of the production factor of knowledge – which Romer (1990, 1994) and Lucas (1988) identified as replacing the more traditional factors as the source of competitive advantage – but also by a very different, but complementary, factor they had overlooked: entrepreneurship capital, or the capacity to engage in and generate entrepreneurial activity. It is not straightforward that knowledge or R&D always spills over due to its mere existence (Audretsch and Keilbach, 2003).

The purpose of this paper is to discuss the distinction between the models of the managed and entrepreneurial economies and to explain why the model of the entrepreneurial economy may be a better frame of reference than the model of the managed economy when explaining the role of entrepreneurship in the contemporary, developed economies. This is done by contrasting the most

---

2. See Carree and Thurik (2003) for a literature survey spanning different strands.

fundamental elements of the managed economy model with those of the entrepreneurial economy model. Building upon Audretsch and Thurik (2000 and 2001), Audretsch, Thurik, Verheul and Wennekers (2002) and Thurik and Verheul (2003), fourteen dimensions are identified as the basis for comparing models of the entrepreneurial and the managed economy. The common thread throughout these dimensions is the more important role of new and small enterprises in the entrepreneurial economy model (as compared to that of the managed economy). Understanding the distinction between the models of the entrepreneurial and managed economies is vital for entrepreneurship education explaining why the causes and consequences of entrepreneurship differ in the managed and the entrepreneurial economies (Wennekers, Uhlaner and Thurik, 2002; Thurik, Wennekers and Uhlaner, 2002). This suggests that the conditions for, and aspects of, teaching entrepreneurship under the model of the entrepreneurial economy may not be the same as under the managed economy model. While the paradigm prevalent across the management curricula was a response to managing production in the managed economy model, the model of the entrepreneurial economy dictates new approaches.

2. The Era of the Managed Economy

Throughout the first three-quarters of the last century large enterprise was clearly the dominant form of business organization (Schumpeter, 1934). The systematic empirical evidence, gathered from both Europe and North America, documented a sharp decreased in the role of small business in the post-war period. This was the era of mass production when economies of scale seemed to be the decisive factor in dictating efficiency. This was the world described by John Kenneth Galbraith (1956) in his theory of countervailing power, where the power of 'big business' was balanced by that of 'big labor' and 'big government'. This was the era of the man in the gray flannel suit and the organization man, when virtually every major social and economic institution acted to reinforce the stability and predictability needed for mass production (Piore and Sabel, 1984; Chandler, 1977).[3] Stability, continuity and homogeneity were the cornerstones of the managed economy (Audretsch and Thurik, 2001). Large firms dominated this economy. Large corporations in the managed economy are described in *The Economist* (December 22nd, 2001, p. 76): "*They were hierarchical and bureaucratic organizations that where in the business of making long runs of standardized products. They introduced new and improved varieties with predictable regularity; they provided workers with life-time employment; and enjoyed fairly good relations with the giant trade unions*". In organization studies this modernism is referred to as Fordism.[4]

3. See Whyte (1960) and Riesman (1950) for a description of the gray flannel suit and the organization man.

Small firms and entrepreneurship were viewed as a luxury, as something Western countries needed to ensure a decentralization of decision making, obtained only at the cost of efficiency. A generation of scholars, spanning a broad spectrum of academic fields and disciplines, has sought to create insight into the issues surrounding this perceived trade-off between economic efficiency on the one hand and political and economic decentralization on the other (Williamson, 1968). These scholars have produced a large number of studies focusing mainly on three questions: (i) What are the gains to size and large-scale production?, (ii) What are the economic and welfare implications of an oligopolistic market structure, i.e., is economic performance promoted or reduced in an industry with just a handful of large-scale firms?, and (iii) Given the overwhelming evidence that large-scale production and economic concentration is associated with increased efficiency, what are the public policy implications?

This literature has produced a series of stylized facts about the role of small business in the post-war economies of North America and Western Europe:

- *Small businesses were generally less efficient than their larger counterparts.* Studies from the United States in the 1960s and 1970s revealed that small businesses produced at lower levels of efficiency than larger firms (Weiss, 1966, 1964 and Pratten, 1971).

- *Small businesses were characterized by lower levels of employee compensation.* Empirical evidence from both North America and Europe found a systematic and positive relationship between employee compensation and firm size (Brown, Hamilton and Medoff, 1990; Brown and Medoff, 1989).

- *Small businesses were only marginally involved in innovative activity.* Based on R&D measures, small businesses accounted for only a small amount of innovative activity (Chandler, 1990; Scherer, 1991; Acs and Audretsch, 1990; Audretsch, 1995).

- *The relative importance of small businesses was declining over time in both North America and Europe* (Scherer, 1991).

4. Early contributions of organization studies have shown that changes in the external organization affect the type of organization that is successful. For instance, Lawrence and Lorsch (1967) show that the more homogeneous and stable the environment, the more formalized and hierarchical the organization.

3. The Emergence of the Entrepreneurial Economy

Given the painstaking and careful documentation that large-scale production was driving out entrepreneurship, it was particularly startling and seemingly paradoxical when scholars first began to document that – what had seemed like – the inevitable demise of small business, began to reverse itself from the 1970s onwards. Loveman and Sengenberger (1991) and Acs and Audretsch (1993) carried out systematic international analyses examining the re-emergence of small business and entrepreneurship in North America and Europe. Two major findings emerged from these studies. First, the relative importance of small business varies largely across countries, and, secondly, in most European countries and North America the importance of small business increased since the mid-1970s. In the United States the average real GDP per firm increased by nearly two-thirds between 1947 and 1989 – from $150,000 to $245,000 – reflecting a trend towards larger enterprises and a decreasing importance of small firms. However, within the subsequent seven years it had fallen by about 14 percent to $210,000, reflecting a sharp reversal of this trend and the re-emergence of small business (Brock and Evans, 1989). Similarly, small firms accounted for one-fifth of manufacturing sales in the United States in 1976, but by 1986 the sales share of small firms had risen to over one-quarter (Acs and Audretsch, 1993).

The reversal of the trend away from large enterprises towards the re-emergence of small business was not limited to North America. It was also seen in Europe. For example, in the Netherlands the business ownership rate (business owners per workforce) fell during the post-war period, until it reached the lowest point at 8.1 percent in 1984 (Verheul et al., 2002). The downward trend was subsequently reversed, and a business ownership rate of 10.4 percent was reached by 1998 (Verheul et al., 2002). Similarly, the employment share in manufacturing of small firms in the Netherlands increased from 68.3 percent in 1978 to 71.8 percent in 1986. In the United Kingdom this share increased from 30.1 percent in 1979 to 39.9 percent in 1986; in (Western) Germany from 54.8 percent in 1970 to 57.9 percent by 1987; in Portugal from 68.3 percent in 1982 to 71.8 percent in 1986; in the North of Italy from 44.3 percent in 1981 to 55.2 percent in 1987, and in the South of Italy from 61.4 percent in 1981 to 68.4 percent in 1987 (Acs and Audretsch, 1993). A study of EIM (2002) documents how the relative importance of small firms in Europe (19 countries), measured in terms of employment shares, has continued to increase between 1988 and 2001. See Figure 1 for the development of the entrepreneurship rates (business ownership rates) in a selection of countries taken from van Stel (2003). A distinct U-shape can be observed for these countries. The upward trend of the entrepreneurship rate is leveling off in such countries as the UK and the US.[5] In the UK this may be due to policy measures favoring incumbent growth businesses rather than startups (Thurik, 2003). In the US this may be due to the high level of economic

5. See van Stel (2003) or Verheul et al. (2002) for precise data and figures of the US development.

development and to shake out of industries that are in a more advanced stage than elsewhere in the area of modern OECD countries.[6]

Figure 1: Entrepreneurship rates (business owners per workforce) in six OECD countries

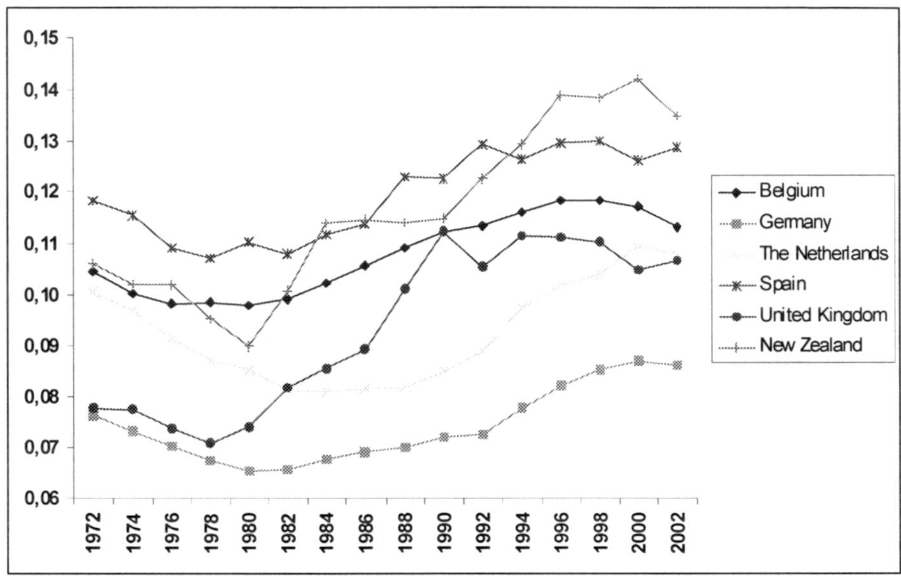

As the empirical evidence documenting the re-emergence of entrepreneurship increased, scholars began to look for explanations and to develop a theoretical basis. Early explanations (Brock and Evans, 1989) revolved around six hypotheses regarding the increased role of small firms:

- Technological change reduces the importance of scale economies in manufacturing.[7]

- Increased globalization and the accompanying competition from a greater number of foreign rivals render markets more volatile.

- The changing composition of the labor force, towards a greater participation of women, immigrants, young and old workers, is more

6. See also Kwoka and White (2001) who observe that despite its importance in absolute and relative terms the small business sector accounts for a diminishing share of US private sector activity. In van Stel (2003) it can be observed that the entrepreneurship rate in countries like Japan and France has dropped over a long period including the 1990s.
7. The influence of technological change on the shaping of business conditions has been widely discussed elsewhere in the late 1980s. See Piori and Sable (1984) and Tushman and Anderson (1986).

conducive to smaller than larger enterprises, due to the greater premium placed on work flexibility.

- A proliferation of consumer demand away from standardized and mass-produced goods towards tailor-made and personalized products facilitates small producers serving niche markets.

- Deregulation and privatization facilitate the entry of new and small firms into markets previously protected and inaccessible.

- The increased importance of innovation in high-wage countries reduces the relative importance of large-scale production, fostering entrepreneurial activity instead.

Audretsch and Thurik (2001) explain the re-emergence of entrepreneurship in Europe and North America on the basis of increased globalization, which has shifted the comparative advantage towards knowledge-based economic activity. They discuss the consequences for economic performance: entrepreneurship capital may be a missing link in explaining variations in economic performance (Audretsch and Keilbach, 2003). An alternative and wider view of this missing link may be that it is the institutional fabric that makes the difference between high and low performance. For example, Saxenian (1994) attributes the superior performance of Silicon Valley to a high capacity for promoting entrepreneurship. While the traditional production factors of labor and capital, as well as knowledge capital, are important in shaping output, the capacity to harness new ideas by creating new enterprises is also essential to economic output.

While entrepreneurs undertake a definitive action, i.e., they start a new business, this action can not be viewed in a vacuum devoid of context. Rather, as Audretsch et al. (2002) show, entrepreneurship is shaped by a number of forces and factors, including legal and institutional as well as social factors. The study of social capital and its impact on economic decision making and behavior dates back to classic economics and sociology literature where it is argued that social and relational structures influence market processes (Granovetter, 1985). Thorton and Flynne (2003) and Saxenian (1994) argue that entrepreneurial environments are characterized by thriving supportive networks that provide the institutional fabric linking individual entrepreneurs to organized sources of learning and resources. Studying networks located in California's Silicon Valley, Saxenian (1990, p. 96/7) emphasizes that it is the communication between individuals that facilitates the transmission of knowledge across agents, firms, and industries, and not just a high endowment of human capital and knowledge in the region: "*It is not simply the concentration of skilled labor, suppliers and information that distinguish the region. A variety of regional institutions – including Stanford University, several trade associations and local business organizations, and a myriad of specialized consulting, market research, public relations and venture capital firms – provide technical, financial, and networking services which the region's enterprises often cannot afford individually. These networks defy sectoral barriers: individuals move easily from semiconductor to disk drive firms or from computer to network makers. They move from established firms to startups (or vice versa) and even to market research or consulting firms, and from consulting firms back into startups. And they continue to meet at trade shows, industry conferences, and the scores of seminars, talks, and social activities organized by local business organizations and trade associations. In these forums, relationships are easily formed and maintained, technical and market information is exchanged, business contacts are established, and new enterprises are conceived...This decentralized and fluid environment also promotes the diffusion of intangible technological capabilities and understandings.*"

Such contexts generating a high propensity for economic agents to start new firms can be characterized as being rich in entrepreneurship capital. Other contexts, where the startup of new firms is inhibited, can be characterized as being weak in entrepreneurship capital.[8]

Entrepreneurship capital exerts a positive impact on competitiveness and growth in a number of ways. The *first* way is by creating knowledge spillovers. Romer (1986), Lucas (1988 and 1993) and Grossman and Helpman (1991) established that knowledge spillovers are an important mechanism underlying endogenous growth. However, they shed little light on the actual mechanisms by which knowledge is transmitted across firms and individuals. Insight into the process of knowledge diffusion is important, especially since a policy implication commonly drawn from new economic growth theory is that, due to the increasing role of knowledge and the resulting increasing returns, knowledge factors (e.g., R&D) should be publicly supported. It is important to recognize that also the mechanisms for spillovers may play a key role and, accordingly, should serve as a focus for public policy enhancing economic growth and development.[9]

The literature identifying mechanisms creating knowledge spillovers is sparse and remains underdeveloped. However, entrepreneurship is an important area where transmission mechanisms have been identified. This will be explained below.

Cohen and Levinthal (1989) suggest that firms develop the capacity to adapt new technology and ideas developed in other firms and are therefore able to appropriate some of the returns accruing to investments[10] in new knowledge

---

8. While this may seem like a tautology, we are using the concept of entrepreneurial capital to characterize locations exhibiting a high degree of entrepreneurial capital.
9. For instance, see Scarpetta et al. (2002) where a firm-level database for ten OECD countries is used to present empirical evidence on the role that policy measures and institutions in product and labor markets play for firm dynamics and productivity. Moreover, different features of entrant and exiting firms across countries are observed.
10. As Audretsch and Feldman (1996) point out knowledge spillovers occur in the context of networks and clusters.

made externally (i.e., outside the own organization). This view of spillovers is consistent with the traditional knowledge production function, where firms exist exogenously, and then make (knowledge) investments to generate innovative output. Audretsch (1995) proposes a shift in the unit of observation away from exogenously assumed firms towards individuals, such as scientists, engineers or other knowledge workers, i.e., agents with endowments of new economic knowledge. When the focus is shifted from the firm to the individual as the relevant unit of observation, the appropriability issue remains, but the question becomes: How can economic agents with a given endowment of new knowledge best appropriate the returns from that knowledge? Albert O. Hirschman (1970) argues that if voice proves to be ineffective within incumbent organizations, and loyalty is sufficiently weak, a knowledge worker may exit the firm or university where the knowledge is created in order to create a new company. In this spillover process the knowledge production function is reversed. Knowledge is exogenous and embodied in a worker and the firm is created endogenously through the worker's effort to appropriate the value of his knowledge by way of innovative activity. Hence, entrepreneurship serves as a mechanism by which knowledge spills over from the source to a new firm in which it is commercialized. There is a large history of people who only started their firms after large firms were disinterested in the innovation. This applies particularly to competence-destroying industries. Chester Carlsson started Xerox after his proposal to produce a new copy machine was rejected by Kodak. Steven Jobs started Apple Computer after his proposal to produce a new personal computer was turned down by Xerox.

A *second* way in which entrepreneurship capital generates economic growth is through augmenting the number of enterprises and increasing competition. Jacobs (1969) and Porter (1990) argue that competition is more conducive to knowledge externalities than is local monopoly.[11] With local competition Jacobs (1969) is not referring to competition within product markets as has traditionally been envisioned within the industrial organization literature, but rather to the competition for new ideas embodied in economic agents. Not only does an increase in the number of firms enhance the competition for new ideas, but greater competition across firms also facilitates the entry of new firms specializing in a particular new product niche. This is because the necessary complementary inputs are more likely to be available from small specialist niche firms than from large, vertically integrated producers. Feldman and Audretsch (1999) as well as Glaeser et al. (1992) found empirical evidence supporting the hypothesis that an increase in competition in a city, as measured by the number of enterprises, is accompanied by higher growth performance of that city.[12]

11. An anonymous referee pointed out that saying that competition is more conducive to knowledge externalities than a local monopoly is not the same as that new firms create more knowledge externalities.

A *third* way in which entrepreneurship capital generates economic output is by providing diversity among firms (Cohen and Klepper, 1992). Not only does entrepreneurship capital generate a greater number of enterprises, it also increases the variety of enterprises in a certain location. A key assumption of Hannan and Freeman (1989) in the population ecology literature is that each new organization represents a unique formula.[13] There has been a series of theoretical arguments suggesting that the degree of diversity, as opposed to homogeneity, will influence the growth potential of a location.

The theoretical basis for linking diversity to economic performance is provided by Jacobs (1969), who argues that the most important sources of knowledge spillovers are external to the industry in which the firm operates and that cities are a source of considerable innovation because here the diversity of knowledge sources is greatest (Audretsch and Feldman, 1996; Jaffe et al., 1993). According to Jacobs (1969) it is the exchange of complementary knowledge across diverse firms and economic agents that yields an important return on new economic knowledge. Jacobs (1969) develops a theory emphasizing the argument that the variety of industries within a geographic environment promotes knowledge externalities and, ultimately, innovative activity and economic growth. In this environment entrepreneurship capital can contribute to growth and development by injecting diversity and serving as a conduit for knowledge spillovers, leading to increased competition. The entrepreneurial economy is characterized by a high reliance on this third role of entrepreneurship capital.[14]

4. Contrasting the Entrepreneurial and Managed Economy Models

The era of the managed economy is being supplanted by the emergence of the entrepreneurial economy. This suggests two contrasting models with differing roles of entrepreneurship. The model of the managed economy revolves around the links between stability, specialization, homogeneity, scale, certainty and predictability on the one hand and economic growth on the other. By contrast, the model of the entrepreneurial economy focuses on the links between flexibility, turbulence, diversity, novelty, innovation, linkages and clustering on the one hand and economic growth on the other. The models of the managed and the entrepreneurial economy can be compared distinguishing between different groups of characteristics, including underlying forces, external environment

---

12. See also Acs (2002) who hints at the dual causality between the growth of cities and that of the number of firms.
13. As opposed to the organizational ecology approach of Hannan and Freeman institutional theorists in organization studies also point to strong pressures on new firms to conform (Dimaggio and Powell, 1983).
14. A different view on the role of knowledge and its spillovers is offered in the "systems of innovations" approach (Nelson, 1993).

characteristics, internal or firm characteristics and policy characteristics. See Table 1 at the end of the present article.

4.1. Underlying Forces

The first group of characteristics contrasts the forces underlying the models of the entrepreneurial and managed economy: localization *versus* globalization; change *versus* continuity; and jobs and high wages *versus* jobs or high wages.

In the model of the managed economy production results from the inputs of labor and capital (Solow, 1956). Geography provides a platform to combine (mobile) capital with (immobile) lower-cost labor (Kindleberger and Audretsch, 1983). In the model of the entrepreneurial economy knowledge is the dominant factor of production. The comparative advantage in the knowledge economy is dependent on innovative activity. Knowledge spillovers are an important source of this innovative activity. Hence, in the model of the entrepreneurial economy local proximity is important, with the region being the most important locus of economic activity, as knowledge tends to be developed in the context of localized production networks embedded in innovative clusters.

While the model of the managed economy focuses more on *continuity* (Chandler, 1977), the model of the entrepreneurial economy provokes and thrives on *change*. Although innovation is present under the conditions of both change and continuity, the locus of innovative activity differs. A distinction can be made between incremental and radical innovations. Innovations are considered incremental when they are compatible with the core competence and technological trajectory of the firm (Teece, Rumult, Dosi and Winter, 1994). By contrast, a radical innovation can be defined as extending beyond the boundaries of the core competence and technological trajectory of the firm. In the model of the managed economy change is absorbed within a given technological paradigm: the average firm excels at incremental innovation. By contrast, in the model of the entrepreneurial economy, the capacity to break out of the technological lock-in imposed by existing paradigms is enhanced by the ability of economic agents to start new firms. Thus, incremental innovative activity along with diffusion plays a more important role in the model of the managed economy. While often requiring large investments in R&D, this type of innovative activity generates incremental changes in products along the existing technological trajectories. In the entrepreneurial economy model, the comparative advantage of the high-cost location demands innovative activity earlier in the product life cycle and which is of a more radical nature.

One of the most striking policy dilemmas in the model of the managed economy is that unemployment can be reduced only at the cost of lower wages. In the model of the entrepreneurial economy high employment can be combined with high wages and a low wage level does not imply high employment.[15] An indication of the absence of a trade-off between high wages and employment is the fact that although corporate downsizing has been rampant throughout the OECD countries, there is a large variance in unemployment rates. Audretsch et al. (2002) show that economies of OECD countries exhibiting characteristics in conformity with the entrepreneurial economy model have been more successful at creating new jobs to compensate for jobs lost in the process of corporate downsizing. Small firms in general, and new ventures in particular, are the engine of employment creation.[16] Under the model of the managed economy the job creation by small firms is associated with lower wages. However, the growth of new firms may not only generate greater employment, but also higher wages. New firm growth ensures that higher employment does not come at a cost of lower wages, but rather the opposite – higher wages. Hence, while small firms generate employment at a cost of lower wages in the model of the managed economy, in the entrepreneurial economy model small firms may create both more jobs and higher wages.[17]

4.2. External Environment

The second group of characteristics contrasts the external environment characteristics of the models of the managed and the entrepreneurial economies. Turbulence, diversity and heterogeneity are central to the model of the entrepreneurial economy. By contrast, stability, specialization and homogeneity are the cornerstones in the model of the managed economy.

Stability in the model of the managed economy results from a homogeneous product demand, resulting in a low turnover rate of jobs, workers and firms. The model of the entrepreneurial economy is characterized by a high degree of *turbulence*. Each year many new firms are started and only a subset of these firms survives. Nelson and Winter (1982) argue that the role of diversity and selection is at the heart of generating change. This holds for both the managed and the entrepreneurial economy model. However, what differs in these models is the management and organization of the process by which diversity is created as well as the selection mechanism. In the model of the managed economy research activities are organized and scheduled in departments devoted to developing novel products and services. The management of change fits into what Nelson and Winter (1982) refer to as the firm's routines. The ability of existing businesses to manage the process of change pre-empted most opportunities for entrepreneurs to

15. An anonymous referee pointed out that, clearly, the trade-off between involuntary unemployment and wages requires a ceteris paribus condition: if the productivity of workers increases than both employment and wages can increase.
16. Carree and Thurik (1999) show that a higher share of small business in European manufacturing industries leads to higher growth of value added in the subsequent years.
17. See Acs, Fitzroy and Smith (2002) and Scarpetta, Hemmings, Tressel and Woo (2002) for illustrating data material.

start new firms, resulting in a low startup rate and a stable industrial structure. In the model of the entrepreneurial economy the process of generating new ideas, both within and outside of R&D laboratories, creates a turbulent environment with many opportunities for entrepreneurs to start new firms based upon different and changing opinions about different and changing ideas.

A series of theoretical arguments has suggested that the degree of *diversity* versus *specialization* may account for differences in rates of growth and technological development. While *specialization* of industry activities is associated with lower transaction costs and, therefore, greater (static) efficiency, *diversity* of activities is said to facilitate the exchange of new ideas and, therefore, greater innovative activity and (dynamic) efficiency. Because knowledge spillovers are an important source of innovative activity, diversity is a prerequisite in the model of the entrepreneurial economy where lower transaction costs are preferably sacrificed for greater opportunities for knowledge spillover. In the model of the managed economy, there are less gains from knowledge spillovers. The higher transaction costs associated with diversity yield little room for opportunities in terms of increased innovative activity, making specialization preferable in the model of the managed economy.

Whereas the trade-off between diversity and specialization focuses on firms, that between *homogeneity* and *heterogeneity* focuses on individuals. There are two dimensions shaping the degree of homogeneity versus heterogeneity. The first dimension refers to the genetic make-up of individuals and their personal experiences (Nooteboom, 1994) and the second dimension refers to the information set to which individuals are exposed. The model of the managed economy is based on homogeneity, that of the entrepreneurial economy on heterogeneity. In a heterogeneous population communication across individuals tends to be more difficult and costly than in a homogenous population: transaction costs are higher and efficiency is lower. At the same time, new ideas are more likely to emerge from communication in a heterogeneous than in a homogeneous world. Although the likelihood of communication is lower in a heterogeneous population, communication is this environment is more prone to produce novelty and innovation. The lower transaction costs resulting from a homogeneous population in the model of the managed economy are not associated with high opportunity costs because knowledge spillovers are relatively unimportant in generating innovative activity. However, knowledge spillovers are a driving force in the model of the entrepreneurial economy, offsetting the higher transaction costs associated with a heterogeneous population.

4.3. Firm Behavior

The third group of characteristics contrasts firm behavior of the models of the managed and the entrepreneurial economy: control *versus* motivation; firm transaction *versus* market exchange; competition and cooperation as substitutes *versus* complements; and scale *versus* flexibility.

Under the model of the managed economy labor is considered as indistinguishable from the other input factors, as long as management is able to extract a full day's worth of energy for a full day's pay (Wheelwright, 1985). It is considered homogeneous and easily replaceable. In the managed economy model firms organize their labor according to the principles of *command and control.* Management styles emphasize the maintenance of tasks through direct forms of employee control. Under the model of the entrepreneurial economy, the command and control approach to labor is less effective as the comparative advantage of the advanced industrialized countries tends to be based on new knowledge. *Motivating* workers to facilitate the discovery process and implementation of new ideas is more important than requiring an established set of activities from knowledge workers. Management styles emphasize the nurturing of interpersonal relationships facilitating rather than supervising employees. In the entrepreneurial economy model the focus of activities is on exploring new abilities, rather than exploiting existing ones. Hence, under the model of the entrepreneurial economy motivating employees to participate in the creation and commercialization of new ideas is more important than simply controlling and regulating their behavior. The distinction between controlling and motivating employees can be traced back to, and corresponds with, McGregor's (1960) Theory X and Y, autocratic versus democratic decision-making (Lewin and Lippitt, 1938), task-oriented versus interpersonal-oriented styles (Blake and Mouton, 1964), and transactional versus transformational leadership (Bass et al., 1996).[18] It has also been suggested that controlling versus motivating employees can be viewed as more masculine versus more feminine management styles (Van Engen, 2001), although a recent study by Verheul (2003) suggests that women are more control-oriented than men when managing employees.

Dating back to Coase (1937), and more recently to Williamson (1975), an analytical distinction can be made between *exchange via the market* and *intra-firm transactions*. Both Coase and Williamson emphasize that uncertainty and imperfect information increase the cost of intra-firm transactions. As Knight (1921) argued, low uncertainty combined with transparency and predictability of information, make intra-firm transactions efficient relative to market exchange. In the managed economy model, where there is a high degree of certainty and predictability of information, transactions within firms tend to be more efficient than market exchange. By contrast, in the entrepreneurial economy model market transactions are more efficient because of the high uncertainty. Since the mid-1970s the economic arena has become increasingly uncertain and unpredictable (Carlsson, 1989; Carlsson and Taymaz, 1994), witnessed by a decrease in both mean firm size and the extent of vertical integration and conglomeration.

18. An anonymous referee refers to Ackroyd and Thomson (1999) for some entertaining examples on the subject within UK firms.

While models of *competition* generally assume that firms behave autonomously, models of *cooperation* assume linkages among firms. These linkages take various forms, including joint ventures, strategic alliances, and (in)formal networks (Gomes-Casseres, 1996 and 1997; Nooteboom, 1999). In the model of the managed economy competition and cooperation are viewed as being substitutes. Firms are vertically integrated and primarily compete in product markets. Cooperation between firms in the product market reduces the number of competitors and reduces the degree of competition. In the model of the entrepreneurial economy firms are vertically independent and specialized in the product market. The higher degree of vertical disintegration under the model of the entrepreneurial economy implies a replacement of internal transactions within a large vertically integrated corporation with cooperation among independent firms. At the same time, there are more firms, resulting in an increase in both the competitive and cooperative interface. The likelihood of a firm competing or cooperating with other firms is higher in the entrepreneurial economy model.

Under the model of the managed economy costs-per-unit are reduced through expanding the scale of output, or through exploiting economies of *scale*. In product lines and industries where a large scale of production translates into a substantial reduction in average costs, large firms will have an economic advantage, leading to a concentrated industrial structure. The importance of scale economies has certainly contributed to the emergence and dominance of large corporations in heavy manufacturing industries, such as steel, automobiles, and aluminum (Chandler, 1977). The alternative source of reduced average costs is *flexibility* (Teece, 1993), characterizing the entrepreneurial economy model. Industries where demand for particular products is shifting constantly, require a flexible system of production that can meet such a whimsical demand.

4.4. Government Policy

The final group of contrasting dimensions of the models of the entrepreneurial economy and the managed economy refers to government policy, including the goals of policy (enabling *versus* constraining), the target of policy (inputs *versus* outputs), the locus of policy (local *versus* national) and financing policy (entrepreneurial *versus* incumbent).

Under the model of the managed economy public policy towards the firm is essentially *constraining* in nature. There are three[19] general types of public policy towards business: antitrust policy (competition policy), regulation, and public ownership. All three of these policy approaches restrict the firm's freedom to

19. As an anonymous referee pointed out: enabling one section in society may entail constraining other sections. For instance, a major policy issue for small businesses in the UK is how government can withhold banks from abusing power in the market from small business banking, thereby fostering an environment in which small businesses can succeed.

contract. Under the model of the managed economy the relevant policy question is: *How can the government withhold firms from abusing their market power?* The entrepreneurial economy model is characterized by a different policy question: *How can governments create an environment fostering the success and viability of firms?* Whereas the major issues in the model of the managed economy are concerns about excess profits and abuses of market dominance, in the model of the entrepreneurial economy the issues of international competitiveness, growth and employment are important. In the managed economy model the emphasis is *constraining* market power through regulation, whereas the focus in the entrepreneurial economy model is on stimulating firm development and performance through *enabling* policies.

Another governmental policy dimension involves targeting selected *outputs* in the production process versus targeting selected *inputs*. Because of the relative certainty regarding markets and products in the model of the managed economy, the appropriate policy response is to target outcomes and outputs. Specific industries and firms can be promoted through government programs. Whereas in the model of the managed economy production is based on the traditional inputs of land, labor and capital, in the entrepreneurial economy model it is mainly based on knowledge input. There is uncertainty about what products should be produced, how and by whom. This high degree of uncertainty makes it difficult to select appropriate outcomes and increases the likelihood of targeting the wrong firms and industries. Hence, the appropriate policy in the model of the entrepreneurial economy is to target inputs, and in particular those inputs related to the creation and commercialization of knowledge.

The *locus* of policy is a third dimension on which the models of the managed and entrepreneurial economy can be compared. Under the model of the managed economy the appropriate locus of policy making is the *national or federal* level. While the targeted recipients of policy may be localized in one or a few regions, the most important policy making institutions tend to be located at the national level. By contrast, under the model of the entrepreneurial economy, government policy towards business tends to be decentralized and *regional or local* in nature. This distinction in the locus of policy results from two factors. *First*, because the competitive source of economic activity in the model of the entrepreneurial economy is knowledge, which tends to be localized in regional clusters, public policy requires an understanding of regional-specific characteristics and idiosyncrasies. *Secondly*, the motivation underlying government policy in the entrepreneurial economy is growth and the creation of jobs (with high pay), to be achieved mainly through new venture creation. New firms are usually small and pose no oligopolistic threat in national or international markets. In the model of the entrepreneurial economy no external costs – in the form of higher prices – are imposed on consumers in the national economy as is the case in the model of the managed economy. The promotion of local economies imposes no cost on consumers in the national economy. Hence, local intervention is justified and does not result in any particular loss incurred by agents outside of the region.

Finally, financing policies vary between the two models. Under the model of the managed economy, the systems of finance provide the existing companies with just liquidity for investment.[20] Liquidity is seen as a homogeneous input factor. The model of the entrepreneurial economy requires a system of finance that is different from that in the model of the managed economy. In the model of the managed economy there is certainty in outputs as well as inputs. There is a strong connection between banks and firms, fostering growth. In the entrepreneurial economy model certainty has given way to uncertainty requiring different (or differently structured) financial institutions. In particular the venture and informal capital markets, providing finance for high-risk and innovative new firms (Gaston, 1989; Gompers, 1999), play an important role in the model of the entrepreneurial economy. In this model liquidity looses its homogeneous image and is often coupled with forms of advice, knowledge and changing levels of involvement.

Storey (2003) has painstakingly documented examples of policies predicted by the entrepreneurial model like access to loan finance and equity capital, access to markets, administrative burdens, managed workspace, university spin-offs, science parks, stimulating innovation and R&D and training in small firms. See Storey (2003, table 3).

5. Discussion

The model of the managed economy seems to characterize most economies throughout the first three-quarters of the previous century. It is based on relative certainty in outputs (mainly manufactured products) and inputs (mainly land, labor and capital). The twin forces of globalization have reduced the ability of the managed economies of Western Europe and North America to grow and create jobs. On the one hand there is the advent of new competition from low-cost, but highly educated and skill-intensive, countries in Central and Eastern Europe as well as Asia. On the other hand, the telecommunications and computer revolutions have drastically reduced the cost of shifting not just capital but also information out of the high-cost locations of Europe and into lower-cost locations around the globe. Taken together, these twin forces of globalization imply that economic activity in high-cost locations is no longer compatible with routinized tasks. Rather, globalization has shifted the comparative advantage of high-cost locations to knowledge-based activities, and in particular intellectual search activities. These activities cannot be costlessly transferred around the globe. Knowledge as an input into economic activity is inherently different from land,

20. See Hughes and Storey (1994), Storey (1994), Reid (1996) and the special issue of Small Business Economics devoted to European SME Financing (Cressy and Olofsson, 1997).

labor and capital. It is characterized by high uncertainty, high asymmetries across people and high transaction costs. An economy where knowledge is the main source of comparative advantage is more consistent with the model of the entrepreneurial economy.

This paper has identified fourteen dimensions that span the difference between the models of the entrepreneurial and managed economies and provides a framework for understanding how the entrepreneurial economy fundamentally differs from the managed economy. See Table 1 below for a overview. Building upon Audretsch and Thurik (2001) these contrasting models provide a lens through which economic events can be interpreted and policy formulated. Using the wrong lens leads to the wrong policy choice. For example, under the model of the managed economy firm failure is viewed negatively, representing a drain on society's resources. In the model of the managed economy resources are not invested in high-risk ventures. In the model of the entrepreneurial economy firm failure is viewed differently, i.e., as an experiment, an attempt to go in a new direction in an inherently risky environment (Wennekers and Thurik, 1999). An externality of failure is learning. In the model of the entrepreneurial economy the process of searching for new ideas is accompanied by failure. Similarly, the virtues of long-term relationships, stability and continuity under the model of the managed economy give way to flexibility, change, and turbulence in the model of the entrepreneurial economy. What is a liability in the model of the managed economy is, in some cases, a virtue in the model of the entrepreneurial economy.

The implication for teaching entrepreneurship is that the role of and context for new and small firms is strikingly different in the entrepreneurial economy than in the managed economy. While small business was a follower in the managed economy, it has emerged as the engine of growth in the entrepreneurial economy. Also, ever more teaching efforts have the small-scaled environment as case example regardless of whether the education aims at training people for small or large firms.

Table 1: Fourteen dimensions of the difference between the model of the entrepreneurial and the managed economy

Category	Entrepreneurial economy	Managed economy
Underlying forces		
	Localization	Globalization
	Change	Continuity
	Jobs and high wages	Jobs or high wages
External environment		
	Turbulence	Stability
	Diversity	Specialization
	Heterogeneity	Homogeneity
How firms function		
	Motivation	Control
	Market exchange	Firm transaction
	Competition and cooperation	Competition or cooperation
	Flexibility	Scale
Government policy		
	Enabling	Constraining
	Input targeting	Output targeting
	Local locus	National locus
	Entrepreneurial	Incumbent

References:

Ackroyd, S. and P. Thomson, 1999, *Organizational Misbehaviour*, London: Sage Publications.

Acs, Z.J., 2002, *Innovation and the Growth of Cities*, Cheltenham, UK: Edward Elgar.

Acs, Z.J. and D.B. Audretsch, 1990, *Innovation and Small Firms*, Cambridge, MA: MIT Press.

Acs, Z.J. and D.B. Audretsch, 1993, Conclusion, in: Z.J. Acs and D.B. Audretsch (eds.), *Small Firms and Entrepreneurship; an East-West Perspective*, Cambridge, UK: Cambridge University Press.

Acs, Z.J., F.R. Fitzroy and I. Smith, 2002, "High-technology employment and R&D in cities: heterogeneity vs specialization", *Annals of Regional Science* 36 (3), 373-386.

Aldrich, H.E. and M. Martinez, 2003, "Entrepreneurship as social construction", in: Z.J. Acs and D.B. Audretsch (eds.), *The International Handbook of Entrepreneurship*, Boston/Dordrecht: Kluwer Academic Publishers.

Audretsch, D,B., 1995, *Innovation and Industry Evolution*, Cambridge, MA: MIT Press

Audretsch, D.B. and M.P. Feldman, 1996, "R&D spillovers and the geography of innovation and production", *American Economic Review* 86 (3), 630-640.

Audretsch, D.B. and M. Keilbach, 2003, "Entrepreneurship capital and economic performance", Centre for Economic Policy Research Discussion Paper DP3678, London: CEPR.

Audretsch, D.B. and A. R. Thurik, 1999, *Innovation, Industry Evolution and Employment*, Cambridge: Cambridge University Press.

Audretsch, D.B. and A. R. Thurik, 2000, "Capitalism and democracy in the 21st century: from the managed to the entrepreneurial economy", *Journal of Evolutionary Economics* 10, 17-34.

Audretsch, D.B. and A.R. Thurik, 2001, "What is new about the new economy: sources of growth in the managed and entrepreneurial economies", *Industrial and Corporate Change* 19, 795-821.

Audretsch, D.B., M.A. Carree and A.R. Thurik, 2001, "Does entrepreneurship reduce unemployment?" Tinbergen Institute Discussion Paper TI 2001-074/3, Rotterdam: Tinbergen Institute.

Audretsch, D.B., M.A. Carree, A.J. van Stel and A.R. Thurik, 2002, "Impeded industrial restructuring: the growth penalty", *Kyklos* 55 (1), 81-97.

Audretsch, D.B., A.R. Thurik, I. Verheul and A.R.M. Wennekers (eds.), 2002, *Entrepreneurship: Determinants and Policy in a European - US Comparison*, Boston/Dordrecht: Kluwer Academic Publishers, 2002.

Bass, B.M., Avolio, B.J. and L.E. Atwater, 1996, "The transformational and transactional leadership style of men and women", *Applied Psychology* 45, 5-34.

Blake, R.R. and J.S. Mouton, 1964, *The Managerial Grid*, Houston: Gulf Publishing Company.

Brock, W.A. and D.S. Evans, 1989, "Small business economics", *Small Business Economics* 1 (1), 7-20.

Brown, C. and J. Medoff, 1989, "The employer size-wage effect", *Journal of Political Economy* 97 (5), 1027-1059.

Brown, C., Hamilton, J. and J. Medoff, 1990, *Employers Large and Small*, Cambridge, MA: Harvard University Press.

Carlsson, B., 1989, "The evolution of manufacturing technology and its impact on industrial structure: an international study", *Small Business Economics* 1 (1), 21-38.

Carlsson, B. and E. Taymaz, 1994, "Flexible technology and industrial structure in the U.S.", *Small Business Economics* 6 (3), 193-209.

Carree, M.A. and A.R. Thurik, 1999, "Industrial structure and economic growth, in: D.B. Audretsch and A. R. Thurik (eds.)", *Innovation, Industry Evolution and Employment*, Cambridge, UK: Cambridge University Press, 86-110.

Carree, M.A. and A.R. Thurik, 2003, "The impact of entrepreneurship on economic growth", in: Z.J. Acs and D.B. Audretsch (eds.), *Handbook of Entrepreneurship Research*, Boston/ Dordrecht: Kluwer Academic Publishers.

Caves, R., 1982, *Multinational Enterprise and Economic Analysis*, Cambridge: Cambridge University Press.

Chandler, A.D., 1977, *The Visible Hand: The Managerial Revolution in American Business*, Cambridge, MA: Harvard University Press.

Chandler, A.D. Jr., 1990, *Scale and Scope: The Dynamics of Industrial Capitalism*, Cambridge, MA: Harvard University Press.

Coase, R.H., 1937, "The nature of the firm", *Economica* 4 (4), 386-405.

Cohen, W.M. and S. Klepper, 1992, "The trade-off between firm size and diversity in the pursuit of technological progress", *Small Business Economics* 4 (1), 1-14.

Cohen, W. and D. Levinthal, 1989, "Innovation and learning: the two faces of R&D", *Economic Journal* 99 (3), 569-596.

Cressy, R.C. and C. Olofsson, 1997, "European SME financing: an overview", *Small Business Economics* 9 (2), 87-96.

Dimaggio, P.J. and W. Powell, 1983, "The iron cage revisited: institutional isomorphism and collective rationality in organizational fields", *American Sociological Review* 48, 147-160.

Dosi, G., 1988, "Sources, procedures and microeconomic effects of innovations", *Journal of Economic Literature* 26, 1120-1171.

EIM, 2002, *SMEs in Europe*, Report submitted to the Enterprise Directorate General by KPMG Special Services, Zoetermeer: EIM Business & Policy Research.

Feldman, M.P. and D.B. Audretsch, 1999, "Innovation in cities: science-based diversity, specialization and localized monopoly", *European Economic Review* 43, 409-429.

Galbraith, J.K., 1956, "American Capitalism: The Concept of Countervailing Power", Boston: Houghton Mifflin Co.

Gaston, R.J., 1989, "The scale of informal capital markets", *Small Business Economics* 1 (3), 223-230.

Glaeser, E., Kallal, H., Sheinkman, J. and A. Schleifer, 1992, "Growth in cities", *Journal of Political Economy* 100, 1126-1152.

Gomes-Casseres, B., 1997, "Alliance strategies of small firms", *Small Business Economics* 9 (1), 33-44.

Gomes-Casseres, B., 1996, *The Alliance Revolution: The New Shape of Business Rivalry*, Cambridge, MA: Harvard University Press.

Gompers, P., 1999, *The Venture Capital Cycle*, Cambridge, MA: MIT Press.

Granovetter, M.S., 1985, "Economic action and social structure: the problem of embeddedness", *American Journal of Sociology* 91 (3), 481-510.

Grossman, G.M. and Helpman, E., 1991, *Innovation and Growth in the Global Economy*, Cambridge, MA: MIT Press.

Hannan, M.T. and J. Freeman, 1989, *Organizational Ecology*, Cambridge, MA: Harvard University Press.

Hirschman, A.O., 1970, *Exit, Voice, and Loyalty*, Cambridge, MA: Harvard University Press.

Hughes, A. and D.J. Storey, 1994, *Finance and the Small Firm*, London: Routledge.

Jacobs, J., 1969, *The Economy of Cities*, New York: Vintage Books.

Jaffe, A., Trajtenberg, M. and R. Henderson, 1993, "Geographic localization of knowledge spillovers as evidenced by patent citations", *Quarterly Journal of Economics* 63, 577-598.

Kindleberger, C.P. and D.B. Audretsch (eds.), 1983, *The Multinational Corporation*, Cambridge, MA: MIT Press.

Knight, F.H., 1921, *Risk, Uncertainty and Profit*, New York: Houghton Mifflin.

Krugman, P., 1991, *Geography and Trade*, Cambridge, MA: MIT Press.

Kwoka, J.E. and L.J. White, 2001, "The new industrial organization and small business", *Small Business Economics* 16 (1): 21-30.

Lawrence, P. and J. Lorsch, 1967, *Organization and Environment*, Cambridge, MA: Harvard Universty Press.

Lewin, A. and R. Lippitt, 1938, "An expirimental approach to the study of autocracy and democracy: a preliminary note", *Sociometry* 1, 292-300.

Loveman, G. and W. Sengenberger, 1991, The re-emergence of small-scale production; an international comparison, *Small Business Economics* 3 (1), 1-37.

Lucas, R.E. Jr., 1993, "Making a miracle", *Econometrica* 61 (2), 251-272.

Lucas, R.E., 1988, "On the mechanics of economic development", *Journal of Monetary Economics* 22, 3-39.

McGregor, D., 1960, *The Human Side of Enterprise*, New York: McGraw-Hill.

Nelson, R.R., (ed.), 1993, *National Innovation Systems: A Comparative Analysis,* Oxford, UK: Oxford University Press.

Nelson, R.R. and S.G. Winter, 1982, *An Evolutionary Theory of Economic Change*, Cambridge, MA: Harvard University Press.

Nooteboom, B., 1994, "Innovation and diffusion in small firms", *Small Business Economics* 6, 327-347.

Nooteboom, B., 1999, *Inter-Firm Alliances; Analysis and Design*, London: Routledge.

Piore, M.J. and C.F. Sabel, 1984, *The Second Industrial Divide: Possibilities for Prosperity*, New York: Basic Books.

Porter, M., 1990, *The Comparative Advantage of Nations*, New York: Free Press.

Pratten, C.F., 1971, *Economies of Scale in Manufacturing Industry*, Cambridge: Cambridge University Press.

Reid, G.C., 1996, "Financial structure and the growing small firm: theoretical underpinning and current evidence", *Small Business Economics* 8 (1), 1-7.

Riesman, D., 1950, "The Lonely Crowd: A Study of the Changing American Character", New Haven: Yale University Press.

Romer, P.M., 1986, "Increasing returns and long-run growth", *Journal of Political Economy* 94 (5), 1002-1037.

Romer, P.M., 1990, "Endogenous technological change", *Journal of Political Economy* 98, 71-101.

Romer, P.M., 1994, "The origins of endogenous growth", *Journal of Economic Perspectives* 8 (1), 3-22.

Saxenian, A., 1994, *Regional Advantage*, Cambridge, MA: Harvard University Press.

Saxenian, A., 1990, "Regional networks and the resurgence of Silicon Valley", *California Management Review* 33, 89-111.

Scherer, F.M., 1991, "Changing perspectives on the firm size problem", in Z.J. Acs and D. B. Audretsch, (eds.), *Innovation and Technological Change: An International Comparison*, Ann Arbor: University of Michigan Press, 24-38.

Schumpeter, J.A., 1934, *The Theory of Economic Development*, Cambridge, MA: Harvard University Press.

Solow, R., 1956, "A contribution to the theory of economic growth", *Quarterly Journal of Economics* 70, 65-94.

Van Stel, A.J., 2003, "COMPENDIA 2000.2: a harmonized data set of business ownership rates in 23 OECD countries", EIM Research Report H200302, Zoetermeer: EIM Business and Policy Research.

Scarpetta, S., Ph. Hemmings, T. Tressel and J. Woo, 2002, "The role of policy and institutions for productivity and firm dynamics: evidence from micro and industry data", OECD Economics Department Working Paper 329, Paris: OECD.

Storey, D.J., 1994, *Understanding the Small Business Sector*, London: Routledge.

Storey, D.J., 2003, "Entrepreneurship, small and medium sized enterprise and public policies", in: Z.J. Acs and D.B. Audretsch (eds.), *Handbook of Entrepreneurship Research*, Boston/ Dordrecht: Kluwer Academic Publishers.

Teece, D.J., 1993, "The dynamics of industrial capitalism: perspectives on Alfred Chandler's "Scale and Scope"", *Journal of Economic Literature* 31, 199-225.

Teece, D.J., R. Rumult, G. Dosi and S. Winter, 1994, "Understanding corporate coherence: theory and evidence", *Journal of Economic Behavior and Organization* 23 (1), 1-30.

Thorton, P.H. and K.H. Flynne, 2003, "Entrepreneurship, networks and geographies", in: Z.J. Acs and D.B. Audretsch (eds.), *Handbook of Entrepreneurship Research*, Boston/Dordrecht: Kluwer Academic Publishers.

Thurik, A.R., 2003, "Entrepreneurship and unemployment in the UK", *Scottish Journal of Political Economy*, 50 (3), 264-290.

Thurik, A.R. and I. Verheul, 2003, "The relationship between entrepreneurship and unemployment: the case of Spain", in: E. Genesca, D. Urbano, J.L. Capelleras, C. Guallarte, J. Verges (eds.), *Creacion de Empresas. Entrepreneurship*, Barcelona, Spain: Servei de Publicacions de la UAB.

Thurik, A.R., Wennekers, A.R.M. and L.M. Uhlaner, 2002, "Entrepreneurship and economic growth: a macro perspective", *International Journal of Entrepreneurship Education* 1 (2), 157-179.

Tushman, M.L. and Ph. Anderson, 1986, "Technological discontinuities and organizational environments", *Administrative Science Quarterly* 31 (3), 439-465.

Van Engen, 2001, *Gender and Leadership: a Contextual Perspective*, Tilburg University: Dissertation Social and Behavioral Sciences.

Verheul, I., 2003, "Commitment or control? Human resource management in female- and male-led businesses", Strategic Study B200206, Zoetermeer: EIM Business and Policy Research.

Verheul, I., Wennekers, A.R.M., Audretsch, D.B. and A.R. Thurik, 2002, "An eclectic theory of entrepreneurship: policies, institutions and culture", in: Audretsch, D.B., Thurik, A.R., Verheul, I. and A.R.M. Wennekers (eds.), *Entrepreneurship: Determinants and Policy in a European-US Comparison*, Boston/Dordrecht: Kluwer Academic Publishers, 11-82..

Vernon, R., 1970, "Organization as a scale factor in the growth of firms", in: J. W. Markham and G. F. Papanek (eds.), Industrial Organization and Economic Development, Boston: Houghton Mifflin, 47-66.

Weiss, Leonard W., 1976, "Optimal plant scale and the extent of suboptimal capacity", in R.T.

Masson and P.D. Qualls, (eds.), *Essays on Industrial Organization in Honor of Joe S. Bain*, Cambridge, Mass.: Ballinger.

Wennekers, A.R.M. and A.R. Thurik, 1999, "Linking entrepreneurship and economic growth", *Small Business Economics* 13 (1), 27-55.Weiss, Leonard W., 1964, "The survival technique and the extent of sub-optimal capacity", *Journal of Political Economy*, 72(3), 246-261.

Wennekers, A.R.M., Uhlaner, L.M. and A.R. Thurik, 2002, "Entrepreneurship and its conditions: a macro perspective", *International Journal of Entrepreneurship Education* 1 (1), 25-64.

Wheelwright, S.C., 1985, "Restoring competitiveness in U.S. manufacturing", *California Management Review* 27, 113-121.

Whyte, W.H., 1960, *The Organization Man*, Hammondsworth, Middlesex: Penguin.

Williamson, O.E., 1968, "Economies as an antitrust defense: the welfare trade-offs", *American Economic Review* 58 (1), 18-36.

Williamson, O.E., 1975, *Markets and Hierarchies: Analysis and Antitrust Implications*, New York: The Free Press.

3. Entrepreneurship and Economic Performance: A Macro Perspective

Roy Thurik
Erasmus University Rotterdam

Sander Wennekers
EIM Small Business Research and Consultancy

Lorraine M. Uhlaner
Erasmus University Rotterdam [1]

Abstract. The present paper provides a theoretical framework of the relationship between rate of entrepreneurship and national economic performance. The first part deals with some aspects of the recent economics literature on the relation between entrepreneurship and small business, on the one hand, and economic growth, on the other. In particular, it gives a summary of some work of the EIM/ CASBEC research group in the Netherlands. In the second part a framework is presented linking entrepreneurship and growth at different levels of aggregation. The last part of the paper illustrates the framework with some historical case studies. The present paper supplements Wennekers, Uhlaner and Thurik (2002) which is concerned with the causes of the rate of entrepreneurship.

Keywords: entrepreneurship, small firms, market structure, growth, economic development, economic history.

1. Introduction

Entrepreneurship and small business are related but not synonymous concepts. On the one hand, entrepreneurship is a type of behavior that concentrates on opportunities rather than resources (Stevenson and Gumpert, 1991). This type of behavior can happen in both small and large businesses but also elsewhere. On the other hand, small businesses can be a vehicle for both Schumpeterian entrepreneurs introducing new products and processes that change the industry and for people who simply run and own a business for a living (Wennekers and Thurik, 1999). The latter group includes many franchisees, shopkeepers and

---

1. The authors would like to thank David Audretsch, Andrew Burke, Martin Carree, Kevin Hindle, Païvi Oinas and Lois Stevenson for comments on an earlier version of the present paper. Earlier versions of parts of the present paper has been read at the *Annual Meeting of the American Economic Association*, Boston, 6-9 January 2000, at the *Round Table on Entrepreneurship for the Future*, Växjö, Sweden, 18 March 2001 and the *Global Entrepreneurship Monitor meeting* at the London Business School, 11 January 2002. Support is acknowledged by the research program SCALES (Scientific Analysis of Entrepreneurship and SMEs), financed by the Dutch Ministry of Economic Affairs. Lorraine Uhlaner acknowledges the support of Eastern Michigan University, Department of Management, Ypsilanti, Michigan for a sabbatical leave at Erasmus University Rotterdam. Finally, the present paper is part of the SNS project on Entrepreneurship and Growth financed by the Marcus and Marianne Wallenberg's Foundation.

This article was originally published in the International Journal of Entrepreneurship Education 1(2): pp. 157-179.

people in professional occupations. They belong to what Kirchhoff (1994) calls 'the economic core'. That both entrepreneurship and small businesses matter is not a new observation. In particular, they are important where they overlap. This is in the area of new, small, and sometimes fast growing businesses. However, the way in which they matter has evolved over time. During the first decades of the twentieth century, small businesses were both a vehicle for entrepreneurship and a source of employment and income. This is the era in which Schumpeter (1934) conceived his *Theory of Economic Development*, emphasizing the role of the entrepreneur as prime cause of economic development. He describes how the innovating entrepreneur challenges incumbent firms by introducing new inventions that make current technologies and products obsolete. This process of creative destruction is the main characteristic of what has been called the Schumpeter Mark I regime.

During the post-World War II years small business still mattered, but increasingly less on the grounds of economic efficiency, and more for social and political purposes such as employment, stability and provision of personal services. Immediately following WWII when large firms had not yet gained the powerful position of the 1960s and 1970s, small businesses were the main supplier of employment and hence of social and political stability. But as trends showed a shift toward larger firm employment, scholars, such as Chandler (1977) and Galbraith (1967) convinced economists, intellectuals and policy makers that the future was in the hands of large corporations; small business would fade away as the victim of its own inefficiencies. During the 1960s and 1970s, policy in the United States was divided between the choices of allowing the demise of small business on economic grounds versus preserving some semblance of a small-enterprise sector for social and political reasons. In choosing for the latter, policy-makers argued that small business was essential to maintaining American democracy in the Jeffersonian tradition. Even earlier, passage of the Robinson-Patman Act by the US Congress in 1936 to supplement the Clayton Antitrust Act (Foer, 2001; Bork, 1978) and creation of the United States Small Business Administration in 1953 were both policy responses to protect less-efficient small businesses and to maintain their viability. These policy responses are typical of what Schumpeter (1942) identifies as a Mark II regime, in which large firms outperform their smaller counterparts in the innovation and appropriation process through a strong positive feedback loop from innovation to increased research and development activities.

The purpose of the present paper is to outline the relationship between entrepreneurship and economic performance using a macro perspective. Whereas in an earlier paper, Wennekers, Uhlaner and Thurik (2002) address the causes of variation in the rate of entrepreneurship across countries and across time, the primary aim of the present contribution is to identify the consequences of entrepreneurship. Carree and Thurik (2002) also provide an extensive literature survey of this area. Section 2 reviews changes in the world's economy since the

1970s and the consequences this change has had on economic policy. Furthermore, Section 2 reviews some recent research on the relationship between entrepreneurship and small business on the one hand and economic growth on the other. Section 3 provides a framework linking entrepreneurship and growth at different levels of aggregation focusing on the triangle restructuring, (new) structure and the process of variety and competition. Section 4 of the paper illustrates the framework with some historical case studies.

2. The Economics of the Consequences of Entrepreneurship

2.1. The Changing Role of Small Business Within the Economy

In today's world, both economists and policy makers increasingly see small businesses, particularly new ones,[2] as a vehicle for entrepreneurship, contributing not only to employment and social and political stability but also to innovation and competition (Wennekers and Thurik, 1999). This replaces the older view that small businesses should be maintained for social rather than economic reasons, even at a net economic cost. Recent empirical evidence reinforces this view. Research across a wide spectrum of units of observation, spanning the establishment, the enterprise, the industry, the region, and the country, verifies the positive and statistically robust link between entrepreneurship and economic growth with a lack of entrepreneurship incurring a cost in terms of forgone economic growth (Audretsch and Thurik, 2000; Audretsch, Carree, van Stel and Thurik, 2002; Carree and Thurik, 1999; Carree, van Stel, Thurik and Wennekers, 2002; Audretsch, Carree and Thurik, 2001).

In short, while small business has always mattered to policy makers, the way in which it has mattered has changed dramatically. Confronted with rising concerns about unemployment, job creation, economic growth and international competitiveness in global markets, policy makers have responded to new research evidence with a new mandate to promote the creation of new businesses, i.e., entrepreneurship (Reynolds, Hay, Bygrave, Camp and Autio, 2000). This trend is fairly recent. Whereas in the late 1980s, European policy makers were relatively slow to recognize these links, since the mid-1990s, European policymakers have rapidly built momentum in crafting general intuitive approaches (EIM/ENSR, 1993, 1994, 1995, 1996, 1997; Audretsch, Thurik, Verheul and Wennekers, 2002). Yet, without a clear and organized view of where and how

2. For instance, in his speech « For a new European entrepreneurship » to the Instituto de Empresa, (Madrid, 7 February 2002) Romano Prodi, President of the European Commission, said: "Our lacunae in the field of entrepreneurship need to be taken seriously because there is mounting evidence that the key to economic growth and productivity improvements lies in the entrepreneurial capacity of an economy."

entrepreneurship manifests itself, policy makers are left in unchartered waters without an analytical "compass". Perhaps, this explains the wide variation in their responses (European Commission, 2000 and 2001). For the evaluation of these responses an understanding of the mechanisms by which entrepreneurship impacts economic performance is needed since this may guide more appropriate responses in the future.

2.2. Evidence of the Change

The shift in policy regarding small business and entrepreneurship was coupled with a shift in economic activity from large firms to small firms in the 1970s and 1980s in the U.S. and in the 1980s and 1990s in Europe. The most impressive and also the most cited is the share of the 500 largest American firms, the so-called *Fortune 500*. Their employment share dropped from 20% in 1970 to 8.5% in 1996 (Carlsson, 1992 and 1999). Though the drop in the large firm employment share does not necessarily imply an increase in that of small firms, indeed the share of entrepreneurship in the US labor force increased from 8% in 1972 to nearly 11% in 1988, remaining practically constant afterwards (Wennekers, Uhlaner, and Thurik, 2002). Furthermore, a study of 23 OECD countries in the period 1974-1998 shows that across the entire sample of nations, the number of business owners grew from about 29 million in 1972 to about 45 million in 1998 (Wennekers, Uhlaner, and Thurik, 2002). In spite of clear evidence of a shift toward more widespread ownership and, concurrently, of a shift toward a larger number of smaller firms, this data also reveals considerable disparity in business ownership rates across countries and over time (Audretsch and Thurik, 2000 and Audretsch, Thurik, Verheul and Wennekers, 2002; Wennekers, Uhlaner and Thurik, 2002). Some countries, including Denmark, France, Luxembourg and Norway, even suffered a steady decline in the business ownership rate during the period under study. Finally, although Japan only had a decline in business ownership in the second period (1984-1998), this decline is particularly noteworthy since its share in total business owners dropped from more than 20% in 1972 to 15% in 1998. This data is presented and discussed in detail in our previous paper (Wennekers, Uhlaner, and Thurik, 2002). In fact, it is precisely this variation across countries what allows us to ask the central question of the present paper: do varying rates of entrepreneurship across countries affect economic performance and if so, why?

2.3. Causes of the Change

Many of the major causes of the shift toward expanded entrepreneurship are discussed by Wennekers, Uhlaner, and Thurik (2002) and thus will not be repeated in detail. At the aggregate level, technology, level of economic development, demographic characteristics, culture and institutions all play a role in determining the opportunities (on the demand side), and the capabilities and preferences (on the supply side) that plant the seeds of nascent entrepreneurship. Wennekers, Uhlaner and Thurik (2002) further elaborate the manner in which nascent entrepreneurship, start-ups and exits combine to establish the actual rate of business ownership in a particular economy. This is further complicated by the notion that the actual rate is a fluctuation of an underlying equilibrium rate of entrepreneurship within a particular economy. Rather than repeat these arguments here, the reader is urged to refer to our earlier paper. Other sources documenting the industrial changes and their causes are Piore and Sabel (1984), Brock and Evans (1989), Loveman and Sengenberger (1991), Carlsson (1992), Acs, Carlsson and Karlsson (1999), Audretsch and Thurik (2000) and Carree, van Stel, Thurik and Wennekers (2002).

2.4. The Consequences of Entrepreneurship

What then are the consequences of the shift toward smallness? The relationship between growth and entrepreneurship at the macro level is a complicated one. In the past, macro-economic models have assumed a two-way causation between changes in the level of entrepreneurship and that of the level of economic development: a "Schumpeter" effect of rate of entrepreneurship enhancing economic growth and a "refugee" or "shopkeeper" effect of low growth levels stimulating self-employment. Audretsch, Carree and Thurik (2001) try to reconcile the ambiguities found in the relationship between unemployment – as the inverse of economic growth - and entrepreneurship. This two-way causation between unemployment and entrepreneurship finds its origins in various parts of the economics literature. On the one hand, the simple theory of occupational choice, which has been the basis for numerous studies focusing on the decision confronted by individuals to start a firm and become an entrepreneur suggests that increased unemployment will lead to an increase in startup activity on the grounds that the opportunity cost of starting a firm has decreased. On the other hand, the unemployed tend to possess lower endowments of human capital and entrepreneurial talent required to start and sustain a new firm, suggesting that high unemployment is associated with a low degree of entrepreneurial activities. A low rate of entrepreneurship may also be a consequence of low economic growth levels, which also reflect higher levels of unemployment. Entrepreneurial opportunities are not just the result of the push effect of (the threat of) unemployment but also of the pull effect produced by a thriving economy as well as by entrepreneurial activities in the past. In addition to unemployment leading to more or less entrepreneurial activity, the reverse has also been claimed to hold. On the one hand, new-firm startups hire employees, resulting in subsequent decreases in unemployment. On the other hand, the low rates of survival combined with the limited growth of the majority of small firms imply that the employment contribution of startups is limited at best, which would argue against entrepreneurial activities reducing unemployment.

Reynolds, Hay, Bygrave, Camp and Autio (2000) take a more direct approach by correlating growth and entrepreneurial activity. The latter approach is simpler in a methodological sense but more sophisticated in that a wider variety of countries is observed and that entrepreneurial activities are measured appropriately. Despite their entirely different approaches both studies show a positive correlation between entrepreneurship and economic growth. Carree and Thurik (2002) cite other studies in their survey of the literature on the role of entrepreneurship in economic growth. Briefly summarizing their conclusions, by and large, research to date suggests that entrepreneurship contributes to economic growth irrespective of how entrepreneurship is measured, which level of aggregation is observed and/or which model is used. However, our knowledge of the drivers, i.e. the intermediate linkages between entrepreneurship and economic performance is weak. We return to this theme in the next section, where we suggest what some of the linkages may be.

3. A Framework Linking Entrepreneurship and Economic Performance

Wennekers, Uhlaner and Thurik (2002) provide a framework of entrepreneurial behavior that addresses both the determinants and consequences of entrepreneurship at the macro-level of analysis (See Figure 1). Their paper focuses primarily on the left-hand portion of the framework: explaining how the various determinants of entrepreneurship, including technology, level of economic development, demography, culture and institutions, exert their influence on nascent entrepreneurship by way of individual occupational choice. Subsequently, their paper provides insight into how nascent entrepreneurship influences the actual rate of business ownership at the aggregate level of analysis, considering various intermediary and conditional variables.

The present paper concentrates on the right-hand portion of the framework: in particular, the relationship between different aspects of entrepreneurial behavior (i.e. nascent entrepreneurship, start-ups, and total business ownership) and economic performance at the individual, firm and macro levels. (See Figure 2).

Figure 1: A Framework of Entrepreneurial Behavior

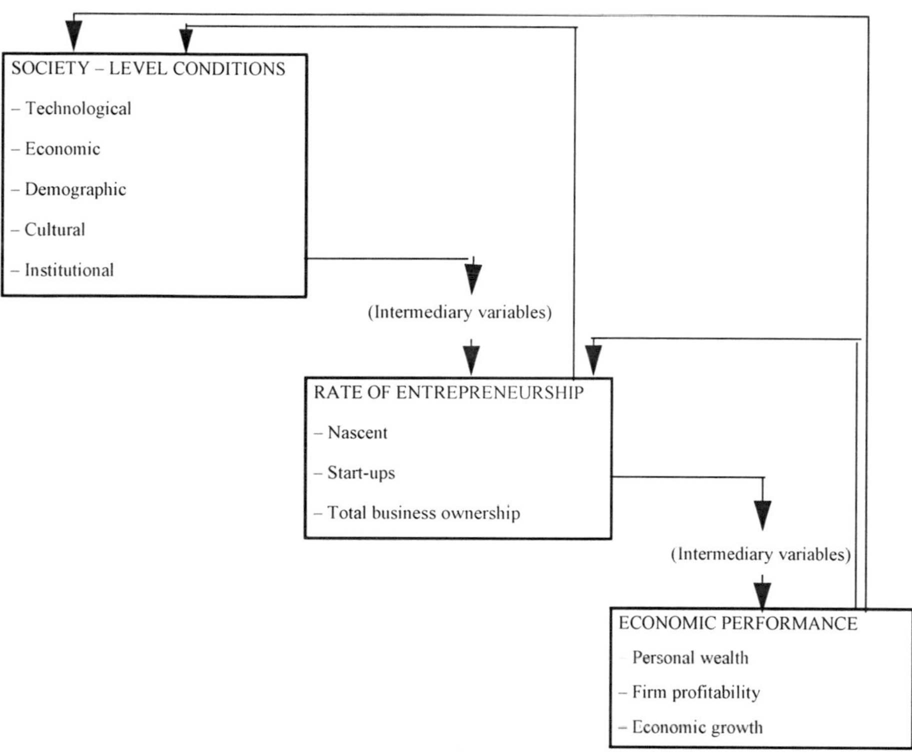

3.1. Nascent Entrepreneurship: the Starting Point

Our discussion of the framework starts from the phenomenon of nascent entrepreneurship, as indicated in the upper left corner of Figure 2. Nascent entrepreneurs are individuals (such as wage earners, unemployed, students and homemakers) who intend and/or actively try to start a new business. Nascent entrepreneurship stands for untapped 'entrepreneurial energy outside the market'. Only a certain proportion of nascent entrepreneurs succeeds in getting a new business up and running. This proportion is represented in our model by the variable, start-ups, which in our model is treated as a firm-level variable. Start-ups represent the firms that enter the market. They affect the level of innovation found at the firm level of analysis. A substantial proportion of (though not all) new firms foster innovation by introducing new products or by finding new ways of producing and/or delivering an existing good or service. This influence is most directly operational at the firm level (as noted by the arrow between innovation and firm performance in Figure 2).

Figure 2: Entrepreneurship and Economic Performance

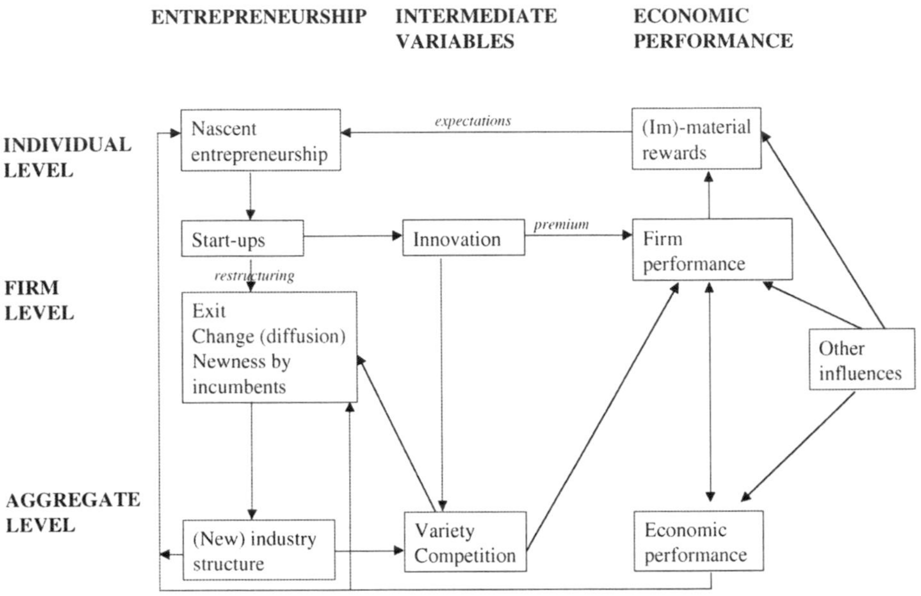

Second, start-ups trigger a restructuring of the economy through a wide array of adaptive reactions including, ultimately, business exits, mergers, re-engineering (diffusion), and new innovations by incumbents. The decisions leading to these reactions are made at the firm level, but their accumulated effects influence the aggregate level as well. In particular, the accumulated effects of these start-ups, exits and mergers change industry structure in terms of the number of businesses (the rate of business ownership) and the firm size distribution of firms.[3] This restructuring takes place at the aggregate levels of sectors, regions and national economies. The (new) industry structure resulting from start-up behavior and decisions taken by the incumbent firms and the innovations brought forward by new firms are also crucial inputs for a (new) round of variety and competition at the aggregate level. New industrial constellations lead to new forms of static as well as dynamic competition, in particular when new products or processes become manifest (innovation). Therefore in Figure 2 arrows are drawn from both (new) structure and innovation

3. Age is also an interesting aspect of industry structure influenced by new firm start-ups. Based upon an extensive investigation into company histories of many of the world's major firms of the past century, Jovanovic and Rousseau (2001, p. 14) conclude: "New technologies and products are usually brought in by young companies and this means that – with some delay – when a new technology comes to market, [the average age of] an economy's leading firms tend[s] to get younger". We will not go deeper into the meaning of age for our framework.

to the process of variety and competition. The static competition depends upon number and size class distribution of firms whereas dynamic competition arises from the variety of products and processes. This variety and competition, in turn, has an effect on the process of restructuring through selection of the most viable firms and the best ideas. In other words, firms are inclined or forced to react to their competitive environment with decisions about exiting, changing or introducing newness. Therefore in Figure 2 an arrow is drawn between the process of variety and competition and that of restructuring. Both the (new) industry structure and the variety and competition process directly or indirectly provide new impulses to nascent entrepreneurship, via second attempts of failed entrepreneurs, via spin-offs from incumbent firms and via new (inexperienced) start-ups following successful examples of entrepreneurship. The indirect impulses of variety and competition on nascent entrepreneurship are rather complex, traveling via the path to firm performance, individual rewards and the expectations of these actual rewards for nascent entrepreneurs. These impulses will be explained below.

3.2. Economic Performance in the Framework

Figure 2 also considers the direct and indirect effects of (new) entrepreneurial decision making on firm performance. Firm performance is influenced in three *direct* ways. First, the variety and competition process resulting from increased start-ups and restructuring of the economy manifests itself as an effect on firm performance. Second, in the short run, innovation often brings a premium to the innovator, in terms of higher growth of sales or higher business profitability (and thus also influencing firm performance). Third, economic performance at the aggregate level itself influences firm performance by creating or destroying opportunities for improved performance at the firm level. A strong economy not only provides a richer resource base for starting and expanding firms but also, ceteris paribus, for high performance. Conversely, an economy (or sector) in recession, will have a generalized dampening effect on individual firm performance. And, of course, the accumulated results of firm performance affects economic performance at the aggregate level. Therefore, the diagram shown in Figure 2 reveals a two-way arrow between firm performance and economic performance.

Figure 2 also shows a relationship between firm performance and the rewards entrepreneurs receive as a result of managing and owning their own businesses. Further such rewards – both material and immaterial – can be shared with the wage earners employed. These rewards can include, for instance, not only growth of personal wealth but also self-realization or sense of achievement for their accomplishments. Figure 2 indicates that *other influences* may directly affect such rewards. These *other influences* may include the taxation and inheritance laws affecting the amount of profits entrepreneurs are entitled to keep.

Of course, exogenous factors may also influence economic growth and firm performance in addition to the endogenous factors indicated in Figure 2. Three important examples are the characteristics of consumer preferences, the growth of scientific knowledge and the invention of new radical technologies. A fourth one consists of deviations between the "optimal industrial" structure and the current one. We will discuss this fourth example below in section 4.2.3.

3.3. Preliminary Assessment of the Framework

Summarizing, our framework discusses several links leading from nascent entrepreneurship to firm performance, economic growth at the macro level as well as material and immaterial rewards at the individual level. Finally, the outcome of these dynamic processes depends also on a set of societal conditions discussed in an earlier article in this journal (Wennekers, Uhlaner and Thurik, 2002). It is likely that there are more feedbacks than those mentioned. Competition and selection in a world of variety enable individuals and firms to learn from both their own and other's successes and failures.[4] Role models implant expectations in future nascent entrepreneurs, while learning processes help individuals to improve their skills and adapt their attitudes. Also, but not explicitly shown in Figure 2, deviations from the "optimal" industrial structure as perceived by policy makers, induce political debate leading to the introduction of new policies and the revision of existing institutions. The outcome of all these so-called "spillovers" may be new entrepreneurial actions, creating a recurrent chain of linkages. Figure 2 must be interpreted as a highly stylized first attempt to describe the links between entrepreneurship and economic performance integrating various aggregation levels. Also, its emphasis on the role of the triangle of restructuring, (new) structure and variety and competition leaves room for alternative points of view. For instance, (new) entrepreneurs may also contribute to economic development by working longer and harder than similarly educated employees.

4. Historical Case Studies

The framework of entrepreneurial behavior and economic development provides a tool for analysis of the long-term economic performance of national economies, and particularly of the rise and decline of nations. In this section we take a closer look at the second industrial revolution – driven by the implementation of electricity and combustion – in the turn-of-the-nineteenth-century United States,

4. Also see Dosi (1988a, p. 235).

and the partly overlapping managerial revolution leading to the age of giant corporations during the years 1930-1970. Second, we examine the modern knowledge economy of the late 20th and early 21st century.

4.1. The Second Industrial and Managerial Revolutions

The Second Industrial Revolution (Landes, 1969, p. 4; Atkeson and Kehoe, 2001, p. 1), driven by inventions such as electricity and the internal combustion engine, was a highly entrepreneurial period in economic history. This revolution was most conspicuous in the United States, although several European countries, notably Germany, also produced many innovations in this period (Landes, 1969, p. 352). The Second Industrial Revolution, while basically concentrated between 1860 and the early 1900s, gave rise to innovations in all walks of life, both in the US and in Europe, over an even longer period of time (Atkeson and Kehoe, 2001, p. 1). We will briefly touch upon this episode, as well as the Managerial Revolution, which began a few decades later and carried into a period ending roughly in 1970 (Chandler, 1977).

The growth in scale economies and the managerial revolution that took place in the decades preceding 1970 were forces that pushed the rate of business ownership downward, suppressing entry of new businesses and other entrepreneurial ventures. In spite of these forces, the economic success of this interim period can however be traced back to individual entrepreneurs. In support of this point, Purrington and Bettcher (2001) tracked the entrepreneurial roots of America's largest corporations at the close of the twentieth century. In particular, they found that out of the *Fortune 200* companies listed in 1997, 197 were either directly (101) or indirectly (96) tracked back to one or more entrepreneurial founders.

The speed of scientific discoveries, technical inventions and ensuing innovations during the second half of the 19th century was remarkable, rivaling or possibly even surpassing that of the so-called "new" economy of the late twentieth century. A sampling of the innovations put to market between 1851 and 1910, and predominantly still in use in the early 21st century, include automobiles, airplanes, telephones, photography, the cinema, the typewriter, electric light, the refrigerator and many other electrical household appliances, aspirin, vaccines, plastics, the safety pin, the zipper, jeans, and toilet paper.[5] One source of dissemination somewhat unique to that period was the popularity of world exhibitions in both America and Europe. In a period where international communication was still quite primitive by today's standards, these international fairs played an extremely important role in the diffusion and adoption of new

5. For a more complete overview of the many innovations of this period, the reader is referred to the catalogue of the exposition "La belle Europe; le temps des expositions universelles 1851-1913", Musées Royaux d'Art et d'Histoire, Brussels 26 October 2001 – 17 March 2002.

innovations. Later, photography and other newer technologies reduced the need for physical display of wares. Also, these fairs came into being at a time of relative calm and political stability among different nation-states.

The late 19th and early 20th century was also a period of high entry rates of new businesses. Many of the companies to dominate commerce for the majority of the twentieth century, such as General Electric, American Telephone and Telegraph (AT&T), General Motors and Boeing, were new entrants to business during this period, becoming listed on the stock market rather quickly upon their initial founding and creating lasting value (Jovanovic and Rousseau, 2001). We conjecture that these were among the firms, also including 'new' German brands[6] such as Siemens (1847), Bayer (1863), Agfa (1873) and Opel (1898), that may have inspired Schumpeter to develop his *Theory of Economic Development* (Schumpeter, 1934), emphasizing the role of the entrepreneur as prime cause of economic development, challenging incumbent firms by introducing new inventions that make current technologies and products obsolete. This process of 'creative destruction' is the main characteristic of the Schumpeter Mark I regime referred to previously.

For the champions of the Second Industrial Revolution, notably the US and Germany, this period was also an era of relatively high economic growth rates. According to Maddison (2001, p. 185, 186), GDP per capita growth between 1870 and 1913 averaged 1.8% per annum in the US. The average economic growth rate in Germany was 1.6%, while the leader of the First Industrial Revolution, the UK, achieved no better than 1.0% per annum. In The Netherlands, the technological frontier of Europe in the 17th century and the richest country of the western world until the early 1800s, economic growth between 1870-1913 did not exceed 0.9%.

At the same time, the evolving separation of business ownership and management roles in the late 19th and early 20th century is a hallmark of the onset of the Managerial Revolution (Chandler, 1977). The introduction of the limited and/or listed company facilitated the development of this separation of roles between ownership and management, first by the railroad and telegraphs industries and later mimicked by a broad range of other sectors including the automobile industry, retailing, and insurance. These changes were also coincident with a giant leap in business scale, the onset of multi-unit firms and the creation of managerial hierarchies. Though reaching a mature stage as early as 1910, the Managerial Revolution continued until roughly around 1970 (Chandler, 1977).

The continued decline of business ownership rate during this period is also attributed to the Managerial Revolution (Phillips, 1962). The scale achieved by many of the early entrants also helped these companies to ride out the Great Depression of the 1930's. For decades following the Great Depression, few firms entered the stock market, exceptions being mature firms, such as Proctor and Gamble and Pfizer that had been founded in the previous century. "Accordingly,

6. Again the reader is referred to the catalogue of "La belle Europe; le temps des expositions universelles 1851-1913", mentioned before.

the largest firms, which in the vast majority of cases were able to ride out the Depression, remained large" (Jovanovic and Rousseau, 2001, p. 15).

In sum, the years before 1910 are characterized as a classical entrepreneurial period with many new radical inventions and high business entry rates (Schumpeter Mark I), while scale economies gradually began to manifest themselves. The decades after 1910 were increasingly committed to technology *diffusion*, a period of about 70 years of ongoing, rapid technical change and accelerated growth in productivity (Atkeson and Kehoe, 2001, p. 1). The high economic growth rates of the 1950s and 1960s seem to be more the result of the spread of the managerial revolution, investments in new capital intensive industrial plants and large firm R&D (the so-called Schumpeter Mark II regime as foresaid in Schumpeter, 1942), rather than of new entrepreneurial formation.

Applying our framework to the period 1860-1970 we see that the triangle of restructuring, new structure and variety is particularly relevant for the decades before 1900 showing the onset of many new industries, resulting in a large wave of new and small firms consistent with the early stage of their product life cycle. The framework seems less applicable to the 1930-1970 years dominated by scale economies and stable technological trajectories giving rise to a relatively large firm-based industrial structure. This latter period is also quite distinct from the late 1970s and the 1980s, during which a more entrepreneurial economy would re-emerge. In the decades before 1900 start-up activity and innovation behavior dominated the explanation of growing economic performance.

4.2. The Knowledge Economy (1975 - ???)

Our second case example is drawn from the most recent economic period. Since the early 1970s many developed economies, beginning with the United States, have witnessed the revival of business ownership and the upsurge of new business start-ups. This section explores how our framework as presented in Figure 2 might be helpful in explaining some consequences of this most recent resurgence in entrepreneurial activity, as well as the large variation that persists across countries.

4.2.1. Global Trends in the Business Environment

In the modern economy, knowledge has replaced raw materials and physical labor as the key resource (Drucker, 2001), thus earning the present era the label of the *knowledge economy* (Audretsch and Thurik, 2000). New information technologies, especially the Internet, allow knowledge to spread quickly, available to anyone with computer access and telephone connections. These new technologies have led to an information technology (IT) revolution characterized by Jovanovic and Rousseau as the “second democratization of knowledge”, the first one being the invention of the printing press in the 15th century (Jovanovic and Rousseau, 2001, p. 22).

One can draw parallels between the Second Industrial Revolution and the present IT revolution. One obvious parallel is the young age of IT entrants on the stock market and the related wave of new products, new firms, and faster productivity growth worldwide than witnessed in the middle part of the 20th century” (Jovanovic and Rousseau, 2001, p. 17). Secondly, governments at both the country and at the supranational level are increasingly being tuned towards fostering entrepreneurship (Stevenson and Lundström, 2001; Audretsch et al., 2002; OECD, 1998; European Commission, 1999). Various nations have instituted labor and capital market reforms, reduction of regulatory and administrative barriers for business start-ups, new competition policies, specific programs and services in support of new and small firms, promotion of entrepreneurship and an increasing attention for entrepreneurship at all levels of the educational system.

The advent of knowledge as a prime input factor weakened incumbent firms depending on more traditional inputs and led to increased start-up activity and innovation behavior. This again led to strong movements in the triangle of restructuring, structure and variety and competition as depicted in Figure 2.

4.2.2. Contemporary Institutional Differences Across Nations

Our earlier analysis[7] of the first part of our framework in Figure 1 suggests that the variation in business ownership across countries partly stems from differences in the level of economic development. Up to a certain stage of economic development more prosperous countries have relatively fewer business owners and a relatively greater large firms sector. Beyond this stage of development a reversal of the declining business ownership rate was seen to occur in several of the economically most advanced nations. Additionally, and partly unrelated to the stage of development, historically rooted cultural and institutional differences contribute to the variation in business ownership.

A brief comparison of the cultural and institutional conditions for entrepreneurship in France with those in the US, further illustrates how our framework of economic performance in figure 2 is embedded in the overall framework of entrepreneurial behaviour in figure 1.[8] Both France and the U.S. rank among the most advanced nations of the world, economically and technically speaking. However, they differ conspicuously with respect to rate of business

7. For a detailed elaboration of our framework on the causes of entrepreneurship the reader is referred to our article in Wennekers, Uhlaner and Thurik (2002).
8. This section is based upon chapters 3 and 6 of Audretsch, Thurik, Verheul and Wennekers (2002).

ownership. Over the last three decades of the twentieth century, France declined in business ownership to an all-time low level of 8.5% in 1998. By contrast, the U.S. rebounded in its rate of business ownership to a rate above 10% of its labor force over the same period. This net gain in ownership masks an even more vibrant entrepreneurial economy: the U.S. economy can be described as turbulent, as reflected in unusually high entry and exit rates, a high prevalence of rapid growth firms, and innovative entrepreneurship, with respect to advanced technologies.

Cultural and institutional differences between these two countries may help to explain theses sharp differences in entrepreneurship rates. For instance, Hofstede's research characterizes French culture as having a high degree of uncertainty avoidance and power distance (Wennekers, Uhlaner and Thurik, 2002). Its institutions also reflect strict government regulations, centralized planning and control. Management positions are often assigned to former students of the elite schools, the so-called *Grandes Écoles*. The French educational system restricts its attention for entrepreneurship to universities and colleges, most prominently in business schools. Labor market flexibility is traditionally limited, causing high opportunity costs of entrepreneurship and restricting the room for business owners to adjust their workforce to market demand. Relative to the United States, France can also be seen as a more centrally-managed economy. It has a centuries-long history of strong government intervention in industrial development. Innovation is strongly dependent upon the government, which is inclined to assign technological projects to large firms. Within technological clusters large firms are often aloof to their immediate environment, thereby inhibiting "technological cross-fertilization". By contrast, the U.S. culture has often been described as supportive of entrepreneurship. Using Hofstede's dimensions, it is characterized by a low rate of uncertainty avoidance. Furthermore, its culture traditionally attaches a high value to self-reliance. Starting a business is easy and considered 'normal'. The social stigma of failure is relatively low. Its institutions also support entrepreneurship. The venture capital market is well developed, the labor market is flexible and intellectual property rights are relatively well protected. Finally, knowledge spills over rather smoothly from universities and large corporations to small and new firms through spin-offs, incubator centers, and rules that often encourage or at least allow for the sharing of information.

4.2.3. Economic Effects of Business Ownership and the Concept of "Disequilibrium"

Business ownership declined over a long time span, clearly documented from at least the late nineteenth century until approximately the 1970s (Wennekers, Uhlaner, and Thurik, 2002). The reversal of the downward trend in business ownership rates since the early 1970s gives rise to the idea that a U-shaped relationship exists between rates of business ownership and economic development. Economists partly explain this reversal as the result of the information communications technology (ICT) revolution, which significantly altered the transaction costs of doing business, leveling the playing field between large and small firms (Wennekers, Uhlaner and Thurik, 2002). However, this technology shift alone cannot sufficiently explain why the extent and timing of this shift varies so much across countries (Brock and Evans, 1989). Thus, a further explanation must take into account the differences in institutions and policies across countries that facilitated a greater and more rapid response to globalization and technological change, along with the other underlying factors, by shifting to a less centralized industry structure in some countries than has been the case in other countries (Audretsch, Thurik, Verheul and Wennekers, 2002). An implication of this high variance in industry restructuring is that some countries are likely to have industry structures that are different from "equilibrium" or "optimal" rate.

Many forces may cause the actual number of business owners to deviate from the "equilibrium" rate.[9] Such a "disequilibium" may result from cultural forces, institutional settings (regulation of entry, incentive structures, functioning of the capital market) and economic forces (unemployment, profitability of private enterprise). A "disequilibrium" may also result from overshooting. This overshooting may have occurred in the last declining stage of business ownership rates, as the upsizing of the business sector and the development of relevant institutions (labor market regulation, social security, tax system, educational system) have symbiotically reinforced each other during the greater part of the last century. During the 1950s and 1960s the actual business ownership rate in many countries may well have decreased to a level below the underlying equilibrium rate. There are several forces in market economies that contribute to a process of adapting towards the equilibrium. An example may illustrate this. A high labor income share and a structurally low number of enterprises contributed to structural unemployment in the late 1970s and 1980s in many Western economies. Such high levels of unemployment may have various consequences. First, unemployment may have a direct effect on self-employment, as unemployed are claimed to be more likely to become self-employed than employees. Second, structural unemployment gradually results in wage moderation helping to restore profitability of private enterprise (lower labor income share). In addition, a perceived shortage of business ownership will

9. As the business ownership rate is by definition inversely related to average firm size, it is straightforward that the "equilibrium" rate may be inversely related to (the development of) scale economies in the various lines of business, and to their relative proportions. At the supply side of business ownership the equilibrium rate is also influenced by real wages, representing the opportunity costs of entrepreneurship (Lucas, 1978). For a generalization see de Wit and Van Winden (1991).

induce policies fostering entrepreneurship, ranging from better access to financing to competition policies (OECD, 1998).

Explanations for economic growth have in recent decades generally been restricted to the realm of macroeconomics. However, a different scholarly tradition links growth to industrial organization (Schumpeter, 1934). According to this tradition, performance, measured in terms of economic growth, depends upon the degree to which the industry structure most efficiently utilizes scarce resources. But what determines this 'optimal' structure? There is a long-standing tradition in the field of industrial organization devoted towards identifying the determinants of industry structure, in particular technology. Chandler (1990), for instance, expands the determinants of optimal industry structure to include other factors next to underlying technology. Dosi (1988b, p. 1157) concludes that "Each production activity is characterized by a particular distribution of firms." When the determinants of the underlying industrial structure are stable, the industry structure itself would not be expected to change. However, a change in the underlying determinants would be expected to result in a change in the "optimal" industry structure. An extensive literature has linked the structure of industries to performance. However, little is known about the consequences of deviating from the "optimal" industry structure. The evidence provided in Audretsch, Carree, van Stel and Thurik (2002) shows that, in fact, there is a cost of not adjusting industry structure towards the "optimal". They define structure in terms of the small business share or the relative number of entrepreneurs and measure costs in terms of forgone economic growth. Since deviations are inevitable due to regulations, scarce input factors, or failing markets, the existence of growth penalties is a relevant phenomenon.

Therefore, these deviations, though not explicitly indicated in Figure 2, are subsumed under the heading of *other influences*.

4.2.4. Empirical Evidence on the Role of Entry and Exit

In recent years some research has been carried out into the relationship between dynamic proxies of entrepreneurship and economic performance. Bosma and Nieuwenhuijsen (2000) studied the impact of firm dynamics on productivity growth in the Netherlands. Their model is based upon a production function framework in which turbulence (the sum of entry and exit as a percentage of the number of incumbent businesses) is incorporated as an additional explanatory variable. Using data for a panel of 40 Dutch regions in the period 1988-1996, they estimate their model for services and manufacturing separately. For the services sector they find a significant and positive influence of lagged turbulence on (total factor) productivity growth. For manufacturing no impact was found.

Audretsch and Frisch (2002), investigate the differences in employment growth rates between 74 West-German regions in the 1980s and 1990s. They distinguish between four growth regimes: the entrepreneurial regime (high start-up rate and high employment growth rate), routinized regime (low start-up rate with high growth rate), revolving door regime (high start-up rate with low growth rate) and the declining or downsizing regime (low start-up rate and low growth rate). When comparing the 1980s and the 1990s they find some striking results. First, regions with revolving door regimes in the 1980s often become entrepreneurial in the 1990s. Second, none of the regions with a routinized regime in the 1980s became entrepreneurial in the 1990s, but many entered the downsizing category. Third, the majority of the regions that were in the entrepreneurial or the downsizing category in the 1980s were of the same type in the 1990s. Finally, when regressing employment change across regions, they find a significant positive influence of high start-up rates in the 1980s on employment change in the 1990s. Audretsch and Fritsch (2002) conclude: 'Small firms and new firm start-ups may not be necessary for regional growth in the short run, but perhaps they are the seeds of future growth and are of central importance for long run economic development'. A similar investigation concerning business start-ups and employment growth in 60 regions of Great Britain confirms these results (van Stel and Storey, 2002).

This and similar research is an example of the influence of the triangle of restructuring, structure and variety and competition on firm performance (Figure 2).

4.2.5. Further Evidence Regarding the Relationship Between Entrepreneurship and Innovation

Small businesses serve as a vehicle for entrepreneurship. In addition, Acs (1992) suggests that small firms also play an important role as a source of innovative activity, as a stimulus for industry evolution and as a source of new jobs. Acs and Audretsch (1990) are the first to extensively investigate the role of smallness in the process of innovation. They found that, contrary to what was generally believed, industries with a large amount of small firms also have an inclination for innovation. Prior to their investigations it was generally thought that large (monopolistic) firms with large laboratories were the main source of economic progress (Chandler, 1977; Galbraith, 1967). As noted in the framework, start-up activity is assumed to be an engine for structural change across different industries and the economy at large. Audretsch (1995) provides examples within the American manufacturing sector. Cohen and Klepper (1992) focus on the impact of the number of firms on variety of the population of firms while this variety is a mechanism for progress: firms as well as consumers tend to reconsider their behavior in the face of alternatives. Baumol (1990) hypothesizes that while the total supply of entrepreneurs varies among societies, the productive contribution of their activities varies much more because of their allocation between productive activities such as innovation and largely unproductive activities such as rent-seeking or organized crime (Baumol, 1990, p. 894). Burke, Fitzroy and Nolan (2000) point at the fundamental difference between factors affecting the number of self-employed and their performance, i.e., between quantity and quality. Their study supports the view that an economy containing more small firms is not necessarily one with a more highly-performing, small-firm sector. For instance, a highly educated work force may produce a smaller total number of successful start-ups but a higher absolute number of highly performing ones. See also Carree and Thurik (2002) for a extensive literature survey of the entire area of entrepreneurship and economic growth.

5. Summary and Conclusions

We concur with the conclusion reached in a recent report that "...remarkably little is known about the relationship between entrepreneurship and economic growth, including how it works, what determines its strength and the extent to which it holds for diverse countries" (Reynolds, Hay, Bygrave, Camp and Autio, 2000, p.11). This lack of information points toward the importance of initiatives such as the EIM/CASBEC research program and the Global Entrepreneurship Monitor in supporting the policy debate to focus more and more on the role of entrepreneurship for economic growth. The richness of the newly arising data material in terms of the variety of countries, the variety with which entrepreneurship can be measured and the large amount of explanatory variables will in due time provide policy makers with indispensable insight in macroeconomic policies and instruments needed to foster solid economic growth.

The present paper attempts to outline the relationship between entrepreneurship and economic performance using a macro perspective: the aim of the present contribution is to identify the consequences of entrepreneurship. It reviews some recent research on the relationship between entrepreneurship and small business on the one hand and economic growth on the other. It provides a tentative framework linking entrepreneurship and growth at different levels of aggregation while it also presents some historical case studies.

Entrepreneurship has played a vital role both in the take-off stages of the European economy and during the First Industrial Revolution.[10] Entrepreneurial formation also played a crucial role during the Second Industrial Revolution. But the growth in scale economies and the managerial revolution that took place in the decades preceding 1970 were forces that not only pushed the rate of business ownership downward, but also suppressed entry of new businesses and other entrepreneurial ventures. In spite of these forces, the economic success of this

10. Moreover, it is likely that economic decline, such as that experienced in 18th century Holland and late 19th and most of 20th century Britain, was aggravated by the cultural and institutional framework becoming less conducive to entrepreneurship (Wennekers and Thurik, 1999).

interim period can however be traced back to individual entrepreneurs of an earlier period.

Finally, the present era is sometimes designated as that of the knowledge economy or the third industrial revolution. From the empirical evidence of increasing new business formation and total business ownership in recent decades, and from econometric analysis of these data, it can be concluded that entrepreneurial formation seems to be regaining the economic relevance of previous industrial revolutions.

We conclude that our framework of the consequences of entrepreneurship seems to be applicable, although apparently the explanatory power of the various determinants and the weight of the various consequences differ between historical periods. However, much needs to be done to explain the links between entrepreneurship and economic growth.

References:

Acs, Z.J. (1992). "Small business economics; a global perspective," *Challenge*, Vol. 35, 38-44.

Acs, Z.J. and D.B. Audretsch. (1990). *Innovation and Small Firms*, Cambridge, MA: MIT Press.

Acs, Z.J. and D.B. Audretsch. (1993)."Conclusion," in Z.J. Acs and D.B. Audretsch (eds.), *Small Firms and Entrepreneurship; an East-West Perspective*, Cambridge, UK: Cambridge University Press.

Acs, Z.J., B. Carlsson and Ch. Karlsson. (1999). "The linkages among entrepreneurship, SMEs and the macroeconomy," in Z.J. Acs, B. Carlsson and Ch. Karlsson (eds.), *Entrepreneurship, Small and Medium-Sized Enterprises and the Macroeconomy*, Cambridge, UK: Cambridge University Press.

Atkeson, A. and P.J. Kehoe. (2001). "The transition to a new economy after the second industrial revolution", NBER Working Paper 8676, Cambridge, MA: National Bureau of Economic Research.

Audretsch, D.B. (1995). *Innovation and Industry Evolution*, Cambridge, MA: MIT Press.

Audretsch, D.B. M.A. Carree, A.J. van Stel and A.R. Thurik. (2002). "Impeded industrial restructuring: the growth penalty," *Kyklos*, Vol. 55, no.1, 81-97.

Audretsch, D.B. M.A. Carree and A.R. Thurik. (2001). "Does entrepreneurship reduce unemployment?", Discussion paper TI01-074/3, Tinbergen Institute, Erasmus University Rotterdam.

Audretsch, D.B. and M. Fritsch. (2002). "Growth regimes over time and space," *Regional Studies*, Vol. 36, 113-124.

Audretsch, D.B. and A.R. Thurik. (2000). "Capitalism and democracy in the 21st century: from the managed to the entrepreneurial economy," *Journal of Evolutionary Economics*, Vol. 10, no. 1, 17-34.

Audretsch, D.B. and A.R. Thurik. (2001). "What's new about the new economy? From the managed to the entrepreneurial economy," *Industrial and Corporate Change*, Vol. 10, no. 1, 267-315.

Audretsch, D.B., A.R. Thurik, I. Verheul and A.R.M Wennekers (eds). (2002). *Entrepreneurship: Determinants and Policies in the New Economy*, Boston/Dordrecht: Kluwer Academic Publishers.

Baumol, W.J. (1990). "Entrepreneurship: productive, unproductive and destructive," *Journal of Political Economy*, Vol. 98, no. 5, 894-911.

Blair, J.M. (1948). "Technology and size," *American Economic Review*, Vol. 38, 121-152.

Bork, Robert H. (1978). *The Antitrust Paradox: A Policy At War With Itself*, New York: Basic Books.

Bosma, N.S. and H.R. Nieuwenhuijsen. (2000). "Turbulence and productivity in the Netherlands", Research Report 9909/E, Zoetermeer: EIM Business and Policy Research.

Brock, W.A. and D.S. Evans. (1989). "Small business economics," *Small Business Economics* , Vol.1, 7-20.

Burke, Andrew E., Felix R. Fitzroy and M.A. Nolan. (2000). "When less is more: distinguishing between entrepreneurial choice and performance," *Oxford Bulletin of Economics and Statistics*, Vol. 62, no. 5, 565-587.

Carlsson, B. (1992). "The rise of small business; causes and consequences," in W.J. Adams (ed.), *Singular Europe, economy and policy of the European Community after 1992*, Ann Arbor, MI: University of Michigan Press, 145-169.

Carlsson, B. (1999). "Small business, entrepreneurship, and industrial dynamics," in Z. Acs (ed.), *Are Small Firms Important?,* Boston/Dordrecht: Kluwer Academic Publishers, 99-110.

Carree, M.A. and A.R. Thurik. (1998). "Small firms and economic growth in Europe," *Atlantic Economic Journal*, Vol. 26, no. 2, 137-146.

Carree, M.A. and A.R. Thurik. (1999). "Industrial structure and economic growth," in *Innovation, Industry Evolution and Employment*, D.B. Audretsch and A. R. Thurik (eds.), Cambridge, UK: Cambridge University Press, 86-110.

Carree, M.A. and A.R. Thurik. (2002). "The impact of entrepreneurship on economic growth," in D.B. Audretsch and Z.J. Acs (eds), *Handbook of Entrepreneurship Research*, Boston/ Dordrecht: Kluwer Academic Publishers.

Carree, M.A., A. van Stel, A.R. Thurik and A.R.M. Wennekers. (2002). "Economic development and business ownership: an analysis using data of 23 OECD countries in the period 1976-1996," *Small Business Economics*, Vol. 19, no. 3, 271-290.

Chandler, A.D. Jr. (1977). *The Visible Hand: The Managerial Revolution in American Business*, Cambridge, MA: Harvard University Press.

Chandler, A.D. Jr. (1990). *Scale and Scope: The Dynamics of Industrial Capitalism*, Cambridge, MA: Harvard University Press.

Cohen, W.M. and S. Klepper. (1992). "The trade-off between firm size and diversity in the pursuit of technological progress," *Small Business Economics*, Vol. 4, 1-14.

Dosi, G. (1988a). "The nature of the innovative process," in G. Dosi, C. Freeman, R. Nelson, G. Silverberg and L. Soete (eds), *Technical change and economic theory*, London and New York: Pinter Publishers, 221-238.

Dosi, G. (1988b). "Sources, procedures and microeconomic effects of innovations," *Journal of Economic Literature,* Vol. 26, 1120-1171.

Drucker, Peter. (2001). "The next society; a survey of the near future," *The Economist,* November 3rd 2001.

EIM/ENSR. (1993). *The European Observatory: first annual report*, Zoetermeer: EIM Business and Policy Research.

EIM/ENSR. (1994). *The European Observatory: second annual report*, Zoetermeer: EIM Business and Policy Research.

EIM/ENSR. (1995). *The European Observator: third annual report*, Zoetermeer: EIM Business and Policy Research.

EIM/ENSR. (1996). *The European Observatory: fourth annual report*, Zoetermeer: EIM Business and Policy Research.

EIM/ENSR. (1997). *The European Observatory: fifth annual report*, Zoetermeer: EIM Business and Policy Research.

European Commission. (1999). *Action Plan to Promote Entrepreneurship and Competitiveness*, Directorate-General for Enterprise.

European Commission. (2000). *The European Observatory for SME: sixth report, submitted to the Enterprise Directorate General*, Luxembourg: KPMG Consulting, EIM Business and Policy Research, and ENSR.

European Commission. (2001). *Implementation Report on the Action Plan to Promote Entrepreneurship and Competitiveness,* Luxembourg: Office for Official Publications of the European Communities.

Foer, A.A. (2001). "Small business and antitrust," *Small Business Economics*, Vol. 16, 3-20.

Galbraith, John Kenneth. (1967). *The New Industrial State*, Boston, MA: Houghton Mifflin.

Hébert, R.F. and A.N. Link. (1989). "In search of the meaning of entrepreneurship," *Small Business Economics*, Vol. 1, 39-49.

Jovanovic, B. and P.L. Rousseau. (2001). "Stock markets in the new economy", Working paper No. 01-W18, Nashville: Vanderbilt University.

Kirchhoff, B.A. (1994). *Entrepreneurship and Dynamic Capitalism*, Westport, CT: Praeger.

Kirzner, I.M. (1997). "Entrepreneurial discovery and the competitive market process: an Austrian approach," *Journal of Economic Literature*, Vol. 35, 60-85.

Landes, D.S. (1969). *The Unbound Prometheus; Technological Change and Industrial Development in Western Europe from 1750 to the Present*, Cambridge, UK: Cambridge University Press.

Lewis, W. A. (1955). *The Theory of Economic Growth*, London: George Allen & Unwin.

Loveman, G. and W. Sengenberger. (1991). "The re-emergence of small-scale production; an international comparison," *Small Business Economics*, Vol. 3, 1-37.

Lucas, R.E. (1978). "On the size distribution of firms," *BELL Journal of Economics*, Vol. 9, 508-523.

Maddison, A. (2001). *The World Economy; A Millenial Perspective*, Paris: OECD Development Centre Studies.

OECD. (1998). *Fostering Entrepreneurship, the OECD Jobs Strategy*, Paris: OECD.

Phillips, J.D. (1962). "The self-employed in the United States", *University of Illinois Bulletin* Vol. 88, Bureau of Economic and Business Research, Urbana: University of Illinois.

Piore, M. and C. Sable. (1984). T*he Second Industrial Divide; Possibilities for Prosperity*, New York: Basic Books.

Purrington, C.A. and K.E. Bettcher. (2001). "From the garage to the boardroom: the entrepreneurial roots of America's largest corporations", National Commission on Entrepreneurship (www.ncoe.org).

Reynolds, P.D., M. Hay, W.D. Bygrave, S.M. Camp and E. Autio. (2000). *Global Entrepreneurship Monitor: 2000 Executive Report,* Kauffman Centre for Entrepeneurial Leadership at the Ewing Marion Kauffman Foundation.

Reynolds, P.D., M. Hay, W.D. Bygrave, S.M. Camp and E. Autio. (2001). *Global Entrepreneurship Monitor: 2001 Executive Report*, Babson College, IBM, Kauffman Center for Entrepreneurial Leadership and London Business School, available through http://www.gemconsortium.org.

Scherer, F.M. and D. Ross. (1990). *Industrial Market Structure and Economic Performance*, Boston, MA: Houghton Mifflin Company.

Schmitz, Jr., J.A. (1989). "Imitation, entrepreneurship, and long-run growth," *Journal of Political Economy,* Vol. 97, 721-739.

Schumpeter, J.A. (1934). *The Theory of Economic Development*, Cambridge, MA: Harvard University Press.

Schumpeter, J.A. (1942). *Capitalism, Socialism and Democracy*, New York: Harper and Row.

Stel, A. van and D. Storey, 2002, "The relationship between firm birth and job creation", Tinbergen Institute Discussion Paper TI02-52/03, Erasmus University Rotterdam.

Stevenson, H.H. and David E. Gumpert. (1991). "The heart of entrepreneurship," in W.A. Sahlman and H.H. Stevenson (eds), *The Entrepreneurial Venture*, Boston: McGraw-Hill.

Stevenson, L. and A. Lundström. (2001). *Patterns and trends in entrepreneurship/SME policy and practice in ten economies, Entrepreneurship Policy for the Future Series, Vol. 3*, Swedish Foundation for Small Business Research.

Wennekers, A.R.M. and A.R. Thurik. (1999). "Linking entrepreneurship and economic growth," *Small Business Economics,* Vol. 13, 27-55.

Wennekers, A.R.M., L.M. Uhlaner and A.R. Thurik. (2002). "Entrepreneurship and its conditions: a macro perspective," *International Journal of Entrepreurship Education*, Vol.1, no.1, 25-64.

Wit, G. de and F.A.A.M. van Winden. (1991). "An m-sector, n-group behavioral model of self-employment," *Small Business Economics*, Vol. 3, 49-66.

4. Entry Barriers and Entry Strategies

Daniel F. Spulber [1]
Kellogg School of Management, Northwestern University

Keywords: barriers to entry, industrial organization, competitive strategy.

1. Introduction

Competition is a dynamic process, with market structures shaped by the entry and exit of firms. The process of entry is costly, as companies incur substantial costs of learning about the market, researching products and production processes, establishing facilities, contacting suppliers, and raising finance capital. Companies entering the market devise strategies to compete with established companies. Companies already established in the industry in turn devise strategies in anticipation of entry. Established firms and entrants alike match their organizational abilities to market opportunities as they try to achieve competitive advantage.[2]

An entry barrier is any competitive advantage that established firms have over potential entrants. An established firm, also known as an incumbent, benefits from an entry barrier because the barrier presumably prevents competition from entrants. Yet, as with competitive advantage generally, entry barriers tend to be temporary. An incumbent firm should not count on building an invulnerable fortress against entry because no specific entry barrier is sustainable for very long. Companies trying to enter markets can seize opportunities created by technological change and by shifts in customer demand. In the following discussion, I examine entry barriers and strategies that entrants can employ to overcome them.

The literature on industrial organization and related work in management strategy identifies two categories of entry barriers, each corresponding to a type of competitive advantage. There may be cost-based entry barriers if an incumbent has a cost advantage over potential entrants, due perhaps to various first-mover advantages or cost efficiencies.[3] There may be product-differentiation-based entry barriers if an incumbent has a differentiation advantage over potential entrants resulting from better products or a strong brand. In addition, a third category of entry barrier can be identified. There may be transaction-based entry

1. Daniel F. Spulber is Director of the International Business & Markets Program at the Kellogg School of Management. He is the Elinor Hobbs Distinguished Professor of International Business and Professor of Management Strategy. I thank Paul MacAvoy for helpful comments.
2. This lecture draws upon some material in Spulber (1998, 2003).

This article was originally published in the Journal of Strategic Management Education 1(1): 55-80.

barriers if an incumbent has a transaction advantage over the entrant due to lower transaction costs or established relationships with customers, suppliers and partners. The term "transaction advantage" is first introduced and defined in Daniel F. Spulber (2003).

These three types of entry barriers are likely to be temporary because they depend on costs, products, and transactions, all of which are subject to the effects of changing market forces and changing technology.[4] Companies can apply creative entry strategies to surmount most entry barriers and enter markets. When managers of a potential entrant perceive that incumbent firms have cost, differentiation or transaction advantages, they must devise appropriate strategies to overcome these advantages. Technological change allows entrants to lower production costs, introduce new products or arrange novel transactions. Growing market demand or changes in consumer tastes also generate opportunities for entry. Therefore, managers should not expect that entry barriers would allow a company to sustain competitive advantages for very long.

In some industries, particular entrants may find that incumbent firms have overwhelming strength by virtue of their experience, financial assets, brand recognition, technological expertise and other attributes. Then, those potential entrants should postpone head-to-head competition if possible. An entrant faced with stronger incumbents should pursue indirect entry strategies by entering markets that are not served or not served well by incumbent firms. In this way, the entrant avoids costly battles with the incumbent and builds strength for a future direct challenge to established firms. Of course, stronger entrants can still challenge incumbents in direct competition, overcoming entry barriers in the ways outlined here.

2. Cost Advantage and Entry Strategies

Potential entrants face a barrier to entry into an industry if they must incur costs that incumbent firms can somehow avoid, see Stigler (1968). There are several types of cost differences that can confer strategic advantages on incumbents. However, innovation tends to erode incumbent cost advantages. This means that

---

3. Proponents of the structure-conduct-performance school identify three basic entry barriers: economies of scale, absolute cost advantages, and product differentiation, see particularly Bain (1956). According to this view, if industries have a concentrated market *structure*, the companies in that industry must have monopoly *conduct*. In turn, monopoly conduct leads to an inefficient economic *performance*. Thus, the fewer the firms, the worse must be the economic performance. The structure-conduct-performance view is refuted by empirical analyses that do not find such a systematic relationship. Game theory also rejects the structure-conduct-performance causation since market structure itself is determined by the strategies of firms.
4. Entry barriers created by government tend to be more permanent and harder to surmount. These include exclusive franchises or licences, technology standards, subsidies, and tariff and nontariff barriers to international trade.

creative entrants can devise competitive strategies to overcome cost-based entry barriers.

To challenge entrenched incumbents, it is necessary for managers of potential entrants to anticipate the actions of established competitors. Managers should try to determine what will be the future strategy of the incumbents. The incumbent will not stand still in the face of entry. Incumbent company managers will anticipate entry and attempt preemptive strategies, such as price cuts or new product introductions. Managers of entrants must make their entry plans in anticipation of these strategic moves. Moreover, managers of entrants must plan ahead for challenges that they in turn will face from future entrants.

The incumbent's performance provides useful information about the costs and earnings of a company operating in the industry. However, managers of companies contemplating market entry should not base their decision to enter on the incumbent's profitability. Instead, the entering firm's managers should consider the expected profits that the entrant will make in competition with the incumbent.

2.1. Sunk Cost

One of the key strategic aspects of entry is the need to make irreversible investments in setting up new operations, including production facilities, marketing, market research, and R&D. Companies that expand their operations also make irreversible investments. These irreversible investments are known as <u>sunk costs</u>. Sunk costs can be perceived as a barrier to entry if entrants need to make irreversible investments in capacity, while incumbents have already incurred these costs.[5]

Sunk costs appear to confer a strategic advantage on incumbents because the decision of an incumbent differs from than of an entrant. Having already incurred the costs of entry, an incumbent writes off those costs, that is, the incumbent does not base future decisions on the costs of entry because the costs are sunk and thus unaffected by later decisions. The incumbent is only concerned about the benefits and costs brought about by future decisions. The incumbent will continue to operate as long as revenues are sufficient to recover operating expenses.[6]

An entrant, in contrast, must decide whether or not to incur the costs of entry. The entrant must anticipate that its earnings after entry will exceed not only operating costs but also the irreversible costs of establishing its facilities. The

5. The definition is commonly applied, see for example Baumol and Willig (1981) and Spulber (1989).
6. There are consequences if incumbent's fail to recover the initial investments made to enter the market. If the incumbent has incurred debt to finance the entry costs, the firm can face bankruptcy, restructuring and possibly acquisition. If entry costs are financed from the sale of equity, a failure to recover initial investments will adversely affect the firm's stock price and increase the firm's cost of obtaining additional financing. Even if an incumbent firm exits the industry due to financial difficulty, productive capacity may still remain employed.

entrant will only enter if expected revenues are sufficient to recover both sunk costs and operating expenses.

An entrant might be deterred by sunk costs under some circumstances. An entrant might anticipate that competing with the incumbent will not generate sufficient revenues to cover entry costs, particularly if the entrant is concerned that a price war will break out after entry takes place. Shakeouts have been identified in a wide range of industries. For example, shakeouts occurred with the entry and exit of Internet start-ups known as the dot coms, who discovered that even electronic commerce entails the need to sink costs. Such price wars are part of the everyday struggle of companies seeking to win markets.

For example, suppose that the sunk costs of entry are $100 and both the entrant and incumbent have operating expenses equal to $2. The potential entrant will not commit to the industry unless the entrant anticipates revenue of at least $102. No matter what prices are before entry, the entrant is concerned that prices will fall below the level required to generate $102 after having entered the market. The incumbent need only earn revenue of little more than $2 to stay in business. In fact, after entering, the entrant will also continue to operate with revenue above $2. If a price war occurs, prices might fall all the way to $2. If prices fell below $102, the entrant would fail to recover the sunk cost of entry.

An established company, having already incurred the entry cost of $100, has written off that cost since it is unaffected by any strategic decisions. Accordingly, if the market price were say $3, the incumbent firm would continue to operate. Before entering the market, a company must anticipate earning $102 or more in revenue to cover its total costs. If the expected market price was below $102, the potential entrant would not choose to enter the market.

In practice, however, the need to sink costs is not necessarily an effective barrier to entry. All competitive markets involve some degree of irreversible investment - whether in purchasing specialized capital equipment, establishing a brand, or carrying out R&D. Entrants normally commit capital resources in markets where they expect to earn at least competitive returns on their investments. Entrants incur sunk costs after incumbents simply as a matter of timing. It is evident that since sinking costs to enter an industry is a routine part of doing business, and since companies are continually entering industries, sunk costs need not be a barrier to entry.

Potential entrants should expect price wars only if entry will result in excess capacity in the industry. If the irreversible investment is embodied in productive capacity, that capacity often stays in service even if the firm that originally constructed the capacity exits the industry. Incumbents and entrants may battle for market share if each believes they can serve customers at the least cost. Duplication of investment and entry of excess capacity can take place when there is uncertainty regarding costs, technology, or market demand. Companies may find they have overinvested in light of increases in industry costs or reductions in market demand. When entry creates excess capacity, this often leads to vigorous competition and industry shakeouts that reduce the profits of incumbents.

However, entrants should not necessarily be deterred by an incumbent's threat of a price war. Such threats are not always credible. After the entrant has invested in facilities, it is on the same footing as other incumbent firms, and competitors will only cut prices to marginal cost if it is in their interest. If the incumbent and entrant have limited production capacity, it is unlikely that they will pursue a price war for market share that calls for production volumes in excess of that capacity.

There are many factors that lessen the likelihood of a price war after entry. If the incumbent and entrant offer differentiated products, price competition tends to be reduced. Both the incumbent and entrant will have the opportunity to earn profits in post-entry competition. Because a lower price than a competitor causes only some customers to switch their purchases, the incumbent and the entrant will not have an incentive to engage in an all-out price war. Since the incumbent and the entrant earn positive profits in competition after entry, it is more likely that the entrant can earn a sufficient margin above operating expenses to recover the sunk costs of entry. Other factors that lessen price wars are customer switching costs, customer brand loyalty, different convenience features, and imperfect information. If these factors are present, the entrant can expect a reduction in the severity of post-entry competition, allowing for the recovery of sunk costs. Therefore, with product differentiation and other factors, sunk costs are less likely to be a barrier to entry.

If the entrant has a differentiation advantage over the incumbent, it has a better chance of recovering sunk costs. An entrant could offer products that deliver sufficiently greater value to the customer than do the products of established companies. In return, the entrant will earn margins that allow for the recovery of sunk costs incurred in entering the market.

An entrant with a transaction advantage over the incumbent need not be deterred by the need to sink costs. Through innovative intermediation between buyers and sellers, the entrant can earn operating profits after entry. By reducing transaction costs, the entrant will earn returns that allow for the recovery of sunk costs. Accordingly, entrants can make investments in information technology, communications systems, customer support, supplier connections, and back office processes, that are recovered through transaction advantages over incumbents.

Generally, with technological change, the need to sink cost is not an insurmountable barrier to the entry of new competitors. If an entrant employs new technologies to reduce its operating costs, it can enjoy a cost advantage over an incumbent operating outdated technology. Even if the incumbent and entrant compete on price, an entrant with an operating cost advantage over the incumbent will earn positive margins that allow for the recovery of sunk costs.

Moreover, sunk costs need not be an entry barrier because the entrant's sunk cost is a matter of strategic choice. The entrant makes various decisions about how much to spend on facilities, marketing, R&D and so on. In particular, the entrant can offer different products from those of the incumbent thus changing the entrant's production costs. The entrant can serve different sets of customers than the incumbent, thus changing the entrant's need for distribution facilities and marketing expenditures. The entrant can adopt different production or distribution technology than the incumbent, often drastically changing the mix of investment and operating costs.

Consider telecommunications for example, where the incumbent local operating companies such as Verizon or SBC Communications have made substantial sunk investments in building legacy wireline networks. An entrant into local telecommunications need not replicate these wireline networks but can offer a different product such as mobile communications, which uses a different technology of wireless transmission. Wireless transmission technology involves substantially lower sunk costs than wireline systems in local exchange telecommunications but provides services that increasingly are able to compete with traditional systems.

Even with similar products and technology, entrants can reduce the risk associated with making investment commitments in a variety of ways. The entrant can lessen the risk of post-entry competition by forming <u>contracts with customers</u> before irreversible investments are made. The entrant can compete with the incumbent for customers before deciding to enter the market and then only incur entry costs if the customer contracts will generate sufficient revenues. The company can find out if its product will be successful before making substantial investments in facilities. For example, aircraft manufacturers such as Boeing and Airbus sign up prospective customers on a contingent basis before starting a production run on an aircraft. Gas pipeline companies sign up customers before building new pipelines.

The success of the contracting strategy also depends on the level of transaction costs. If the transaction costs of contacting with customers are relatively low in comparison with sunk costs of entry, then testing the waters through contracts is worthwhile. The entrant can use contracts to establish prices and customer orders before entering the market thus reducing the risk of irreversible investments and avoiding price wars after entry. Thus, efficiencies in contracting can mitigate the impact of entry costs. Accordingly, entrants can use contracts as an entry strategy when sunk costs are substantial.

2.2. Scale Economies and Absolute Cost Advantage

Economies of scale are sometimes alleged to confer a cost advantage on incumbents that creates a barrier to entry. When production technology has economies of scale, an established firm with a higher output than an entrant will have lower unit costs than the entrant. Were this situation to persist, the incumbent firm would be a cost leader and the entrant might be priced out of the market. However, there are various entry strategies to overcome the effects of scale.

When economies of scale are critical, challengers need to invest in the required productive capacity and to undertake the necessary marketing to build a sufficient level of sales. For example, in producing automobiles, a challenge to General Motors, Ford or Toyota requires a startup scale in the millions per year. Yet, the opportunity to realize economies of scale is equally available to entrants and incumbents. New companies are just as capable of discovering technological efficiencies as are established companies. Entrants are equally able to apply management skills to achieving production economics. Moreover, entrants are certainly equally able to build large scale facilities as are established companies. Other sources of economies of scale such as the separation of function and division of labor or automation and information technology can be purchased commercially by entrant and incumbent alike. There is little that is inherent in increasing returns technology that acts as a barrier to entry.

If the entrant and the incumbent operate the same technology with equal efficiency, greater output results in greater scale economies. However, scale economies do not confer any inherent advantage in attracting customers. By pricing competitively, the entrant has the opportunity to attract customers away from the incumbent, thus reducing differences in sales and allowing the firms to have similar unit costs of production. Even if the scale economies were on the marketing and distribution side rather than in production, entrants could benefit from those same economies to mount a substantial sales effort.

The entrant may have different technology than the incumbent. Even if the incumbent benefits from significant scale economies, an entrant that operated with greater efficiency could price to build market share and successfully enter the market. For example, if the incumbent produces 100 units at a unit cost of $5, an entrant that operated more efficiently might produce 100 units at a unit cost of $3. Such an entrant could profitably price below the incumbent's cost and attract the 100 units of sales away from the incumbent. Moreover, if the entrant were more efficient the entrant might reach a lower unit cost at a smaller output, thus achieving lower cost than the incumbent with lower sales.

As a small-scale new entrant into the steel industry, Nucor's enterprising adoption of a new technology, known as thin-slab casting of steel, surprised incumbents such as USX or Bethlehem, larger-scale, traditional producers of steel, Ghemawat (1993, 1995). SMS, a German supplier of steel making equipment, developed the technology and widely publicized it within the steel industry. Other steel producers were slow to adopt the new technique despite its cost savings. Nucor established minimills that achieved efficiencies from small-scale production of steel from scrap, Ghemawat (1993, 1995).

The impact of economies of scale is also offset by product differentiation. If the entrant offers a superior product, it obtains a differentiation advantage allowing the entrant to charge a price premium over the incumbent. A sufficient price premium would allow the entrant to overcome any advantage the incumbent derives from higher sales and lower unit cost.

The impact of scale economies also can be offset if entrants can gain a transaction advantage. The Barnes and Noble superstores seemed to offer significant scale that would difficult for entrants to challenge. Online booksellers, including Amazon.com and a host of smaller bookstores, were able to enter the retail book business by offering convenient transactions through the Internet.

If economies of scale are significant relative to the size of the market, there may only be room for one or two firms in the market. This means that it is more efficient for the market to be served by one or two large firms with economies of scale than by a fragmented industry of small firms with high unit costs. This does not imply that significant economies of scale function as an entry barrier because entrants can displace incumbent firms. If an entrant has greater cost efficiency, superior products or lower transaction costs, it can successfully enter at the expense of incumbents.

Consider the case in which the efficient scale of the incumbent firm is sufficient to serve the entire market demand when price is equal to unit cost, a situation known as natural monopoly. The market demand at a price of $5 equals 100 units and the market demand at a price of $4 equals 120 units. Suppose that with economies of scale, the incumbent can produce 100 units at a unit cost of $5, and 120 units at a unit cost of $4.50. Then, the incumbent may be said to have a natural monopoly. The incumbent could sell 100 units at a price of $5 and exactly break even. However, suppose that a more efficient entrant comes along who can produce 120 units at a unit cost of $3. The entrant could then displace the incumbent by selling 120 units at a price of $4 and still make a profit. Therefore, natural monopoly does not prevent the entry of more efficient competitors. [7]

When an incumbent has an absolute cost advantage over entrants, entry is indeed deterred unless entrants can overcome that advantage with product differentiation or innovative transactions. Yet, cost leadership by incumbents is not a permanent entry barrier. As with all competitive advantage, such deterrents are temporary. Technological change in manufacturing technology, product design and transaction methods allows entrants to address cost advantages and challenge incumbents. If the incumbent's cost advantage is difficult to overcome rapidly, potential entrants can find ways to avoid head-to-head confrontations through indirect strategy, as will be shown in Section 5.

Michael E. Porter (1982) introduces the concept of strategic groups as groups of firms within an industry that follow similar strategies. For example, some firms in a given industry may pursue low-cost strategies while other firms pursue

---

7. Even if technology exhibits natural monopoly characteristics, competitors may compete to serve the market, Demsetz (1968). Moreover, if an incumbent firm prices above cost, entrants can compete for customers. Thus, an industry can still be contestable even if the technology exhibits natural monopoly, Baumol, Panzar and Willig (1982). Even if the incumbent prices at cost there are still some situations in which an incumbent monopoly cannot find prices that sustain its position against entry.

product differentiation strategies, thus creating two industry groups. An industry might be divided into a group of large firms and a competitive fringe of smaller firms. Some firms may be specialized with a narrow product scope while others may offer a full line of products and services. Some firms may be vertically integrated while others may outsource much of their manufacturing and other operations. Companies within the same industry may differ along many dimensions at once.

Porter further defines mobility barriers as barriers within industries that prevent the companies that are in an industry from moving among the groups in that industry. For example, such mobility barriers might prevent a company following a low-cost strategy from developing better products and switching to a differentiation strategy. When mobility barriers are present within an industry, some groups of firms may have competitive advantages over other groups of firms in terms of costs, product differentiation or transactions. The group of firms with competitive advantages operate within a more profitable market segment.

Intra-industry mobility barriers that limit the ability of established firms to enter market segments are similar to industry entry barriers that deter the entry of new competitors. Just as market entry barriers can be temporary, so can industry mobility barriers. Innovation and creative strategies help established companies within an industry surmount mobility barriers. Accordingly, through innovation and other strategies, established firms may change their strategies and reposition their company to serve different market segments within their industry.

With growth in customer demand, the advantages of scale can be increased or reduced. If incumbents have considerable excess capacity, an expansion in demand allows even further lowering of average costs. However, if incumbents are operating near full capacity, expanding production can raise average costs, creating opportunities for entrants. In such a situation, entrants do more than take up the slack, they can take a substantial market share by price competition with incumbents. By carving out a market niche, entrants can avoid some the costs of full-service incumbents, allowing the entrant to overcome the incumbent's apparent economies of scale and absolute cost advantages. Southwest Airlines entered the market with a different route structure that allowed it to compete with the major airlines.

The presence of industry groups does not in itself indicate that there are mobility barriers. A key premise of management strategy is that the actions of firms can differ considerably within the same industry. The complexity of competition implies that there are many alternative strategies to choose from. Company differences also reflect the different abilities and resources within their organizations. Company differences are due to diversity in historical experiences as well as the divergent perceptions of their managers. With global competition, company differences often reflect each company's country of origin, which affects business practices, management strategy, and corporate structure. Thus, industry groups can result from differences in the characteristics and strategies of firms.

3. Differentiation Advantage and Entry Strategies

Managers of entering firms may perceive that an incumbent firm has a differentiation advantage that acts as an entry barrier. A differentiation advantage allows incumbent firms to command a price premium while deterring entry because customers recognize the incumbent's brand and product quality. Established firms have well-known brand names while start-up entrants are necessarily unknown. Yet there are many entry strategies to address a perceived differentiation advantage. Entrants have successfully launched new brands that compete with those of incumbents and often displace them.

3.1. Product Differentiation and Brand Advantage

Incumbent firms maintain highly recognized brand names by consistent delivery of high-quality products. Incumbent firms build brand equity through marketing and customer service. A company contemplating entry into the beverage industry must contend with the Coke and Pepsi brands. A company trying to enter into insurance must deal with such brands as Allstate, State Farm and Prudential.

A potential entrant may face a situation in which technological advances and imaginative designs contribute to the attractiveness of the incumbent firm's products. Entrants into the microprocessor industry must take account of the high quality of Intel's microprocessors. Entrants into electronics must deal with Sony's popular product designs.

Yet, despite these clear advantages, product differentiation in itself need not be an entry barrier. Entrants are limited only by their creativity in devising new products, marketing their services, and building customer trust. Start-ups can distinguish their products from the familiar characteristics of the incumbent's brand by offering better quality, higher durability, greater safety, or other enhanced features. The strength of an incumbent's brand name does not guarantee competitive advantage .

Indeed, product differentiation is the key to competitive entry. Entrants can launch a new brand through investment in marketing. By creating a new brand, entrants are able to distinguish their offerings from the incumbent. If customers perceive that the new brand has more attractive features, then they will switch from the incumbent's product to that of the entrant. Price discounts and promotions can attract early interest. Over time, entrants can build up confidence in new brands. Even though IBM had a brand synonymous with computers, and personal computers are still referred to as IBM-compatible, companies such as

Compaq and Dell were able to launch successful brands. The American big three automakers, GM, Ford and Chrysler, also seemed invulnerable until the Japanese automakers successfully developed such brands as Toyota, Nissan, Honda, Lexus, and Infinity.

There are few limits to creativity in product differentiation strategies. The strengths of an incumbent firm's brands are often its weaknesses. Because leading brands have clearly defined features, new brands can easily distinguish their products relative to those brands. If incumbents offer "one-size-fits-all", entrants can offer customized services. Such a strategy can go undetected until the incumbent discerns that the entrants are pursuing a mass customization strategy. If incumbents offer confusing contracts, entrants can cut through the complexity and offer clarity. In long distance telecommunications, pricing plans offered by AT&T, Sprint and MCI/Worldcom became increasingly complicated, allowing entrants to attract customers with simpler pricing plans. If incumbents sell strictly through stores, entrants can offer their product through new channels such as catalogs and Internet shopping. Clothing retailer J. Crew found that it could enhance sales relative to its competitors by a combination of store sales, catalog sales and online sales, Tedeschi (2002).

Companies with established brand equity in other markets, can expand into new markets under their existing brand. For example, although there were many established brands of coffee in the supermarket such as Folgers and Hills Brothers, Starbucks built its brand name through its coffee shops and then was able to enter the supermarket as an established brand in coffee. Alternatively, an entrant can acquire an established brand and invest in further improvements in product performance and sales.

Companies with an established brand name may use that name as an umbrella to enter into related markets. For example, Nestlé, the world's largest food company, sells a variety of products around the world under locally known brands, with the Nestlé brand name as an umbrella brand. In 1985, Nestlé acquired Carnation Milk, which had been marketed since 1907 as "Milk from Contented Cows". Nestlé markets the company's products as Nestlé's Carnation Evaporated Milk, Dry Milk, and Condensed Milk.[8]

If the entrant believes that the incumbent has a significant product differentiation advantage, the entrant may elect to pursue a price-leadership strategy. By entering a market at the low-end, companies may find they face little initial challenges from higher priced high-end competitors. The entrant can avoid directly challenging established competitors by offering the low-price product in a different market segment than the incumbent's product.

Companies that produce generics are a good example of low-end entry. Supermarkets have higher margins on some lower-cost generic products, from prepared foods to detergents. Costs are kept lower through reduced marketing and

8. http://www.nestle.com/all_about/at_a_glance/index.html

sales expenditures as well as lower production costs. In many categories, the major producers of brand-name products did not see the generics coming. The major brands did not believe that generics posed a significant challenge to the sales strength and reputation of their brands. Eventually, companies such as Procter & Gamble had to adapt to the incursions of generic versions of household cleaning products and other goods by consolidating brands, reducing price variability associated with promotions, and lowering prices consistently.

There are many different ways for an entrant to distinguish its product offerings from that of an incumbent. For example, companies can enter the market by concentrating on one aspect of the business and executing better than incumbents. Domino's Pizza became the leading pizza delivery company because it only delivers, deciding early on that combining delivery with restaurants would lower the service quality of delivery. This allowed them to compete effectively against incumbents that offered a combined restaurant and delivery approach.

3.2. Entry and Position

Managers of potential entrants may be concerned if incumbents offer a great variety of brands. Established companies may offer complete product lines with many different product features. Also, established companies may offer diverse product lines suited for different market segments. The existing brands may cover the range of prices and features serving customers with different willingness to pay levels.

Brand proliferation, the crowding of the brand space by established companies, need not create a barrier to entry. The established firm obtains a differentiation advantage only if an entrant finds it difficult to improve on its set of products. A brand proliferation strategy can be vulnerable to entry strategies.

If a company offers many brands, the customer base will be tend to be narrow for each brand. The company's own brands will compete with each other, a process known as fratricide. In addition, crowding the brand space is costly. The established company will have high costs of designing, manufacturing and marketing many different brands. The established firm may obtain economies of scope from producing multiple brands, but they may forego economies of scale from producing higher outputs of a smaller variety of products. Moreover, there are high costs of distributing many brands and resellers may have limited shelf space. Managers may not be able to devote sufficient attention to critical market segments if they are handling too many brands.

Therefore, a company that offers too many brands can be vulnerable to an entrant who offers fewer brands. The entrant can lower costs by taking advantage of standardization. The entrant can also offer greater simplicity and lower transaction costs to retailers and wholesalers. Also, an established company with too many brands will be vulnerable to companies that target specific segments and serve them better. An incumbent that tries to be all things to all people can face competition for specialized entrants.

Established companies often add and retire brands. Procter & Gamble (P&G) divested Oxydol because the brand "no longer provided a strategic fit".[9] Entrants also should avoid a brand proliferation strategy. When food-giant ConAgra launched its $1 billion flagship brand Healthy Choice, the brand appeared almost simultaneously throughout the grocery store taking on competitors in canned soup, dairy products, frozen foods, and other products. While sales jumped, the company faced targeted retaliation by companies dominant in each segment, creating lower returns. Entrants should target specific market segments for the launch, and then progressively extend the brand to other market segments.

3.3. Network Effects

The phenomenon of critical mass appears to influence many types of economic and social behavior. Neighborhoods improve or deteriorate due to self-confirming expectations, social conventions become self-enforcing, and prophecies become self-fulfilling, Schelling (1978). Do critical mass effects imply that consumer choices collectively create market inefficiencies? Are market outcomes subject to the phenomenon of <u>tipping</u> in which inferior products are purchased by all due to problems of coordination? Critical mass effects create benefits to consumers that have access to a network. The more consumers that join a communications network, for example, the greater the benefits from access since a consumer can potentially interact with many other people.

<u>Network effects</u> have been said to constitute another type of entry barrier arising from the demand side of the market. One type of network effect arises from complementary goods. Companies selling computers benefit from the availability of compatible software while companies selling software benefit from sales of computers that use the software. The more users that adopt a particular type of computer, the better off they will be because there will be more software made available for that type of computer.[10] Do leading firms gain an advantage from network effects?

Leading firms often offer products that set technology standards, creating substantial value for customers because of the benefits of product standardization. Also, companies offering complementary products benefit from conforming to a widely accepted standard. However, when such standards are proprietary, competing companies often must either obtain licenses from the established firm

---

9. A start-up company named Redox founded by former employees of P&G purchased the brand with the intention of building a company out of brands divested by other companies, see Trivedi (2000).
10. For a discussion of network effects as externalities see Katz and Shapiro (1985), and Church and Gandal (1993, 2000). For a discussion of why network effects should not be considered externalities, see Liebowitz and Margolis (1994, 1995, 1999).

or offer alternative products that conform to a different standard. The question of whether such technology standards reduce competition is the subject of some controversy.

In the computer industry, technological standards are referred to as platforms. Platforms have shown market concentration and persistence, particularly the IBM compatible platform with Microsoft's Windows/DOS personal computer operating system and Intel microprocessors. The popularity of Windows sets a standard in operating systems. Such a standard benefits consumers because personal computer makers and software application designers can reduce their production costs by standardization. Moreover, computers can communicate more easily and consumers need only learn to use one system. However, competitors have complained about barriers to entry resulting from the widespread use of the Windows operating systems. Yet, there has been substantial entry into the computer industry by many different types of companies supplying many varieties of both hardware and software.[11] Standardization of technology and product features not only creates economies of scale and scope, it stimulates the growth of product variety and the supply of complements.

Because standardization creates value it is sometimes viewed as a source of competitive advantage. Managers may perceive that there are substantial difficulties in entering a market where the incumbent owns the technological standards. Yet, such advantages tend to be temporary because as technology changes so do product standards. The greater the rate of technological change, the faster opportunities arise for entrants. For example, the analog standard in cellular phones gave way to digital transmission, allowing the entrant Nokia to surpass the established market leader Motorola. Moreover, the development of digital personal communications services, with new paging and telephone equipment and newly released spectrum, created opportunities for a wide range of companies supplying digital communications services and all sorts of wireless devices.

History is replete with dominant technological standards being surpassed and replaced, yet another illustration of the competitive process of creative destruction. As the advantages of the alternative become apparent to consumers and exceed the costs of switching, a new product can rapidly overtake a market leader. The VHS standard for video cassette recorders appeared dominant, but was rapidly replaced by digital video discs (DVDs). Technological change of this type creates opportunities for entrants to supply the new product (DVD players), and complementary products (DVD disks and peripherals).

Technology standards need not be set by the first mover. Entrants can learn from the limitations of the product offered by established companies and change the market standard. Thus, standard setting sometimes benefits entrants, casting doubt on whether standard setting and network effects are entry barriers.

---

11. Bresnahan and Greenstein (1999) look at the market structure of the computer industry over a thirty year period and argue that entry barriers were low for firms if not for platforms.

Sometimes the incumbent gets it right and sometimes later entrants innovate more effectively.

For example, in the market for handheld electronic organizers, there was a series of incumbents, including Psion in 1984, Sharp in 1987, Atari in 1989, and Apple with the notorious Newton in 1993. Despite these established companies, Palm Computing's 1996 Palm Pilot sold over a million within a period of 18 months, selling "faster than the VCR, the color television, the cell phone and the personal computer," Girard (2001). Palm's operating system set a market standard, adopted by applications developers and phone designers. Despite being the market leader, Palm itself faced challenges from Pocket PCs offered by Hewlett-Packard, Compaq, Casio, and others based on Microsoft's CE operating system and the advent of handheld devices with wireless communication.

If proprietary standards are seen to benefit incumbents, entrants can pursue a strategy of promoting open standards. Such a strategy puts pressure on incumbents to open their proprietary standards and to seek alliances with prospective entrants and suppliers of complementary products. IBM pursued such a strategy by promoting open computing and investing in open computing standards for hardware and software, such as spending $1 billion in a single year to support the Linux operating system. Microsoft's CEO Steve Balmer understood the strategic threat: "Linux is our enemy No. 1".[12]

Network effects often benefit entrants rather than incumbents. Although incumbents can realize demand growth attributed to network effects, such growth helps entrants as well. For example, companies in the personal computer industry realized substantial growth due to standardization. However, the advent of the Internet created growth opportunities for a vast number of new companies providing everything from infrastructure hardware and software as well as a host of companies engaged in e-commerce. The network effects that stimulated the growth of the Internet created expansion in demand for the services of entrants and incumbents. Accordingly, network effects need not create barriers to entry because they can be overcome by creative strategies.

4. Transaction Advantage and Entry Strategies

Managers of entering firms may believe that they face an entry barrier if the incumbent has a <u>transaction advantage</u>. By acting as an intermediary, the company lowers transaction costs for its customers and suppliers.[13] By acting as an entrepreneur, the company creates new combinations of buyers and sellers.[14]

12. The Linux operating system is an open computer standard based on the Unix operating system, see Holstein (2001).
13. For additional discussion of the theory of the firm as an intermediary see Spulber (1999).
14. Schumpeter (1997, p. 229) emphasizes the role of entrepreneurs in creating new combinations of transactions.

Transaction advantages are likely to erode quickly limiting their potential effects as entry barriers. Entrants devise strategies to address the incumbent's transaction advantage. Entrants create their own innovative transaction methods or they identify new combinations of buyers and sellers.

4.1. Transaction Cost and Entry Strategies

To surpass incumbent advantages, an entrant must lower transaction costs relative to incumbents or create greater value for suppliers and customers. At the most basic level there may be economies of scale and scope in the transaction technology itself. Retail stores have fixed costs of transactions, that is, costs that do not depend on the volume of transactions, such as computers, cash registers, bar coding, point-of-sale terminals and other information-processing equipment. These cost economies need not translate into barriers to entry. As with production cost advantages, the entrant can apply innovations in transaction technology to produce transactions at a lower costs. For example, an entrant could apply new types of enterprise software, point-of-sale equipment, or communications devices, as means of lowering transaction costs.

Transaction technologies such as back-office information technology or point-of-sale systems can involve substantial sunk costs. Entrants may perceive an entry barrier if incumbent firms may have made substantial irreversible investments in such transaction technology. However, sunk costs in transaction technology can be overcome by continued innovations. Moreover, entrants can pursue different distribution channels that lower transaction costs.

A critical transaction advantage stems from identifying innovations and bringing them to market faster than competitors. However, incumbent firms that achieve success from such a strategy often build their business by producing products based on a particular generation of technology. The successful incumbent has an incentive to stick with a particular generation of technology to provide service to its installed base of customers. The incumbent may choose to incrementally improve its products since continually changing their basic technology would involve substantial investment and costs of adjustment. As a result, entrants can gain a transaction advantage by embracing later generations of technology. For example, Cisco Systems appeared to have a distinct transaction advantage in incorporating new technologies into its products, but entrants were successful in penetrating the market for Internet routers.

Entrants may perceive that the incumbent firm has a transaction advantage resulting from supplier and customer relationships that are difficult to duplicate. Moreover, the established firm may have experience in coordinating its supplier and customer transactions. For entrants to overcome such advantages, it is necessary to offer different types of transactions that improve upon existing types of exchange. For example, Amazon.com was able to enter the retail book business by selling through the Internet even though established bookstores had long-standing relationships both with customers and with publishers.

4.2. Intermediary Strategies

One type of entry strategy, the go-between strategy, requires interposing the company between buyers and sellers who are currently transacting.[15] For the strategy to be effective, the company must improve on the existing transaction costs that buyers and sellers face. The go-between strategy competes with the direct transactions between buyers and sellers, see Figure 1 below.

Figure 1: The Go-Between Strategy

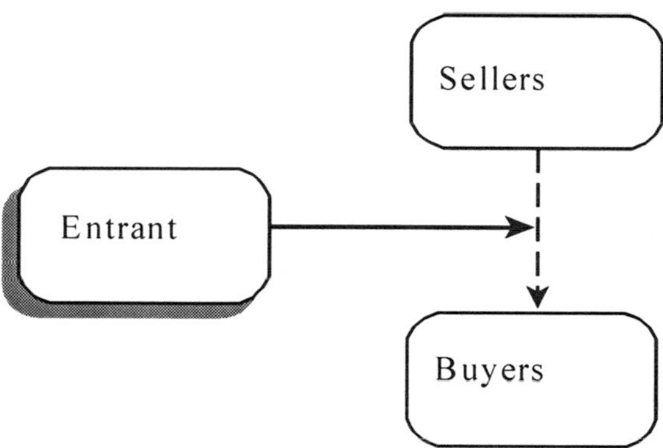

Managers of the potential entrant begin by identifying existing combinations of buyers and sellers and targeting particular market transactions. For example, the entrant can become a wholesaler by helping manufacturers that are selling directly to retailers. An entrant can become a supply chain manager by helping manufacturers manage their purchases from suppliers.

Then, the entrant contemplating a go-between strategy surveys its own resources and attempts to create innovative ways to carry out the transactions at lower costs. An important part of the go-between strategy is to get close to the customer. The entrant improves and bypasses competing marketing channels and converts established sellers into suppliers. By controlling access to the customer, the go-between is in a position to receive economic rents from suppliers seeking

15. The go-between strategy is introduced in Spulber (1998).

to sell their products. For example Charles Schwab entered the market for brokerage by going between mutual fund companies and individual investors.

The go-between strategy involves many different methods of improving transactions. By consolidating the demand of many different buyers and sellers, the entrant reduces marketing and distribution costs for sellers and shopping costs for final customers. If the entrant can handle a greater volume of transactions, the company can achieve economies of scale in the back office that are not available to buyers and sellers that deal directly with each other. The entrant pursuing a go-between strategy may be able to offer improved market information. If sellers and buyers rely on negotiation, the entrant might offer the convenience of posted prices or dynamic price adjustment methods such as auctions. The posted prices save on the time costs of bargaining and remove the inherent uncertainty in negotiation. Therefore, by clearly posting prices, the intermediary can attract customers and suppliers away from a high-transaction cost market that involves bargaining.

An entrant using a go-between strategy can create markets when it is costly for buyers to monitor the quality of products offered by sellers. With decentralized exchange, there can be variations in product quality. Consumers are uncertain about the efficacy of pharmaceuticals, the durability of appliances, or the quality of automobiles. Suppliers generally have better information about the products they offer than do their customers. The entrant can develop innovative methods for testing products and use the test results to certify product quality.

By dealing with many buyers and many sellers, the entrant following a go-between strategy can offer immediacy and other market making services to improve upon existing transactions. By consolidating transactions, the entrant gains an advantage over direct exchange between buyers and sellers. For example, the Internet auctioneer Ebay entered the market by improving upon direct transactions between buyers and sellers in markets for collectibles and resold goods. The leading international reseller of computers and other technology products, Ingram Micro, entered the computer market by going between manufacturers and resellers of computer hardware and software. Ingram Micro sources over 145,000 products and services through affiliates in 31 countries and serves 100,000 resellers in 120 countries.

Another type of entry strategy that attempts to overcome transaction advantages of incumbent firms involves consolidation of fragmented distribution networks or supply chains.[16] Entrants pursuing a bring-together strategy attempt to reduce industry transaction costs by acquiring small or specialized distributors or by rationalizing supply chains. Such consolidation creates economies of scale and scope that allows the entrant to lower transaction costs relative to established firms. Moreover, by consolidating distribution, the entrant may enhance efficiency by greater coordination of purchases and sales.

---

16. The bring-together strategy is introduced in Spulber (1998).

When distributors resell the goods of many diverse sellers, the bring-together strategy offers a supermarket approach to distribution, selling a wide variety of products and services. Customers gain from one-stop-shopping where they can select from a wide variety of products, choosing the best products by comparison shopping at one central location. Customers that purchase multiple products also gain from the lower costs of putting together a market basket of goods and services. Thus, the entrant can improve on the offerings of distributors that handle only a few products or services.

The bring-together strategy allows the entrant to achieve economies of scope by handling multiple products. The company saves on the overhead and other costs that multiple distributors would incur. This increased efficiency allow the company to lower prices relative to independent distributors. Consolidating distribution can require a substantial initial investment to provide a broad range of products and services, contracting with a wider range of suppliers or customers than competing firms. Entrants can merge with or acquire existing distributors to bring their markets together. Alternatively, the strategy can be carried out through targeting a market segment and diversifying the firm's offerings over time. Dole Food Company entered the fresh-cut flower industry by consolidating part of the wholesale distribution channel.

The returns to the bring-together strategy are evident in the growth of superstores and category killers. Book superstores such as Barnes and Noble and Borders brought together in one place the books offered by a host of specialty bookstores. By adding recorded music, Barnes and Noble attracted customers who buy both books and music, competing with independent music stores. Electronic superstores such as Best Buy combined a variety of products, outperforming specialized stores selling computers, cameras, or stereos. These companies took advantage of scale and scope in distribution to outperform specialized suppliers that were already established in the market.

5. Incumbent Strengths and Indirect Entry Strategies

If the managers of the potential entrant believe that the incumbent firms have competitive advantages that cannot be profitably overcome, they can pursue an <u>indirect entry strategy</u> by avoiding or delaying direct confrontation with incumbents. The entrant builds bridgeheads in market niches where they are less likely to be observed or understood by competitors. The entrant maximizes value added by serving neglected markets, meeting unmet needs, increasing product variety, and providing innovative goods and services.[17]

The firm's objective is not competition itself, the goal is winning markets. Head-to-head competition is an expensive proposition, involving lower revenues from price reductions, and higher costs for promotion, advertising and enhanced

17. This section draws upon Spulber (1998, chapter 8).

services. Indirect strategy increases profits by reducing the costs of direct confrontation. The entrant can concentrate its abilities, management effort, marketing and sales on a targeted market segment while neutralizing the competitive advantages of an established incumbent. By serving markets with less competition, entrants build strength in preparation for direct competition with established incumbents.

Entrants pursuing an indirect strategy choose markets that are not served, or not served well, by established competitors. Such market segment may yield low revenues but require correspondingly lower costs, so that profits are higher than in hotly contested markets. In some cases, a market that is difficult to serve can be profitable if the costs of service have deterred other firms from providing service.

There is a high cost to direct conflict. It is measured in terms of economic returns that companies could have earned by investing their capital and resources in other markets. The key to avoiding direct conflict is to discover opportunities to serve customers not perceived by others. The firm will earn arbitrage rents, without costly price wars.

A competitive battle with an entrenched incumbent could be highly costly in terms of marketing and product design expenditures. The entrant might better invest money in developing new products and services for other markets. A price war can lead to economic losses and industry shakeouts. Managers should only enter into such a direct confrontation if they are sure their company has the necessary cost efficiencies, superior product performance. or transaction efficiency.

By serving undefended markets or market segments, a start-up company builds strength. The entrant develops expertise in purchasing, distribution, marketing, production, product design, and R&D. The company identifies talented managers and employees and forms market networks of suppliers and distributors, and develops relationships in financial markets. The entrant eventually broadens its markets and takes on established rivals.

Economic frictions resulting from transaction costs make it possible to pursue indirect strategies. The economy is full of imperfections and asymmetric information. Changes in consumer tastes and technology continually create new opportunities. It is easy to imagine that no other manager has yet observed a particular market opening. Finding such unmet needs takes creativity and talent, which are not available in unlimited supply in business, as in any other endeavor. Moreover, identifying opportunities is costly, requiring market research and technical know-how. If companies differ in their research costs, those with greater research efficiencies will find different opportunities. There is also a large element of chance, so that discerning an unmet need may be fortuitous. This means there are always many unexplored opportunities. If the firm can bring buyers and suppliers together in a new way, selling products and services to customers that have not been served before or purchasing inputs for new types of production or distribution, the firm captures economic rents.

Identifying unmet needs is a critical management skill. The undefended territory can be entered simply by bringing new products and services to a geographic region not served by others. Alternatively, entry can be acheived by serving a customer group, distinguished by age, gender or other aspects, whose needs for a particular product are being ignored. The point of entry may be a low-cost generic service or a high-quality service, but need not be a niche market. A sufficiently innovative product or service for a mass market can be supplied without initially encountering rivals. During its early expansion in small towns, Wal-Mart was "too small and insignificant for any of the big boys to notice", Walton (1992).

6. Conclusion

Entrants perceive the presence of entry barriers if they believe that incumbent firms have competitive advantages. However, cost advantages, differentiation advantages, and transaction advantages tend to be temporary. They are subject to the effects of technological change in production processes, product features, and transaction methods. Moreover, changes in customer preferences create opportunities for entrants to provide new types of products and services.

Managers of companies that are contemplating entry should identify specific competitive advantages of incumbents and devise counter strategies based on adopting product and process innovations, adapting to changing consumer preferences, or creating innovative transactions. Although the process of entry is costly, there are many strategies that an entrant can employ in attempting to overcome barriers to entry. Entrants can overcome cost advantages by embracing technological innovations before incumbents, by introducing products that add sufficient value to surpass cost advantages, or by transaction innovations. Entrants can target product differentiation advantages by applying technological innovations or by introducing product varieties that satisfy unmet needs. Entrants can address transaction advantages by developing innovative transaction methods, by reorganizing supply chains and distribution channels, and by creating new combinations of buyers and sellers.

References:

Bain, J. S., (1956), *Barriers to New Competition*, Cambridge, MA: Harvard University Press.

Baumol, W. J. and R. D. Willig, (1981) , "Fixed Cost, Sunk Cost, Entry Barriers and Sustainability of Monopoly," *Quarterly Journal of Economics*, 95, August, 405-431.

Baumol, W. J., J. C. Panzar and R. D. Willig, (1988), *Contestable Markets and the Theory of Industry Structure*, rev. ed., New York: Harcourt Brace Jovanovich.

Bresnahan, T. and S. Greenstein, (1999), "Technological Competition and the Structure of the Computer Industry," *Journal of Industrial Economics,* March, 47, 1-40.

Church, J. and N. Gandal, (1993), "Complementary Network Externalities and Technological Adoption," *International Journal of Industrial Organization*, 11, 239-260.

Church, J. and N. Gandal, (2000), "Systems Competition, Vertical Merger and Foreclosure," *Journal of Economics & Management Strategy*, 9, Spring, 25-51.

Demsetz, H., 1968, Why Regulate Utilities, *Journal of Law and Economics*, 11, April, 1968, 55-65.

Ghemawat, P., (1993), "Commitment to a Process Innovation: Nucor, USX and Thin-Slab Casting," *Journal of Economics & Management Strategy*, 2, 135-161.

Ghemawat, P., (1995), "Competitive Advantage and Internal Organization: Nucor Revisited," *Journal of Economics & Management Strategy*, 3, 685-717.

Girard, K., (2001), "The Palm Phenom," *Business 2.0*, April 3, 74- 81.

Holstein, W. J., (2001), "Big Blue Wages Open Warfare," *Business 2.0*, April 17, 62- 65.

Katz, M. L. and C. Shapiro, (1985), "Network Externalities, Competition, and Compatibility," *American Economic Review*, 75, June, 424-440.

Liebowitz, S. J. and S. E. Margolis, (1994), "Network Externality: An Uncommon Tragedy," *Journal of Economic Perspectives*, 8, 133-150.

Liebowitz, S. J. and S. E. Margolis, (1995), "Path Dependence, Lock-In and History," *Journal of Law, Economics, and Organization*, 11, 205-226.

Liebowitz, S. J. and S. E. Margolis, (1999), *Winners, Losers and Microsoft: Competition and Antitrust in High Technology*, Independent Institute, 1999.

Porter, M. E., (1982), *Competitive Strategy: Techniques for Analyzing Industries and Competitors*, New York: Free Press.

Schelling, T. C. (1978), *Micromotives and Macrobehavior*, New York: Norton.

Schumpeter, J. A., (1997), *The Theory of Economic Development*, New Brunswick, NJ: Transaction Publishers.

Spulber, D. F., (2003), *Management Strategy*, New York: McGraw Hill, forthcoming.

Spulber, D. F., (1998), *The Market Makers: How Leading Firms Create and Win Markets*, New York: McGraw Hill.

Spulber, D. F., (1989), *Regulation and Markets*, Cambridge, MA: MIT Press.

Stigler, G. J., (1968), *The Organization of Industry*, Homewood, IL: Irwin.

Tedeschi, B., (2002), "The Catalog Business J. Crew Reaches A Milestone as its Sales over the Web Exceed Sales from its Catalog," *New York Times*, March 25, C6.

Trivedi, K., (2000), "Chips Off the P&G Block," *New York Times*, August 5, B1.

Walton, S. with J. Huey, (1992), *Made in America: My Story*, New York: Bantam Books.

5. A Lecture on Integrating the Treatment of Uncertainty in Strategy [1]

Hamilton W. Helmer [2]

Keywords: strategy, uncertainty, risk, mental model, adaptive, Helmer Principle, tuning, transforming, Design School, Porter, Mintzberg, Knight, Keynes, subjective probability, shareholder value, Sony, Hewlett-Packard.

1. Introduction

Uncertainty permeates business. Ask any astute businessman about an opportunity's prospects and you will get a conditional reply and, the further in the future or the more uncommon the opportunity, the more restrictive the conditions. This is not dissemblance but rather a reflection of the certainty of uncertainty.

To be more specific, to prospectively assess an opportunity, it is necessary to understand the future disposition of four fundamentals: a firm's own *capabilities*, the intent and abilities of the *competition* (actual and potential), the wants and needs of *customers*, and a firm's bargaining strength in its *chain of value*. Substantial lack of specificity regarding any one of these "Four C's" can be correctly characterized as uncertain.[3]

Uncertainty takes on special relevance in Strategy, because many of the most important opportunities for increasing shareholder value[4] will exhibit just such a characteristic. A few well-known examples of dramatic increases in shareholder value illustrate this point:

1. In this lecture I will use "Strategy" to denote the intellectual discipline and "strategy" to denote a specific business or corporate strategy.
2. Hamilton W. Helmer is the Managing Director of Strategy Capital, an investment firm utilizing Strategic Arbitrage™, an investment approach that capitalizes on the convergence of market prices of publicly traded equities to the value predicted by Power Dynamics, a proprietary theory of prospective value based on Strategy precepts. Mr. Helmer has been an active business strategist for over twenty years, first with Bain & Company and then with his own firm. His clients have included Adobe, Hewlett-Packard, Mentor Graphics, John Hancock, Raychem and Pinkerton. Mr. Helmer is a Director of American Science and Engineering (AMEX: ASE) where he serves as Chairman of the Audit Committee. Mr. Helmer received his Ph.D. in Economics from Yale University in 1978.
3. In the section that follows I will give a more precise definition of uncertainty. In the terms developed in that section, the reason these situations are uncertain is that this lack of knowledge makes impossible a meaningful attribution of a probability function to outcomes of interest.

This article was originally published in the Journal of Strategic Management Education 1(1): 93-114.

- *IBM into mainframes*. When IBM went into the mainframe business a commissioned market study predicted that the eventual worldwide market would be limited to a double digits number of these machines. So there was huge customer uncertainty. There was also substantial uncertainty on the competitive front: IBM was following the early entrance and strong brand recognition of Remington Rand's Univacs. Mainframes for IBM went on to become one of the most successful businesses in history.

- *GE into financial services*. GE started its financial services arm as a facilitator to its appliance business. It was not viewed as a potential major source of income, nor was the diversity of financing that it would pursue in its later years even vaguely imagined. This business faced uncertainty in all of the Four C's. GE Capital now accounts for about half of the profits of one of the largest market cap companies in the world.

- *Hewlett-Packard into inkjet printers.* When HP started to pursue inkjet printers, it was completely unclear whether a technical solution could be found (capabilities uncertainty) or how successfully competitors would pursue inkjet (Canon had some important patents) or how other printing technologies would evolve. Inkjet printers have gone on to represent about half of the income of this Fortune 25 Company.

- *Microsoft into application software.* Microsoft is such a juggernaut that it is hard to remember that it was not always so. At one point Lotus Development (the owner of Lotus 123) was perceived to be a much stronger company. It was not at all clear that an operating system and language company had the skills necessary to compete in applications, and the reaction from its well-entrenched competitors (Lotus, WordPerfect and Ashton-Tate) was impossible to predict. In FY2000

---

4. It is the objective of a strategy to delineate the path likely to maximize shareholder value. Increasing shareholder value can be looked at from the perspective of financial markets or company performance. The financial market perspective would assert that increasing shareholder value means increasing stock price. This involves presenting the financial community with sufficient evidence of a new source of cash flow that had not previously been capitalized into the share price. Most opportunities not exhibiting uncertainty are already well-known by management and the financial community and are, therefore, already in the stock price. This would argue that, from a financial market perspective, uncertain opportunities represent a particularly rich vein for growing shareholder value. The company performance perspective looks to how to change the NPV of cash flows. This is the perspective I take. The examples listed below illustrate just such a dramatic increase in NPV. I should confess that my many years of successful stock market investment have left me as a "soft fundamentalist": relative stock prices tend to eventually reflect relative differences in underlying financial performance.

applications accounted for about 40% of revenues of this 300B market cap company.

Just these four examples represent many hundreds of billions of dollars of new shareholder value[5] and yet each was steeped in uncertainty. The natural question that arises is "To what extent can Strategy substantially advance such high value efforts?"

At first blush, one's expectations would be high due to the rich intellectual heritage in Finance and Economics on the treatment of Uncertainty and Risk. Nobel Prizes have been awarded to professors at Yale, Stanford, Princeton and Harvard in this area and a diverse set of valuable constructs have emerged: portfolio theory (Harry Markowitz and James Tobin), capital asset pricing (William Sharpe), option pricing (Myron Scholes and Robert Merton), game theory (John Nash), and state preference analysis (Kenneth Arrow).

However, this expectation has not been fulfilled. Ironically, the availability of these powerful parallel concepts has proven to be a burden in the practical treatment of uncertainty in Strategy. The problem is analogous to the driver of a powerful sports car in icy conditions. It is hard to resist using the power and stepping on the gas, even though this will preclude control. Beyond this there has been an additional impasse to the effective treatment of uncertainty in Strategy: the well-entrenched traditions of strategy development in corporations typically follow an approach that is inimical to advancing opportunities with uncertainty.

This lecture will start with a clearer characterization of the nature of uncertainty. I will follow this with a brief overview of the current practice of strategy development and the barrier that it creates to accommodating uncertainty. I will then explore the key problems exhibiting uncertainty faced by corporations and use this understanding as a guide to how Strategy can contribute.

2. The Nature of Uncertainty in Strategy

There is a rich body of work on the meaning of uncertainty and its relation to risk. It is well beyond the scope of this lecture to review and comment on that body.[6] However, for purposes here, it is important to carefully characterize what I mean by uncertainty, as this will usefully narrow the set of possible ways to approach the problem posed by this lecture.

---

5. There are also many instances in which a significant amount of shareholder value is destroyed by forays into new areas. This further buttresses the desirability of usefully employing Strategy in such situations.
6. The New School website http://cepa.newschool.edu/het/home.htm has been a very useful resource for me. I am not an academic economist, and the format they have developed helped me quickly brush up on past developments in related areas. In particular, their sections on risk and uncertainty were of value.

Ex ante, an opportunity will display one of three mutually exclusive dispositions:

> *Certainty*. The relevant dimensions[7] of its outcome are completely known.
>
> *Risk*. Some relevant dimensions of its outcome are not known, but it is possible to meaningfully[8] attribute a known probability function to those dimensions.
>
> *Uncertainty*. There are some relevant dimensions that are not known and for which it is impossible to meaningfully attribute a probability function.[9]

There are two ways in which it is possible to meaningfully assign a probability function to a phenomenon. The first is to realize that the phenomenon in question is sufficiently similar to an analogous phenomenon for which we can develop a probability function. More formally this determination by *association* is possible if all of the following conditions[10] are met:

> *Non-uniqueness*. The variable of interest ex ante must be identical to another variable for which we have ex post observations.[11]
>
> *Repeatability*. The variable observed ex post must have had enough instances so that a meaningful distribution can be constructed.
>
> *Continuity*. The future must be identical to the past in the ways relevant to this variable.[12]
>
> Assignment by association is the approach often used in financial models such as modern portfolio theory. This approach uses an ex post

---

7. NPV is an example of a relevant dimension.
8. "Meaningful" here is taken as meaning that the probability function so assigned is a reasonably accurate reflection of the impact of the possible variation faced. I do not want to descend into a discussion here of whether or not such an objective probability actually exists or not.
9. By this definition, lack of certainty must result in either risk or uncertainty but not both. Accordingly in this formal sense, uncertainty is not identical to lack of certainty. It is this specific meaning of uncertainty that this lecture will use. As noted later in this lecture, this definition is based on the work of Knight and Keynes.
10. As Edmund Helmer has pointed out to me, the extent to which these conditions are satisfied may themselves be subject to probabilistic assessments.
11. I will state these conditions in their stronger form. In practice, the softer form is really the constraint. The softer form would require, for example, not perfect identity but rather that it be sufficiently close.

observation of volatility[13] as a measure of exposure. This is extremely powerful, when valid, because it is observable and in many cases there are a sufficient number of data points to be statistically robust. This has found real world application in a number of areas such as option pricing and portfolio management.

A probability function may also be meaningfully assigned by *calculation*, rather than by association. If the outcomes of relevance are caused in a defined way by variables for which we have probability functions (or specific values), then we can reasonably calculate an expected probability function even though we do not have an analogous phenomenon.

The above distinction between risk and uncertainty is very much in line with that made by Keynes and Knight.

> By 'uncertain' knowledge, let me explain, I do not mean merely to distinguish what is known for certain from what is only probable. The game of roulette is not subject, in this sense, to uncertainty...The sense in which I am using the term is that in which the prospect of a European war is uncertain, or the price of copper and the rate of interest twenty years hence...About these matters there is no scientific basis on which to form any calculable probability whatever. We simply do not know.[14]

> The practical difference between the two categories, risk and uncertainty, is that in the former the distribution of the outcome in a group of instances is known (either through calculation a priori or from statistics of past experience), while in the case of uncertainty this is not true, the reason being in general that it is impossible to form a group of instances, because the situation dealt with is in a high degree unique.[15]

Any breakthrough that would eliminate all uncertainty by converting it to risk would be highly desirable. In the theory of choice, the notion of subjective probability does just that. The roots of this idea, that an individual's disposition is reflected in the probability that they attribute, can be traced back at least as far as Reverend Bayes' famous essay on conditional probability:

> After having observed for some time the course of events it would be found ... that the operations of nature are in general regular, and that the powers and laws which prevail in it are stable and permanent. The consideration of this will cause one ...to produce a much stronger expectation of success in further experiments than would otherwise have been reasonable; just as the frequent observation that things of a sort are disopposed together in any place would lead us to conclude,

---

12. This condition has in turn three separate necessary conditions: the set of factors that influence the variable does not change; the frequency of occurrence of those affecting factors does not change; and the function determining the value of the variable from these conditions does not change as you go forward into the future from when the ex ante prediction was made.
13. This is represented by the standard deviation, if you assume a normal distribution.
14. As cited on http://cepa.newschool.edu/net/essays/uncert/intrisk.htm, Keynes (1937).
15. Page 233, Knight (1967).

> upon discovering there any object of a particular sort, that there are laid up with it many others of the same sort.[16]

Subjective probability was very successfully formalized by Savage and others[17] as an answer to the indeterminacy of uncertainty. Simply put, the argument is something like this: you may face uncertainty, but nevertheless you make choices; these choices are based on a subjective assessment of the future and hence reveal a subjective probability function. Uncertainty and risk are therefore the same. Uncertainty does not come from the lack of a probability function but only your unwillingness to state it.

This is a powerful approach in modeling choice, but not very useful in business. The reason is that there is an objective reality to the exposure faced by a business opportunity, and thinking it otherwise will not change it. To give the reader a concrete example of why a subjective formulation can miss the point, consider entrance into a new business. In my several decades of observing and being a part of such efforts, I can comfortably say that there is often a "grass is greener" phenomenon at work: those less familiar with the entry area are likely to attribute ex ante higher probability of success to such an effort than those old hands, who have a sense early on of all the challenges ahead.[18] Put in other terms, in this situation, which is quite common, the subjective probability attributed by the naïve is more favorable than that by the experienced. Who would you bet on?[19]

This leads again to Keynes who says that what we are really dealing with is the lack of knowledge.[20]

> In the sense important to logic, probability is not subjective. It is not subject to human caprice. A proposition is not probable because we think it so. When once the facts are given which determine our knowledge, what is probable or improbable in those circumstances has been fixed objectively, and is independent of our opinion.[21]

---

16. Page 19, Bayes (1763).
17. c.f., Savage (1972).
18. This suggests a violation of the Harsanyi Doctrine that two individuals who receive the same knowledge will assign the same probabilities. One might get around this by arguing that "naïve" and "old hand" are themselves characterizations of the extent of their knowledge and so they in fact are not presented with the same knowledge.
19. Interestingly, not only are the naïve disadvantaged in their ex ante assessment of a situation but they are also disadvantaged in their ability to execute going forward. It is this double barrel "risk" that underlies venture capitalists making team assessment their first focus in due diligence.
20. This view would argue that even the ability to predict a coin toss is an informational issue: specific characterization of the force vectors of an individual toss, the mass distribution of the coin, wind conditions, etc.
21. Page 4, Keynes (1957).

Keynes' point is that it is a lack of knowledge that prevents subjective probabilities from reflecting an underlying objective probability[22]. The knowledge of the old hands is more complete than that of the newcomers, so the probability attributed by the old hands is closer to correct. A good business person should not consider their views equivalent.

Knowledge deficiency is not only the condition that prevents a probability function from being accurately estimated. The extent of this knowledge deficiency also determines the shape of the objective probability function[23] and influences the degree of uncertainty.[24] In this vein I need to make one additional distinction, that between intrinsic and firm-specific knowledge deficiency. Intrinsic deficiency is the extent to which knowledge is not available at acceptable cost to the most informed player, whereas, firm-specific deficiency is the additional degree faced by a specific firm. For example entering the digital camera business would represent far less firm-specific deficiency for Hewlett-Packard than for General Motors.[25] Or, going back to the grass is greener example, the naïve entrant faces higher firm-specific deficiency than the old hand. In both cases, the greater knowledge deficiency can be said to result in higher uncertainty.

Before leaving this topic I should note that there is a dynamic relationship between risk and uncertainty. As one moves from the initial ex ante time closer and closer to the ex post time of interest, the factors named earlier that make uncertainty the right framework (as opposed to risk) diminish. In particular, as some of the largest question marks are eliminated, the activity moves closer to satisfying the conditions named earlier of non-uniqueness, repeatability and continuity. At some point a threshold[26] may be passed such that the opportunity is no longer uncertain but merely risky.[27]

The example of Hewlett-Packard's effort in ink-jet printers will help to demonstrate what I mean. At one point, this business was merely a gleam in the

---

22. For example, the difference between guessing about mortality rates compared to having detailed actuarial studies.
23. If those entering a new business, for example, have less knowledge then we would expect the objective probability function to have a lower mean and greater variance.
24. The degree of uncertainty can be objectively assessed ex ante, although only approximately. It is also a quality that usually diminishes as an activity moves forward in time (although not uniformly). A good guideline is that the more an anticipated activity diverges from existing activities, then the higher the uncertainty.
25. These are objective and not subjective uncertainty. They may not be able to be measured precisely, but they can be estimated based on the systematic assessment of a family of related factors, e.g., "Does the new business area share customers with a business area you are already in?"
26. The most useful meaning of "greater" and "lesser" uncertainty is whether a situation is further or closer to this threshold than some other situation.
27. It is possible to move from uncertain to certain with no transition through risky. Predicting a terrorist attack using a weapon of mass destruction is a problem of this nature. In business, however, such a transition is less likely because business has been around for so long in so many places that if you come close to certainty it is quite likely you will be in the realm of reasonably analogous prior parallels.

eyes of its inventors, John Vaught, Dave Donald, John Meyer[28] and others. At that time, the cluster of challenges was so unique that it was not possible to meaningfully characterize their chances of success with a known success probability function based on other histories. This barrier lessened as each major hurdle was passed: understanding cavatation with superheating, nozzle fabrication, combining the printhead with the ink cartridge, gauging customer acceptance with the failure of the Thinkjet and so on. If I had to guess, I would say that this could have been reasonably thought of as risky rather than uncertain once the Deskjet was released[29] in 1987, *nine years* after the original work began. The point here is that there is a normal progression out of the cloud of uncertainty into the light of risk and finally on to the finality of certainty.

In sum then, this paper concerns the use of Strategy in situations that are uncertain, where that means the complete lack of the ability to meaningfully attribute a probability function to outcomes. These situations can involve large investment outlays with significant upside or downside returns. The specific examples given earlier of IBM, Hewlett-Packard, General Electric and Microsoft can all be characterized as exhibiting uncertainty because each represented a cluster of unknowns unmatched by repeated other situations. More generally, one could reasonably argue that one of the distinguishing characteristics of new high profit ventures is that they are unique[30] and thus violate the conditions necessary for them to be considered "risky" in their early stages.[31]

3. Strategy Traditions Preclude Uncertainty

Strategy, as we now think of it, was propelled sharply forward in the 1960's and 1970's by the twin (and occasionally antagonistic) forces of academia and management consulting. The development and advocacy of the Experience Curve by the Boston Consulting Group forever changed the way corporations viewed the asset of market share. Their success and the subsequent success of their spin-off, Bain & Company, made it clear that strategy development was a highly saleable service and could attract the best and the brightest out of the leading MBA programs.

---

28. I wish to thank Dr. John Meyer for an extensive interview on the development of the ink-jet printer.
29. As a businessman, the transition from uncertainty takes place, not when I can articulate the probability function with great precision (something that is rare in most business decisions), but rather when approximations of probability reasonably reflect the underlying reality.
30. This is the argument that Porter makes in pages 61-78, Porter (1996).
31. A more mature unique phenomenon may be considered risky rather than uncertain, because its own history (perhaps over a number of business cycles) may provide the analogous phenomenon from which it draws its prospective probability function. This is the approach used for example in CAPM treatment of stock prices. Beta is calculated based on the stock's own history.

On the academic side, the publication in 1980 of Professor Michael Porter's *Competitive Strategy* established the intellectual pedigree of Strategy and further heightened its respectability. Professor Porter studied at Harvard under the exceptional Industrial Organization economist Richard Caves, and Porter's seminal insight was "...in turning IO economics on its head."[32] The "market imperfections" that IO sought to identify as the cause of differential returns were the very same sources of enduring advantage any good strategist would seek. This profound insight immediately rooted Strategy in a well-established rigorous body of thought.

These two developments and the subsequent movement of the largest corporations to each have their own strategy had a profound and lasting influence on corporate method. Strategy development became accepted practice within almost all large corporations and a standard methodology evolved:

- Strategy development became an activity done separately from day to day business.
- It was done only periodically either as part of a formally established cycle (strategic planning) or as an episodic event on an as needed basis.
- Those leading the development of strategy were initiates in the discipline of Strategy, or they hired consultants who were initiates.
- The strategy team would utilize their knowledge of drivers of differential returns and apply that to an existing or prospective opportunity faced by the corporation.
- The outcome of these efforts was the development of a formal strategy, approved by the board of directors, to be implemented by management, who were made responsible for it in the years to come.[33]

This method has come to be called the Design approach and is essentially identical regardless of whether it was undertaken by external consultants or internal staff experts. Over my decades of experience as a member of the former, I have not seen a single effort that significantly diverged from the description above.

This Design approach is insidiously alluring. It is rational, logical and built on a strong intellectual foundation. It resonates with business sense of what makes money. It is accepted practice and empowers groups that endlessly preach its merits and pursue its application.

The problem with the Design approach is that it precludes effective treatment of new and different opportunities beset with uncertainty. It assumes that the drivers of differential returns are identifiable *ex ante* by the strategy team. For an

---

32. Page 23, Rumelt, Schendel, and Teese (1994). This is a lucid review of the genesis of modern strategy.
33. A variant of this was scenario planning, which developed several alternatives futures and planned accordingly.

established business this may be true, but for a highly uncertain prospect it is not. The brilliantly reasoned critique of the Design approach by Professor Henry Mintzberg argued persuasively that the factors the Design School focuses on may be valid as *ex post* explanations of why an existing business exhibits high returns but are not useful as an *ex ante* framework for a business person hoping to create new high return opportunities.

A look at our earlier examples gives anecdotal support to Mintzberg's point that, at the onset of uncertain endeavors, the critical future sources of strategic strength cannot be anticipated. Could Microsoft have seen that its control of a common graphical user interface (Windows) would give it insurmountable synergy in applications? Could IBM have known that a bet-the-farm redesign from the ground up (System 360) would give it long term architectural control? Could Hewlett-Packard have foreseen that high switching costs would have led to a highly profitable supplies business (ink cartridges)? The answer is that no amount of study ex ante could have revealed these keystones of future success.[34]

Despite this criticism, well-reasoned by example, the Design approach has held sway, partially because of the allure mentioned above but also because no viable alternative has been put forward. It is the purpose of this lecture to present such a viable alternative.

4. Transforming is the Key

After twenty years as a practicing business strategist and investor, I have come to realize that there are two distinctly different ways of creating shareholder value: *tuning* and *transforming*. Tuning examines what you currently do and asks "What can we do better?"[35] Tuning takes an existing business and improves it, encompassing cost cutting, financial structuring, divestitures, and incremental growth. Tuning has great appeal: it is more or less predictable, and its results can be dramatic and achieved within a reasonable time. Tuning is about efficiency, and it will always be important.

Transforming is the alternative way of creating shareholder value. It is an answer to the question "What can we do next?" Transforming launches a major

---

34. I recommend Mintzberg (1994) for a thorough treatment of this theme as well as an excellent debate presented in Mintzberg et al (1996). The views expressed by Mintzberg and others of this bent have come to be known as the Emergent approach. As discussed later these examples make it clear that part of strategy development is invention rather than discovery. This is an additional element beyond knowledge deficiency that contributes to its uncertain character. Further, both its invention and discovery components may depend on future occurrences beyond prediction.
35. Over the years this has proved a very valuable distinction for corporations to make. A full blown explanation of this is beyond the scope of this lecture but the reasons are rooted in the fact that although each represent major on-going sources of shareholder value, the type of leader, the needed aperture, the time constant, the degree of uncertainty, and the relevance of current organizational structures differ considerably between tuning and transforming.

new value proposition. All the examples of uncertainty given at the beginning of this lecture represent transforming.[36] Tuning is to transforming as editing is to composing. The differences could not be more stark.

Because tuning builds on an established business model and is incremental, it is much less likely to be uncertain. Transforming, on the other hand, does the opposite: it establishes new quite different sources of shareholder value. Accordingly, uncertainty is an essential quality of transforming at its outset. In the case of Hewlett-Packard's inkjet printers we saw earlier that this uncertainty probably lasted nine years or so. At the heart of developing a successful treatment in Strategy of uncertainty is the understanding that transforming is by far the most important domain of uncertainty in corporations. If this is an accepted proposition, then I can move forward to build a new understanding of how Strategy can really make a difference in situations with uncertainty. My approach will be to progressively peel back layers of the onion of transforming until eventually Strategy's potential contribution is evident.

5. Origination: the Heart of Transforming

Transforming is outside of the scope of a corporation's "normal" activities and as a result usually lacks a formal organization.[37] Nevertheless there is an implicit transforming architecture comprised of five major tasks: (1) delineating a promising space, (2) coordinating the resources necessary for transforming[38], (3) originating new meritorious programs, (4) acting as an investment gatekeeper for transforming programs, and (5) effectively carrying out a well-developed business plan.

Although each of these has an important role to play, origination (3) is clearly the heart of transforming. It is its first cause – without origination transforming never even begins. With this insight we can then restate the problem of incorporating uncertainty in Strategy: "Can Strategy significantly bolster origination?"[39]

To better understand the character of origination, I will briefly recite the history of a well-known example, the genesis of the Sony Playstation.

Ken Kutaragi joined Sony directly after graduating from the University of Electro-Communications in Tokyo in 1975. Compared to other major Japanese corporations, Sony appeared exceptionally forward-thinking. CEO Akio Morita,

---

36. An independent analysis done by the author and Scott Judd estimated that, of the top 25 market cap companies in the US in 1999, approximately 60% of their profits came from businesses they were not originally in, that is, from transforming.
37. Many corporations have a Business Development function and some have an Advanced Projects group. Nevertheless these rarely contain the bulk of the resources necessary to succeed at transforming.
38. This takes on special importance because of the lack of a formal transforming organizations.
39. Strategy also has a role in scoping and review, but these are ancillary.

one of Sony's most visible external symbols, was a high profile, internationally-savvy iconoclast and not at all of the drab-suited, tradition-minded mold typical of Japanese senior executives of his time, and Sony had a history of breakthrough products: the transistor radio, the Betamax, and the Walkman. So it seemed a good choice for Kutaragi, as his brilliance, independence and cheek were already evident.

Kutaragi's role in origination at Sony began in earnest in 1984, when he attended the demonstration of some new graphics technology developed by Sony's Information Processing Research Center at Atsugi.

> It was September of 1984, in a room at a Sony factory in Atsugi, Japan. An incredibly stunning picture was taking form on a monitor before Ken Kutaragi's eyes. On the screen was the image of a person's face. The image changed shape at the touch of a slide control...The computer graphics system – called System "G" (Japanese for "image") – was revolutionary in that it was capable of real-time texture mapping.[40]

System G was developed for generating special effects in broadcasting. Kutaragi's interest lay elsewhere, however. On seeing System G, he was immediately struck by what an incredible video game engine the System G technology would make. This insight became a driving passion that would consume him for the next 15 years and propel him into the senior ranks of Sony's management.

Origination, however, did not stop with this initial insight. Rather it involved the long agonizing process of sustaining the commitment of Sony and finding the right path over many years: there were the doubts over the ability to put System G on a single chip; there was the highly fractious aborted attempt to work with Nintendo; there was the disdain for digital technology by the better-regarded analog mavens; there was the simmering resentment caused by Kutaragi's take-no-prisoners style; there was the initial complete disinterest of the 3rd party developer community; and so on. The outcome, however, was well worth the travail. By 1999 video games represented 39% of Sony's operating profits and probably represented its major growth opportunity, and this dramatic result was for a business that only had its first product in 1994.

This is a classic example of origination. The persistent uncertainty is palpable and Kutaragi and Sony's response to this is instructive. Success was not the result of ex ante strategy development followed by inflexible implementation, but rather of maintaining momentum over a long period of time and intelligently adapting when key new knowledge did become available.[41] Many of the critical problems

40. Page 3, Asakura, (2000).
41. One could characterize this in terms of options theory. According to the Black-Scholes formulation, an option is uniformly more valuable if variability is increased and/or the duration of the option is increased. Transforming represents a high variance activity over a long period of time. Maintaining the ability to adapt is preserving the value of options.

faced by Sony, much less their solutions, were not evident early on and no amount of analysis could have made them so.[42] A useful perspective in transforming is "The rudder only works when the ship is moving."[43]

Even apparently modest improvements in the efficacy of adaptation can have a powerful impact on transforming. A simple calculation supports this. Suppose a transforming effort took five years and, in each of those years, four critical directional decisions were made. If the original likelihood of making the correct choice was 80% for each choice, then the likelihood of ending up with in the right place is about 1.15%. If somehow we could improve the likelihood by just five percentage points at each decision, then the final success probability increases to almost 3.9%. This may not seem like much but it is an improvement of almost 250%!

The challenge before us then is "Can Strategy improve the adaptive process central to origination?" To answer that we must better understand how adaptation proceeds.

6. The Nature of Adaptation

When someone like Sony's Kutaragi sees an opportunity, what is really going on? A useful starting place can be found in the philosophical consideration of the nature of Reason. A.N. Whitehead's formulation is particularly apropos:

> One main law which underlies modern progress is that, except for the rarest accidents of chance, thought precedes observation. The novel observation which comes by chance is a rare accident and usually wasted.[44]

A simple way to state this is that you see what you are looking for. Casual observation suggests there is a lot of truth in this view that perception is shaped by past learning. For example, my brother, who is a builder and developer, can look at a building or a real estate deal and see problems and opportunities that are completely opaque to me.

The Scottish psychologist Kenneth Craik developed this idea in a more scientific way with the theory of "mental models".[45] His view was that individuals held internal mental models that were used to receive and interpret

---

42. A frequent problem in large corporations is analysis paralysis, the inevitable outcome of applying a Design approach to situations with uncertainty. At each bend in the road, the corporation requests new cash flows, another market study, further review. This back and forth is inimical to transforming because it damages both flexibility and the speed of response.
43. The value of adaptive behavior extends to the risky as well as the uncertain. As noted earlier, the higher the variance the greater the value of an option.
44. Page 72, Whitehead (1969).
45. Craik, (1943). An extensive bibliography of mental model publications can be found at http://www.tcd.ie/Psychology/Ruth_Byrne/mental_models/publications.html.

external stimuli. These mental models allow one to perceive something interesting that would be missed by another observer.

Kutaragi of Sony apparently had the right type of mental model, so how did he look at things?[46]

> Whenever he came across an interesting idea, his thoughts quickly turned to how the technology could be successfully commercialized.[47]

In other words, Kutaragi's mental model was not just about how advanced the technology was or whether Sony had the ability to develop the product but rather how these pieces fit into a much broader picture of whether this could be a successful business. Certainly it would be a lot easier to utilize a mental model that was much narrower; the model could be simpler and the information needed sparser. With tuning you can get away with that, but, unfortunately, with transforming you cannot; the necessity for such a broad field of view like Kutaragi's follows inexorably from transforming's necessarily wide aperture.

7. Strategy as a Mental Model

So where does that leave us? For a lucky few like Kutaragi, experience and disposition have led to an effective transforming mental model already. Our attention, however, must turn to the vast majority of originators who are not so fortunate. What can they do? It would be nice if they could get a Parietal Lobe download from someone like Kutaragi. Unfortunately, despite the rapid advances in medical technology, it will be a long wait before this service becomes widely available. So instead we must ask "What existing perspective might serve as an effective mental model that covers these higher level drivers of business success?"

A financial approach such as expected NPV won't work, because of the inability to meaningfully determine the numbers. A marketing model won't work because it is focused on market acceptance rather than the underlying drivers of profitability. For similar reasons, a technical evaluation model won't work because it focuses on technical feasibility, not broad success. It turns out that Strategy is exactly the mental model one would like to have. This is evident when one considers that the purpose of a strategy is to identify the determinants of long term superior returns.

---

46. A good mental model is necessary but not sufficient. "Seeing" transforming opportunities of great merit depends on adequate mental models and also on exposure to the right kinds of information. Had Kutaragi not been carefully following the development of family computers or if he had not had substantial digital design training and experience, then his witnessing of System G would have been akin to my looking at a house, the origination spark would not have occurred.
47. Page 6, Asakura (2000).

When Kutaragi is thinking about what it takes for a technology to be "successfully commercialized", he is really pondering a strategy problem. This is the answer to the formulation of Strategy to account for uncertainty. In the highly uncertain adaptive terrain of transforming, following the traditional Design path of developing a strategy is counterproductive. Instead, an entirely different approach must be undertaken: to help the origination frontliners develop a sufficient understanding of Strategy so that it can serve as a mental model.

This is a powerful insight, and with it comes the convergence of the Design and Emergent approaches. In situations of uncertainty Strategy can play a vital role as a cognitive framework for the innovator. The rich understanding of desirable ends developed by the Design proponents (and Industrial Organization) now has the potential of energizing the formative process correctly described by the Emergent proponents. Or, to put it more succinctly,

With uncertainty, Strategy is useful whereas strategy is not.

This is the answer to the puzzle and the heart of Strategy under uncertainty.[48] This insight is good news for the Design School and its foundation, Industrial Organization. It means that their powerful body of knowledge can extend its practical usefulness into areas of uncertainty. It is also good news for the Emergent proponents as their thoughtful description can now shape a potent prescription.[49]

Strategy, like Medicine, is a prescriptive discipline: its purpose is to develop a body of thought that will assist business people in making better decisions.[50] What this means is that Strategy consists of an understanding of *both* the qualities of good decisions and what practical process can best achieve these qualities. In situations of uncertainty, the better process is to enable successive intelligent choices rather than attempting to delineate a fixed path in advance. The Strategy problem then is no longer to develop a strategy but rather the higher order concern of continuously and flexibly informing many decisions over a long period of time. Accordingly, the advance of Strategy to make it a useful contributor in uncertain situations does not come from furthering its description of the implications of uncertainty but rather by making it more useful in an adaptive process.

---

48. I should note that this conclusion is not just theoretical but also practical. I have trained many innovators in Strategy to quite good effect.
49. Having put this solution forward, it is not clear to me how the Strategy Elite will react. There is no question that it will dramatically change their role from "fishing" to "teaching how to fish". It is also true that some beloved centers of privilege may be diminished and that the natural reaction of any guild is lack of transparency. However, on the plus side of the ledger, those of the Strategy Elite that can adapt and become teachers and mentors will now see the value of their ideas dramatically expand. Only time will tell.
50. At a deep level this is why subjective probability is unsuitable.

8. Strategy and Uncertainty

With this insight in hand, I will now offer some guidance regarding how Strategy must advance to make it suited to fulfill this promising role.[51] To do this I will briefly characterize what types of constructs are best suited for mental models and then compare Strategy to this benchmark to uncover the areas that most need attention.

To best act as the foundation of an effective mental model, an intellectual framework needs to fulfill five requirements. It must be:

1. *Relevant*. The framework seeks to solve the right problem.
2. *Valid*. The framework does in fact solve the problem.
3. *Complete*. The framework applies to nearly all situations faced.
4. *Simple*. The framework is simple enough to be remembered and used.[52]
5. *Practical*. The information needed to use the framework is available.

This structured view answers the question as to why Strategy is such a good candidate as a transforming mental model: it seeks to characterize the broad drivers of success, so it is relevant; there has been enough empirical work to make one comfortable that, although not precise, it is valid[53]; and it is a well-studied area, so there are at least some models of Strategy that are complete.

Strategy, when used as a mental model, is also practical. The Design approach was rejected earlier because it was not practical in transforming. To be more specific, the sources of strategic strength were not identifiable at the time of the Design exercise (ex ante). What has changed to make us believe that the using Strategy as a mental model makes it practical?

To answer this we must answer, "Why are the sources of strategic strength not observable in a Design process?" There are two reasons. First, certain key foundation developments have not yet occurred. For example, much of Microsoft's strength came from its control of the GUI (Windows). At an early

---

51. Some of the better Strategy models, though not perfect, are already able to start being used in this way. Accordingly, this section is not about how to make the use of Strategy mental models possible at all but rather how to make them better.
52. The requirement of simplicity is not that the fully articulated framework is simple but rather that a reasonably inclusive distillation can be stated simply. Getting to this distillation may require considerable complexity – force equals mass times acceleration is simple, but the derivation of Newtonian mechanics is not.
53. It is beyond the scope of this paper, but it would also help Strategy's value as a mental model if it improved its understanding of dynamics, as this is so central to transforming's success.

stage, the many technical and market developments that even made such an approach feasible were not known. Second, developing strategy is not just discovery but also invention[54]. Invention is the result of a potent confluence of intention, intelligence, knowledge, serendipity and elbow grease. Only rarely do these elements converge in a group formed to develop a strategy – the confluence cannot be forced. Strategy as a mental model gets past both these concerns by putting Strategy in the mind of the inventor[55]. By so doing it increases the chances that, *when the time is ripe*, the best strategy choices will be observed/ created and that they will be pursued.

This leaves simplicity. In science, there is Occam's razor that states that the simplest complete explanation of observed phenomena is probably the correct explanation. In contrast, there is Helmer's Principle: a simple explanation will triumph in business. This Principle is so powerful that often incorrect, simple explanations gain precedence over more accurate but more complex ones. This is not because business people have limited intellectual capacity, but rather because alignment within a business involves persuasion and complexity defeats this. The practice of strategy development has a long history of embracing incomplete (or even wrong) constructs because they are simple.[56] Thus in advancing the use of Strategy as a mental model, great care must be taken to not overly compromise completeness or validity for the sake of simplicity.

It is my view that simplicity (retaining sufficient completeness and validity) is the quality of Strategy that could most use improvement to achieve suitability for mental models.[57] This leads us to the unorthodox conclusion that, as a practical matter, advancing Strategy to account for uncertainty does not involve layering in complex constructs borrowed from Finance or Economics but actually going in exactly the opposite direction of greater simplicity and transparency.[58]

---

54. This is the point Henry Mintzberg makes pages 66-75, Mintzberg (1987).
55. By "inventor" I mean that to include not just technical inventions, but business inventions of all types whether they be technical, channel, process, whole product, etc.
56. For example, the Experience Curve that was mentioned earlier, though simple, was incomplete.
57. It is my view that Professor Porter's Five Forces and positioning framework comes the closest to being both complete and simple, although it could still use additional distillation to get maximum leverage as a mental model. It also is lacking in its treatment of dynamics, as Porter recognizes.
58. I have focused on Strategy's primary role in transforming: a mental model for origination. In support of this is Strategy's value as the basis of gatekeeping criteria. In the traditional model, gatekeeping often appears like a black box to originators. This leads to a lost opportunity for guidance, poor decisions and frustration. Instead, the criteria used by gatekeepers should be transparent, known in advance and based on the same principles of Strategy that the originators have been taught. So established, a positive spiral can be established, whereby the gatekeeping function can serve as strong reenforcer of the use of Strategy as a mental model and thus lead to better opportunities being brought forth.

9. Summary and Conclusion

As a practitioner of Strategy, not an academic, my concern has always been to develop frameworks that are useful in the development of strategies for making high return investments.[59] Accordingly, this lecture is focused on trying to get past the barriers that have prevented constructive use of Strategy in uncertain situations. My starting place was to understand that wholesale adoption of a Design approach is antithetical to adequate treatment of uncertainty and that we need to be inductively guided by the understanding that transforming is the principal domain of uncertainty.

Building on these insights I dissect the process of "transforming", first realizing that origination is its heart, then learning that adaptation is the hallmark of origination and finally recognizing the central role in adaptation played by mental models. I then asked, "Can Strategy form the basis of a mental model for transforming?" The answer to this is strongly affirmative. This opens up a novel way for Strategy to contribute in uncertainty: not as a set of concepts that allows the ex ante development of a strategy but rather as an internal compass that helps guide transforming to a positive outcome. This use of Strategy puts some demands on the future development of the discipline. In particular, the honing of constructs so that they are teachable must be a major goal.

In closing, I should state that the prescription offered in this paper for Strategy and uncertainty is only part of a larger theme. Strategy is about the identification and realization of fundamental drivers of business success. As such it is not a subject that should be reserved for a privileged few. Instead Strategy should become like accounting. While few business people are expert in the intricacies of GAAP, almost all understand the basics of income statements and balance sheets. So it should be with Strategy. Such a penetration of Strategy, into the core of decision-making, would result in a powerful distributed intelligence[60] that would bode well for the future creation of shareholder value.[61]

---

59. As a practitioner, I cannot claim to be fully conversant in many of the academic articles on Strategy, so I ask for the reader's forbearance in the scarcity of my references.
60. I would argue that distributed rather than centralized approaches, if implementable, are superior in complex systems. The triumph of capitalism over central planning and the downfall of a "Le Courbousier type" urban planning are good examples. The work of Institutionalists, such as Douglas North, has shown, however, that the secret to successful decentralized systems is carefully laid out and enforced ground rules (e.g., property laws in capitalism). In the case of transforming the rules that make decentralization work come from two sources: the external logic of shareholder value creation and the internally enforced gatekeeping criteria. As mentioned before, part of the secret of energizing transforming is designing gatekeeping criteria that are consistent with an understanding of Strategy and uncertainty.
61. In my view Microsoft and GE already have a measure of this distributed Strategy intelligence.

References:

Asakura, R. (2000), *Revolutionaries at Sony: The Making of the Sony PlayStation and the Visionaries Who Conquered the World of Video Games,* New York, NY: McGraw-Hill Companies, Inc.

Bayes, T. (1763), "An Essay Towards Solving a Problem in the Doctrine of Chances", web site http://www.stat.ucla.edu/history/essay.pdf.

Craik, K. (1943), *The Nature of Explanation*, Cambridge, MA: Cambridge University Press.

Keynes, J. (1937), web site http://cepa.newschool.edu/het/essays/uncert/intrisk.htm.

Keynes, J. (1957), *A Treatise on Probability*, London, Great Britain: Macmillan & Company Limited.

Knight, F. (1967), *Risk, Uncertainty, and Profit*, New York, NY: Sentry Press.

Mintzberg, H. (1987), "Crafting Strategy", *Harvard Business Review* 65(4): 66-75.

Mintzberg, H. et al (1996), "The 'Honda Effect' Revisited", *California Management Review* 38(4): 78-117.

Mintzberg, H. (1994), *The Rise and Fall of Strategic Planning,* New York, NY: The Free Press.

Porter, M. (1985), *Competitive Advantage: Creating and Sustaining Superior Performance*, New York, NY: The Free Press.

Porter, M. (1996), "What is Strategy?", *Harvard Business Review* 74(6): 61-78.

Porter, M. (1980), *Competitive Strategy: Techniques for Analyzing Industries and Competitors*, New York, NY: The Free Press.

Rumelt, R., Schendel, D., and Teese, D. (1994), *Fundamental Issues in Strategy*, Boston, MA: Harvard Business School Press.

Savage, L. (1972), *The Foundations of Statistics*, New York, NY: Dover Publications, Inc.

Whitehead, A. (1969), *The Function of Reason*, Boston, MA: Beacon Press.

6. The Rise and Fall of the Dot Com Enterprises

Des Laffey
Kent Business School

Abstract. This paper looks at the dot com phenomenon drawing mainly on examples from the USA where the boom started and was most pronounced, but also from the UK which had a number of high profile dot coms. It starts by asking the question, 'Who were the dot coms?'. It then goes on to consider the factors which led to the emergence of the dot coms such as the emergence of the commercial Internet, the lowering of entry barriers which followed from this and the funding available for new businesses through venture capital. The article also looks at the reasons why it was believed that the dot coms represented a threat to established businesses. The article then looks at the booming IPO market for dot coms and the opportunities this provided for exit by venture capital investors. The crash of 2000 is considered, lessons are drawn for entrepreneurs and investors and finally the article looks at future prospects for the dot com sector.

Keywords: dot coms, business shakeouts, venture capital, e-commerce.

1. Introduction and Objectives

On 7th December 1998 the front cover of Fortune announced: 'Internet or bust'. This hyperbolic statement was made at the height of the dot com boom. Traditional companies felt vulnerable, as many observers believed that the start-up companies – the so-called dot coms – would threaten established ways of doing business. However, just a year and a half later the dot com bubble had burst.

This paper looks at the dot com phenomenon drawing mainly on examples from the USA where the boom started and was most pronounced, but also from the UK which had a number of high profile dot coms. It will consider the following points:

In section 2 this paper will ask the question 'Who were the dot coms?'. Section 3 will go on to consider the factors which led to the emergence of the dot coms such as the emergence of the commercial Internet, the lowering of entry barriers which followed from this and the funding available for new businesses through venture capital. Section 4 will look at the reasons why it was believed that the dot coms represented a threat to established businesses. Section 5 will analyse the nature of the dot com IPO frenzy of the late 1990s and the gains made by venture capital firms. Section 6 will explain the collapse in dot com share prices in 2000, drawing on academic theory and empirical data. Lessons that can be drawn for entrepreneurs and investors are covered in section 7, which looks at examples of success and failure in the dot com sector. Finally, in section 8 future prospects for the dot com sector will be examined.

This article was originally published in the International Journal of Entrepreneurship Education 2(2): pp. 167-202.

2. Who Were the Dot Coms?

In the USA in the mid to late 1990s a large number of new firms emerged through the medium of the Internet. These so-called dot coms included the high profile firms, Amazon, Yahoo and eBay. It is no coincidence that these companies emerged in a nation at the forefront of what Audretsch and Thurik (2001) identified as the newly emerging entrepreneurial economy.

The entrepreneurial economy is described in terms of a number of trade-offs with the previously dominant managed economy and is characterised by greater uncertainty, turbulence and 'an increased role for new and small enterprises' (Audretsch and Thurik, 2001, p270) which sets the scene for the growth of these companies.

Whilst the dot com phenomenon was most apparent in the USA, European entrepreneurs also emerged, albeit on a smaller scale, with such well publicised examples as Boo.com (a retailer of sports goods), and Lastminute.com (enabling customers to purchase unsold travel inventory).

But before one talks about dot coms in any depth it is necessary to be clear about what they are and how they vary in characteristics. Chaffey (2002, p54) defines dot coms as start-up businesses "whose main trading presence is on the Internet", thus distinguishing them from established firms such as Lands' End – the catalogue retailer of clothes – which open an Internet channel; such firms being referred to as multi-channel, or clicks and mortar, firms.[1]

The dot coms, however, require further categorisation which can be done by defining the type of buyer and seller.

2.1. Business to Consumer - B2C

These dot coms offer products to consumers and include the classic dot coms such as Amazon and Boo. It is this category which the media generally tends to refer to when it discusses dot coms.

2.2. Consumer to Consumer - C2C

This type of dot com allows consumers to trade in marketplaces with other consumers. eBay is the best known example through the online classifieds and auctions they provide.

---

1. It is noted here that there is some debate over the use of the term dot com. Ryanair, the European low cost airline offers an example of a firm that trades mainly over the Internet, selling 94% of tickets online, but would not usually be referred to as a dot com. This is because Ryanair moved their business online over time rather then emerging as an Internet based start-up.

2.3. Business to Business - B2B

These dot coms trade with other businesses. Many dot coms tried to extend the eBay idea of marketplaces, also known as exchanges, for whole business sectors where procurement was seen as a fragmented and inefficient process. FreeMarkets, for example, operate auctions for industrial parts and raw materials. B2B has a far lower profile than B2C, but is nevertheless by far the larger part of e-commerce.

2.4. Consumer to Business - C2B

This final category of dot com enables consumers to initiate transactions with business. This is exemplified by Priceline who operate reverse auctions in which the consumer states a price for a product, and vendors then compete for their business.

Dot coms may not fit exclusively into any one of these categories. Amazon, for example, started as a B2C company and then diversified into auctions, a C2C activity.

3. What Factors Led to the Rise of the Dot Coms?

3.1. The Growth and Commercialisation of the Internet

What was to eventually became known as 'The Internet' was developed in the 1960s through funding by the US military in order to find a means of enabling communication in the event of nuclear conflict (Schneider and Perry 2000).

Until the early 1990s, however, the Internet was the domain of academics and researchers as commercial use was prohibited. A process of commercialisation started in the late 1980s and the wider use this encouraged was to be given a further boost with the emergence of the World Wide Web in the early 1990s. The release of the easy to use Mosaic browser in 1993 at the National Center for Supercomputing Applications (NCSA) at the University of Illinois which enabled Web pages to be viewed in a graphical format in colour then brought the benefits of the Internet to a much wider population. The World Wide Web was to then grow at a rapid rate both in terms of the number of websites and users as shown in Figures 1 and 2. This alerted some in the business community to its potential as a means of communication and as a sales and marketing channel. Indeed, Marc Andreessen, who had been involved in the development of Mosaic was to form Mosaic Communications Corporation with the businessman Jim Clark. The company was renamed as Netscape and the interest in it would start the dot com

IPO frenzy in 1995 when it raised $140 million and the share price more than doubled in its first day of public trading (Ritter, 2002).

Figure 1: US Online population 1995 - 2003

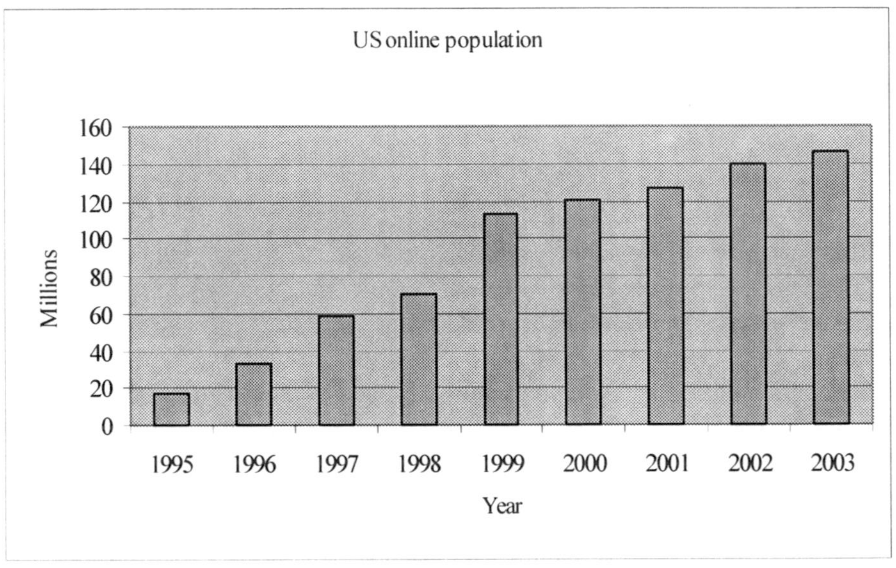

Source: www.harrisinteractive.com. Date accessed May 2004

Figure 2: Growth in the number of Websites from 1990

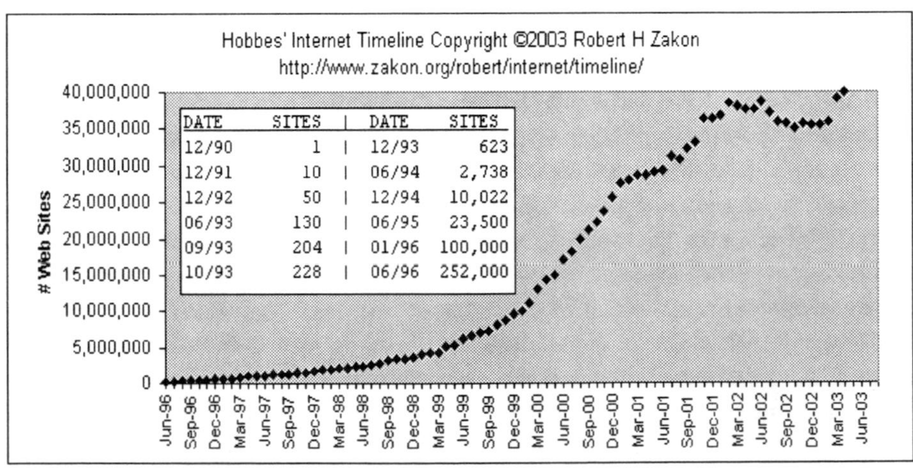

Source: Hobbes' Internet Timeline Copyright (c)1993-2003 by Robert H Zakon, http://www.zakon.org/robert/internet/timeline. Date accessed May 2004.

3.2. The Lowering of Entry Barriers Through the Internet

One would-be entrepreneur alerted by the growth of the Internet was Jeff Bezos, a Vice President with D.E. Shaw and Co, a New York trading firm. Spector (2000) describes how in 1994 after Bezos was told by his employers to research potential categories for retail on the Internet, he placed books at the top of the list. After rejection Bezos decided to pursue the idea himself, giving up his highly paid job and founding Amazon in 1994.

The initial founding of Amazon through Bezos' own resources illustrates how the Internet lowered barriers to entry in many markets. The World Wide Web offered access to a wide market without the investment in retail outlets across the whole country that would have brought with it a need for much larger funding at an early stage and a concomitantly higher risk.

3.3. Venture Capital

New firms require financing to grow and as Audretsch and Thurik (2001, p304) argue, in the entrepreneurial economy "traditional means of finance are no longer appropriate" as they are based on the notion of lower risk. This statement leads us to the crucial role played in the funding of the dot coms by venture capitalists and also by informal capital sources, for example wealthy individuals and firms.[2]

As the American National Venture Capital Association[3] (NVCA) state, in their most typical arrangement venture capitalists raise capital from investors, who may be University endowment funds, wealthy individuals or organisations, known as limited partners, which forms a fund to be invested in a range of companies which demonstrate the possibility of explosive growth, in return for an equity stake.

The role of the general partners, the venture capitalists who manage the funds, is to judge which firms to invest in and to then oversee the investment with the ultimate goal of exit through either the glamorous route of an IPO or a sale to another firm. The venture capitalist typically looks at a timescale of five to seven years to reap their returns, though the late 1990s were not typical times, and investment horizons were reduced considerably.

The motivation which leads investors to become limited partners is shown by an article published in the Notre Dame (University) magazine in summer 2000 (Cohen, 2000). This describes how the University made a strategic decision to move some of its investment portfolio away from conservative investments, such as bonds and shares in large companies, into venture capital in search of higher

---

2. Examples of such firms were Dell and Intel who each had their own specialist venture capital arms. As the 1990s progressed dot coms themselves would also become active investors.
3. http://www.nvca.org

returns. Consequently, in 1993 Notre Dame invested $3 million in a fund set up by Sequoia Capital, the famous venture capital firm.

3.3.1. The Funding Process

At some point, depending on their resource requirements and desire for credibility, new firms will look to obtain the involvement of venture capital. The funding provided can be categorised as being in a number of stages – seed/start-up, early, expansion and later stage – which reflect the development of the enterprise.

As these stages progress, with other things remaining equal, the uncertainty of the firm as an investment prospect decreases and consequently the price paid for a stake in the firm increases as its prospects become much clearer. The overall levels of these investments, valuations given and stages will depend on the opportunities for quick and easy exits.

3.3.2. Seed/Start-Up Stage

The start-up of a dot com is, by its nature, high risk with the resources typically provided by the entrepreneur and/or friends and family, as occurred when Pierre Omidyar founded AuctionWeb, which would be renamed eBay, with his own resources in 1995.

Conversely, Bronson (1999) describes how the venture capital firm Draper Fisher Jurvetson (DFJ) invested at the seed/start-up stage to the tune of $300,000 for a stake of 15% in an idea for a free email service, which would become the ubiquitous Hotmail.

3.3.3. Early Stage

Early stage is where venture capital will generally start to get involved. Early successful examples from the leading venture capital firms, which became part of the dot com legend, include:

- The investment by Sequoia Capital in Yahoo in 1995, as described by one of its limited partners Notre Dame University, "For a total investment of less than $2 million Sequoia received nearly a third of the company" (Cohen, 2000).

- The investment by Benchmark Capital, itself a new firm, of $5 million in 1996 for a stake of 22% in eBay (Southwick, 2001).

- In the UK, Apax Partners invested $12 million in QXL, a European version of eBay, for an undisclosed stake in 1999 (QXL, 2001).

Fuerst and Geiger (2003) state that early stage investment will typically be used to complete the development of the product, pull together a professional management team and develop the marketing side of the business. As these investments are higher risk the venture capital firm will generally want to take an active role in overseeing their investment by taking a seat on the board. The start-up will now need to deliver on its potential to achieve further funding when the initial capital is exhausted, something the venture capitalist can use as a form of control.

Entrepreneurs also actively seek the involvement of elite venture capital firms to gain credibility. Stross (2000) cites the example of eBay whose founder Pierre Omidyar already had sufficient resources to fund further development through personal wealth gained from the sale of an earlier entrepreneurial venture and from the early profitability of the firm. Instead he had looked for venture capital involvement in order to attract an experienced CEO which then led to the investment by Benchmark and the subsequent recruitment of Meg Whitman, an experienced senior executive.

3.3.4. Expansion Stage

An example of the expansion stage was the investment of $25.4 million in E-Loan, the online mortgage company, in 1998 by Yahoo, Softbank Technology Ventures, Softbank Holdings Inc. and Sequoia Capital (E-Loan, 1998). Early stage funders usually look for the involvement of others to finance this stage, 'other people's money', though they may continue their involvement.

3.3.5. Later Stage

An example of a later stage investment was the $102.6 million invested in 1-800-Flowers.com, an online seller of flowers, by Softbank Capital, Benchmark and Forum Holdings in 1999 (Kawamoto, 1999). The falling post IPO performance of this firm demonstrated how later stage investments can be at the mercy of the market.

The economic environment of a booming stock market in the 1990s was ideal for such activity and US venture capital funds showed impressive growth culminating in an average return of 160% in 1999 (Fuerst and Geiger, 2002, p204). Attracted by these returns venture capital investment in the USA soared in the 1990s as shown in Figure 3.

Figure 3: Venture capital investment in the USA 1991 - 2003

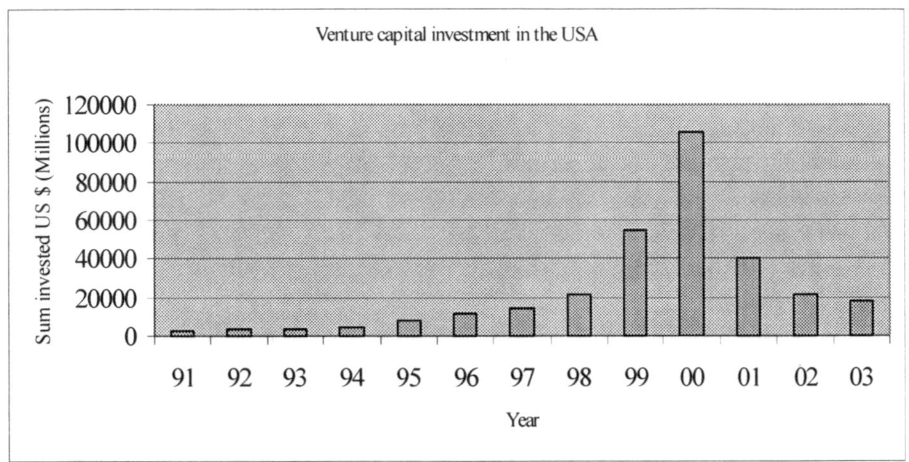

Source: Developed using data from National Venture Capital Association. http://www.nvca.org. Date accessed May 2004.

4. The Threat of the Dot Coms

The dot com impact was wide ranging. It was believed by some that the Internet was about to transform the basis of competition across the whole economy and that the leading firms in this area could become the new Microsofts in terms of market domination. This section will consider the reasons why it was believed by many that the dot coms offered a superior way of doing business.

4.1. The Economics of the Dot Com Model

Table 1 which follows illustrates the seeming undeniable logic of the dot com way as illustrated by Amazon; a combination of wide consumer choice (once freed from the constraints of the physical bookstore), low costs and high sales.

A more extreme example of the way in which disintermediation could occur lies in digital products, that is any product which can be represented in computer readable form, for example, music and news. With such products the Internet enabled the disintermediation of further parts of the value chain, by removing the need even for physical production and distribution. This threatened to radically change the economics of such industries by lowering the scale required to compete in the industry.

Table 1: Business model comparison of Amazon versus a Land-based retailer

	Land-based	**Amazon.com**
Superstores	439	1
Titles per superstore	175,0002,	500,000
Occupancy costs (% of sales) [a]	12%	<4%
Sales per operating employee	$100,000	$300,000
Inventory turnover	2-3X	50-60X
Sales per square foot	$250	£2,000
Rent per square foot	$20	$8.00

[a] Includes Rental, Depreciation, Amortization, and Pre-opening expenses

Source: William J. Gurley, "Amazon.com: The Quintessential Wave Rider", Deutsche Morgan Grenfell, June 9, 1997, taken from Katz L. E. (2002) Amazon.com Going Public, in Gompers P. A and Sahlman W.A. *Entrepreneurial Finance: A Casebook,* New York, John Wiley and Sons, 538-568.

4.2. Enhanced Levels of Customer Service

Porter and Millar (1985, p7) argue "that most products have had a physical and information component". They define the information component as "everything that the buyer needs to know to obtain the product and use it to achieve the desired result" (p7). Where products have a high information content – for example, banking, books, newspapers and travel and tourism – the Internet should be able to provide an enhanced service.

But a website can be more than a source of generalised information, it can provide 'personalisation'. When a user enters a website their preferences can be noted through registration and/or the use of cookies – files that a website visited creates and stores on the visitor's computer, enabling tracking of their website activity which can be fed back to them at their next visit. Mendelson and Meza (2001) describe how Amazon uses these technologies to offer a personal storefront to returners to the site, featuring products from categories they have purchased previously. This was taken a step further with comparison of purchasing patterns, meaning that Amazon could recommend products to customers that had been bought by consumers with similar tastes, both through the website and through targeted emails. The increase in sales revenue from under $16 million in 1996 to over $2.7 billion in 2000 (Amazon, 2001) showed the attraction of this innovative approach to the consumer.

The advantages discussed above are undoubtedly positive aspects of dot coms, but such services can be offered just as readily by established firms who set up Internet channels. Many established companies, feeling under threat by these upstart companies, thus sought to react to the threat by establishing their own Internet offerings either by extending their own operations to offer Internet services or by setting up their own dot coms. It was believed, however, that existing firms would face the problem of cannibalisation, whereby existing customers would merely be diverted to the new channel with the addition of a new cost layer. This was a factor in Barnes and Noble's sluggishness in responding to the threat of Amazon, failing to open their Internet subsidiary until 1997.

In addition to this existing channels – both internal and/or external – could fight against any migration to the Internet, a situation known as channel conflict. This occurred when Compaq had their products removed from the leading retail outlets in Australia when they decided to sell online (Coltman, Devinney, Latukefu and Midgley, 2002).

4.3. The New Economy – First Mover Advantage and Network Economics

Much emphasis was placed on the idea of a 'new economy' and how first mover advantage using the Internet would lead to market dominance. The term 'new economy' as used in the dot com arena was in part a popularisation and distortion of the ideas expressed by Arthur (1996) on the phenomenon of dominant firms in high technology markets. A central tenet of his argument was the idea of network effects, which other writers refer to as network externalities, which occur when there are wide benefits from the use of a product.

A network effect can be seen clearly in eBay, which is attractive for those looking for online auctions as it offers a wide variety of products for sale. This increase in demand then leads to increased supply as the site becomes more attractive to sellers. Great importance was thus placed on speed to market to achieve such network effects.

5. The Dot Com IPO Frenzy

The venture capital investments discussed in section 3.3 enabled the dot coms to grow but many of them would go on to launch IPOs to provide further resources and credibility in the marketplace.

Significantly, an NVCA press release in January 2000 (NVCA, 2000) revealed that 50% of IPOs in 1999 were venture capital backed, which illustrated the opportunities for early stage investors. As John Fisher of DFJ stated:

> With the stock market valuing internet-based companies at huge multiples compared with revenues, companies can go from start-up to initial public offering in under two years, compared with a more sedate five-year period with traditional high-tech start-ups. (Quoted in Foremski, 1999)

The late 1990s were to see explosive IPO debuts by many of the dot coms and the phenomenon of the 'day trader', whereby individuals would make short term investments in hot shares, gave a further momentum to share prices, as illustrated in table 2.

Table 2: Selected dot com IPOs in the USA

Company	Description of company	Date of IPO	Offer Value	First Day Share Performance from IPO Price
Ariba	B2B marketplace	June 1999	$115 million	291%
Ask Jeeves	Search engine	July 1999	$42 million	364%
eBay	Auction and classified site	September 1998	$63 million	163 %
FreeMarkets	B2B marketplace	December 1999	$173 million	483%
iVillage	Women's Portal	March 1999	$88 million	234%
Neoforma	B2B marketplace	January 2000	$91 million	303%
Priceline	Reverse auction pricing website	March 1999	$160 million	331%
theglobe	Hosting service for websites	November 1998	$28 million	606%
Yahoo	Portal and search engine	April 1996	$34 million	154%

Source: Developed using data from http://bear.cba.ufl.edu/ritter, http://www.ipodata.com, http://www.forbes.com http://www.ipocentral.com. Date accessed May 2004.

To confirm the impression of a booming IPO market in the late 1990s Ritter (2002) states that in 1999 119 IPOs doubled in value on their first day compared to 39 in the previous 24 years combined, though the last half of 1998 had seen 10 such events as the market started to overheat. To give some sense of perspective Amazon had gone public in 1997 and recorded a relatively 'low' first day gain of 31% which reflected the difficult market for Internet related IPOs in that year.

In Europe similar forces were at work, although on a smaller scale, as "the number of technology companies listed on Euro.NM, an alliance of five new European equity markets, doubled in 1999" (Aragon and Raik-Allen, 2000). One extreme example of this was the case of the UK dot com JellyWorks – a firm set up by the 24 year old entrepreneur Jonathan Rowland to invest in dot coms – moving from incorporation in October 1999 to a flotation in December valuing the company at £10 million. Within 3 days the company's value had increased to £200 million (BBC, 1999).

These share price gains thus produced valuations which defied traditional thinking "about profits, multiples, and the short-term focus of capital markets" (Desmet, Francis, Hu, Koller and Riedel, 2000, p1). Traditional measures such as p/e ratios could not be used for many of these firms as these required profits, and even for those firms with profits these ratios were extremely high[4]. As Canzer (2003) states, average historic p/e ratios for the Standard and Poor index had varied considerably from 5.9 in 1944 to 35 in 1999, reflecting the future prospects of the general economy at these times. However, many of the dot coms were trading at enormous p/e ratios with Jaffe (1999) reporting values of 1,400 for eBay and 470 for Yahoo in September 1999.

This led analysts to use measures which looked at future potential. Metrics looking at sales growth and website traffic would thus became important. If companies could demonstrate rapid growth it was argued that they could justify higher than normal valuations. The sales growth many dot coms had shown offered some support to high valuations though at some point they would have to deliver profits.

Valuations of 1999 dot coms are placed in perspective by the comparison of eToys, the online seller of toys, as opposed to its established bricks and mortar rival Toys R Us, undertaken in August of that year by a US asset management firm, as illustrated in Table 3.

Table 3: Comparison of the valuations of eToys and Toys R Us in 1999

	eToys 99 (Estimated)	**Toys R Us 99 (Estimated)**
Sales	$100 Million	$11.5 Billion
Earnings	($123 Million)	$400 Million
Earnings per Share	($0.91)	$1.61
Price to Earnings	Loss	10x
Market Valuation	$4.9 Billion	$4 Billion

Source: http://www.centman.com. Date accessed May 2004.

Table 3 places in clear perspective the gap which had emerged between performance and valuation; eToys, with estimated losses of $123 million in 1999 and less than 1% of the sales of ToysRUs, was valued at more than 20% greater than its rival which had estimated profits of $400 million.

4. The price of a share of a company's public stock divided by the company's earnings per share. For most companies normal p/e ratios would be somewhere between 10 and 20. However, if a company is expected to show strong future profitability a 'high' p/e ratio can be justified as the profit growth will ultimately bring the ratio back to more normal levels.

5.1. Harvest

The early stage investors were thus sitting on enormous gains, provided the share levels did not collapse before the expiry of the lock in after the IPO. Venture capital firms historically had made their names through 'home runs' – obtaining an equity stake in a new firm and eventually harvesting an enormous profit for themselves and their limited partners. Benchmark Capital, scored its home run with the 49,900% gain Bob Kagle, a general partner of the firm, revealed his firm had made on their original investment in eBay (Himelstein,1999).

Dot coms could avoid an IPO by the alternative route of the trade sale. As Schultz and Zaman (2001) state, the amount raised through IPOs was smaller than that received through the sale of private Internet companies, an example of this being the sale of Hotmail to Microsoft for a reported $400 million in 1997 (Perkins, 1998).

With the well publicised successes of venture capital an increasing number of investors tried to get access to the new larger funds announced by venture capital firms. There was also a pronounced shift in venture capital funding towards early stage riskier investment. As Sussis (1999) made clear, "Interestingly, an ever increasing number of investments are early stage. From 1995 to 1999 (YTD) 53% of investments in technology/Internet-related companies came in the early stage while only 28% of investments in non-Internet related companies came in early."

Valuations were also rising at each stage as entrepreneurs gained the upper hand over venture capitalists keen to use their large funds and overcrowded marketplaces required large brand building programmes. 1999 was thus to see record investments in single rounds of funding which included a $275 million round for Webvan, the online grocery firm (NVCA, 1999).

The hype that accompanied the dot com phenomenon played an enormous part in the rise of these firms with sports style coverage of dot com shares on the main US TV networks feeding the frenzy. Analysts from investment banks – for example, Henry Blodget of Merrill Lynch – were tipping dot com shares whilst their firms were simultaneously advising the same firms. This represented a potential conflict of interest as Treanor writes:

> The accusation is that the analysts inflated their recommendations on shares so that their investment banking employers could earn lucrative business from the companies whose shares were being touted. (2002)

A further charge made against investment bankers was that the allocation of IPO shares and pricing decisions were made to obtain future business. With the enormous first day gains access to shares at the IPO was seen as a route to quick financial gain, and was unsurprisingly not available to all. In a practice known as 'spinning' investment bankers would allocate shares to firms to gain future business.[5] Loughran and Ritter (2002) also argue that IPOs were underpriced by underwriters in the late 1990s to increase the potential value of the allocations.

6. Industry Shakeouts

It is normal for innovations as dramatic as e-commerce to lead to many new entrants as entrepreneurs and investors aim to make profits. Whilst the threat to the incumbents appeared real enough, at some point the dot coms would need to deliver on their promise. One way or the other there would be a shakeout, either of the old order, or of the new entrants if the status quo was not seriously challenged.

Day (1997) analyses the process of consolidation, which is typical across industries and identifies two types of business shakeout, boom-and-bust and seismic-shift.

6.1. Seismic-Shift

According to Day the seismic-shift syndrome strikes stable, mature industries with relatively high profit levels which have been sheltered from the ravages of competition through the existence of what he calls 'isolating mechanisms', which in conventional language are barriers to entry. Examples of isolating mechanisms given by Day are patents, regulatory barriers, close personal relationships which exist in an industry and local tastes which could be added to with other factors such as economies of scale. The impact of the seismic shift is to remove one of these isolating mechanisms and shake up the existing market.

Day gives four common triggers for a seismic-shift; deregulation, globalisation, technological discontinuity and competency predator. Of these triggers 'technological discontinuity' best describes the potential impact of the dot coms on many stable industries such as retail banking, music and the media as seen in the late 1990s. It appeared that the Internet lowered the minimum efficient scale and enabled enhanced services to be offered by the new entrants.

However, there was no such seismic shift in any of these sectors. To use a term from a later related article by Day et al (2003) this is because these were re-formed markets, where new technology does not change the fundamental principles of how the market operates. In this case the Internet makes the industry more efficient rather than transforming it, and therefore does not represent a threat to the dominance of existing players. Day et al (2003) illustrate this by using the example of the booming market for business-to-business exchanges in the late 90s as new entrants thought they could replace existing practices. By July 2002 57%

---

5. This issue has recently been under the spotlight, with Credit Suisse First Boston (CSFB) paying $100 million to settle charges of how allocations were made, without accepting any wrongdoing, and Frank Quattrone, the former head of technology banking at Credit Suisse First Boston being found guilty of obstructing investigations into the matter (USA Today, 2004).

of the independent exchanges had exited the market indicating the existence of the boom and bust syndrome which we shall now examine.

6.2. Boom and Bust

Day states that the boom-and-bust syndrome is typical in hot emerging markets – an accurate description of the dot com phenomenon – or in highly cyclical businesses, such as construction. As a boom develops, "an unsustainable glut of competitors is attracted to the market at a rate which overshoots the industry's long-term carrying capacity" (1997, p94).

At some point however, a reality check enters the picture and a shakeout then occurs as excess supply impacts on margins and firms exit the industry.

Markets as diverse as groceries, pet supplies, toys and furniture saw many new entrants as the early pioneers were copied. These entrants believed that the Internet had fundamentally changed the dynamics of these markets (seismic-shift) and that they could benefit from this. If this had been the case, there would still have been a boom-and-bust shakeout of the new players. In reality, however, all that was really seen was the latter syndrome at work.

Day et al (2003) also consider breakthrough markets, only made possible through the advent of new technology, which include search engines, portals and online auctions. New entrants in such markets will not have to take market share from existing players, rather there will be competition from the new players entering the market. According to their thinking this would lead to a large number of firms entering breakthrough markets, and a few survivors after a boom-and-bust shakeout. A look at the history of the search engine market does indeed show many entrants and some exit and consolidation but not a shakeout on the scale Day et al would have us believe, which is probably due to the relatively low costs in running a search engine.[6] Even in the area of portals, where the need for updated content represents a major expense, whilst the big players (AOL, MSN and Yahoo) dominate the market, both in terms of users and advertising revenues, players whose demise was predicted in 2001 such as Walt Disney's Go still exist. This all suggests that the shakeout forces in breakthrough markets may operate in a different manner to that suggested.[7]

---

6. This is a point made by Danny Sullivan, the editor of Search Engine Watch, at http://www.searchenginewatch.com
7. Day's 1997 article does offer a plausible reason for the lack of a more severe shakeout in the portal market. He uses the term 'inhibitors', which is effectively another term for barriers to exit, to describe the factors which may lead a firm to stay in a market. In the portal case with Walt Disney's Go the inhibitors are probably the loss of face from exit and the belief that the market is too strategically important to exit.

6.3. The April 2000 Crash

As we have seen there were always strong business fundamentals that would lead to the eventual downfall of many of the dot coms. From a peak of 5048.62 reached on 10th March 2000 the Nasdaq, where most of the dot coms were listed, fell as illustrated in Figure 4.

Figure 4: The value of the Nasdaq index January 1996 – May 2004

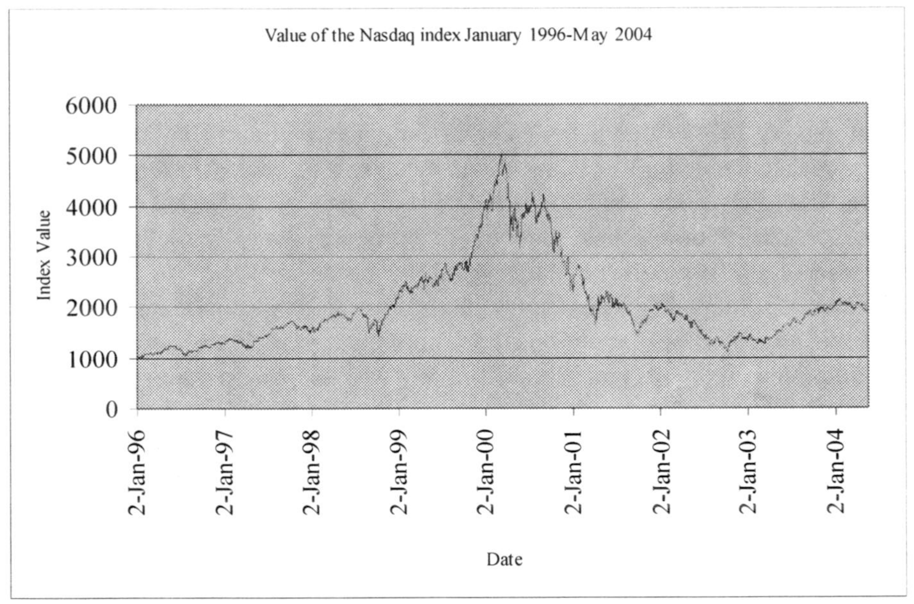

Source: Developed using data from Yahoo Finance, http://finance.yahoo.com/
Date accessed May 2004.

The sustained falls which came after 27th March 2000 were to see the four largest one day falls in the history of the index as investors sought safe havens for their money. In aggregate these falls lowered the value of the Nasdaq by over 34% from its peak to a low point in April 2000. Whilst the market did recover temporarily in April this was to prove a false dawn as the trend was firmly downwards. By the end of 2000 the Nasdaq had fallen over 50% from its peak and worse to come with the lowest point being reached in October 2002 by which time it had lost 77% of its peak value.

The dot coms had flourished along with the technology boom. As the boom appeared to be ending investors were thus more likely to sell 'risky' shares which led to falls in dot com share prices as illustrated in Table 4.[8]

Table 4: Changes in selected dot com share prices 27th March - 20th April 2000. (All data adjusted for dividends and splits).

Company	**Change in share price 27th March – 20th April 2000**
Amazon	-28%
Ariba	-44%
Ask Jeeves	-62%
eBay	-37%
FreeMarkets	-68%
iVillage	-40%
Neoforma	-76%
Priceline	-26%
theglobe	-52%
Yahoo	-39%

Source: Developed using data from Yahoo Finance. http://finance.yahoo.com. Date accessed May 2004.

However, the dot coms had always lived volatile lives – for example, in July to August 1999 many of these dot coms had experienced considerable falls in their share prices, as illustrated in Table 5.[9]

8. Amazon which was not included in Table 2 because of its relatively low first day share performance is included in this table and subsequent tables because of its importance as a dot com stock.
9. This volatility was not new as Katz (2002) quotes research by Morgan Stanley which showed that nearly 75% of dot com IPOs from August 1995 to April 1997 were trading below their offer prices in May 1997.

Table 5: Changes in selected dot com share prices 2nd July – 4th August 1999. (All data adjusted for dividends and splits) N/A These companies were not public at this time.

Company	Change in share price 2nd July – 4th August 1999
Amazon	-29%
Ariba	-39%
Ask Jeeves	-61%
eBay	-47%
FreeMarkets	N/A
iVillage	-42%
Neoforma	N/A
Priceline	-41%
theglobe	-40%
Yahoo	-32%

Source: Developed using data from Yahoo Finance. http://finance.yahoo.com. Date accessed May 2004.

The difference was that in 1999 most of them had bounced back (illustrated in Table 6), whilst after April 2000 share prices simply collapsed.

Table 6: Changes in selected dot coms share prices: 4th August – 31st December 1999. (All data adjusted for dividends and splits). [a] For those companies not public on August 4th the change in price is calculated from the IPO offer price to 31st December. N/A This company was not public at this time.

Company	Change in share price 4th August – 31st December 1999
Amazon	72%
Ariba	393%
Ask Jeeves	303%
eBay	65%
FreeMarkets	611%[a]
iVillage	-41%
Neoforma	N/A
Priceline	-28%
theglobe	-26%
Yahoo	258%

Source: Developed using data from Yahoo Finance. http://finance.yahoo.com/ Date accessed May 2004.

Market sentiment had also turned against a number of the higher profile dot coms well before the downturn of April 2000. Webvan, the online grocery store, had launched their IPO in November 1999 and after a fall and then rise of one third, the share price began to follow a sharply downward trend, leading to its eventual bankruptcy in August 2001.

6.3.1. What Burst the Bubble?

The basic reason for the collapse of the dot coms was a generic trigger listed by Day (1997) – they ran out of money. Few of the dot coms had positive cash flows as the emphasis had been gaining market share and increasing the number of visitors to the site, to gain first mover advantage and network effects. Without profits in sight the dot coms could only survive for as long as they had the support of their funders, which required confidence in the future value of their holdings. The triggers which have been put forward for the crash can be summarised as follows:

Overvalued stock

With the US on a long bull market and recording massive gains, particularly on technology shares with the Nasdaq up 84% in 1999, many were predicting a general market correction and a collapse of dot com values which had reached ludicrous levels. These valuations were reliant on investor confidence which, with the influx of amateurs, could easily change. The credibility of etailers selling physical goods had been hit by their fulfilment performance in the Christmas of 1999, with the prime example being eToys. As a consequence of this adverse publicity eToys and Amazon both suffered falling share prices after the holiday season.

The end of the technology boom

Laudon and Traver (2002) identify the resolution of millennium bug issues and price wars in the telecoms sector as making the technology sector less attractive, leaving dot coms vulnerable. In addition to these factors, the ruling that Microsoft had acted as a monopolist in the browser market hit market confidence in technology, corresponding with the third largest ever fall in the Nasdaq index.

Poor financial judgement

Quinn Mills (2001, p23) argues that a "perverse public-private partnership led by Wall Street and the Federal Reserve" first created the dot com bubble, and then destroyed it. He argues that fears of a recession brought on by the millennium bug led to a loosening of monetary policy in 1999 which merely led to players in Wall Street adding to the dot com feeding frenzy. The last quarter of 1999 was indeed to see a further spike in valuations and IPOs which made a hard landing more likely.

However, whilst interest rate policy may have exacerbated the boom and initiated the bust it appears hard to see how any macroeconomic policies could prevent the collapse of firms who were basing their hopes on transforming entire industries.

In all likelihood, a combination of the above factors leading to a loss of confidence is the most plausible explanation of the timing of the crash. At some point investors would inevitably sell dot com shares to take profits, though with the day traders adding to market irrationality it was hard to say precisely when that would be.

Once share prices started falling fear of further falls became a self-fulfilling prophecy, with the irrational exuberance that had driven the market up giving way to a blind panic that brought the market crashing down. Dot coms rapidly run out of money, as venture capitalists were unwilling to back them, whilst money raised through IPOs was used up fast – if it was not already gone.

For firms who had not yet taken the IPO route this source of finance was now far more difficult, as the UK company Boo found out when plans for an IPO were cancelled in April, with the company going bust in May 2000. The trigger event in the UK appeared to be the IPO of Lastminute.com in March 2000, whose shares launched at £3.80, and after a quick spike increasing by 28% (BBC, 2000) fell rapidly down in value, to a low of £0.18 in 2001.

Initially it was thought this slump was confined to consumer based dot coms and that the sturdier B2B sector was still a safe investment. However, this was to be an incorrect assumption as not only was the whole Internet sector (however loosely defined) savaged, but so too was the technology sector. The wider economy would be affected too, with the indexes of stock markets across the world falling, as the world was engulfed in a long bear market.

7. Lessons for Entrepreneurs and Investors

Section 6.3 considered the triggers to the dot com collapse in March 2000. However, there were fundamental problems with the dot com sector which would have eventually brought a correction. This section will cover these problems and in doing so offer some insights into successful versus unsuccessful dot coms, both within and across sectors.

7.1. Lack of Scale

What was often forgotten in the hype about the dot coms was their lack of size in terms of revenue. Schultz and Zaman (2001) in a study of a sample of 299 Internet publicly traded stocks in 1999 found that less then 25% had sales of $25 million in the previous quarter.

Whilst a minority of dot coms such as Amazon had large revenues most were small players. A fundamental problem that the B2C e-commerce firms dealing with physical goods were faced with was their lack of scale in areas such as logistics.

Focus on Amazon and Warehousing

Amazon started off without any of its own warehouses and aimed for a zero inventory model. However, in order to guarantee availability and combine books from different suppliers in one package they had to develop capabilities and hold their own inventory (The Economist, 2000). To quote from the Amazon annual report 1999 "We grew worldwide distribution capacity from roughly 300,000 square feet to over 5 million square feet in less than 12 months" (Amazon, 2000, p2). Whilst Amazon have developed a reputation for effective delivery this has clearly come at a significant price.

A solution to Amazon's problem is to offer warehousing services to other firms, as shown by the sale of Toys R Us merchandise through Amazon's site. The effort to expand from books to other products such as videos and CDs also offers lower costs through economies of scope.

The Amazon case throws light on the failure of other dot coms which operated at much smaller scale. Webvan, the online grocery firm, developed a state of the art warehousing and distribution infrastructure which would enable them to cost effectively deliver to individual households. However, they were unable to attract sufficient demand and in 1999 operated at just 20% of capacity (Banks et al 2001). The economics of delivery to single households are also not attractive and require large, regular order sizes to be viable, something Webvan could not persuade enough people to do. Delivery of physical goods also has to face the realities that working people are not at home during the day, congestion problems and the issue of returns.

Markets with rigid inefficiencies can however be targeted by dot coms. The low cost airline sector offers a good example as Web based distribution strips out costs by avoiding the margins of travel agents enabling the new players to effectively compete on point-to-point travel where customers will accept more basic levels of service. An example of a recent entry to the low cost sector enabled by the Internet is the Spanish Vueling Airlines launched in 2004 with 30 million Euros of funding, the main backer being the UK venture capital firm Apax Partners.[10] The London based consultancy Aviation Economics (www.aviationeconomics.com) writes that standard software to run such websites can be bought from companies such as Navitaire for less than £1 million UK pounds which substantially lowers the barriers to entry. Full service airlines find it difficult to compete against such rivals as they risk upsetting the relationships they have with travel agencies, though some of them have moved to Web based distribution and/or set up of their own low cost operations.

7.2. The Costs of Reaching Customers

The development of brand names assumed great importance as many markets went through an overcrowded boom phase. To quote John Doerr of Kleiner Perkins Caufield and Byers at the height of the Internet boom, "We are living in the Internet land-grab era." (Perkins, 2000). This led to dot coms pursuing extravagant advertising campaigns, some even buying TV advertising at the Super Bowl at a cost of $2.4 million per slot (The Economist, 2001).

In contrast to the dot coms, established firms already had marketing campaigns across the whole range of media which could be expanded, at marginal cost, to include their e-commerce operations simply by adding their Web address. Furthermore, their existing off-line campaigns are where most of the potential e-commerce customers can be reached. The severe costs of customer acquisition that the dot coms thus faced are shown by the experience of Bank One in the United States which set up the Internet only bank Wingspan. To quote Andrew Hilton "Bank One spent US $150 million last year on marketing Wingspan which works out at around US $18,000 a year to acquire each customer" (2000, p12).

7.3. Customer Behaviour is Hard to Change

After the euphoria of the Internet boom it became apparent that behaviour is harder to change than had been anticipated. Many of the opportunities that had been envisaged did not materialise as consumers did not move their expenditure online as fast as predicted, for example in the purchase of music or in the real

---

10. The source for this is www.apax.com

estate sector. In the B2B sector Day et al (2003) explain that even though B2B exchanges offered great potential efficiency savings they ignored the trends across manufacturing towards reducing the number of suppliers and also the inertia which comes from the risk of change.

There is a related fundamental problem for the B2C segment. Many people like to shop in 'real stores' whether to examine products or for more intangible social reasons (shopping on-line lacks that certain 'feel-good' factor). However, this does not mean there are not enough consumers to make e-commerce viable, rather that the target market needs to be clearly defined and marketed to effectively.

7.4. Planning

Any new business has to gain credibility, whether it is a new café or a dot com. Many dot coms, however, overpromised and underdelivered, with poor or late delivery of products being a common complaint. The UK fashion retailer Boo was a particular example of poor planning with a high profile campaign for the launch of their website being wasted when the site was not ready on time (Laudon and Laudon, 2002).

7.5. The Multi Channel Future?

There is evidence that many of the population prefer a multi channel experience. McKenzie (2003, p32) in a study of banking quotes Christine Skouenberg, an analyst at the research consultancy Datamonitor, "The greatest change in bank's approach and strategy in multi-channel banking is the fact that the branch is coming back into focus". Many consumers may use the Web for researching their purchases and then choose to buy in a face-to-face environment, which is more likely to be the case for higher value products.

7.6. The World Wide Wait

The dot coms, and many other firms who moved to adopt e-commerce, had overly optimistic views on the ease of use of websites. For multi-channel firms this was an annoyance but for dot coms it threatened their only source of revenue. A general issue was the lack of broadband connections that enable fast download of websites including graphics and video. During the dot com boom the vast majority of the population in the UK and USA had narrowband connections, dial up using a modem, which are far slower. It was estimated in 2000 that less than

10% of Internet users in the USA had broadband connections and less than 1% in the UK (Harris Interactive, 2000, Ofcom, 2003)

Thus many customers who attempted to use websites gave up in frustration, faced with slow and complex websites. The Boo website, for example, demonstrated how the use of a great many graphics made the site too slow. Indeed, 40% of visitors on the day of launch could not access the site (Laudon and Laudon, 2002), the equivalent of finding the doors to a high street store locked!

Another factor that inhibited the growth of e-commerce was the fear of fraud, even though most websites use encryption methods to secure data and moreover publicised this fact.

7.7. Adaptive Survivors?

Day et al (2003) suggest that in re-formed markets only what they term 'adaptive survivors' – those who find a protected niche by retooling their strategy and enhancing existing relationships – will survive. They give the example of Neoforma, which started as an independent exchange for the medical industry. As demand for such exchanges did not grow as anticipated, due to the factors discussed in section 6.1., Neoforma transformed itself into supplying and operating marketplaces to support existing purchasing activity in the industry. This links in well with the advice of Sahlman (2002, p90) who advises that one should sell "ammunition to all sides of the war without end" – in this context facilitating and improving existing activity – rather than engaging in direct combat, which here means replacing existing activity.

7.8. Competing Using the Unique Features of the Internet

Some sectors, however, particularly those that are concerned with the exchange of information offer a more optimistic view for dot coms in re-formed markets. The key principle here is that new players add value using the unique features of the Internet in a way existing players find difficult to counteract.

- *Lastminute.com*, the UK firm which emerged selling excess travel inventory, has continued to grow and in November of 2002 declared its first quarterly pre-tax profit. It showed a steadily recovering share price which peaked in November 2003 at £3.13 after strong growth and on rumours of a takeover bid. The threat of forward integration, or disintermediation, from suppliers selling discounted tickets on their own websites has not happened to any significant degree. As Martha Lane-Fox, a co-founder who later left the company, stated in an interview "Companies can't do it on their own website because they fear cannibalisation" (Quoted in Chaffey, 2002, p58). Lastminute.com also gained much needed credibility by its appointment of Alan Leighton, the former Chief Executive of the Asda UK supermarket chain which, as its Chairman, thus bringing in some 'old economy' skills to the company. The company has also grown to achieve economies of scale through acquisitions and diversified through its purchase of a car hire firm to enable it to offer a comprehensive travel service.

- *Netflix*, which describes itself on its website (www.netflix.com) as "the world's largest online DVD movie rental service" provides an example of a firm successfully entering a re-formed market. The company competes through offering a subscription service which enables members to choose from the 20,000 titles through its site which are then delivered free through the post. Subscribers can rent 3 titles at a time which can be kept as long as they want, the only limit being that 3 more titles can only be rented on return of the previous selection. This service has 2 million subscribers attracted by its wide choice – five times the selection of a typical store, no late fees and convenience. The service attacks the reliance of the conventional rental business on the contribution of late fees to revenue, estimated at 18% for Blockbuster in 2002 (Ellis, 2002). The company raised $82.5 million through its IPO in May 2002 with the share price rising 12% from the offer price on its first day and in May 2004 traded at over twice the offer price. High street players such as Blockbuster have responded with similar offerings and whilst the future for Netflix is uncertain it provides an example of a new entrant shaking up a sector.

Other dot com firms who have succeeded in re-formed markets through e-commerce include financial information sites, dating sites and pornographic sites. The latter two categories are perhaps a reflection of today's busy world and are encouraged by the anonymous nature of the Internet, given that such services can be used without any of the embarrassment that their use in the real world might result in.

7.9. Dominating Breakthrough Markets Through First Mover Advantage

Day et al (2003) emphasise the importance of first mover advantage in breakthrough markets.

- *eBay* is clearly an example of a winner as demonstrated by its first quarter results of 2004 available on its website which reported sales of

> $756 million, up 59% year on year and profits of $200m up 92% from the corresponding quarter last year. Its continued dominance of its market, facing off challenges from both Yahoo and Amazon, who attempted to cross sell auctions to their existing customers and attract eBay customers, is an indication of the strength of its network effects. There has also been a realisation of the need to react to a changing market. Growth has been achieved by diversifying into a wide range of auction categories, such as cars with eBay now being the largest used car market in the United States. Moreover, the company has recognised that asynchronous auctions can be a tedious format and reacted by offering a 'buy it now option' and diversified into fixed price sales through its acquisition of Half.com. Finally, large retailers such as IBM have been invited to sell at eBay through the development of the eBay stores format.

Being the first mover does not guarantee continued dominance of a market, in online as well as in conventional markets. Interestingly, Day and Fein in an earlier related paper (2001) listed Yahoo as an example of a pure play winner, which few would have disagreed with at the time. After Yahoo's early dominance of the search engine market Google, who were founded in 1998, have gone on to provide serious competition. Yahoo now have only a narrow lead (26% versus 23%) in consumer searches in the United States, whilst Google have actually drawn ahead in worldwide English searches (33% versus 24%) (ClickZ Stats, 2003).[11]

How did Google pull this off, given that Yahoo appeared to be doing all the right things, offering portal services, such as news and email, to keep users on their site? In the early days of the Internet it was also believed that Yahoo's manual indexing of relevant websites to improve searching added value for inexperienced Web users. However, Google was very attractive to people who just wanted effective search facilities. Firstly Google developed superior search engine technology which rated sites using a number of measures, for example how many links they have in other documents. Secondly, they went against received wisdom by not offering portal like services – the search engine equivalent of 'stick to the knitting'.

The Google experience shows that Yahoo have weak if any network effects in the area of search services. There are no benefits for consumers from wide usage by others, in fact quite the opposite if it slows the service down! In short, the search engine environment had changed as the volume of information grew, users have become more demanding and a rival innovative product has emerged.

---

11. From 2000 Google supplied their Web Crawler software which travels the Web indexing relevant websites to Yahoo. Yahoo used this to enhance the results from their manually generated directory until the relationship was terminated in 2004.

- *Betfair*, the C2C gambling website in the UK, set up in 2000 by former professional gambler Andrew Black and Investment Banker Edward Wray, is a further excellent example of a dot com establishing dominance in a breakthrough market. The Betfair website[12] explains that 'users can either bet in the normal way (back) or offer odds to other punters (lay)' and effectively become a bookmaker, which to quote company spokesman Mark Davies "couldn't happen without the internet" (BBC, 2003). Betfair thus avoids the risk function of the bookmaker as it merely facilitates gambling between its users, taking a commission of between 2% and 5% from the winner. The main attractions to users of this site are the better odds on offer and strong network effects as it has reached a critical mass quickly. Betfair declared annual profits of £8.45 million on revenues of £32.3 million (UK) for the year ending April 2003 up from £1.07 million in 2002, which represented an impressive pre-tax profit margin of over 25% (Pratley, 2004).

7.10. The Revival in Dot Com Fortunes

After all the gloom which had engulfed the sector, October 2002 saw the start of a dramatic increase in the value of many dot com companies. The gains shown by the companies we have covered from October 2002 to August 2003 are illustrated in Table 7, although the high percentage growth is because they were at such a low value. Of the ten firms in this table, five were above the offer price at their IPO in August 2003. Revealingly, all these five firms are consumer websites suggesting that the B2B sites are being held down by a combination of low corporate IT spending and an unwillingness to change established practices. However, to place the optimism for consumer dot coms in perspective by the summer of 2003 only eBay had managed to trade at close to its previous peak value. Not only that, it appeared that the market might be overshooting again with p/e ratios on 1st August 2003 of Yahoo 107.34, Ask Jeeves 581.67 and eBay 93.30. However, this general revival in the share prices of most of the consumer based dot coms continued (until May 2004) with significant gains in share prices from eBay – who surpassed their previous all time high, Yahoo, iVillage and Ask Jeeves. The strong performance of search engines has been driven by their ability to monetise search activity. This is done by the use of context specific advertising whereby advertisers pay to be top of a list for specific keywords which then appears along with the normal results of a search, for example with Google on the right hand side.

12. http://www.betfair.com

Table 7: Changes in selected dot coms share prices 1st October 2002 – 1st August 2003. (All data adjusted for dividends and splits).

Company	Change in share price 1st October 2002 – 1st August 2003	Share price on 1st August 2003 as a percentage of the previous peak value
Amazon	+136%	38%
Ariba	+64%	2%
Ask Jeeves	+1531%	9%
eBay	+97%	86%
FreeMarkets	+27%	2%
iVillage	+197%	2%
Neoforma	+31%	2%
Priceline	+244%	3%
theglobe	+1678%	4%
Yahoo	+224%	13%

Source: Developed using data from Yahoo Finance. http://finance.yahoo.com/. Date accessed May 2004.

What attracted investors was that in general the dot coms had demonstrated the ability to grow in a sluggish market and an increasing number of them were achieving profitability. The path to profit and a regaining of credibility has also been through more rigorous cost controls, as illustrated by the following quote from A. George "Skip" Battle, the CEO of Ask Jeeves:

> Finally, across the entire company we've worked strenuously to reduce costs. Counting the people in the businesses we've acquired, we've reduced our headcount from 850 in December 2000 to 346 at the end of February 2003. Other costs also have been dramatically reduced. We'll average about $22.5 million in expenses per quarter in 2003, as compared to $44 million in Q4 2000. (Ask Jeeves, 2003, p5)

8. The Future for Dot Com Entrepreneurs

The previous section has discussed the reasons for the dot com failure, and has made it clear that in most sectors multi-channel firms have the advantage due to their scale and their established channels. However, it is possible to offer some ideas for the future of the dot com sector.

8.1 Lack of Venture Capital Funding

The funding environment for dot com entrepreneurs has remained challenging with venture capital funding falling for two years quarter on quarter after the abnormal peaks of 1999 and 2000. The NVCA reported in July 2003 that funding appeared to have stabilised, though was cautious about a dramatic upturn (NVCA, 2003). Such an upturn would be dependent on the health of the wider economy and the IPO market. Some commentators believe that the decision by Google to go public in 2004 – with a valuation on the firm of up to $20 billion – would help kick start venture capital activity again. The S-1 filing by Google to the SEC[13] revealed that Google made a net profit of $105.6 million in 2003 on revenues of $961.9m and that first quarter profits for 2004 had doubled year-on-year mainly through the growth of context specific advertising. This made impressive reading but the competitive threat of a resurgent Yahoo and the likely entry of Microsoft into the search market means that continued success is by no means certain.[14]

A successful Google float could help to restore confidence to the market, although it seems improbable that venture capital activity of the type seen at the peak of the dot com boom will be achieved again. This is no bad thing as the last thing the sector needs is an oversupply of new entrants forcing down prices and increasing advertising costs.

Funding is still available, albeit more difficult to achieve, with FreshDirect – an online grocery operation – raising over $100 million from private investors including Mercantile Capital Partners (Business Week, 2003). After the Webvan experience the FreshDirect funding is somewhat surprising even though the entrepreneur behind the company, Joe Fedele, has a successful track record in previous innovative food ventures which were predicted to fail.

8.2. The Continued Growth of E-commerce

A factor which has driven the share prices of dot coms forward is that B2C e-commerce is continuing to grow in both the USA and UK. USA B2C Internet sales, for example, grew 26% in 2003, although most of these sales are to multi channel firms (BBC, 2004).

In the area of physical products, success is difficult due to the problems discussed in section 7.1. There are, however, some success stories in the sale of physical goods outside of the standard, easy-to-ship categories such as books and

13. Available at http://www.sec.gov/Archives/edgar/data/1288776/000119312504073639/ds1.htm. Date accessed May 2004.
14. In a break from tradition Google intend to sell their shares through an auction. This is designed to overcome the problems highlighted earlier on the allocation of shares and to allow the general public the chance to purchase shares.

CDs, which offer optimism for the future. One such example is Blue Nile, the online retailer of diamonds and jewels, which confounds the view that only low value standard products can be sold online. The company website[15] explains that it offers a wide choice of diamonds at 20-40% below retail price, and the ability to 'design your own' earnings and pendants using the website. The company states that growth has been driven by customer service, with word of mouth recommendation, rather than by expensive advertising campaigns. Sales of $72 million in 2002 up 48% on 2001, with a net profit indicate the success of this approach. This performance enabled the company to raise $76.7 million at its IPO in May 2004 with its shares gaining 39% on their first day and ending the month over 60% above the offer price.

The BlueNile experience suggests that the early stereotyping of the online consumer is misplaced. Whilst some products may be harder to sell per se there are people who are happy to buy this way and/or who prefer not to visit shops.As sales volumes grow economies of scale will become easier to achieve. A supporting industry will also develop offering better services: in the UK, for example, logistics firms such as iForce and M-box are emerging to offer an outsourced solution to this cost disadvantage of operating at low levels of capacity.

From the customer perspective use of the Web is something people become more familiar with over time and as broadband connections continue to grow usage is given a further fillip.

8.3. Charging for Content

Historically, the Internet was seen as a vast free resource. This situation is changing, and as less content is available free, it is self-evident that charging for content will become easier. The endoffree.com website documents sites that are moving over to a charging approach. High profile examples include McKinsey with their Quarterly Magazine and The Economist website's archive.

Even in the field of music where copying has been such a problem the initial success of Apple's iTunes service has indicated a willingness to pay, though it has been reported that users have found a way of copying and sharing files from the site.

As organisations begin to charge for previously free products, they will do well to learn from Shapiro and Varian's advice (1999) on the marketing of digital products (or content).

- Offering a free basic service and payment for the full product, which comes with enhanced features. One example of this is Hotmail where

15. http://www.bluenile.com

for an annual payment the payee receives enhanced services, such as greater storage and no account expiration.

- The free service comes with annoyance features, for example reminders that it is not as good as the full product.

- Offering samples free of charge, such as abstracts of articles or a sample copy (see, for example, the International Journal of Entrepreneurship Education!).

The general point is to attract users with a lesser version of the product and then convert them to paying customers.

8.4. Global Reach for Niche Products

The Internet with its global reach offers the opportunity to make niche markets viable.

One example of this is the business of Nick Spurrier, whose second-hand online bookshop now enjoys global reach, whereas previously it relied on a single retail outlet in an isolated British town. The Internet is ideal for such a business as buyers are often searching for books which are out of print and thus difficult to find. This enabled Spurrier to charge higher prices online than he could in his shop which he decided to close.

To quote Spurrier:

> I really loved having a bookshop, but the economics of owning it just didn't add up. I was paying someone £40 a day to work in the shop but I wasn't taking more than £100 a day. At the same time from the Internet I was making at least £1000 a week. The number of customers has almost trebled since I went online. (BBC, 2001)

Whilst Spurrier was not a start-up his experience offers clear lessons to those who may venture into the dot com arena.

9. Conclusion

In conclusion we have looked at the emergence of the dot coms, their meteoric rise, apparent collapse and their recent revival. This article has also attempted to draw out some lessons for the future for aspiring dot com entrepreneurs.

The bankruptcy of so many firms should not be any surprise as any textbook on small business will emphasise how high the casualty rate of new start-ups is. The last few years have also demonstrated that, in most cases, the Internet is not a disruptive technology which 'changes the rules of business', but rather an enabling technology (Porter, 2001) which is generally best utilised by existing firms. Thus one now generally sees increases in e-commerce B2C sales benefiting multi-channel firms who have considerable scale advantages.

However, if a weakness can be identified in existing markets successful dot coms can emerge. The firms which emerge in the new breakthrough markets such as eBay and Betfair can establish dominance if network effects are present, but the extent of this phenomenon should not be overstated.

References:

Amazon, (2000), "1999 Amazon.com Annual Report", *Amazon.com, http://media.corporate-ir.net/media_files/irol/97/97664/reports/123199_10k.pdf.* Date accessed May 2004.

Amazon, (2001), "2000 Amazon.com Annual Report", *Amazon.com*, http://media.corporate-ir.net/media_files/irol/97/97664/reports/00ar.pdf. Date accessed May 2004.

Aragon L. and Raike-Allen, G. (2000), "Benchmark to raise $500 million European fund", *Red Herring*, 7th March 2000, http://www.vault.com/nr/main_article_detail.jsp?article_id=51253&cat_id=0&ht_type=5. Date accessed May 2004.

Arthur, W. B. (1996), "Increasing Returns and The New World of Business", *Harvard Business Review 74(4): 100-109.*

Ask Jeeves, (2003), "2002 Ask Jeeves Annual Report", *Ask Jeeves*, http://www.irconnect.com/askjinc/files/askjeeves_ar_02.pdf. Date accessed May 2004.

Audretsch, D.B. and Thurik, A.R, (2001), "What's New about the New Economy? Sources of Growth in the Managed and Entrepreneurial Economies", *Industrial and Corporate Change 10(1): 267-315.*

Banks, D., Driessen, O., Oh, T., Scipioni, G., and Zimmerman R. (2001), "Webvan: Reinventing the Milkman", in Afuah, A. and Tucci, C. L. *Internet Business Models and Strategies: Text and Cases.* Boston, McGraw Hill Irwin, 192-201.

BBC, (1999), "Jelly Works rapid rise", *BBC News Online*, 23rd December 1999, http://news.bbc.co.uk/1/hi/business/576530.stm. Date accessed August 2003.

BBC, (2000), "More trouble for Lastminute.com", *BBC News Online*, 31st March 2000, http://news.bbc.co.uk/1/low/business/697058.stm. Date accessed May 2004.

BBC, (2001), "Still making the net pay", *BBC News Online*, 6th September 2001, http://news.bbc.co.uk/1/hi/uk/1525293.stm. Date accessed May 2004.

BBC (2003), "The gamble that paid off", *BBC News Online* 15th June 2003, http://news.bbc.co.uk/1/hi/business/3047739.stm. Date accessed May 2004.

BBC, (2004), "US online sales hit $50bn in 2003", *BBC News Online*, 23rd February 2004, http://news.bbc.co.uk/1/hi/business/3515287.stm. Date accessed May 2004.

Bronson, P. (1999), *The Nudist on the Late Shift and Other True Tales of Silicon Valley*, New York, Random House.

Business Week, (2001), "Online Extra: Q&A with Amazon's Jeff Bezos", *Business Week Online*, 26th March 2001, http://www.businessweek.com/print/magazine/content/01_13/b3725027.htm?mz. Date accessed May 2004.

Business Week, (2003), "The Start of a Dot-Comback?", *Business Week Online*, 24th January 2003, http://www.businessweek.com/smallbiz/content/jan2003/sb20030124_6345.htm. Date accessed May 2004.

Canzer, B. (2003), *E-Business - Strategic Thinking and Practice*, Boston/New York, Houghton Mifflin.

Chaffey, D. (2002), *E-Business and E-Commerce Management, Strategy, Implementation and Practice*, Harlow, Financial Times - Prentice Hall.

ClickZ Stats, (2003), "Google Grabs Globe, U.S. to Yahoo!", *ClickZ Stats*, 1st May 2003, http://www.clickz.com/stats/big_picture/applications/article.php/1301_2200171. Date accessed May 2004.

Cohen, E. (2000), "A Billion Dollars in Nine Months", *Notre Dame Magazine*, http://www.nd.edu/~ndmag/endws00.htm. Date accessed May 2004.

Coltman, T., Devinney, T., Latukefu, A. and Midgley D. (2002), "E-Business: Revolution, Evolution or Hype?" *California Management Review* 44(1): 57-85.

Day, G. S. (1997), "Strategies for Surviving a Shakeout", *Harvard Business Review 75 (2), 92-102.*

Day, G.S. and Fein A. J. (2001), "Shakeouts in Digital Markets", *The Wharton School, University of Pennsylvania*, Working Paper, http://hops.wharton.upenn.edu/ideas/pdf/SHAKEOUTS%20IN%20THE%20NEW%20ECONOMY%20v3.pdf. Accessed May 2004.

Day, G.S., Fein, A. J. and Ruppersberger, G. (2003), "Shakeouts in Digital Markets: Lessons from B2B Exchanges", *California Management Review 45 (2): 131-150.*

Desmet, D., Francis, T., Hu, A., Koller, T.M, and Riedel, G. A., (2000), "Valuing dot-coms", *The McKinsey Quarterly 1: 148-157.*

Ellis J. (2002) "Strategy", *Fast Company*, November 2002, http://www.fastcompany.com/online/64/jellis.html. Date accessed May 2004.

E-Loan, (1998), "E-Loan Receives $25.4 Million from Yahoo!, Softbank, and Sequoia Capital", *E-Loan*, 14th September 1998, http://ir.thomsonfn.com/InvestorRelations/PubNewsStory.aspx?partner=6400&storyId=86264. Date accessed May 2004.

Foremski, T. (1999), "Survey - Financial Times Information Technology: Living In The Golden Age", *The Financial Times*, 5th May 1999, http://search.ft.com/search/article.html?id=990505003754&query=living+in+the+golden+age&vsc_appId=powerSearch&offset=0&resultsToShow=10&vsc_subjectConcept=&vsc_companyConcept=&state=More&vsc_publicationGroups=TOPWFT&searchCat=-1. Date accessed May 2004.

Fuerst, O. and Geiger, U. (2003), *From Concept to Wall Street: A complete guide to entrepreneurship and venture capital*, New York/London, Financial Times Prentice Hall

Harris Interactive (2000), "Plenty of Demand for Broadband, According to Harris Interactive Consumer TechPollSM", *Harris Interactive*, 28th November 2000, http://www.harrisinteractive.com/news/allnewsbydate.asp?NewsID=197. Date accessed May 2004

Hilton, A. (2000), "Internet banking: A fragile flower - Where's the killer app", *Centre for the Study of Financial Innovation.*

Himelstein, L. (1999), "Benchmark's Venture Capitalists Take the Valley by Storm", *Business Week Online*, 15th February 1999, http://www.businessweek.com/1999/99_07/b3616103.htm. Date accessed May 2004.

Jaffe, S. (2002), "For Dot.Coms, Second Place Isn't So Bad", *Business Week Online*, 21st September 1999, http://www.businessweek.com/bwdaily/dnflash/sep1999/sw90921.htm. Date accessed May 2004.

Katz, L. E. (2002), "Amazon.com Going Public", in Gompers P. A and Sahlman W.A. *Entrepreneurial Finance: A Casebook*, New York, John Wiley and Sons 538-568.

Kawamoto, D. (1999), "Flower sites' IPOs blossom", *CNET News.com*, 21st May 1999, http://news.com.com/2100-1017-226208.html. Date accessed May 2004.

Laudon, K.C. and Laudon, J. P. (2002), *Management Information Systems: Managing the Digital Firm*, 7th Edition, New Jersey, Prentice Hall.

Laudon, K. C. and Traver, C. G. (2002), *E-Commerce: Business, Technology, Society*, Boston, Addison Wesley.

Loughran, T. and Ritter, J. (2003), "Why Has IPO Underpricing Changed Over Time?", *University of Florida*, 6th August 2003, http://bear.cba.ufl.edu/ritter/work_papers/Whynew.pdf, Working Paper. Date accessed May 2004.

McKenzie, H. (2003), "Multi channel banking", *Banking Technology 20 (2): 32-37.*

Mendelson, H. and Meza, P. (2001), "Amazon.com: Marching towards profitability" (Case Number EC-25), *Graduate School of Business, Stanford University*, 27th July 2001, http://www.gsb.stanford.edu/cebc/pdfs/EC25.pdf. Date accessed May 2004.

NVCA, (1999), "Venture Capital Investment Has Record Breaking 3rd Quarter with $12.98 Billion; Q3 Provides Considerable Growth Among all Industry Sectors", *National Venture Capital Association*, 28th October 1999, http://www.nvca.com/VEpress10_28_99.html. Date accessed May 2004.

NVCA, (2000), "Venture-Backed Companies Account for Half of All IPOs In 1999", *National Venture Capital Association*, http://www.nvca.org/VEpress01_07_00a.html Date accessed May 2004.

NVCA, (2003), "Venture Capital Investments Stabilize in Q2 2003, Early Stage Investing Finally Begins to Rise", *National Venture Capital Association*, 29th July 2003, http://www.nvca.org/nvca7_29_03.html. Date accessed May 2004.

Ofcom (2003), "International benchmarking study of Internet access (dial-up and broadband)", Ofcom, 4 June 2003, http://www.ofcom.org.uk/static/archive/oftel/publications/research/2003/benchint_1_0603.htm. Date accessed May 2004.

Perkins, A. B. (1998), "May The M&A Force Be With You", *Red Herring, May 1998*, http://www.redherring.com/Article.aspx?a=9537. Date accessed May 2004.

Perkins, A. B. (2000), "The Angler- The Advertising Frenzy of E-Commerce Companies", *Red Herring*, January 2000, http://www.redherring.com/mag/issue74/mag-angler-74.html. Date accessed May 2004.

Porter, M. E. (2001), "Strategy and the Internet", *Harvard Business Review 79 (3): 63-78*

Porter, M.E. and Millar, V.E. (1985), "How Information Gives You Competitive Advantage", *Harvard Business Review 63 (4): 149-160.*

Pratley, N. (2004), "Betfair profits leap", *Guardian Unlimited*, 1st June 2004, http://sport.guardian.co.uk/horseracing/story/0,10149,1228711,00.html. Date accessed May 2004.

Quinn Mills, D. (2001), "Who's to blame for the bubble", *Harvard Business Review 79 (5): 21-22.*

QXL, (2001) "*QXL Annual Report*", QXL.com, http://www.qxl.co.uk/contents/uk/qxlmediacenter/data/QXL2000.pdf. Date accessed May 2004.

Ritter, J.R. (2002) "Big IPO Runups of 1975-December 2002", *University of Florida*, October 2002, http://bear.cba.ufl.edu/ritter/RUNUP750.pdf. Date accessed May 2004.

Sahlman, W.A. (2002), "Some thoughts on business plans", in Gompers P. A and Sahlman W.A. *Entrepreneurial Finance: A Casebook*, New York, John Wiley and Sons, 80-111.

Schneider, G.P. and Perry, J. T. (2000), *Electronic Commerce*, Cambridge, Massachusetts, Course Technology.

Schultz, P. and Zaman, M. (2001), "Do the Individuals Closest to Internet Firms Believe They Are Overvalued", *Journal of Financial Economics 59 (3): 347-381.*

Shapiro, C. and Varian, H.R. (1999), *Information Rules: A Strategic Guide to the Network Economy*, Boston, Massachusetts, Harvard Business School Press.

Southwick, K. (2001), *The Kingmakers: Venture Capital and the Money behind the Net*, New York, John Wiley and Sons.

Spector, P. (2000), *Amazon.com: Get Big Fast*, New York, London, Random House.

Stross, R. E., (2000), *eBoys*: *The first inside account of venture capitalists at work*, London/New York, Texere.

Sussis, D. (1999), "Trends in Funding at the End of 1999", *e-commerce guide.com*. 29th December 1999, http://ecommerce.internet.com/news/insights/econsultant/article/0,3371,10418_270201,00.html. Date accessed May 2004.

The Economist, (2000), "Too Few Pennies From Heaven", *The Economist*, 1st July 2000, http://www.economist.com. Date accessed May 2004.

The Economist, (2001), "Is there life in e-commerce?", *The Economist*, 2nd March 2001, http://www.economist.com. Date accessed May 2004.

Treanor, J. (2002), "Wall Street faces $1bn dotcom fine", *Guardian Unlimited*, 23rd November 2002, http://www.guardian.co.uk/business/story/0,3604,845846,00.html. Date accessed May 2004.

USA Today (2002), "Ex-star banker Quattrone asks for new trial", *USAToday.com*, 25th May 2004, http://ecommerce.internet.com/news/insights/econsultant/article/0,3371,10418_270201,00.html. Date accessed May 2004.

7. You Say You Want a Revolution? A Case Study of MP3.com

Andrew Burke
Cranfield University School of Management

Chris Montgomery
MP3.com/VivendiUniversal

Abstract: Mp3.com was a revolutionary venture set up in an attempt to break the mold of the music recording industry. The case study documents the venture's impressive growth and the factors affecting its performance. A deep understanding of the case requires the reader to draw from a wide spectrum of economics, new venture management theory, and both antitrust and copyright laws.

Keywords: music industry, dot.com venture, new venture economics, copyright law.

1. Introduction

Michael Robertson decided he was going to launch a venture that involved traveling along a well worn path that was littered with business failures. He was going to start a firm in a market that had a poor survival record for start-ups. The music recording industry had a long history of seeing new firms come and go without threatening the major record labels' dominant control of the market (see Table 1 below for UK market share data). The record company sector of the music industry was big business. It was a large market that was highly concentrated. For example, MBI (2001) estimated that the top five record companies accounted for 77.5% of the global market in 1999; equivalent to combined revenues of $25 billion[1].

The fundamental economics of the music industry ensured that most new start-ups would eventually fail to compete with large incumbents or would see their interests – if not survival – dependent on being taken over by a major record label. In effect, because of economies of scale in manufacturing, distribution, and marketing, minimum efficient scale (MES) in the recording industry was relatively high. However, the advantage of the large incumbents over smaller entrants did not stop there. The mass appeal of western culture and the globalization of the industry alongside the highly dynamic level of product differentiation innovation (with concomitant viral marketing effects) implied that

1. The MBI World Report 2001, London.

This case study has been written for classroom discussion rather than as an illustration of either effective or ineffective handling of a situation. This case was originally published in the International Journal of Entrepreneurship Education 1(1): pp. 107-132.

artists with potential faced a large but short window of opportunity. Thus, artists had to rapidly disseminate their music to a large market while their product still had a shelf life. All of this pointed towards competitive advantages for large multinational companies who would have the financial clout to launch artists on such a scale. These same companies were more liquid than independent SME record companies and faced less financial risk by being able to spread the risk involved in music investment across a wide array of artists. Thus, apart from rare exceptions such as Geffen in the US, and Virgin in the UK, most independent record companies had posed no real threat to the dominance of the major record labels. Furthermore, if past history was anything to go by, most new record companies were destined to fail and a common belief in the industry held that "the major record labels *always would* dominate the industry because the major record companies *always had* dominated the industry".

But Michael Robertson thought differently, not only was he going to survive in the music industry, he was going to shake it up! He believed it was possible to launch a successful new venture, which could challenge the dominance of the major record companies.

Table 1: UK record company album market share 1985-2000

Albums % Units	*1985*	*1990*	*1995*	*2000*
PolyGram (Universal 2000)	14.5	23.2	20.6	20.5
EMI	13.4	15.9	13.4	10.7
CBS-Sony	15.0	10.4	12.0	11.6
WEA-Warner Music	12.2	12.1	9.9	11.7
Virgin	8.0	7.4	8.3	7.2
RCA-BMG	5.4	4.7	8.1	8.7
Total	**68.5**	**73.7**	**72.3**	**70.4**

Source: BPI Yearbooks. PolyGram data excludes Universal except for year 2000

2. Background

At 32 years of age, Michael L. Robertson founded MP3.com, and served as the Chief Executive Officer and Chairman of the board from March 1998 to August 2001. From September 1995 to March 1998, Robertson operated several web sites that focused on merging search technologies with commerce. From September 1995 to September 1996, Robertson was President and Chief Executive Officer of Media Minds Inc., a developer of digital picture software. From January 1994 to August 1995, Robertson was President and Chief Executive Officer of MR Mac Software, a developer of networking and security tools. Robertson received his Bachelor of Arts from the University of California, San Diego.

Directly prior to the formation of MP3.com Robertson started a company called Filez.com. File sharing technology was emerging as an interesting little business back in 1997. All types of document and image files were flying across the Internet. While working on this venture, Robertson was joined by Greg Flores who was a former business broker and had a keen interest in computers. Flores actively tried to be alert to new business opportunities; both searching out Michael Robertson as a business contact and playing a significant role in observing the growing interest in mp3 files (see box 1 opposite).

In early 1998, Robertson and Flores soon realized that the trading of a file-type with the extension .mp3 was growing exponentially over the Internet. That file type .mp3 represented a convenient way to compress any song or audio track by eleven times its normal size, thus making it much easier to send over the Internet. A normal four-minute pop song that was once 40-50MB in size was now 3.5-4MB. Although at the time dial up modems (<56k speeds) were common, users were still sending files often taking over one hour to send and receive. For those users who had access to a broadband connection (cable modem, ISDN, DSL) the transfer times were shortened significantly. Soon hard drives across the technology sector began filling as users converted existing CDs to .mp3 files and trading their files with friends and colleagues.

Robertson, who had no formal music industry experience, soon realized that the music industry's distribution chain was vulnerable. Robertson never perceived MP3.com to be a "record label" in the typical sense. His vision was to create the most efficient vehicle that would connect music with music fans. Essentially, to create all the tools and a system without offering many of the competencies that major labels possess – namely, marketing and promotion, A&R/talent development, and financial support. Robertson believed that although the music industry created the stars they did not understand how new technologies would make distribution and marketing more efficient.

Box 1: What's in an idea and a domain name?
An interview with Greg Flores

"I worked in the brokerage business for 13 years but I always stayed connected to computers. I bounced from BBS to BBS (bulletin boards) explored Prodigy and AOL in the mid-1980's while things were just getting started for the World Wide Web. I decided to leave the brokerage business and start my own company in 1996. *Can Do Computing* was a computer consulting company specializing in helping people purchase, setup and use computers to explore the Web. I worked one on one with mostly affluent individuals interested in getting connected to AOL and other services.

In 1997, my wife had the opportunity to head a division in California and I figured that I could do the computer consulting from anywhere so we moved to San Diego. In August of 1997, I spotted an insert in the Tribune featuring the "Top 25 Cool Companies of San Diego" and a little company called Filez.com was mentioned in the article.

I found the number for the company, called and spoke to Michael Robertson, and he and I met the next day for lunch to talk about Filez and some other ideas he had brewing. We talked about Filez and the other concepts involving other search technologies with the main idea being to help consumers easily find things to purchase on the web. The things that struck me about Michael were his different way of looking at the Internet and his belief that traditional business methods weren't going to work on the Internet. One example is the traditional way of marketing a business which does not work when applied to an Internet company. He told me that he thought we could build a great company together and he'd like me to come on board. There was just one problem, he couldn't pay me anything but he was willing to give me some equity in the company and I agreed to take the chance. Bottom line, I didn't buy into a concept or group of concepts, I bought into Michael.

My two main roles at Filez.com were to generate revenue and find creative ways to drive traffic to the site. In order to generate traffic, I used to keep my eyes out for growing trends in site ranking charts. Instead of looking at the top of the heap and trying to copy what was at the top, I would watch what was climbing the charts and MP3 file sites had really started to move up the charts. I also looked at the search logs for Filez and noticed that MP3 searches were on the rise. I decided to explore the MP3 thing and downloaded my first MP3 file. Since I was on a cable modem, the download process was pretty fast but finding a song to actually download was more challenging.

I e-mailed an MP3 file to Michael and he was also blown away by the file size and the quality of the sound. We found that MP3.com had already been registered but wasn't live on the Internet. We e-mailed the owner and told him we were interested in buying the domain name. He asked why and we told him we wanted to setup an MP3 site. He e-mailed back, "what is MP3?". We asked him why he had registered MP3.com if he didn't know what MP3 was. He said that he registered because it was the "handle" that Network Solutions had assigned to him when he had registered a previous name and he thought it would be "cool" to register his handle. His name is Martin Paul and Network Solutions had assigned him the handle of MP3. We offered him $1,000 for the domain name and after a little bit of haggling, we purchased the domain for $1,500. While all this was going on, I set out on the Net to find someone with an MP3 site to run the site for us since we didn't yet know that much about MP3. I compared lots of sites that were giving information about MP3 but weren't actually allowing people to download pirated files and the one that we ended up purchasing was MP3shoppingmall.com. MP3shoppingmall was an information site about MP3 only and the guy running it lived in Scandinavia. We paid him a couple of hundred dollars and a small monthly salary to work on MP3.com.

A few days later after the ownership transfer had taken place and we had the webmaster for MP3shoppingmall in place, we turned MP3.com on and Michael and I were shocked by the amount of traffic. In the first 24 hours, we had over 10,000 unique users and this was especially amazing because MP3.com wasn't yet registered in any search engines. People where solely finding MP3.com by typing the URL in the address bar of a browser. We knew immediately that we where on to something. Within the first 18 hours, I received my first call from a company wishing to purchase advertising and I sold them $5,000 in advertising. The name of the company was Xing Technology and they were later acquired by Real Networks. We more than paid for the domain purchase and the new webmaster purchase in the first day of the site."

Traditionally, record companies (labels) and their parent distributors (RCA Records/BMG Entertainment for example) did not utilize direct communication with music fans. The reality of a dialogue between a consumer and a record label has seldom existed in the past, save for a few niche independent labels. When a consumer leaves the high street record store, no further contact is generally made. So understanding the consumer is very difficult. Record companies have in actuality relied on B2B marketing – via radio promotion and in-store marketing and promotion. Without these two elements, consumers would not be made aware of new recordings. But two major factors were beginning to change the music industry marketing landscape, namely the internet and a consolidating radio industry in the United States.

As the Internet grew and reached more consumers, so too did the ability to track consumer behavior and subsequently communicate with them. On-line retailers, such as Amazon.com and Barnes & Nobel increasingly sold more product, tracked behavior, created consumer profiles (that consisted of music, books, videos and other consumer purchases) and matched those profiles against hundreds of thousands of other consumers. This type of artificial intelligence and predictive research expanded the possibilities for further monetization of the consumer.

As a result of the centralization of radio programming in the US market, the need became very apparent. Since it is increasingly difficult to add new songs (with extremely high initial fixed costs) to a wide number of radio stations, labels needed new ways to communicate with music fans. An artist's 'fan web site' is a good start, but the aggregation of many fan sites is necessary.

The Majors have always been powerful and never believed that any small technology company or independent label could threaten their business. That was until the .mp3 file came along. Instead of embracing the format for its efficiencies and the data associated with the tracking of the consumer's *entire* listening, they tried to block the diffusion of the technology.

The first high profile lawsuit by the Recording Industry Association of America (RIAA) came in the last quarter of 1998, when Diamond Multimedia Systems, Inc. (San Jose, California) launched a new product called the Rio PMP300 portable mp3 player. Much like a Sony Walkman™, the Rio allowed consumers the opportunity to transfer mp3 music files from their PC onto a small hand-held device. The popularity of the Rio portable device played a major role in promoting the mp3 music file format. The Rio PMP300 held just under one hour of CD audio quality music, would never skip and could pause and stop much like a common CD player. But the music files were in a format that the industry had no control over and fears of piracy escalated.

The RIAA attempted to prove that the Rio was a 'two-way' device that would facilitate and promote the illegal distribution of music. Diamond Multimedia successfully proved that the Rio was in fact a one-way device, meaning that music could go in to the player and not be set up to re-distribute the music to a friend with a PC or another Rio player.

Initial reactions by many of the industry executives were extremely negative towards the Rio player. But over time an understanding of the technology and the new distribution channels caused executives to participate on one level or another with the new music economy. In this external environment, Robertson and a small band of revolutionaries set out to create MP3.com.

3. The Initial Management Team

Robertson was in need of a management team that would make this vision become a reality and built one that was more akin to a large multinational than a new start-up. Robin Richards was brought in to serve as President and COO. Richards prior experiences included Managing Director of Tickets.com, Inc., an Internet ticketing company, a founder and President and Chief Executive Officer of Lexi International (a teleservices company) and a director of Cash Technologies Inc., a publicly-held company that provides solutions for coin and currency handling, cash management and electronic commerce transactions. He also held a Bachelor of Science degree from Michigan State University.

Next came Paul Ouyang and Steve Sheiner. Ouyang was named the company's Chief Financial Officer. He had served as Chief Financial Officer and Executive Vice President of Operations of Tickets.com, Inc., as a consultant to UDP Inc., (a company involved in dental practices management) as Chief Financial Officer and Executive Vice President for Cheap Tickets, Inc., and as the

Managing Director of Corporate Finance at KPMG Peat Marwick LLP. He also held various positions with J.P. Morgan & Co., Inc. culminating with Vice President of Corporate Finance. He received a BA from Amherst College and an MBA from Wharton (University of Pennsylvania).

Sheiner was named Executive Vice President, Sales and Marketing. Sheiner previously served as Vice President Business Development at Aegis Communications, Inc., a telecommunications company and as a direct marketing consultant, including President of Sheiner Direct Marketing & Advertising, Inc. Sheiner holds a Bachelor of Arts degree from Concordia University (Montreal, Canada).

Table 2: MP3.com, Inc. Organization Chart, Pre-IPO (headcount in parentheses)

CEO (Robertson)

COO (Richards)

MP3.com Ventures (Spiegel)	**CFO (Ouyang)**	**Pres/SBU (Alofs)**	**EVP Sales & Mktg (Sheiner)**	**EVP?CTO Engineering (Dotson)**
M & A (4)	Controller (7) Finance (3) HR (6) Legal (3) IR (1) Analysis (2) Facilities Mgmt (2)	SBU (28) Artist Services/ Account Mgmt (6) Tours, Special Events (8) Label Relations (2) Marketing (4) Artist Services/ Content Mgmt (28) Customer/ Artist Support (3) CD Fulfilment (1)	Sales & Bus. Dev. (26) Including SVP: Flores	Engineering (25) QA (9) Web Development (24) Project Management (6)

Paul Alofs was named President of the Strategic Business Units. Alofs was formally executive vice president and general manager for The Disney Store, Inc., a wholly owned subsidiary of The Walt Disney Company, and a president of BMG Music Canada, (a division of Bertelsmann).

Thomas Spiegel was named as an executive officer of the company. Spiegel was chief executive officer of Columbia Savings and Loan Association, a financial institution based in Beverly Hills, California. He also founded the Columbia Charitable Foundation, a not-for-profit organization that funds education, medical and social causes.

Other Board of Directors included Mark Stevens, a general partner of Sequoia Capital MP3.com's leading Venture capital firm, Lawrence F. Probst III, President and Chief Executive Officer of Electronic Arts, Inc., and Ted Waite, President and Chief Executive Officer of Gateway Computer.

Robertson and his crew thought that their innovation would be embraced by the music industry due to its distribution efficiencies. They did not realize that the music industry was steeped in a monopolistic tradition. This was a physical product world where Compact Discs (CDs) reigned supreme and the notion of sending a digital file of music to consumers via the Internet was alien. So, Robertson had no choice but to 'hit the streets' himself in hope of finding musicians who would like to share their music via the Internet and potentially reach new fans – due to the fact that most of these independent musicians had no record contract, distribution or marketing competencies.

Many musicians rejected Robertson's early attempts, agreeing with the music industry executives. So MP3.com began doing all the work for the artist. They would convert songs, scan images of bands and artists, build out web pages on MP3.com's web site. As you can imagine, this was very labor and time intensive work. In an attempt to reduce the long term costs of this process MP3.com attempted to alleviate the burden by introducing a new system. The result was a "touchless" system that allowed artists to take on the role of uploading music onto the site thereby freeing MP3.com to concentrate resources on other areas of the business.

MP3.com created a series of "templates" that were user-friendly and empowered all artists with the ability to create a web page on the MP3.com web site in a matter of hours. All that the artist needed was one song in an mp3-file format, a band image and small amount of biography text to be eligible for a place on the MP3.com web site. Artists assigned a genre classification to each song and MP3.com assumed a pure intermediary role, making no comments on song quality or other subjective references to the music.

This "touchless" system helped spur an extremely rapid growth. From late 1998 to July 1999 (IPO) the artist community grew to over 15,000 artists with nearly 100,000 songs posted on the MP3.com web site. That number has grown to over 150,000 artists and over 1,000,000 songs posted within a two-year period of time (see figures 1 & 2).

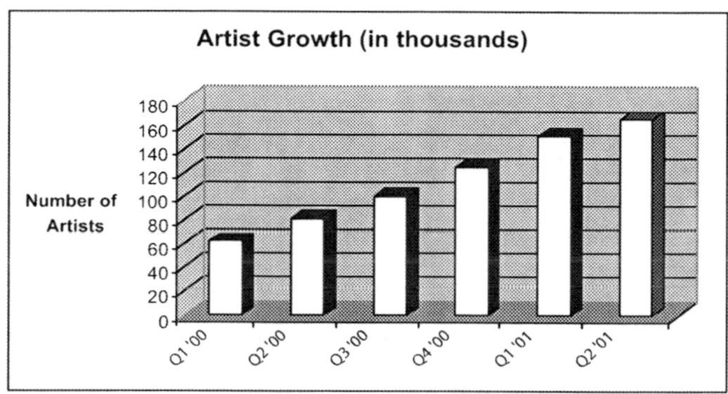

Figure 1

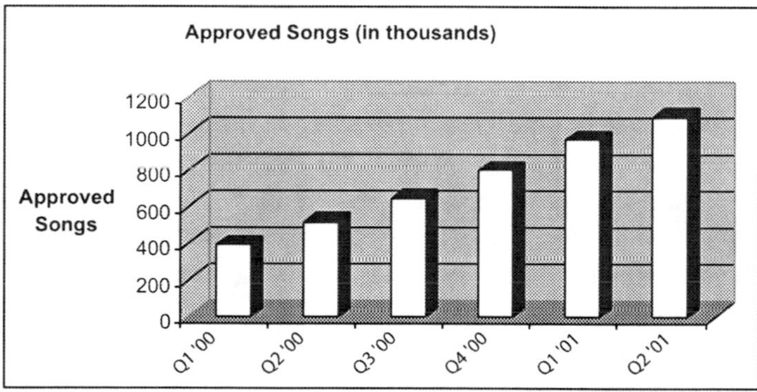

Figure 2

MP3.com achieved a significant milestone in the second quarter of 2001 when it exceeded the million-title level with total approved songs ending the quarter at 1,095,050. Although not a music publisher itself, the significance of the 1 million threshold is apparent when one considers that MP3.com's single source of independent music titles was now comparable in size to the largest rosters of the major record companies' publishing divisions.

Table 3: Major Music Publishing Company Stockholdings of Music Titles: 1996

Company	*Number of titles*
Warner	>1 million
EMI	>1 million
BMG	500,000
PolyGram	270,000
MCA	100,000
Sony	100,000

Source: MBI World Report 1996

3.2. Initial Legal Hurdles

Content management played a key function in the maintenance of the MP3.com web site. With an ever-increasing number of artists and songs being submitted, the risk related to posting illegal content increased. As a safeguard measure to protect the intellectual property rights of the creators of music, artists had to complete an on-line Submission Agreement which states that they possess among other things, the two main intellectual property rights associated with any song – that being the rights for master use and the publishing rights. MP3.com also created two departments – Musicology and Genre Management. As songs were submitted to the site, the Musicology staff (all possessing music industry background) verified that each song was original, not a copy of "Hey Jude" (McCartney/Lennon) for example, and that the file was not corrupted or technically defective. If there was any question about validity, the song was put on hold until positive verification was made.

Once it passed Musicology, the Genre Managers, (also possessing music industry background) listened to each song, confirmed that it was correctly classified and contained no offensive language. Those that were offensive were assigned to the 'Adult Material' section of the site. This is similar in concept to the use of stickers on offensive CDs by record labels.

MP3.com grew to be the home of over 100 music genres, ranging from Pop & Rock to obscure indigenous music.

3.3. Technical and Human Resources

MP3.com was fortunate to have a large number of gifted programmers and engineers join the company during its early growth stage. Many of them once worked for Netscape (who had just been acquired by AOL prior to the AOL/Time

Warner merger) and other Silicon Valley start-ups. The motivation for employees was high: a rebellious Internet music technology company located in San Diego, California (not part of the Silicon Valley cluster), a group of people who shared Robertson's vision and a looming IPO that could create fortunes. MP3.com attracted highly productive personnel from the technology, investment and music industries. The company paid attractive base salaries that could compete with Silicon Valley but the corporate culture of a music revolutionary was also irresistible to many. With that attraction, the company grew from under 50 employees in early 1999 to over 200 at its IPO. Robertson believed that it is was more efficient to have 250 skilled employees who constantly innovate than to boast of 1,000 semi-challenged staff. The outcome was that MP3.com generated a web-based technology which competitors – including the Major record companies – found difficult to replicate.

4. The Market and Competitors

While continuing with technical innovation, MP3.com needed to be fully aware of whom their customers were. MP3.com recognized that they were serving two masters: the artist and the consumer/music fan. Both had different needs and wants. It was essential that the company continue to develop systems, interfaces and user experiences that satisfied everyone. Thus, just as in the case of developing a user-friendly system for its suppliers (i.e. the aforementioned "touchless" system for content management), MP3.com also had to achieve the same objective for its consumers.

Since the consumer was essentially a low-tech individual with a basic knowledge and a dial-up modem, MP3.com developed a user-friendly strategy for accessing, listening and storing a consumer's music collection (see appendix 1 for a full listing of MP3.com's products). Other competitors who assumed a more advanced knowledge by the consumer often criticized this. In fact, there had been a huge number of entrants into the digital music space beginning in 1998. The following is a list of a few of these competitors which reads more like a casualty list, with only a few survivors: icast.com, spinrecords.com, N2K, listen.com, liquidaudio.com, musicboulevard.com, riffage.com, mjuice.com, mxgonline.com, countrysong.com, beatnik.com, scour.com, gig.com, aMP3.com, amplified.com, cductive, cdbaby.com, rollingstone.com, getmusic, emusic.com, Cdnow, MusicBank and rioport.com. Those involved in MP3.com believed that it was largely because of this low-brow approach (to both providers and users of music) that MP3.com could boast 800,000 unique visitors and over 2.1 million song streams each day by the first quarter of 2001. A total which they claim is greater than the sum of all their competitors combined.

5. The Business Model

Getting music users and providers onto a web site was one thing but generating a revenue and ultimately a profit from it was quite another. MP3.com faced a number of options. One of these was based on Digital Rights Management (DRM) and was the model favored and supported by the Majors. DRM involved encryption of music files that could then be securely distributed to approved users. Consumers could acquire a key to decrypt and ultimately listen to the music if they had secured a license for this purpose. The DRM option also included 'watermarking' where music files could include auxiliary information that allowed music providers to track use and to identify who the rightful owners of a music recording are. The DRM option always faced some threat of an encryption code being 'cracked' with subsequent 'open' files being made available. Nonetheless, the DRM solution offered artists a means of selling digital music files online on a pay per track, per album, or rental basis.

The only problem was that few consumers were willing to pay for music in this form – preferring to buy CDs. The main impediments were the lack of Hi-Fi to play digitally downloaded files, the lack of bandwidth that made the process very slow and later (mainly in 2000) the availability of free pirated music on sites such as Napster. In a nutshell, consumers viewed online music as a poor substitute to offline alternatives. Thus, they were willing to sample music online but opted to purchase CDs if they really wanted to buy. Similarly, established artists faced major cannibalization of offline revenues by making music available online; especially with consumers' low willingness to pay for online music. Not surprisingly, the major record labels showed little enthusiasm for making their comparably higher priced content available online. DRM based online music business models were either a non-starter or before their time.

However, from the outset MP3.com had decided not to use the DRM business model not only because they viewed it as unprofitable but also because it went against the whole ethos of what MP3.com thought they were about. Their key objective was to enable and satisfy the music user – and DRM was all about restricting what the consumer could do. Thus, copyright was not at the heart of MP3.com's philosophy as it was with the major record companies. Instead, MP3.com wanted to leverage its user base in order to generate advertising revenue. They sought to sell advertising to non-music industry companies (such as a $150 million deal with Group Arnault) and to music suppliers who wanted to take advantage of the fact that MP3.com had a captive audience who were browsing music and maybe intending to buy CD versions later. In order to maximize value added for advertisers, MP3.com introduced many innovations such as direct email marketing to users (who could be organized by zip code, music tastes, age, gender etc) and payola options where artists were slotted strategically into music charts. In addition, they also adopted various forms of traditional web site banner advertising.

Part of their strategy to offer a flexible service to music providers generated a small but significant revenue stream, namely DAM – their CD on demand service (see section 6). This took advantage of new technologies that were eroding the economies of scale originally inherent in CD manufacture.

At the time of the IPO in 1999, MP3.com reported that 91% of its 1998 net revenues were accounted for by advertising. The customer base for the firm was also very concentrated with MP3.com reliant on a small number of advertisers. For example, 27% and 70% of first quarter advertising revenue in 1999 were accounted for by the top 2 and top 10 accounts respectively. In subsequent years MP3.com would continue to rely heavily on advertising revenue. In the first six months of 2001 87.8% of MP3.com's revenue was accounted for by advertising while the comparable figure for 2000 was 88.4%. Figure 5 opposite plots the revenues over the last six quarters to 2001Q2.

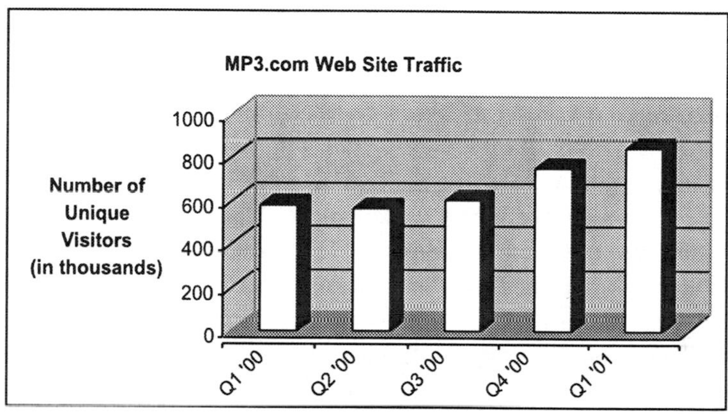

Figure 3

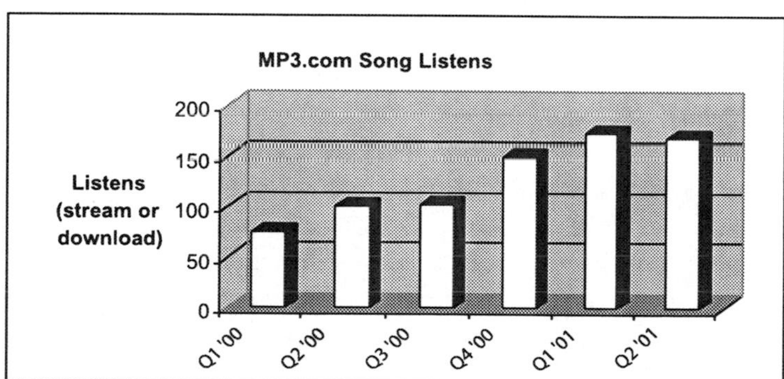

Figure 4

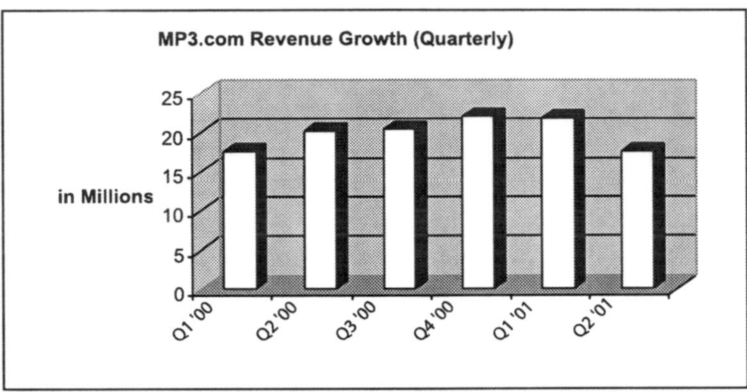

Figure 5

6. The Need to Grow and the Necessity to Innovate

Independent musicians created and accounted for 99% of the music on MP3.com. Many criticized the web site for its lack of success in securing Major label content for distribution or marketing campaigns. Therefore, the innovation of new and unique product and services that served and benefited consumers, artists and music fans was essential. Perhaps with the creation, experimentation and validation of new distribution, marketing and consumer relationship tools, the Major labels would view MP3.com as a friend and not a rebel. But one often-cited setback was the view by the Major labels that Robertson was an arrogant outsider who was interfering in a mature and powerful international industry.

Innovation was achieved through product development practices. Open weekly discussion forums were used for idea generation. Once an idea had reasonable support, the use of Matrix Team management was used to deliver the product to market in a timely fashion. Matrix teams usually involve at least one member from various departments who work together on a common project before moving to another project. Once that specific project or task was completed, those employees were assigned to a new team. This helped to eliminate any 'down time' for a particular department andcontinually utilized as many skills across the company as possible. An example of a MP3.com matrix team is shown in Table 4.

Typically, an employee would be involved in multiple projects, therefore part of multiple matrix teams. In cases where a large project required extensive engineering or web development, up to 100% of an employee's day might be allocated to delivering the task. Gant charts were often used to view the complete project and insure that timelines were met.

One advantage of the matrix team structure was that because of the small and often intimate nature of the group, employees had the opportunity to voice opinions, add suggestions or generally comment on ways to enhance or alter the development process. Since the nature of product development at a technology company such as MP3.com was extremely fluid, input from various team members was absolutely vital.

Table 4: A Matrix Team

# of Employees	*Department*	*Duration*
1	Marketing	2 days (develop and execute marketing plan) 2 weeks to monitor and evaluate final product
1	Accounting	1 day (payment systems, revenue recognition, accrual, etc.)
1	Legal	4 days (draft legal contract)
5	Engineering - Programming/coding - Creative design - Quality Assurance	1 week (design, build, and execute)

After an initial level of internal evaluation MP3.com frequently tested the viability of new innovations on the market directly. They were able to pilot new web based innovations by simply 'switching on' the device or service online. If music users or providers responded positively it was adopted. If not, the innovation was adapted in order to meet user demands more succinctly and/or altered in order to deal with functional shortcomings. Alternatively, if obstacles proved to be too immense or users were simply not interested the innovation was withdrawn. MP3.com's business model was developed in this chunky, evolving trial and error manner.

One of the most innovative early products developed by MP3.com was the Digital Automatic Music (DAM) CDs, which are compact discs, produced on-demand only using a proprietary just-in-time manufacturing process. This system allows an artist to create a record (CD) using part of the template system for content management. The main benefits for the artist are that there is no inventory risk, little to no initial investment apart from recording, and the flexibility to modify the product to suit consumer demand and/or focus.

The process follows this path:

1) Artist uploads multiple tracks to MP3.com web site via the "template" content management system.

2) Artist designates which tracks to appear on the DAM CD.
3) Artist creates a title for the CD and assigns a price point.
4) Artist designates the song order of tracks.
5) Artist uploads cover art via .jpg image file. (Artists may currently upload inside booklet graphics as well)
6) MP3.com and artist agree to share revenue evenly: 50/50 split.
7) When a consumer orders DAM CD, product is created through the just-in-time process: CD burned, booklet/artwork printed.
8) Consumer pays shipping and handling costs.

Another innovative product developed by MP3.com in May 2000 was the On-Demand Music Subscription Model. Thought to be the first of its kind on the Internet, MP3.com launched the Classical Music Channel as a response to the 'vaporware' that permeated the press releases of major labels and many of their technology partners. The afternoon of the official launch saw Sony Music announce their plans to launch a subscription channel by the end of 2000.

The Classical Music Channel allows consumers the ability to listen to a large body of musical works on-demand, whenever he/she chooses to. The initial offer contained over 400 CDs worth of music for a $9.99/month price following a two-week trial period with the ability to stream and/or download the content to a subscribers hard drive and potentially move it to a personal mp3 playback device (such as a Rio Player). Other offers have been experimented such as year long subscriptions. This valid proof of concept then grew across the MP3.com web site.

A month following this product release the 'Children's Channel' was launched. MP3.com then turned the system over to its artist community. It was now possible for any artist or label of any size to create a subscription service offering. They would control pricing, selection of tracks, stream or download functionality and would benefit from a centralized payment/accounting management system, robust delivery platform and log-in security. Although MP3.com has never publicly discussed the numbers of subscribers for any or all channels, they have stated that artists and labels have created over 4,000 channels.

But perhaps the most innovative and controversial product suite created by MP3.com was based on the Beam-it™ technology. Those products are Beam -it™ and Instant Listening™. These two services were at the root of the controversial MP3.com copyright infringement lawsuits.

Beam-it™ technology allowed a consumer access to CD recordings online that they already own by simply inserting the CD into the CD-ROM tray on their computer. MP3.com technology recognized each CD and if it is contained in the MP3.com database, allowed that consumer access to the said recording when they were logged onto their My.MP3 account. This eliminated the need to upload a complete album, which on a slow dial-up modem connection could take many hours. Beam-it™ technology used server-side security (vs. client-side, such as Liquid Audio) and restricted the number of people permitted to log into any one My.MP3 account.

Instant Listening™ is a derivative of the Beam-it™ technology. Used in conjunction with designated retail partners, a consumer could purchase a CD on-line and listen to that CD once the financial transaction was complete. The physical CD was then mailed to the consumer, but the consumer received immediate benefit for the purchase via their My.MP3 account. This basic philosophy of helping consumers aggregate and access their musical collections from one central location has been a thread since the early days of MP3.com.

6.1. The Music InterOperating System (IOS)

Officially launched in January 2001, the Music IOS was perhaps the cornerstone to the differentiation and value that MP3.com had created. One original MP3.com corporate philosophy was Michael Robertson's notion of the Music Service Provider (MSP) model. The basis of the early MSP model and subsequent Music IOS was the need to connect disparate communities, who create, market or distribute music. Once musical content is added to the IOS hub, business rules are assigned which permit the use(s) of that content. For example, if a song is added by label XYZ, it could then be accessed by on-line retailers, software or hardware manufacturers, special promotional offerings, subscription music services or consumers who have formerly purchased the recording or pre-order an advance copy.

In order for this IOS to grow into compelling consumer applications, MP3.com developed a set of APIs (application protocol interface) that allowed software developers access to a limited amount of music while creating new ways to experience music. These applications ranged from auto mp3 players to mobile phone, personal data assistants (PDAs) to other web sites.

Another way of viewing this IOS is to look back at the early days of personal computing when DOS was the most common computer language. Various word processing, spreadsheet and database programs existed but it was very difficult to integrate them into one master document. Once Microsoft and Apple announced their respective operating systems software developers began designing compatible software. This helped to advance the pace of growth significantly.

MP3.com's innovations proved successful on two fronts. First, the company demonstrated an ability to produce innovations which customers – both music users and musicians – wanted. Secondly, MP3.com demonstrated that it had core technological competencies which rivals had difficulty replicating. After the initial success and subsequent growth of MP3.com, competitors began to encroach on MP3.com's market space. Two main groups of mp3 music web sites began to appear. The first group merely aggregated music that was available in a mp3 file format. For example, Rioport.com was established as a 'filling station' for the highly popular Diamond Rio PMP 300 mp3 player. Thousands of tracks were manually added to the site by Rioport.com staff and organized by genre for consumer ease of navigation. The major drawbacks were that little major label content was available and that uploading was labor intensive and expensive. This was in contrast to the 'template' system used by MP3.com. Rioport subsequently shifted its direction towards providing infrastructure services to web sites and retailers and the sale and distribution of Major label content.

Riffage.com adopted another aggregation start-up strategy. Ken Wirt who was a former marketing executive from Diamond Multimedia (parent company of RioPort.com) founded this company. Riffage.com not only intended to compete directly with MP3.com but also attempted to establish an on-line record label. Riffage.com lacked finance and the competencies associated with becoming a record label. It subsequently closed its operations.

The second group of competitors attempted to offer similar services to the artist community that MP3.com had developed. For instance AMP3.com also competed directly with MP3.com, offering artists the ability to upload their own music. Consumers and artists could also create stations, read news and product reviews. One unique differentiating factor with AMP3.com was their attempt to insert audio advertising before every track - offering to pay the artist a percentage of that revenue. The major labels were unenthusiastic and due to lack of financing AMP3.com has apparently closed operations, although the web site does remain live on the Internet.

As a competitor to the My.MP3 service, Myplay.com established a locker service. However, this service required consumers to upload their own 'previously purchased' CDs or tracks to the Myplay locker. This was extremely time consuming and often proved to yield consumer dissatisfaction. Myplay was subsequently taken over by BMG. Sony also launched the Sony Digital Locker - a multi-media storage product.

Search engines (such as Lycos.com, Launch.com, Gig.com, Yahoo.com) also played a key role in the successful brand building of MP3.com. During late 1998 to mid-1999 mp3 was one of the top searched words/phrases on the Internet. MP3.com also secured all top level mp3 spots on these search engines.

Essentially, MP3.com viewed itself as an infrastructure company and therefore, allocated resources towards building an engineering firm. These resources, which included over 150 dedicated engineers, helped bring new products to market at an extremely fast pace. As we have read, it was this approach to product development that helped to create sustained differentiation. Coupled with powerful financial resources and Michael Robertson's vision, MP3.com was able to create a first mover advantage.

7. Financing Innovation and Growth

As with any company experiencing rapid growth, Robertson, Richards and Ouyang realized that additional funds were necessary to grow. The economics of their industry indicated the importance of first mover advantages associated with network externalities. This in itself was an impetus for fast growth even at the expense of sustained initial losses. However, Robertson's grand plan would involve technology development too. Thus, up front loss making was copperfastened by a significant R&D component. At the end of 1998 MP3.com had just $39,509 cash assets and an asset book value of just under half a million dollars. By the end of March 1999, MP3.com secured venture finance and private funding to take the company to an asset value of over $11 million with over $9 million in cash. However, this was not nearly enough for a new music industry upstart who intended to challenge the Majors and in July 1999 MP3.com raised nearly $350 million in an historic IPO on the NASDAQ (see www.sec.gov for an online copy of the IPO S-1 filing).

After the flotation MP3.com's stockholders represented a portfolio of MP3.com customers (including advertisers such as Arkaro holding, a subsidiary of group Arnault[2] and stock reserved for music users), key music providers (such as Tori Amos and Alanis Morisette), employees (with stock options ranging from 11 cents to $6.67). In effect, suppliers and buyers were given a return for trading with the new venture. Financiers took their share too. The early venture capital firm of Sequoia Capital (Menlo Park, California) was no stranger to technology IPOs. In return for venture capital, Stevens received 14.5% of shares outstanding upon the IPO. In June 1999, Cox Interactive Media, Inc. invested $45 million and formed a joint venture with MP3.com. In return for the cash injection, Cox received 9.4% of shares outstanding upon the IPO.

The IPO was one of the largest single Internet flotations on the NASDAQ. MP3.com's shares were placed at a value of $28 dollars, valuing the company at approximately $1.9 billion. The proposed use of the funds (see appendices) was loosely defined and allowed the management significant strategic flexibility.

8. Legal Problems: The Empire Strikes Back

In January 2000, MP3.com launched its controversial new music locker service. The premise of the service was to allow consumers to register for a secure storage locker where their music collection could be stored. This would include music from four main sources: (1) free promotional content on MP3.com's web site, (2) subscription music channels where they pay a monthly or yearly fee for access, (3) CDs that they previously own using the Beam-it™ software or, (4) CDs that

2. Groupe Arnault is a French corporation with interests in diverse companies such as LVMH, Moet, Hennessy, Louis Vuitton and others.

they purchase from an on-line retailer by way of Instant Listening™.

In order for the consumer to add music to their personal online music locker account only 3 and 4 above created legal concerns. In order to facilitate the inclusion of a CD in a music locker account, MP3.com purchased 45,000 CDs and created a secure database from which consumers access the music. It was this act of creating a single unauthorized copy of each work that the US court system found to be willful and subsequently in violation of the Copyright Act. The plaintiffs (including Arista Records, BMG Music, EMI Music, Universal Music, Warner Music Group, and Sony) would seek damages of up to $150,000 per CD violation and injunctive relief prohibiting MP3.com from using any reproductions of the plaintiff's copyright material. MP3.com defended that the new locker service made a "fair use" of the copyrighted recordings, since they believed that it was a consumer's right to listen to their music anywhere or any time they desired. They argued unsuccessfully that the rights that a consumer purchases relating to a recording should be transferable to the Internet.

The overall settlement payments to major labels to date have been estimated to be approximately $150 million. However, with undefined waters in terms of copyright enforcement in the Internet; particularly in the areas of violation, fair use and compensation, the future was far from certain. The fight for survival was at the core of these activities with a rising number of plaintiffs (now including independent record labels and music publishers). The September 2000 ruling in the case of *MP3.com v. Universal* where the Court ruled that Universal should be compensated to the tune of $25,000 per CD copied did not auger well. Pressure on MP3.com's share price (already battered from the dot.com crash) and a massive erosion of cashflows due to actual and potential lawsuits reduced the strategic options facing the company.

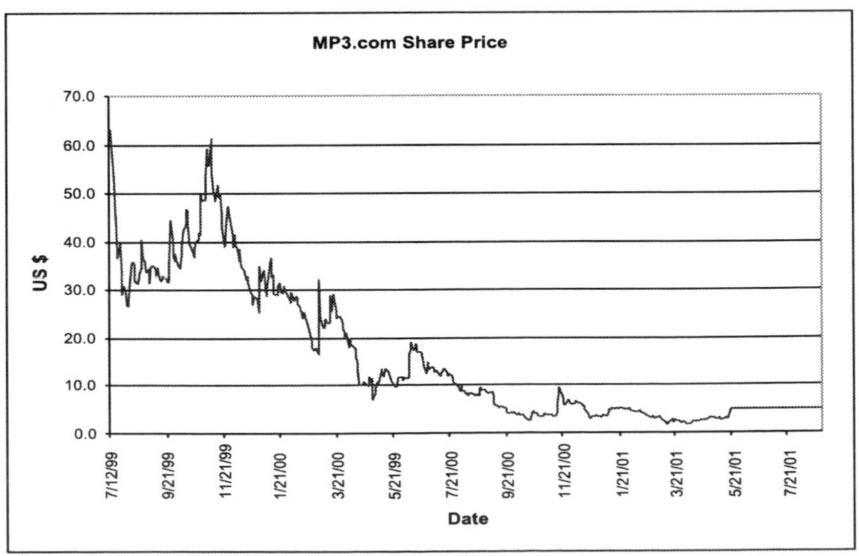

Figure 6

9. Harvest and Exit

In May 2001 Michael Robertson sold the company to one of the Major record companies, namely the French owned Universal/Vivendi. MP3.com was sold at a value equivalent to $5 per share which was significantly less than the 1999 IPO flotation offer price of $28. At the time of writing Michael Robertson had stood down as CEO of MP3.com and had already announced a new venture (Lindows) which planned to produce a computer operating system to compete with Microsoft Windows. Vivendi split MP3.com into 2 divisions. The first concentrated on generating revenues from online music and the second focused on MP3.com's technological competencies. MP3.com had become the powerhouse of Vivendi's online music strategy.

APPENDIX 1:

MP3.com Products

MP3.com's primary focus has been on products targeted at two groups of users: the artist community and global music and entertainment fans. The following is a list of some of the main products offered by MP3.com (as of October 2001) in the order of (1) products for the music providers (2) products for the music user (3) revenue streams from products. For more detail the reader is directed to inspect the web site at MP3.com.

(1) Products for Music Providers (encompassing artists, labels, managers and publishers)

Promotional Tools

- *Premium Artist Services* (see Subscriptions under the Revenue section below)
- *Auction.* Artists or their representatives may bid for promotional advertising slots throughout the MP3.com web site.
- *New Music Army (NMA) Program.* This program rewards individuals who act as representatives for artists on MP3.com. MP3.com subsequently rewards this activity with 5% of any revenues due to the respective artist.

Content Management Tools and Opportunities

- *Payback for Playback (P4P).* This royalty payment program was launched in early 2001. $1 million per month is paid on a pro rata basis to content owners for activity generated on the web site. Example: If artist A generates a higher number of song streams and/or song downloads than artist B, artist A will receive a larger percentage of the $1 million.

- *CD Program (originally called DAM CDs).* This revolutionary just-in-time (JIT) manufacturing process was developed and launched by MP3.com in order to enable artists with the opportunity to produce a CD recording without the potential inventory risk and need to be signed by a large record label. The official name for the program and the technology is DAM (digital automatic music).

- *Business Music Services (BMS).* Similar in concept to a Muzak delivery model, where retail and business establishments may, for a monthly fee, play songs by MP3.com artists. Artists receive Payback 4 Playback. The important features that differentiate this service from the competition is: (a) the ability to program play lists of music from a central location or at each and every individual store location and, (b) the ability to insert audio advertising which may help to offset or generate revenue for the service.

- *Music Licensing Program.* Licensing music for movies, advertising campaigns or compilation use has always been a significant source of revenue for the music industry. Using a searchable database, music and film supervisors for example, may find music for a film sequence. Artists categorize their own music by mood, instrumentation, vocals, tempo and others in order to streamline the search process.

- *Copyright Wizard.* Artists are able to submit works for a fee, directly to the US Copyright Office via MP3.com.

(2) Products for consumers

- *Searching for music*
  - Top 40 Chart and musical Genre Charts
  - Explore by genre or geographical location
  - Browse Local Events (search globally for music and live shows)

- *Managing your music*
  - My.MP3.com
  - Premium Listener Services (PLuS) (See below)
  - Messenger: consumers may receive new music, direct to their email address on a daily, weekly or monthly basis.
  - Notify Me! Consumers are notified whenever their favorite artist's page is modified (new music, new images, new concert information).

- *Stations.* Music fans, artists and labels are encouraged to create their own music stations on the web site. It is an excellent way to create thematic play lists that may be shared with the entire global music community via MP3.com.

(3) Revenue Streams

- *Advertising, sponsorship and promotion.* MP3.com's main revenue streams come in the form of consumer-base advertising, sponsorship and promotional activity. Referring to the initial S-1 it is stated that Groupe Arnault and MP3.com would enter into a $150 million, three-year relationship which would promote the Groupe's suite of brands. Given the rise in popularity of the web site and the historic IPO, many of America's leading brands also chose to include MP3.com as a marketing and promotional vehicle.

- *Subscriptions.* Three basic subscription models exist on MP3.com: Subscription Music Channels, Premium Listener Services (PluS) and Premium Artist Services (PAS).

- *Subscription Music Channels.* In May 2000, MP3.com created and launched the first on-demand music subscription channel on the Internet – The Classical Music Channel. It featured over 400 albums of musical repertoire, fully downloadable or streamable for a fee of $9.99 per month, following a two-week free trial offer. Experimentation with various pricing models occurred during the first year of service until $29.99 per year and $9.99 per month options were instated.

  The Artist Community on MP3.com is encouraged to create subscription channels, market them and sell them to music fans. Artists and/or their labels designate the content which may reside in a channel, control the functionality (stream and/or download) and the monthly pricing. To date, thousands of channels have been created.

- *Premium Listener Services (PLuS).* During 2001, MP3.com launched PLuS. Pricing was set at $2.99 month or $29.95 per year. Two of the important features of the PLuS are the ability to turn off advertising (banner, portals, etc.) and being able to download a small software application that runs on a computer desktop, without a browser, such as Internet Explorer or Netscape.

- *Premium Artist Services (PAS).* Early in 2000, MP3.com launched PAS. Pricing was set at $19.99 per month and targeted at the artist community. Some of the benefits include participation in the Payback for Playback royalty program, bold listing on MP3.com charts and priority placement in the Featured Songs section in each genre section on the web site.

APPENDIX 2:

Use of Proceeds as Outlined in the 1999 IPO Offering

We estimate that our net proceeds from the offering will be approximately $290.2 million (based upon an assumed initial public offering price of $25.00 per share) after deducting the estimated underwriting discount and commissions and estimated offering expenses ($321.5 million if the over-allotment option is exercised in full).

We expect to use approximately $10 million of our net proceeds for marketing and promotional activities, $8 million for capital expenditures, $4 million for concert sponsorships and tours, and $2 million for planned facilities expansion and related improvements. We intend to use the remaining net proceeds for general corporate purposes, including working capital. A portion of the net proceeds may also be used for strategic partnerships, including joint ventures, or to acquire or invest in complementary businesses, technologies, product lines, content or products. We have no current agreements or commitments and we are not currently engaged in any negotiations with respect to any acquisitions. The amounts we actually expend for general corporate purposes may vary significantly and will depend on a number of factors, including the amount of our future revenues and the other factors described under "Risk Factors". Pending these uses, the net proceeds of this offering will be invested in short term, interest-bearing, investment grade securities.

We have no current plan for a significant portion of the proceeds of this offering, and our management will retain broad discretion in the allocation of the net proceeds of this offering.

The principal reasons for this offering include:

- establishing MP3.com as a public company;
- increasing the visibility and brand recognition of our products and services;
- positioning our company to be better able to take advantage of strategic opportunities in the future;
- making a trading market available to our existing stockholders; and
  providing us with capital sufficient to enable us to implement our business plan.

APPENDIX 3:

Summary of MP3.com's Consolidated Statements of Operations (in US$000)

Six months ended:	*June 2001*	*June 2000*
Net Revenues:	39,283	37,673
Cost of Revenues	9,077	7,568
Gross Profit	30,206	30,105
Operating Expenses:		
Sales and Marketing	17,384	28,963
Engineering & Product Development	10,854	11,404
Administration	11,601	14,359
Charges relating to Lawsuits	44,698	–
Charges relating to Copyright claims	–	150,000
Acquisition activities	3,160	1,704
Amortization of Stock based compensation	1,717	6,336
Total Operating expenses	89,414	212,766
Operating profit (loss)	**(59,208)**	**(182,661)**

Source: IPO S-1 filing: www.sec

8. Towards an Integrative Theory of Organizational Success and Failure:Previous Research and Future Issues

Eric G. Flamholtz

Anderson School of Management, UCLA

Abstract. This paper provides a survey of research to develop and empirically test of a holistic model of organizational success and failure in entrepreneurial organizations at different stages of growth. It builds upon previous work by Flamholtz (1995) to develop a model of organizational success and failure and by Flamholtz et.al. to assess the models validity empirically (Flamholtz and Aksehirli, 2000; Flamholtz, 2001; Flamholtz and Hua, 2002A, 2002B). The initial model proposes that there are six key factors or "strategic building blocks" of successful organizations, and the six key variables must be designed as a holistic system, which has been termed "The Pyramid of Organizational Development".

Keywords: strategy, organizational development, infrastructure, financial performance and organizational success.

Acknowledgement. The author gratefully acknowledges that the research reported in this paper was partly supported by the Harold Price Center for Entrepreneurial Studies in the Anderson School at UCLA.

1. Background

In recent years, most industries throughout the world have witnessed successes and failures of seemingly similar companies. Organizations such as Microsoft, Southwest Airlines, Nike and Wal-Mart become dominant forces in their industries while other comparable organizations such as Apple Computer, People Express, LA-Gear, and K-Mart have experienced difficulties and decline after a period of promising initial growth (Flamholtz & Randle, 1998).

The result is an increased need for a better understanding of the management of organizational growth and the determinants of success and failure over the long term. More specifically, why do some organizations continue to be successful over the long term while others, with equally promising starts, experience difficulties and even failure?

To help answer this question, Flamholtz (1995) presented a framework entitled the "Pyramid of Organizational Development" that identified six key "strategic building blocks" of successful organizations. Subsequently, Flamholtz et.al., have engaged in a program of empirical research to assess the validity of the model and various hypotheses and implications derived from it.

This article was originally published in the International Journal of Entrepreneurship Education 1(3): 297-320.

The next section provides a review of the key aspects of the framework relevant to this research. The third section will survey the empirical research which has been conducted to date to assess the validity of various hypotheses derived from the framework. Finally, the implications of this research for theory and practice will be considered in the final section.

2. The Theoretical Framework

The framework consists of four key parts: 1) a "strategic organizational development" model, 2) a life cycle model, 3) a model of the levels of strategic organizational development required at each stage of growth, and 4) a framework for the dysfunctional consequences which occur when suboptimal strategic organizational development occurs. These are described, in turn, below.

2.1. The Model for Strategic Organizational Development

The initial premise or hypothesis underlying this framework is that organizations must perform certain tasks to be successful at each stage of their growth. The six key tasks of strategic organizational, all of which have been supported by previous research are:

- Identification and definition of a viable market niche (Aldrich, 1979; Brittain and Freeman, 1980; Freeman and Hannan, 1983),

- Development of products or services for the chosen market niche (Burns & Stalker, 1961; Midgley, 1981),

- Acquisition and development of resources required to operate the firm (Pfeffer & Salancik, 1978; Brittain & Freeman, 1980; Carroll & Yangchung, 1986),

- Development of day-to-day operational systems (Starbuck, 1965),

- Development of the management systems necessary for the long-term functioning of the organization (Child & Keiser, 1981; Tushman et.al., 1985),

- Development of the organizational culture that management feels necessary to guide the firm (Peters & Waterman, 1982; Walton, 1986).

Each of these key tasks will be discussed in detail below.

2.1.1. Identification of Market Segment and Niche

The first challenge for a new venture in organizational survival or success is to identify a market need for a marketable service or product. The chances of organizational success are enhanced to the extent that the firm is successful in this step (Flamholtz, 1995).

The challenge is not merely in identifying the market but also, if possible, to capture a "market niche," a relatively protected place that would give the company sustainable competitive advantages. Failing to define a niche or mistakenly abandoning the historical niche can cause an organization to experience difficulties and even failure. The process of identifying the market involves the development of a strategic market plan to identify potential customers and their needs and the creation of a competitive strategy (Flamholtz, 1995).

2.1.2. Development of Products and Services

The second challenge or strategic building block involves the development of products and/or services. This process can also be called "productization," which refers to the process of analyzing the needs of customers in the target market, designing the product and developing the ability to produce it (Flamholtz & Randle, 2000). For a production firm this stage involves the design and manufacturing phases, whereas for a service firm, this stage involves forming a system for providing services to the customers (Flamholtz & Randle, 2000).

The success this stage is highly related to the previous critical task, proper definition of the market niche (Flamholtz, 1995). Unless a firm fully understands the needs of the market, it cannot satisfy those needs in productization.

2.1.3. Acquiring Resources

Success in identifying a market niche and productization will create increased demand for a firm's products or services. Consequently, the resources of the firm will be spread very thin (Flamholtz, 1995). The organization will require additional physical, financial and human resources. This is the point at which the entrepreneur/s should start thinking about the long-term vitality of the firm and procure all the necessary resources to survive the pressure of current and future increase in demands (Flamholtz & Randle, 2000).

2.1.4. Development of Operational Systems

The fourth critical task is the development of basic day-to-day operational systems, which include accounting, billing, collection, advertising, personnel recruiting and training, sales, production, delivery and related systems (Flamholtz, 1995). Entrepreneurial companies tend to quickly outgrow the administrative systems available to operate them. Therefore, it is necessary to develop sufficient operational systems, on time, to build a successful organization. In contrast, large established companies might have developed overly complicated operational systems. In this case, the success of the organization depends on the reengineering of operational systems (Flamholtz, 1995).

2.1.5. Development of Management Systems

The fifth step is to develop the management systems, which is essential for the long-term viability of the firm (Flamholtz & Randle, 2000). Management systems include systems for planning, organization, management development and control. Planning systems involve planning for the overall development of the organization and the development of scheduling and budgeting operations. It includes strategic planning, operational planning and contingency planning (Flamholtz, 1995). The mere existence of planning activities does not indicate that the firm has a planning system. A planning system ensures that planning activities are strategic and ongoing.

Organizational structure involves the ways in which people are organized and activities are coordinated. As with the planning activities success depends, not on the mere existence of a structure, but on the match between the structure and business strategy (Flamholtz, 1995).

The process of planned development of the current and future managers is Management Development Systems. Control systems is the set of processes (budgeting, goal setting) and mechanisms (performance appraisal) that would encourage behavior that would help achieve organizational objectives (Flamholtz, 1995).

2.1.6. Developing Corporate Culture

Just as people have personalities, organizations have cultures, which are composed of shared values, beliefs and norms. Shared values refer to the importance the organization attaches to the aspects of product quality, customer service, and treatment of employees. Beliefs are the ideas that the people in the organization hold about themselves and the firm. Lastly, the norms are the unwritten rules that guide interactions and behavior (Flamholtz, 1995).

2.1.7. The Model as a Whole

A second premise or hypotheses is that each of these tasks must be performed in a stepwise fashion in order to build a successful organization. Taken together, then, these six tasks lead to a hierarchical model of organizational development (Exhibit 1 on page 302).

Similar hierarchical views are present in the previous literature. Woodward discussed a similar relation between market niche and product, and structure and culture. In addition, Chandler's (1962) book, "Strategy and Structure," suggests that a firm's structure follows from its long-term strategy.

It should be noted that the pyramid shape does not imply that the key tasks are carried out independently. All six tasks are vital for the health of the firm, and must occur simultaneously. However, the relative emphasis on each task or level of the Pyramid will vary according to the organization's stage of growth (Flamholtz, 1995), as noted below.

Another hypothesis is that the top four levels of the pyramid, which form the "infrastructure" of the firm, are less susceptible to imitation (Flamholtz, 1995) and, accordingly, provide the basis for long-term sustainable competitive advantage. Thus, although competition between firms takes place at all levels, long-term sustainable advantage is primarily found at the top three levels.

EXHIBIT 1

The Six Key Building Blocks of Successful Organizations:
Pyramid of Organizational Development

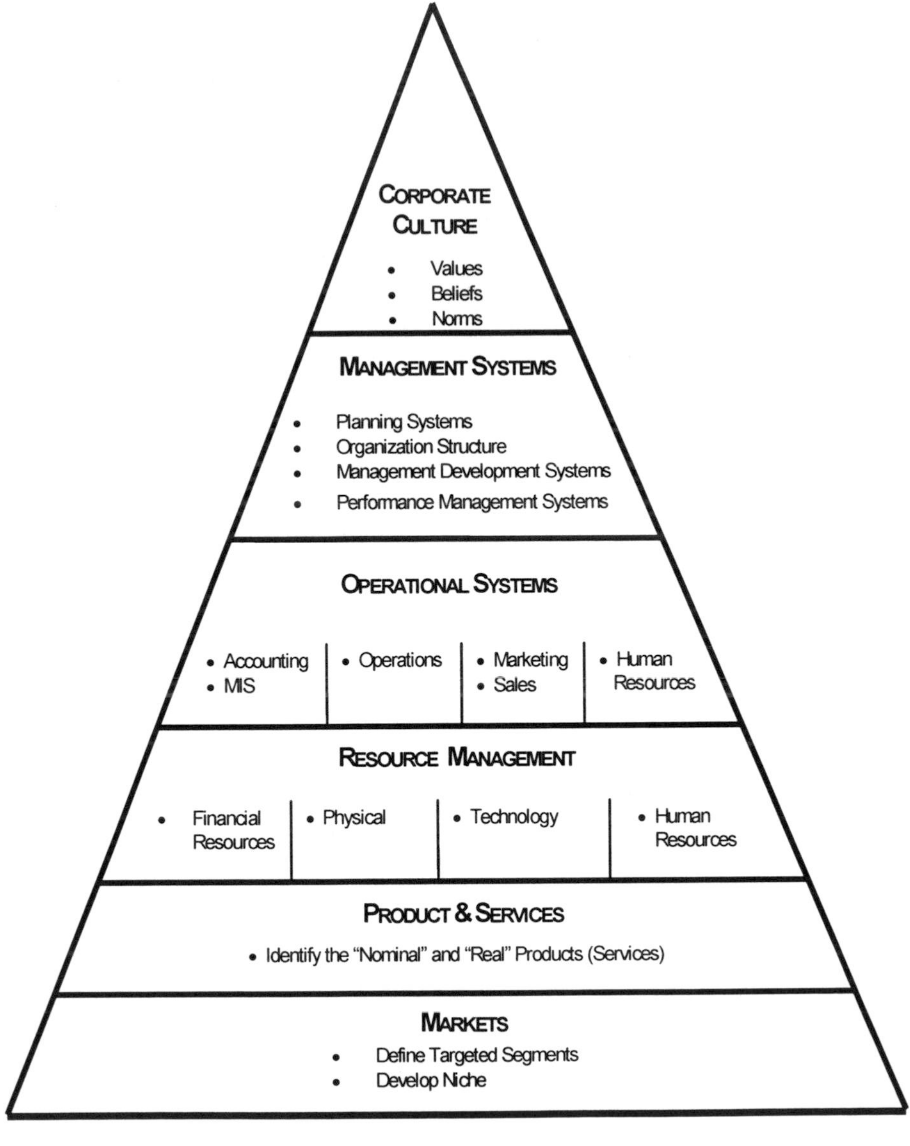

2.2. Strategic Organizational Development at Different Stages of Growth

The emphasis that should be given to each task differs depending on the size of the firm. Organizations experience developmental problems if their infrastructure is not consistent with their size. The parallel relationship with size and organizational structure leads to an organizational life cycle model that complements the Organizational Development Pyramid (Flamholtz, 1995), as shown in Exhibit 2 below.

EXHIBIT 2

Stages of Growth

Stage	Description	Critical Development Areas	Approximate Size	Organizational (sales: US$)
			Manufacturing Firms	Service Firms
I	New Venture	Markets and products	Less than $1million	Less than $0.3 million
II	Expansion	Resources and operational systems	$1 - $10 million	$0.3 - $3.3 million
III	Professionalisation	Management systems	$10 - $100 million	$3.3 - $33 million
IV	Consolidation	Corporate culture	$100 - $500 million	$33 - $167 million

As seen in Exhibit 2, each stage of growth is viewed as having a set of critical developmental tasks. For example, the critical tasks at Stage I are markets and products, while at Stage III the critical task is the development of management systems.

2.3. Dysfunctional Consequences of Suboptimal Strategic Organizational Development

In this framework presented above, strategic organizational development equilibrium occurs when there is a fit between the organization's strategic development of the six key building blocks of organizational success and its size or stage of development. When this fit does not occur, the organization will experience a variety of "organizational growing pains". These growing pains are symptoms of organizational distress and an indication of the need to change, if the organization wants to continue to operate successfully.

2.3.1. The Classic Growing Pains

Based upon our experience in working with a wide variety of organizations, we have identified ten classic symptoms of organizational growing pains (Flamholtz, 1995) and (Flamholtz & Randle, 2000). These growing pains, which are summarized in Exhibit 3 and described below, were derived from observations and assessments conducted with a wide variety of organizations (different sizes and industries).

EXHIBIT 3
Ten Classic Growing Pains

1. People feel that "there are not enough hours in the day."
2. People spend too much time "putting out fires."
3. People are not aware of what other people are doing.
4. People lack understanding about where the firm is headed.
5. There are too few good managers.
6. People feel that "I have to do it myself if I want to get it done correctly."
7. Most people feel that "our meetings are a waste of time."
8. When plans are made, there is very little follow-up, so things just don't get done.
9. Some people feel insecure about their place in the firm.
10. The organization continues to grow in sales but not in profits.

1. People feel that there are not enough hours in the day.

People feel they can work 24 hours a day, seven days a week and still not get all the required work done. When employees believe that they are being endlessly overworked morale problems can occur. People may simply decide they can no longer operate under these conditions and may leave the organization. This will result in significant turnover costs and replacement costs related to recruiting, selecting, and training new people.

2. People spend too much time "putting out fires".

This means that people are faced with an almost endless series of crises or "fires." Examples of "putting out fires" problems are easy to find.

"Fires" or crises were so prevalent at one $50 million manufacturing company in the U.S. that 33 managers began to refer to themselves as "fire fighters", and senior management rewarded middle management for their skills in handling crises. When it became apparent that managers who had been effective in "fire prevention" were being ignored, some of them became "arsonists" to get senior management's attention.

3. People are not aware of what other people are doing.

This creates a situation in which people and departments do whatever they want to do and say that the remaining tasks are "not our responsibility". Constant bickering between people over responsibility for things not getting done may ensue.

4. People lack understanding about where the firm is headed.

Employees may complain that "the company has no clear direction". When insufficient communication is combined with rapid changes, employees may begin to feel anxious. If anxiety increases to the point where it becomes unbearable, employees may begin leaving the firm. It should be noted that turnover of this kind could be very costly to the company.

5. There are too few good managers.

Although the organization may have many people who hold the title of "manager", it may not have *good* or effective managers. Rapid growth at Apple Computer led Steven Jobs to bring in "professional managers" to help manage the company because it had not developed a cadre of managers as it grew. However, this led to the inevitable culture clash, and to Jobs' resignation.

6. People feel that “I have to do it myself to get it done correctly”.

Increasingly, as people become frustrated by the difficulty of getting things done in an organization, they come to feel that “if I want to get something done correctly, I have to do it myself”. Operating under this mindset departments become isolated from one another and teamwork becomes minimal.

7. Most people feel “our meetings are a waste of time”.

Unfortunately, at many companies, meetings have typically no planned agendas, and often they have no designated leader. As a consequence, the meetings become a free-for-all, tend to drag on interminably, and seldom result in decisions.

Other complaints about meetings involve lack of follow-up on decisions that are made. Meetings are also ineffective if people ignore the goals that have been set or fail to monitor their progress toward these goals.

8. When plans are made, there is very little follow-up so things just don’t get done.

Recognizing that the need for planning is greater than in the past, a CEO may introduce a planning process. People go through the motions of preparing business plans, but the things that were planned just don’t get done. In some cases, there is no follow-up because the company has not yet developed systems adequate to monitor its goals. In other cases, follow-up does not occur because personnel have not received proper training in setting, monitoring, and evaluating goals.

9. Some people feel insecure about their place in the organization.

Sometimes the Board has become anxious about problems facing the organization and has therefore hired a “heavy-weight” manager from outside. This action may have been accompanied by the termination of one or more current managers. Employees begin to wonder if whether they will be the next to “get the axe”. In an attempt to protect themselves, they keep their activities secret and do not “make waves”. This results in isolation and a decrease in teamwork. When anxiety becomes too high, it may result in morale problems, turnover, or a very political environment.

10. The organization continues to grow in sales but not in profits.

If all the other growing pains are permitted to exist, this final symptom may emerge. In some instances, sales continue to increase while profits remain flat, so that the company is succeeding in only increasing its workload. In the worst cases, sales increase while overall profits decline.

This set of classic growing pains are not only problems in and of themselves, we believe that they are symptoms of a deeper problem, and a "signal" or warning that the organization needs to make a fundamental change in its infrastructure, as explained below. Although it is tempting to look at growing pains from a binary ("yes" or "no") perspective, as we shall explain below it is more useful to view them on a continuum, i.e., the degree to which they exist in a particular organization.

2.3.2. Nature and Causes of Organizational Growing Pains

Growth, though essential to organizations over the long term, creates its own set of problems: the growing pains described above. These growing pains are symptoms that something has gone wrong in the growth and development of a business enterprise. They are a symptom of organizational distress, and an early warning or leading indicator of future organizational difficulties, including financial difficulties.

Growing pains indicate that the "infrastructure" of an enterprise (i.e., the internal operational and management systems it needs at a given stage of growth) has not kept up with its size, as measured by its revenues. For example, a business with $200 million (U.S.) in revenues may only have an infrastructure to support the operations of a firm with $50 million in revenues, or one-fourth its size. This type of situation typically occurs after a period of growth, sometimes quite rapid growth, where the infrastructure has not been changed to adjust to the new size and complexity of the organization. The result, as shown in Exhibit 4 (page 308), is an "organizational development gap," (that is, a gap between the organization's actual infrastructure and that required at its current size or stage of development) which produces the growing pains.

EXHIBIT 4
Organizational Development Gap

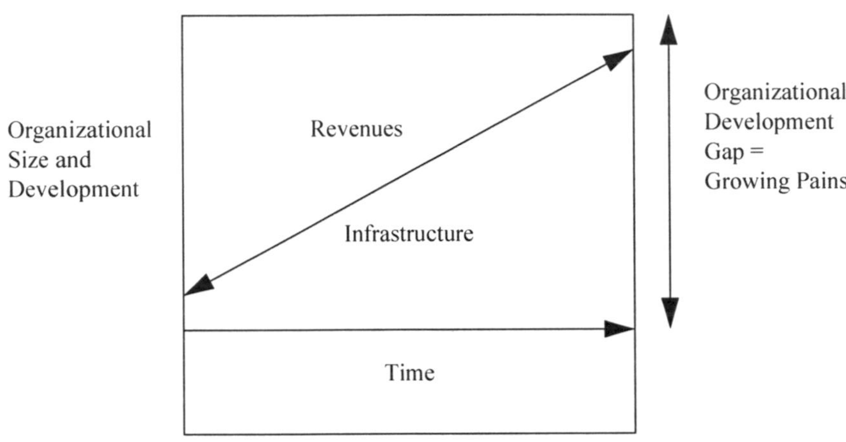

As a rule of thumb, whenever an organization doubles in size (as measured by its revenues), it is essentially a different company and requires a new infrastructure to support its operations. If the infrastructure has not been adjusted to reflect the increased size a variety of classic growing pains will be experienced.

Growing pains can and do occur in organizations of all sizes, including the largest industrial enterprises. However, they are most characteristic of early stage entrepreneurial companies, even in those organizations where revenues exceed $1 billion. Although growing pains are the result of organizational success (i.e., successful development of a market and product), they can lead to great difficulties and even foreshadow failure. For example, Osborne Computers, a pioneer in the portable "personal" (micro) computer business, achieved $100 million in revenues after being in business for only two years, but went into bankruptcy in year three!

3. Empirical Research to Assess the Validity of the Framework

To assess the validity of the framework presented above and to provide empirical support for its proposed implications, Flamholtz et.al. have been engaged in a program of empirical research. In the following section, the empirical research to date to test the model's predictive validity and its related hypotheses will be summarized.

3.1. Strategic Organizational Development and Financial Performance

Flamholtz and Aksehirli (2000) proposed a link between the organizational success model and the financial success of organizations. To test this hypothesized relationship, they analyzed financial and non-financial information relevant to the hypothesized model for eight pairs of companies in different industries. Each company was evaluated in terms of the six key strategic building blocks, and scores were assigned to indicate the degree of the organization's development. Average Return on Equity was used as an indicator of financial performance. Using the Friedman Two-way Analysis of Variance and a regression analysis, they found a statistically significant relationship between the proposed model of organizational success and financial performance.

The major implication of this research is that is provides empirical support for the use of the Pyramid Model as a managerial tool, as we proposed in the previous section.

3.2. Strategic Organizational Development and Financial Performance: Additional Evidence

In addition, Flamholtz and Hua (2002A) report the results of an empirical test of the hypothesized relationship regarding financial success and the degree of development of six key variables (or "strategic building blocks") included in the organizational development pyramid within a *single* firm. The research site was a U.S.-based, medium-sized industrial enterprise. The company is a parts manufacturer for industrial, truck, and other automotive businesses. It is a supplier of parts for such companies as Ford Motor Company, Navistar, and Dana Corporation.

To assess this issue, they compared divisional data the degree of organizational development with divisional "EBIT" (earnings before interest and taxes), a classic measure of financial performance for 18 divisions. Specifically, they ran a regression between: 1) the degree to which each division was perceived as being developed on the six key strategic building blocks as a whole (i.e., the average pyramid development score), and 2) EBIT. This regression was statistically significant. This result supports the hypothesis of a relationship between the degree of strategic organizational development and the financial performance of organizations.

Another question concerned the thresholds of strategic organizational development for profitability of individual companies or operating units. Specifically, they wanted to identify potential "benchmarks" of organizational development to serve as guideposts for developing the six key strategic building blocks. Stated differently: What are the levels of strategic organizational development required for profitability and superior profitability in companies?

They found that all of the six divisions with strategic organizational development scores greater than 3.0 were profitable. In contrast, for the nine divisions with strategic organizational development scores less than 3.0, six were profitable and three were "unprofitable" (i.e., negative EBIT).

This study has implications for the level of strategic organizational development required for optimal profitability. One major implication of this study is, that it provides additional empirical support for the use of the Pyramid model as proposed earlier in this article. Another major managerial implication of this study is that there is a high (in this study 100%) probability of profitability for organizations will Pyramid scores greater than 3.0. Similarly, it also suggests that there is a 33% chance of being unprofitable for organizations with Pyramid scores less than 3.0. While a level of development of 3.0 seems to be the threshold for being profitable, most organizations want to achieve superior financial performance.

3.3. Corporate Culture and Financial Performance

In addition to the overall tests of the strategic organizational development model, there has also been an empirical test of the effects of corporate culture on financial performance (Flamholtz, 2000). "Corporate culture" is one of the six key building blocks included in the Pyramid framework. It is also hypothesized to be the critical developmental factor at Stage IV (see Exhibit 2).

Previous authors (Kotter and Hesket, 1992) have suggested that culture has an impact on financial performance. Unlike previous studies, which have only examined the effects of culture on financial performance using cross-sectional data, Flamholtz (2000) did a study of the impact culture has on financial performance in a single organization.

The study involved developing statements describing the core values of the desired culture of the company as a whole, as well as determining the extent to which the divisions' culture was consistent with the stated desired culture. This was measured by using a survey with a Likert scale (Flamholtz, 2000). This data was then used as an input to address the question concerning the impact of corporate culture on financial performance. The hypothesis was that the greater the degree of agreement of the divisional culture with the overall desired corporate culture, the greater financial performance. Financial performance was measured as EBIT.

The results, using a regression analysis, indicate that there is a statistically significant relationship between culture and financial performance (measured by 'EBIT,' or earnings before interest and taxes). Thus these results provide support for the previously hypothesized relationship between culture and financial performance, with significant implications for management theory and practice.

One of the major implications concerns the potential sources of competitive advantage. One of the hypotheses is that the top four levels of the pyramid, which form the "infrastructure" of the firm, are less susceptible to imitation (Flamholtz, 1995), and, accordingly, provide the basis for long-term sustainable competitive advantage. Culture is one of the key components of organizational infrastructure, and if there are demonstrable differences in culture across business units, which are associated with differences in profitability, this provides support for the notion that organizations compete not only in products and markets but in infrastructure as well.

3.4. Infrastructure and Competitive Advantage

One of hypotheses presented above is that the top four levels of the pyramid, which form the "infrastructure" of the firm, are less susceptible to imitation (Flamholtz, 1995), and, accordingly, provide the basis for long-term sustainable competitive advantage. At present there is no published research on this issue. However, Flamholtz and Hua with the assistance of Aksehirli (2003) have conducted research on this issue. They have found empirical support for this hypothesis.

The major implication of this study is that it challenges the convention paradigm of strategy, which focuses almost exclusively upon external forces. The reserarch by Flamholtz, Hua, and Aksehirili (2003) indicates that competitive advantages can occur within "the black box" systems internal to an organization.

3.5. Growing Pains and Financial Performance

As discussed above, when an organization grows it will almost inevitably experience a classic set of "growing pains". These growing pains are "symptoms" that something has gone wrong in the process of strategic organizational development, and an "early warning" of significant future problems. More specifically, strategic organizational development equilibrium occurs when there is a fit between the development of the six key building blocks of organizational success and the organization's size or stage of development (Flamholtz, 1995).

When this fit does not occur, the organization will experience a variety of "organizational growing pains".

Flamholtz and Hua (2002B) performed an empirical test of the hypothesized relationship between "organizational growing pains" and corporate financial performance. They also addressed the question: are there benchmark levels of growing pains which might be used to predict which organizations will be profitable versus those which are likely to be unprofitable? Previous to this research, the hypothesized relationship between growing pains and performance in previous literature has been conceptual in nature; in contrast, this study presents some very specific "benchmarks" for growing pains in relation to successful organizational financial performance.

To study whether there is a statistically valid predictive relationship between growing pains and EBIT, they calculated a regression equation based upon these two variables. The results of this statistical test indicate that there is a statistically significant relationship between growing pains as a predictor of EBIT. This means that growing pains are a predictor of financial performance or the "bottom line" (EBIT).

An analysis of the relationship between specific growing pains scores and financial performance was also conducted to determine benchmark levels of "safe" versus "unsafe" growing pains. The results suggest that there appears to be a maximum level of growing pains beyond which organizational financial health is at risk. This suggests that there is a "maximum healthy growing pains score" to provide the highest probability of success, and confirms that there do appear to be thresholds levels of growing pains which might be used to predict which organizations will be profitable versus those which are likely to be unprofitable.

The data derived from this study provide empirical support for the notion that growing pains have an impact on financial performance, and that there are threshold levels of growing pains that are "unsafe" or "unhealthy" for future financial performance. The results of the analysis suggest that there is a (very strong) statistically significant relationship between growing pains and financial performance.

The major implication of this research is that there appears to be a maximum level of growing pains beyond which organizational financial health is at risk. Specifically, the maximum "healthy" level of growing pains appears to be "32". This means that to optimize the chances of being profitable an organization ought to keep its growing pains score less than 32 (Flamholtz and Randle 2000).

4. Summary of the Framework's Implications

Several implications can be derived from the framework described above. These are summarized below:

1. The initial premise or implication from this framework is that organizations must perform certain tasks to be successful at each stage of their growth.

2. A second premise is that each of these tasks must be performed in a stepwise fashion in order to build a successful organization.

3. Another implication is that the top four levels of the pyramid, which form the "infrastructure" of the firm, are less susceptible to imitation (Flamholtz, 1995), and, accordingly, provide the basis for long-term sustainable competitive advantage.

4. Each stage of growth is viewed as having a set of critical developmental tasks. For example, the critical tasks at Stage I are markets and products, while at Stage III the critical task is the development of management systems.

5. Strategic organizational development equilibrium occurs when there is a fit between the organization's strategic development of the six key building blocks of organizational success and its size or stage of development. When this fit does not occur, the organization will experience a variety of "organizational growing pains". These growing pains are symptoms of organizational distress and an indication of the need to change, if the organization wants to continue to operate successfully.

4.1. Implications for Management, Boards, Auditors and Researchers

The proposed model and empirical research findings presented above have significant implications for management theory and practice. The specific implications of each individual research study have been stated above. However, this section examines the broader implications of the model and research as a whole for management, boards, auditors, and researchers.

4.1.1. Strategic Organizational Development and Financial Performance.

The data derived from the set of empirical studies surveyed above provides an indication that the proposed model of strategic organizational development does have an impact on financial performance. This has important implications for management theory and practice. It is one thing to assert that organizational development is a significant factor of organizational success and quite another to be able to demonstrate that the effective management of these variables can enhance profitability.

Managers can have confidence in using the framework to assess the strategic development of their companies as well as to plan for its future development. This suggests that the strategic planning process ought to be based upon the pyramid as a "strategic lens" for the development of organizations. Although all six functions that make up the pyramid should be managed successfully in order to achieve good financial performance, practitioners can incorporate the organizational life cycle model to decide which tasks to emphasize at each stage of growth.

Another implication for management is the fact that the organizations are competing at each level of the pyramid. Since markets can be easily entered and products can be easily copied, the real competition goes on at the top four levels of the pyramid. This is the area where organizations can develop sustainable competitive advantages.

4.1.2. Corporate Culture and Financial Performance.

The data derived from the set of empirical studies surveyed above provides an indication that the corporate culture does have an impact on financial performance. This has important implications for management theory and practice. It is one thing to assert that corporate culture is a significant factor of organizational success and quite another to be able to demonstrate that the effective management of this variable can enhance profitability.

One of the major implications concerns the potential sources of competitive advantage. One of the hypotheses is that the top four levels of the pyramid, which form the "infrastructure" of the firm, are less susceptible to imitation (Flamholtz, 1995), and, accordingly, provide the basis for long-term sustainable competitive advantage. The data indicate that there is a statistically significant relationship between culture and financial performance (measured by 'EBIT', or earnings before interest and taxes). Thus these results provide support for the previously hypothesized relationship between culture and financial performance.

Culture is one of the key components of organizational infrastructure, and since there are demonstrable differences in culture across business units, which are associated with differences in profitability, this provides support for the notion that organizations compete not only in products and markets but in infrastructure as well. Culture, then, is a potential source of competitive advantage, and, in turn, differential financial performance.

4.1.3. Growing Pains and Financial Performance.

In addition, as we have seen, organizational growing pains can directly influence financial performance or the so-called "bottom line". As a result, management needs: 1) to understand the nature and causes of growing pains, 2) to have a method of measuring them, 3) a template to assess their severity, and 4) a strategy for managing them.

Variations exist, but it is clear that organizations of all sizes and types experience some growing pains. Severity of these problems can be affected by the rate of growth experienced by the organization. Managers of rapidly growing companies of any size or type must learn to recognize organizational growing pains and take steps to alleviate them so that their organizations can continue to operate successfully. The payoff will be reduced growing pains and an increased likelihood of a positive "bottom line".

What should an organization do to minimize or avoid the problems associated with growing pains? Most entrepreneurs are always concerned with the risk of failure if revenues are insufficient to cover expenses. However, many ignore the equally damaging risks of choking on their own rapid growth. To avoid the problems accompanying hyper-growth, a company must have an infrastructure that will absorb that growth. If a company anticipates rapid growth, then management must invest in building the required infrastructure *before* it is actually necessary. It is very difficult, and sometimes impossible, to "play catch-up" with organizational infrastructure. Some companies, such as Starbucks Coffee, Compaq Computer, and PacifiCare had a strategy of having their infrastructure in place prior to their explosive growth and reaped the benefits of this investment. In contrast, Boston Markets, Osborne Computers, and MaxiCare, did not have their infrastructure in place prior to explosive growth and all three have experienced bankruptcy. Thus the ideal strategy for a firm that anticipates rapid growth is to build an infrastructure sufficient for the size of the organization it anticipates becoming, prior to actually reaching that size.

This strategy of building the infrastructure prior to growth is not merely appropriate for large companies, but for relatively small entrepreneurships as well. For example, several years ago, the author met with the president of a U.S. service firm specializing in insurance-based benefit programs for executives when the firm had approximately $3 million in annual revenues. At that time, the author of this article advised the CEO that it was probably premature to build the infrastructure to the extent that was being contemplated. However, the CEO indicated that he wanted his firm to grow to $50 million in revenue within five years. He then proceeded to invest in building the infrastructure of his company before it was actually necessary. This was a wise move, because the company actually grew to more than $65 million in revenue within five years.

Given the research findings about growing pains cited above, it appears that growing pains can be used as leading indicators of future financial performance. The U.S. Federal Reserve monitors leading indicators of economic activity to predict the direction of GNP and inflation. Similarly, growing pains might be used as leading indicators of future changes in organizational financial performance. In addition, our findings concerning the maximum level of growing pains in relation to the levels of profitability are, at a minimum, suggestive of the need to control or at least minimize growing pains.

Since growing pains can be measured and we have shown that they are clearly linked to financial performance, it would be useful to report growing pains to the Board. This would be done on a comparative basis across time. Independent auditors might also find this information useful as a signal to look for organizational problems. These findings also have implications for Boards of Directors and external auditors. Recent experiences in the U.S., with Enron, Waste Management, and other publicly traded enterprises suggest the need for improved methods of control (Flamholtz, 1996; Nilsson and Olve, 2001). There are complex issues involving the balance of power among management, Boards, and auditors not only in the U.S., but throughout Europe and Asia as well (Hooghiemstra and Van Manen, 2002). What is required are tools that can help identify potential problems *before they occur.*

4.2. Future Research

From an academic perspective, the results reported here are preliminary but promising. The results of the research surveyed here represent the first attempt in the empirical analysis of Organizational Development Pyramid framework and should be supplemented with further studies. It would be valuable for future research to replicate the current study, not only in North American environment but in Europe and Asia as well.

This paper also suggests that the level of strategic organizational development, as well as the level of growing pains, can be used to estimate the future financial success of the firm. Although the results reported here are promising, it remains for future research to examine this phenomenon with a longitudinal study using time series analysis.

4.3. Conclusion

The Organizational Development Pyramid framework can be a promising tool in predicting the future performance of the companies. In combination with stages of growth, the Organizational Development pyramid can be used to assess a company's success in fulfilling the critical tasks for each stage of growth. In addition, as we have seen, organizational growing pains can directly influence financial performance or the so-called "bottom line".

This framework offers the basis of a different paradigm of organizational success and failure for organizations at different stages of growth, from new entrepreneurships to established companies. Although the research is not definitive, it offers some promising findings and opens the way to new questions.

References:

Aldrich, I. (1979). "Organizational Passages: Diagnosing and Treating Life Cycle Problems in Organizations". *Organizational Dynamics*, Summer, pp. 3-24.

Brittain, J.W., Freeman, J. (1980). "Organizational Proliferation and Density-Dependent Selection", In J.R. Kimberly, R.H. Miles and Associates (eds.), *The Organizational Life Cycle Issues in the Creation, Transformation, and Decline of Organizations*, pp. 291-338. San Francisco: Jossey-Bass.

Burns, T. and Stalker, G.M. (1961). *The Management of Innovation.* London: Tavistock.

Caroll, G.R. and Yangchung, P.H. (1986). "Organizational Task and Institutional Environments in Ecological Perspective: Findings from the local Newspaper Industry". *American Journal of Sociology*, v91, pp. 838-873.

Chandler, Alfred Dupont (1962). *Strategy and Structure: Chapters in the History of the Industrial Enterprise*. Cambridge: M.I.T. Press.

Child, J. and Keiser, A. (1981). "Development of Organizations Over Time", in P.C. Nystrom and W.H. Starbuck (eds.) *Handbook of Organizations: Adapting Organizations to Their Environments*, pp28-64. New York: Oxford University Press.

Cook, T.D. and Campbell, D.T. (1979). *Quasi-Experimentation: Design and Analysis Issues for Field Settings.* Boston: Houghton Mifflin Company.

Flamholtz, E. (1995). "Managing Organizational Transitions: Implications for Corporate and Human Resource Management". *European Management Journal*, v13, n1, pp. 39-51.

Flamholtz, E. (2001). "Corporate Culture and the Bottom Line". *European Management Journal*, v19, n3, pp. 268-275.

Flamholtz, Eric G. and Aksehirli, Zeynep (2000). "Organizational Success and Failure: An Empirical Test of a Holistic Model". *European Management Journal*, 18, (5) 488-498.

Flamholtz, E. and Hua, Wei (2002A). "Strategic Organizational Development and the Bottom Line: Further Empirical Evidence". *European Management Journal*, 20 (1), 72-81.

Flamholtz, E. and Hua, Wei (2002B). "Strategic Organizational Development, Growing Pains and Corporate Financial Performance: An Empirical Test". *European Management Journal*, 20 (5), 527-536.

Flamholtz, E. and Hua, Wei with the assistance of Aksehirli, Zeynep (2003). "Searching for Competitive Advantage in the Black Box", *European Management Journal,* forthcoming (2003)

Flamholtz, E. and Randle, Y. (1998). *Changing the Game: Organizational Transformations of the First, Second, and Third Kinds.* New York: Oxford University Press.

Flamholtz, E. and Randle, Y. (2000). *Growing Pains: Transitioning from an Entrepreneurship to a Professionally Managed Firm,* (New, rev. ed.). San Francisco: Jossey-Bass.

Freeman J. and Hannan, M.T. (1983). "Niche Width and the Dynamics of Organizational Populations". *American Journal of Sociology*, v88, pp. 1116-1145.

Hooghiemstra, R. and Van Manen, J. (2002). "Supervisory, Directors, and Ethical Dilemma: Exit or Voice". *European Management Journal*, 20 (1), 1-9

Kotter, J.P. and Hesket, J.L. (1992). *Corporate Culture and Performance.* New York: The Free Press.

Midgley, D.F. (1981). "Toward a Theory of the Product Life Cycle: Explaining Diversity". Journal of Marketing, v45, pp. 109-115.

Nilsson, F. and Olve, N. (2001). "Control Systems in Multi-National Companies: From Performance Management to Strategic Management". *European Management Journal*, 19 (4), 344-358.

Peters, T.J., and Waterman, R.H. (1982). *In Search of Excellence.* New York: Harper & Row.

Pfeffer, J. and Salancik, G.R. (1978). *The External Control of Organizations: A Resource Dependence Perspective.* New York: Harper & Row.

Quinn, R.E., Cameron, K. (1983). "Organizational Life Cycle and Shifting Criteria for Effectiveness: Some Preliminary Evidence". Management Science, v29, n1, pp. 33-51.

Randle, Y. (1990). *Towards an Ecological Life Cycle Model of Organizational Success and Failure.* Los Angeles: unpublished Ph.D. dissertation, UCLA.

Robalo, A. and Pinto, J.A. (2002). "Organizational Development, Life Cycle, and Success: an empirical test of the Flamholtz Framework". Unpublished working paper.

Siegel, S. (1956). *Nonparametric Statistics for the Behavioral Sciences*. New York: McGraw-Hill Book Company.

Starbuck, W. (1965). *Organizational Growth and Development*, In J.G. March (ed.) Handbook of Organizations, pp. 451-533. Chicago: Rand McNally.

Tushman, M.L.; Virany, B.; Romanelli, E. (1985). "Executive Succession, Strategic Reorientation, and Organization Evolution: the Minicomputer Industry as a Case in Point". *Technology in Society*, v7, pp. 297-313.

Walton, R.E. (1986). "A Vision-led Approach to Management Restructuring". *Organizational Dynamics*, Spring, pp. 9-16.

9. Credit Constraints on Small Businesses: Theory Versus Evidence

Robert Cressy
Cass Business School

Abstract. We describe the prevailing theories of credit constraints, empirical tests of the theories and their policy implications. Theories and empirical tests are then evaluated in the context of small businesses and the likelihood of encountering credit constraints in practice is assessed. Private and public sector responses to perceived credit constraints are then evaluated on both theoretical and empirical grounds and broad conclusions reached about the relevance and effectiveness of policy initiatives. The paper is a written-up version of a lecture that I deliver as part of a course taught to second year students on the BSc degrees at Cass Business School, London. The only prerequisite for the course is that the students should have taken Elementary (Micro and Macro) economics.

Keywords: credit constraints, small business, policy response.

1. Introduction

Billions of dollars are spent annually by governments of a variety of political persuasions around the world to alleviate perceived credit constraints on small, young businesses. The rationale for this activity is certainly questionable, but as Keynes once remarked, it is surprising how much policy-making is influenced by 'the ideas of some [defunct] economist'. So this paper, a written-up version of a lecture that I deliver as part of a course taught to second year students on the BSc degrees at Cass Business School, London, attempts to outline the work of (largely non-defunct) economists in this area and to draw out whatever policy conclusions seem to be both logical and supported by the facts. The 'lecture' itself is based on the concept of 'active learning': I intersperse my delivery with class exercises, usually done in pairs ("Talk to your neighbour"), followed by audience response and finally my own answers, which are distributed as part of the Lecture Notes for the course – after the lecture. The only academic prerequisite for the course is that the students should have taken Elementary (Micro and Macro) economics.

2. Learning Objectives

The learning objectives of the topic are as follows:

This article was originally published in the International Journal of Entrepreneurship Education 1(4): 515-538.

1. To understand the nature of credit constraints and why small and young firms are more likely to experience them than large and old firms.

2. To be able to understand and evaluate the academic literature on credit constraints.

3. To have the intellectual tools to judge if credit constraints exist in practice.

4. To understand whether policy intervention is required as a result of identifying credit constraints and if so what form this should take.

To be able to achieve these objectives we need to have an understanding of the nature of small businesses and their finances.

3. Definition

There are many definitions of a small firm, but most rely on the numbers of employees of the firm falling below a certain threshold. We shall not attempt to define the concept of a small firm any further in this lecture (an earlier lecture is devoted to the subject) but assume that the reader has an intuitive grasp of what a small firm is and refer him or her to the various government definitions should they wish to understand the focus of government policy in this area.

4. Small and Large Firms

Small firms are profoundly different from large firms. This difference manifests itself in a number of ways, and ultimately impacts on the financing they use, the topic of interest in this lecture.

Firstly, small firms are informationally opaque. This is exemplified (and possibly encouraged) by the fact that the financial reporting requirements on them are lighter. Unincorporated businesses, which are the majority of small businesses, are not obliged to publish accounts information at all. Even limited companies, usually thought of as more sophisticated businesses, are often required to publish only summary accounts – in the UK for example, they do not have to publish a profit and loss account. Furthermore, small firms' accounts are not eagerly and regularly poured over by teams of stock analysts, attempting to divine their economic destiny, as are the accounts of the PLCs. Even small companies financed by venture capital (a tiny minority of businesses) produce regular financial reports to their financiers only because they are required to do so as a precondition of funding, and their financiers are careful to make sure that such information does not reach the public light of day[1].

Secondly, small firms are often young firms and for this reason have no track record. This extends to their management, sales, costs and borrowing performance. Combined with the absence of information on their accounts, the absence of a track record makes it difficult for banks to assess their prospects when considering a lending proposal.

Thirdly, small, young firms are more risky than big, old firms. The evidence for this proposition has been ground out in a large number of empirical studies and is incontrovertible, though definitions of failure may vary somewhat from one study to another[2]. This excess riskiness often stems from the fact that small firms often rely on one customer, one product, and one supplier. Naturally under these circumstances they are highly vulnerable to changes in the environment. They also have limited sources of finance available in a liquidity crisis, which may occur in the early stages of their lives and is particularly likely in an economic downturn. In the latter situation they will be likely to experience what economists call 'the flight to quality' among the banks, i.e. a switch in lending towards their less risky, larger counterparts as the failure rate amongst small businesses starts to rise and banks try to protect their rates of return.

Case Study: Failure & the Bespoke Tie Manufacturer

An ex-colleague of mine, Andrew, in the training arm of a well-known business school recounted to me the story of the failure of his own business. He had set up in a boom period a firm that manufactured highly artistic, multicoloured, extrovert neckties. These were attractive especially to extrovert wealthy business people. They therefore sold in good numbers at a considerable premium over the mass-produced varieties during the boom period of the late 80s. However, not a high proportion of profits were retained in the process. When the downturn eventually came (as it inevitably does) in 1990-1 their customers chose either to buy less ties altogether (keeping existing neckties longer) or switched to cheaper, mass-produced varieties e.g. from Marks and Spencer[3]. Thus demand for Andrew's bespoke ties fell dramatically in a short period of time and the company, which had borrowed to expand in the boom period, was suddenly plunged into bankruptcy. Looking back on the sorry affair Andrew could see that the main reasons for the failure of the business were (a) an

1. There is some exception to this: Venture Economics and Venture One, two commercial data agencies make available certain kinds of financial information to their paying subscribers.
2. In the definition of failure we need to distinguish carefully between solvent business closure and bankruptcy or insolvency. Ceasing to trade is typically not accompanied by bankruptcy for small businesses since the majority of a given cohort of startups does not borrow, even on overdraft.
3. Recall the concept of income elasticity of demand from first year Micro. Would you say the demand here is elastic or inelastic? Recollect what happens to revenue if there is a fall in demand and the income elasticity is greater than one. Would you expect it to rise or fall or remain constant?

> excessive dependence on one product; (b) the sensitivity of demand for the product to consumer income levels. On examination Andrew realised that the sensible strategy would have been to have diversified quickly. He might either have developed two products, one mass-produced, the other bespoke, or have developed in addition to the latter an entirely different product, less sensitive to income changes which would provide a minimum turnover in the downturn.

Another reason for the vulnerability of the small firm is that their entrepreneurs often lack human capital: skills, business acumen, vocational qualifications, etc. that are necessary for success. This deficiency conspires against the small firm in financial markets. For example, banks, recognising the excess risk of lending to small firms, will treat their lending proposal differently from one from a large firm, especially in a recessionary environment, often requiring seemingly excessive collateral as security, and charging a much higher margin over Base or Prime[4]. Figure 1 opposite shows a simulation of the failure curve of a small business with the two underlying distributions of profits growth rates[5]. The curves differ only by the initial amount of capital in the firm. It is clear that a better capitalised business (the light curve) has a more favourable profile than a cash-starved startup (the dark curve): the honeymoon period (zero failure rate) is longer, and the peak failure rate is lower[6].

---

4. We should not expect the rates charged by the banks to small and large firms to be the same even if there were no differences in default risk. This is because generally large firms borrow more, and the bank is able to offset the fixed costs of lending to them against a larger loan size, reducing unit costs. This in turn (in a competitive market) will reduce margins relative to those of small firms.
5. The curve is the failure density as a function of time trading and the area under the curve typically (though for obscure mathematical reasons, not necessarily) sums to one. The height of the curve gives the chance that a firm taken at random will fail at this time during its life. The firm must generally fail at some time between now and eternity.
6. A theoretical model that produces this curve as a result of a value-maximisation process by the manager can be found in Cressy (2003).

Figure 1: Initial Capitalisation and Failure

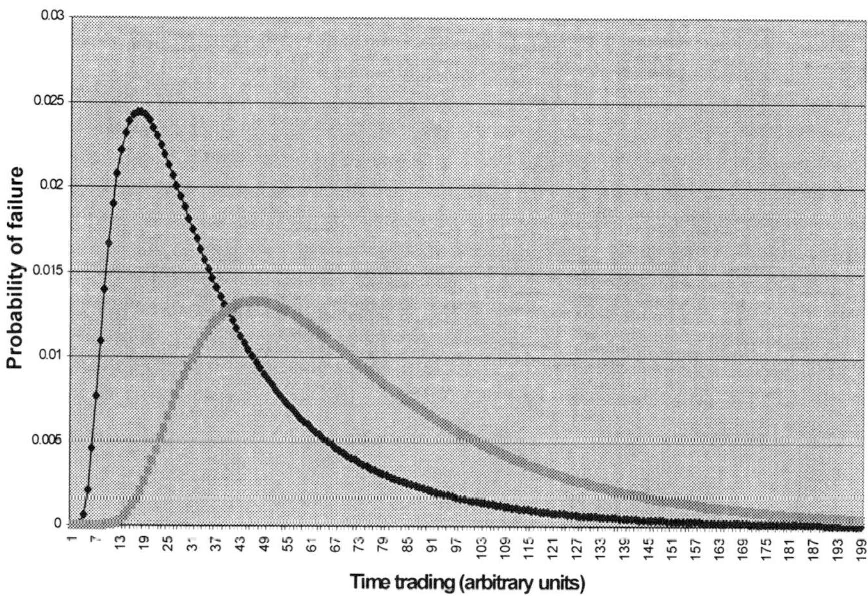

Source: Cressy 1999

Fourthly, small firms have fewer collateralisable assets than large firms. This is partly a function of their stage of development: as the firm grows, it may use retained profits to purchase fixed assets, especially if it is manufacturing products. It may also grow by the purchase of other enterprises, acquiring their fixed assets in the process. Therefore larger firms typically have a longer history of asset acquisition and in consequence possess more collateralisable assets as the basis for loans or overdrafts.

Finally, another potential reason for small firms having a smaller proportion of fixed assets is the possibility of capital constraints: Because of the need to raise relatively large amounts of capital to start a manufacturing business startups typically gravitate to the service industries where the proportion of fixed to total assets is lower – for technical reasons.

Case Study: Constraints and the Choice of Business Sector

Peter, a one-time colleague of mine at prestigious British business school had been made redundant from a large firm and decided to start a business in the Tool Hire industry. This was in the early 1980s, when the industry was in its infancy and just about to embark on a growth trajectory. He chose Tool Hire partly because his redundancy money allowed him to adequately capitalise a business in this sector. (The sector's high returns and growth prospects had also not escaped Peter's notice). If Peter had wanted to go into manufacturing his redundancy lump sum he decided would not have been enough to properly fund his startup.

Question: Does this constitute an example of a capital-constrained entrepreneur or a capital-constrained business or neither?

Answer: Peter started a business, so *he* (the entrepreneur) was not completely constrained by finance. But even if he was not totally constrained we can still ask on grounds of economic efficiency whether he started a business with the *highest* expected return given the limit he perceived on funds. On the one hand, given his limited funds, Peter dismissed the possibility of a manufacturing startup from consideration! On the other, it was clear from Peter's background, predominantly in Service industries rather than Manufacturing, that his skills were more geared to success in Services. So from the point of view of human capital, perhaps Peter did make the right choice after all, and might (optimally) have made the same decision even had he had sufficient financial capital to go into manufacturing.

5. Bank Lending Rules

Most Western banks have simple lending rules for small, young businesses: They typically lend to a firm *in proportion to the value of its assets* e.g. one third of their estimated market value[7]. These assets are required as security or *collateral* for the loan. In 'perfecting' this security the bank will typically take a *fixed* or *floating charge* over the firm's assets. This means that it has a claim on a specific asset (fixed charge) or can choose the asset it wishes to use to pay off the loan when the default occurs (floating charge). Under default it can sell these assets and hope to recover the value of the loan and interest.

What kind of assets will the bank use? Banks are suspicious of intangibles, things that can't be touched or seen and of items with short or passing lives. One bank manager is famous for saying that the problem with service firms is that the assets are their people, and so they tend to go home at 5 o'clock! So banks are likely to ask as the basis for security tangible (rather than intangible) and fixed (rather than current) assets. Classic examples of tangible fixed assets would be land, plant and buildings. Contrast this with intangible assets such as patents and copyrights. A computer program would typically be protected by a copyright (since it consists of lines of *written* code in which the author has obtained a *right to prevent unauthorised copying*.) The code might be worth literally millions of dollars but its value is often difficult to certify and therefore would not typically form the basis of loan collateral. Likewise, the patent on a new drug would not typically be suitable for this purpose. This again might be ultimately highly

7. This is by no means always the case, but in Toivanen and Cressy (2001) we showed that 60% of small business term loans were collateralised. However, loans that were not collateralised were almost certainly to customers with some track record with the bank. See below under Relationship Banking.

valuable, but the bank would tend to regard it as problematic from the point of view of immediate saleability.

So land, machinery and buildings are tangible, fixed assets. They have relatively long lives and larger used values, particularly in the case of land and houses located in 'good' residential areas. Current assets by contrast are items such as stocks of goods and work in progress, debtors and current interest earnt. These might in the event of default have a low or zero value. Debtors might be valueless if the company to whom the products or services were sold, and who currently owed money for them in return, were to go bust. Half-finished goods are of little worth on the open market and even finished goods may need to be sold in distressed conditions, reducing their value substantially. Hence, little weight is placed on them by the banker in deciding the value of collateral.

On the principle of matching assets and liabilities[8] banks may however be prepared to offer short term loans or overdraft facilities on the basis of current assets like debtors. The receipts from these sales are legally valid documents and in the last resort payment can be extracted from the purchaser by court action. On the bank's asset side, overdrafts are in principle repayable on demand: in other words, within 24 hours notice from the bank. Therefore, the risk associated with debtors used as collateral for lines of credit is not great.

Exercise: Constraints & Bank Lending Rules (I)

Consider the following: A firm has no assets at all to place as security for a loan it requests. If the bank lends half the value of assets what will be the value of the loan? Is the firm credit-constrained?

Answer: The answer to the first part is of course "zero". For the second part the questions to ask yourself are: Does the firm have a viable project? Has it approached all potential sources of finance? Assuming that both these are true, then the firm *will* be credit-constrained. The problem, of course, is: *Who* makes the assessment of the project's viability? *When* is the assessment made?

Exercise: Constraints & Bank Lending Rules (II)

Two entrepreneurs, one with high productivity (High) and one with low productivity (Low), have searched efficiently amongst a set of banks for funding for their *viable* projects. They find that only one will lend to them. In the judgement of the bank the each firm has £10,000 worth of fixed assets. The bank's judgement is based on its estimate of the distressed value of these assets when sold on the market. The entrepreneurs on the other hand claim to have discounted profits to the value of £20,000 and £40,000 respectively. The bank

8. This is a well known technique for reducing financial risk. See any standard text (e.g. Brealey and Myers, (2003) for a discussion of the details.

has a lending rule that says it will lend to an entrepreneur on the basis of 1/2 the value of assets. It thus offers a loan of £5,000 to both. However, the High entrepreneur wants a loan of £8k whilst the Low entrepreneur wants one of merely £3k.

Is either entrepreneur credit-constrained?

Answer: It all depends. Consider the two entrepreneurs.

1. High Productivity Entrepreneur

To maximise profits this entrepreneur wants to borrow *more* than the bank will allow given her assets, i.e. £8,000 > £5,000. So she *is* credit-constrained: raising her asset base would allow more borrowing and *increase* the NPV of the firm. This means that the economic arrangement cannot have been optimal i.e. value-maximising.

2. Low Productivity Entrepreneur

To maximise profits this entrepreneur wants to borrow *less* than the bank will allow given her assets, i.e. £3,000 < £5,000. So she is *not* credit-constrained: her profits are as high as they could be *regardless of the bank's lending rule.* In the language of linear programming, the constraint doesn't 'bite': Offering her more money would not increase her profits. The money would presumably be used for some non-profit making activity e.g. buying a BMW for personal use.

6. Theory and Tests of Credit Constraints

Evans and Jovanovic (1989) developed an empirical test for the existence of credit constraints. This was based on the idea of a bank lending rule discussed above.

They argued that firms were credit constrained if and only if a relaxation of the lending rule (or equivalently an unanticipated increase in fixed assets) increased business survival rates[9]. What might be the reasoning behind the Evans and Jovanovic (EJ) argument?

9. More accurately they argued that credit rationing exists if and only if more assets increased the probability of a person moving into self-employment from some other labour market state. This is the mirror image of the proposition discussed in the text which is couched in terms of survival (probability of staying in business) rather than moving into business.

Chart 1: Relation Between Overdraft, House Equity, Turnover and Entrepreneurial Age, 1988

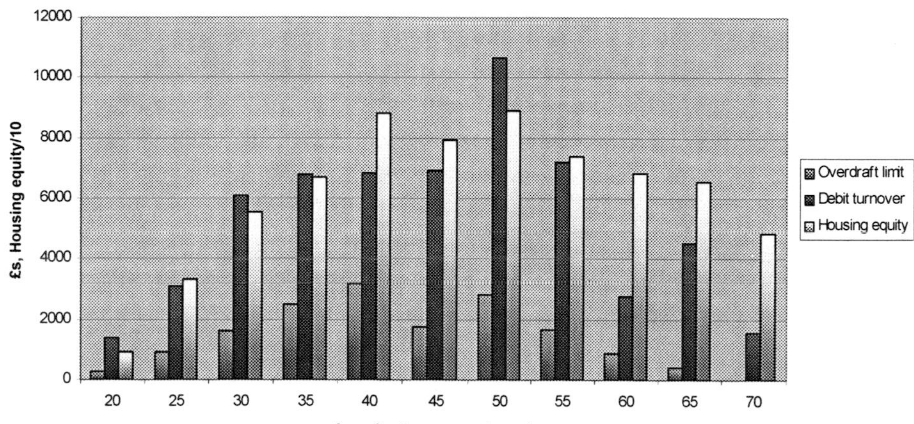

If on average an increase/decrease in assets increases/decreases business survival then bank borrowing based on asset values keeps profits artificially low. Hence for the 'marginal' business (the one just slipping into bankruptcy) an increase in assets allows an increase in borrowing. This increases profits and prevents failure. Hence, in summary: A relaxation of the lending rule reduces business failure rates or equivalently increases business survival rates.

7. Spurious Correlation? Alternative Explanations

The Evans and Jovanovic theory argues that on average bank lending rules *limit borrowing below economically desirable levels.* But what if observed correlation is caused by a third factor, age of the entrepreneur? This would explain the observed relationship of:

- *Borrowing to age* (Chart 1): Older borrowers (until about the age of 50) borrow more because they have more housing assets to place as collateral. Younger borrowers and those reaching retirement have either not accumulated assets or have started to consume their assets. In either case they have less assets to place as collateral and so (being constrained) borrow less.

- *Age to survival* (Chart 2): Older entrepreneurs with more maturity, realism and access to networks are more likely to survive in business (partly perhaps because their wealth enables them to borrow more).

On this theory, experience is the prerogative of age, and energy of youth. The productivity effects of these two forces (one positive and one negative) will cancel out in the mid-50s age range. Thus we should expect an inverse-U shaped relationship of survival to age of the entrepreneur (Chart 2). Because more experienced entrepreneurs will sell more, and require more working capital in consequence, borrowing levels will be positively related to sales; and hence increase with age up to a certain point, declining thereafter as declining energy begins to outweigh greater experience and skills (Chart 1). Assets likewise will behave according to the lifecycle consumption theory implying an inverse U-shaped relation of assets to age (Chart 1): Older entrepreneurs have accumulated more assets; these begin to be consumed after a certain age is reached. Thus we have explained why survival, sales and borrowing are positively correlated with each other via the age factor.

Exercise: Effects of Age on Business Characteristics

> Compare the position of two firms A and B which differ simply in terms of the average age of the owners, 20 years and 50 years respectively using chart 1. How do business survival, sales, housing equity and overdraft borrowing figures differ between the firms?

But what does this imply for the existence of capital constraints. Returning now to the discussion of the Evans and Jovanovic theory, we may ask: Under the alternative hypothesis of human capital driving the correlation of assets and survival, what would we expect to find in the data? We would expect of course to find the concave relationships with respect to age for all three variables we have observed above. However, using more sophisticated statistical techniques, we should expect also to find *one important difference:* once we hold human capital *constant* the effect of assets on survival should drop out. Why? Because it occurs *only because of the correlation of assets and survival with age.* If this happens then we should conclude that capital constraints do *not* exist: the correlation of assets and survival is spurious.[10] The correlation of human capital and survival is the primary *causal* relationship.

10. This is a technical term meaning that the simple correlation between X and Y is positive but the partial correlation (controlling for relevant variables) is zero.

Chart 2: Business Survival by Age of Proprietor

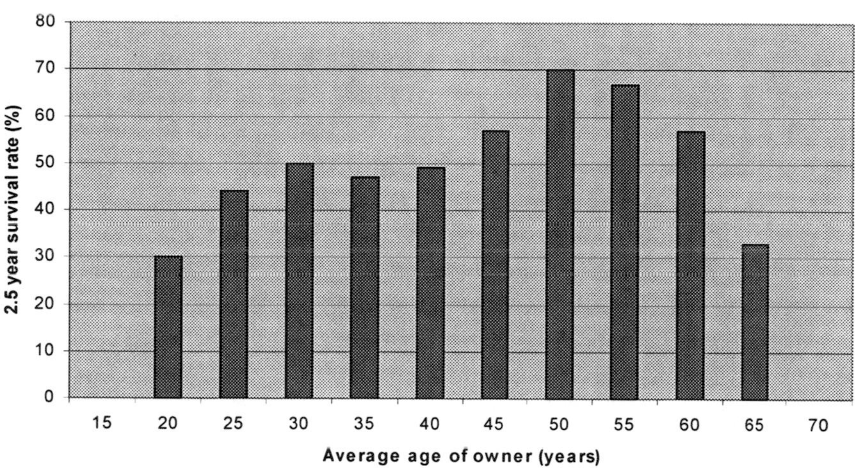

So what are the empirical facts? In Cressy (1996) I performed a regression of survival on Assets alone; Human capital (HC) alone; and finally Assets and HC together. As expected both assets and HC individually were positively correlated with survival, but once the effect of HC was controlled for, assets *dropped out of the equation*. I concluded that startups were not financial capital-constrained, but might indeed be human capital-deficient. Other studies have concluded much the same thing, e.g. Aston (1991) (at most 6% constrained); Cambridge (1998) (no quantitative estimate but little evidence of constraints); Cressy (2003b) (at most 3% constrained).[11]

8. Decreasing Absolute Risk Aversion (Dara)

You don't have to take my word for it! There is another explanation for the EJ finding also which does not imply credit constraints either. It depends merely on some plausible assumptions and limited evidence about human tolerance of risk. It is commonly believed (and there is evidence to show) that people in general *dislike* risk. Studies of the stock market show that people need to be offered higher returns to invest in more risky securities. This is consistent with risk aversion. Likewise, most people take out some kind of insurance policy against fire, theft etc. which involves the payment of a premium. This also suggests dislike of risk since by the mechanism of insurance the risk is transferred to another party.[12]

11. Whilst there is empirical evidence for the positive effects of inheritance on business startups controlling for measures of human capital (e.g. Burke, Fitzroy and Nolan, 2000) this is not necessarily evidence for the existence of capital and specifically credit constraints. The phenomenon of control aversion may well explain these effects (see later).

Imagine, then, that when I increase your assets you become less risk averse, i.e. you become more willing to take risks. This is quite a plausible phenomenon if you think about it: What it means is that if I offer you simultaneously an increase in your wealth W by £1 and a bet which yields +£1 with probability ½ and -£1 with probability ½, *with your additional assets* you are now *more* likely to take the bet than before. In the language of economics this means your utility of income function displays decreasing absolute risk aversion (or DARA)! Bearing in mind that entrepreneurship tends to be more income-risky than employment, this means that the marginal entrepreneur (one for whom the expected costs *just outweigh* the expected benefits) would switch into self-employment should she receive a windfall gain. There is furthermore some empirical evidence to support the assumption that entrepreneurs have decreasing absolute risk aversion (see Guiso, and Paiella, 1999).

9. Asymmetric Information and Its Effects

An understanding of much of the modern literature on credit constraints presupposes a grasp the concept of asymmetric information and its implications for credit markets. The following provides some of the basics for the lay reader.

Perfect or symmetric information in a market is a situation where the market participants know all the relevant facts regarding the motivations of the participants, the objects traded, the prices at which these objects are traded and the participants costs of trading. In a credit (rather than product or factor) market this means that firms wishing to borrow money know the price of credit (interest rates, charges etc), the collateral requirements (if any), the repayment schedule, etc, of all the banks (and other potential sources of finance[13]) in the market. They also know their own chances of repaying the loan and their own cost function (including of course, input prices etc). In addition to that they know (if relevant) how many other applicants there are in the market for funds, and so on. *Symmetry* of information arises because the banks and other competing financial institutions know *exactly the same things.* By contrast, *a*symmetric information is a regime in which one side to the (potential) transaction *knows less than the other.* Thus for example, if the firm knows more about its own projects than the bank (e.g. because the bank finds it too costly to monitor the firm's activities closely) then this might mean that the bank does not know the firm's probability of default but the firm does.[14] This is in fact a common assumption of models of the credit market including the celebrated Stiglitz-Weiss (1981) model of credit rationing.

---

12. There are of course counterexamples. The most glaring is the fact that huge numbers (millions) of people, often the poorest, engage in regularly in an unfair bet, namely the national lottery. This is inconsistent with risk aversion.
13. E.g. hire purchase rates.
14. More generally, the bank may have a less precise estimate of that probability than the firm.

So what are the implications of this possible asymmetry of information? There are two main phenomena that this may give rise to. The first is called *adverse selection*, a phenomenon that arises, for example, where 'bad' borrowers (those with high probability of default) dissemble, pretending to be 'good' borrowers (those with a low probability of default). At first the bank cannot tell the difference and offers them good and bad alike the same contract terms (e.g. a low rate of interest). Since in reality the default probability of the bad borrowers is higher than the bank imagined, this policy results in the bank making an overall loss on its lending. To solve this problem the bank will redesign the good borrower's contract to make it less attractive to the bad borrower. This is typically done with collateral requirements for the loan. The good borrower then ends up as the scapegoat, placing collateral on an otherwise uncollateralised loan, since collateral requirements dissuade the bad borrower from dissembling. Thus by the use of collateral the bank is able to separate the sheep (good borrowers) from the goats (bad borrowers).

The second effect of asymmetric information, is a phenomenon, familiar to students of insurance for many years, called *moral hazard*. This arises when borrower effort is unobservable to the bank. Effort is important to the bank as it influences the chances that its loan will be repaid. Because effort is unobservable, however, the lending contract cannot specify that a certain level of effort is necessary from the borrower to get the interest rate offered. The result is once more that the side with more information can exploit this. In consequence the entrepreneur will be able to get a loan on the basis of how hard she will work, but afterwards buys a BMW, puts her feet on the desk and allows the business to slide into bankruptcy. She can do this with some confidence, knowing full well that the bank will not detect her behaviour and that limited liability and the absence of collateral will protect her from the bailiffs.

The bank is, however, once more playing a repeated 'game', and will soon wise up to the moral hazard problem as it once more experiences losses on its loan portfolio. The manager will find after some thought that collateral is again a way to get the entrepreneur's (suspected) feet off the desk. This is a particularly powerful instrument of persuasion if you require that the loan is secured on the entrepreneur's house![15] So once again moral hazard issues can be resolved by collateralising the loan. Of course, like the use of collateral to solve the adverse selection problem, its use in solving the moral hazard dilemma is not costless: as a result of the good borrower needing to place collateral, she will have lower expected utility or profits. Thus, there is a loss of utility to the 'innocent' party and to society as a whole, by comparison with the symmetric information situation.

In the next section we will see how the costs of asymmetric information are built into an analysis of credit constraints.

15. Typically a personal rather than business asset ('outside' collateral), thus overcoming limited liability issues.

10. The Investment-Cashflow Relationship and Rationing

Fazzari, Hubbard and Petersen (1987) (henceforth FHP) found a positive correlation of small business' cash flows and their investment decisions. This, it was argued, was consistent with the hypothesis that internal funds were cheaper than external ones and firms would tend to substitute the latter for the former as the constraint on internal funds was relaxed (as would happen when the value of the firm increased with the extra cash inflow.). Moreover, their results showed that the marginal effect of cash flow on investment varied systematically with the size of firm, so that smaller firms seemed to face tighter constraints. This would seem to be consistent with the idea that smaller firms are constrained by imperfect capital markets to rely on internal finance to fund their operations. Figure 2 opposite shows the model underlying this hypothesis. We note that the competitive supply curve of funds is horizontal at the bank's cost of capital, r. The actual supply curve by contrast starts to turn upwards once internal funds have been exhausted and as moral hazard and adverse selection premia are priced into the cost of capital (at Q*). The optimal amount of lending (Q**) is therefore greater than the actual amount.

Figure 2 : Effects of Markets Solving Informational Problems on the Pricing and Availability of Credit (after Fazzari et al, 1987)

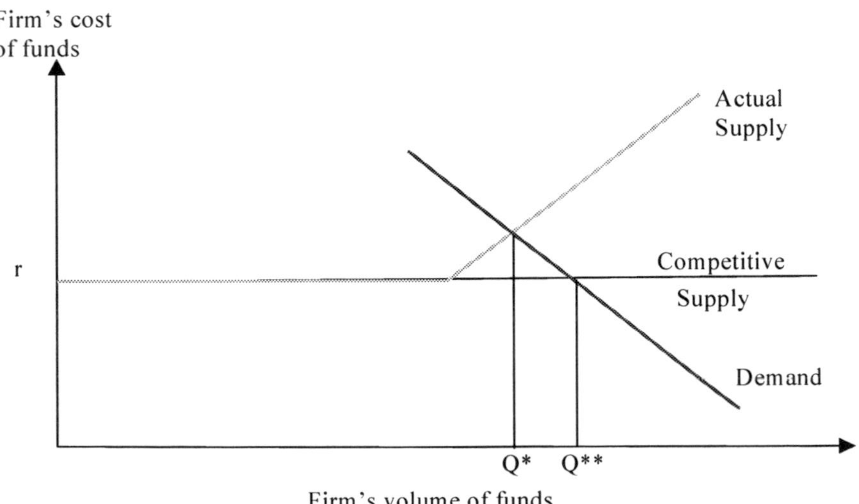

Does the existence of an upward sloping supply-curve for funds imply the need for government intervention? Not necessarily, according to the authors, since the costs of asymmetric information that are priced into this curve are *real* costs. They cannot be wished away. Government intervention might seem justified if the cost to society of the intervention was less than the welfare loss from doing nothing. This, however, is not necessarily the case. Therefore, in some sense we may be observing an *optimal* allocation of resources given the real costs of dealing with asymmetric information (see Cressy, 2002 and the symposium papers contained therein for a discussion of these issues).

11. Alternative Explanations: Control Aversion

It is possible however, to interpret the FHP results in a different way. Entrepreneurs of smaller firms are well-known to be *control averse*: they do not like any kind of interference in their operations, in particular by Big Brother in the form of the local bank manager. (Cressy, 1996). For this (and other reasons) they tend to borrow little[16]. In the language of economics this means that the psychological costs of borrowing outweigh the benefits (at the margin) for the entrepreneur of the smaller firm. As firms get larger things get less personal, management tends to be rewarded by salaries rather than simply profits, and the aversion to perceived bank interference starts to wane. But at the level of the Micro business (one with less than 10 employees) control-aversion restricts borrowing *from the demand side*. The equilibrium tradeoff is illustrated in Figure 3 where the black line indicates profits of the firm as a function of borrowing. This represents the utility function of the financial manager of a larger firm. By contrast the grey line represents an indifference curve for the entrepreneur of a small firm. Whilst profits are a 'good' (yield positive marginal utility) borrowing is 'bad' (yield negative marginal utility). Thus the indifference curve is upward-sloping – its slope being the ratio of the marginal utility of borrowing to that of profits[17]. Utility is therefore increasing as we move to the North-West of the diagram with higher profits and lower borrowing. The highest indifference curve attainable with the black profit constraint is the grey one. The optimum for the larger firm is where profits are maximised, at L*. The optimum of the control-averse entrepreneur, equates the marginal disutility of borrowing with the marginal utility of profits, yielding the smaller borrowing amount L**.

---

16. In Cressy, 1993) I showed that only 1/3 of businesses borrowed even on overdraft at startup. This grew to ½ within 3 years, but was still a minority of (surviving) businesses. Indeed, the attrition rate in the sample was considerable (many businesses closed within 3 years) but the propensity to borrow amongst survivors, and the average amount borrowed, increased over time.
17. The standard formula for the slope of an indifference curve is $-MU_x/MU_y$ where x and y are the two commodities yielding utility to the consumer.

Figure 3: Effects of Control Aversion on the Amount of Borrowing

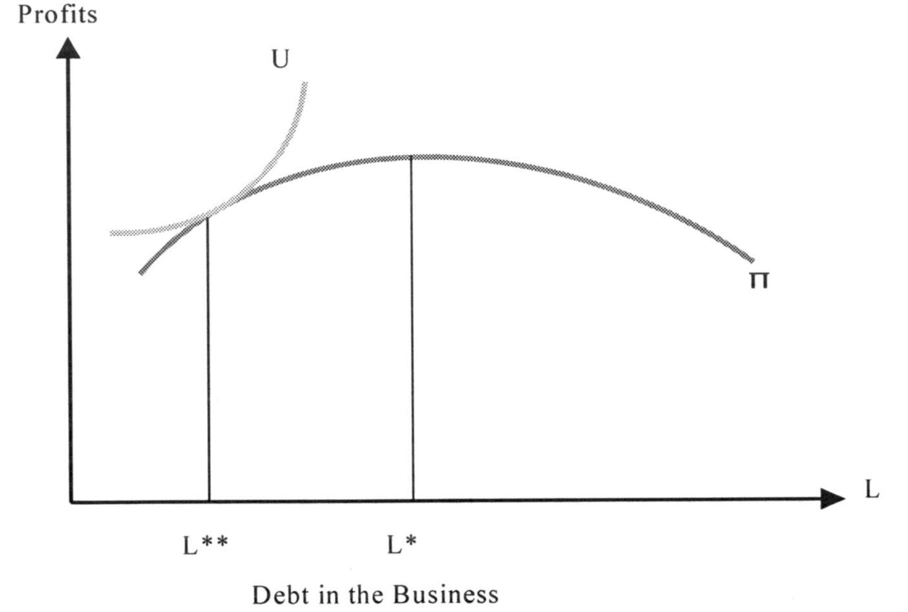

Profits

U

Π

L

L** L*

Debt in the Business

12. Rationing, Bank Heterogeneity and Borrower Search

One feature of the definition of credit rationing is that we assume that the potential borrower has approached all potential lending sources and discovered that none will lend to her. In the simplest competitive model of course, all banks are identical, potential borrowers are costlessly aware of offers of funds and therefore search becomes unnecessary. However, we can imagine a world (the real world!) in which banks are heterogeneous, information is costly to the entrepreneur to acquire and that as a result a she approaches only a subset of potential lenders.[18] This might arise for example, if manager ability (experience) is in short supply and distributed unevenly across banks. Then some banks will be more informed than others[19]. This may in turn lead to one bank rejecting the firm's request and another to accepting it, when approached. But once again, if the supply of credit from any bank is elastic, and search is costless, firms will find the banks that are more informed about their profitable project and borrow from them, so the banks that are less informed will make losses[20]. It is only if firms do not know the 'best' bank and there are costs to finding this out that they may end up starved of funds

18. Indeed empirical research in the UK shows that it is highly likely that banks do *not* all have the same beliefs about a given project.
19. Information is of course a two edged sword: one can learn that a firm's project is good or bad.
20. We can imagine that the anticipation of such losses would lead to banks competing up the price of scarce informed managers by their attempting to attract them away. And so on.

for good projects. But this does not have to be a market imperfection: if at the margin the costs of search are equated to the expected benefits, then just the right number of projects will be funded.

13. Market Solutions: (I) Relationship Banking

Relationship banking is the situation in which a bank manager through his/her relationship with the entrepreneur(s) acquires information about the firm that will be material to his/her lending decisions. Empirically, small firms rarely switch banks – the cost of so doing is too high. And the result is that the typical firm has a relationship of some 10 years with its bank. Relationship banking would seem to have the advantage to a high quality firm in that it should expect better credit facilities and perhaps less rationing when the economy is in recession. By contrast a low quality firm might expect progressively less favourable treatment over time. In practice, the evidence is that relationship banking results in a lower requirement for collateral, and more credit availability but little affect on the interest rates charged. (Petersen and Rajan (1996), Berger and Udell (1998)).This empirical finding seems consistent with theory. In a simple model (Cressy, 2001) it can be shown that relationship banking will eliminate any initial information asymmetry with the result that firms will *never* switch banks, and all banking is therefore 'relationship banking'. The argument goes as follows. Suppose there are two types of borrowers, High and Low, with qualities (success probabilities) $p_H > p_L$. Each project has a two-point distribution of returns, as usual, and requires $1 to get off the ground. Borrowers join a bank now with the prospect of borrowing in 1 year's time to fund their project. Hs and Ls occur with equal probability in the borrower population. To fix ideas suppose that p_H=3/4 and p_L =1/4. There are n competitive banks each with opportunity cost of lending r. Wealth of borrowers, and therefore collateral, is zero. Banks know the distribution of borrower quality and can learn about their own borrowers' quality after lending to them. Under complete information on borrower types the bank prices according to the rule $\alpha = r / p$[21] where r is the bank's cost of capital and α the interest rate it charges on the risky loan. This yields $\alpha_H = 4r/3$ and $\alpha_L = 4r$. In the present, borrowers are allocated randomly to banks. In one period's time the firm's own bank learns with certainty their quality whilst other banks know only the average quality of the borrower pool. It would seem that the Hs would stay with their own banks whilst the Ls would prefer to search, since the latter's return to switching would be a lower interest rate $\alpha_L' = 2r < 4r$. However, *the fact of switching itself conveys information about borrower type:* only the Ls switch. Hence the welcoming bank instead of charging 2r will now charge 4r to the new applicant – just as did the firm's own bank. This means that

21. This assumes that lending is a 'fair bet' i.e. that on average banks only cover their cost of funds, as would be the case under a competitive banking system.

both the Hs and Ls in fact stay put and *all* lending is done on a relationship basis[22]. What has happened, however, is that perceptions of firms credit risk have changed and this has enabled the bank to make more informed judgements about its clients loans and to price them accordingly[23].

14. Market Solutions (II): Mutual Guarantee Schemes

A mutual guarantee scheme (MGS) is an arrangement whereby firms in a given locality or industry pay a membership fee to join an association one of the main benefits of which is insurance against loan default. The arrangement is that when any member firm approaches a bank to borrow, the MGS will guarantee the firm's risk to the bank. Obviously the chances of the MGS not being able to pay the bank are less than that of any individual firm, though the precise probability that an MGS itself will default depends on how large its membership is and the upper limit to borrowing by any given member. MGS societies have a strong incentive to monitor potential and actual members to avoid unscrupulous behaviour and scrupulous risk. However, such monitoring is feasible only within a reasonably well-defined and tightly knit group of firms, e.g. in a given locality and industry or craft. Furthermore, these 'collective' approaches to borrowing may be more successful in some countries than others due to cultural reasons. For example, it appears that the Southern countries of the EU together with France (which straddles Northern and Southern regions) are more open to MGS than the Northern ones. The colder countries of Northern Europe, where collective action is less of a tradition, are less willing hosts to this kind of organisation.

---

22. This model relies of course on a number of simplifying assumptions. For example, the length of relationship a borrowing firm has with its bank (namely the time taken to gain perfect knowledge about the borrower) is arbitrarily set here at 1 period and the bank learns with certainty the firm's quality at the end of the period. We have also assumed that the cost to the bank of learning the information about borrower quality is zero. Most of these assumptions can be relaxed without altering the qualitative conclusions. For example, making the cost to the bank of being informed a fixed cost per $ lent simply alters the bank's cost of funds from r to r+f and interest rates to (r+f)/p. All else remains the same. Likewise the discrete distribution of borrower quality is inessential: if the distribution of borrower quality is made continuous we get exactly the same result. This means that under SW assumptions the marginal borrower is profitable and so there is initially deficient credit in the market. Once relationships are established the marginal borrower is then offered funds that are priced correctly and no rationing occurs. Under DMW assumptions this same logic leads to elimination of surplus funds.
23. This would predict that the average credit spread for a bank increases with the length of the relationship. I am not aware of any empirical test of this hypothesis however.

15. Market Solutions: Outside Equity?

If debt cannot easily be raised by a small firm due to absence of collateral then one might imagine that equity would be the alternative and indeed more suitable form of finance. Outside equity funding involves the purchase by an outside organisation or individual of shares in the firm. However, despite its seeming attractiveness there are insurmountable problems with this proposal.

Firstly, outside equity is by definition irrelevant to the majority of small businesses who are unincorporated and hence cannot (legally) issue equity.

Secondly, control aversion operates even more strongly in the case of equity rather than debt to discourage most small firms from gaining finance this way.[24] If they dislike even the minimal interference associated with a bank loan, what will the owners of a family business do if outsiders propose to muscle in and take seats on the Board?! One dares not think about it.

Thirdly, venture capitalists or Business Angels, the likely source of such finance are not interested in buying equity in the vast majority of small firms (Limited Companies) as they offer no prospects of capital gain of the order they are used to. VCs are always concerned about exit routes, in other words, ways of harvesting their investments and gaining profits. Traditionally they have (*ex ante*) rates of return of 30% or above on a per annum basis on their investments[25]. These rates of return are only possible however if the firm grows very fast and in a short time (3-5 years) ends up with a stock market flotation or a trade sale. The VC will typically exit her investment (sell her shares in the company) in 5-7 years. Needless to say, the overwhelming majority of small companies do not shape up to these requirements, run by relatively unambitious management teams and being slow- or no-growth in orientation and performance.

16. Government Solutions: Loan Guarantee Schemes

If relationship banking only works within a time horizon of 5 years or more and MGS schemes require specific local and cultural conditions to be successful in the solution of credit shortage, we might conclude that government intervention is desirable at least for the well-defined subset of young, small firms under consideration. And one of the most popular remedies proposed by governments eager to please (their electorate?!) is the Loan Guarantee Scheme or LGS. But we shall see that these schemes are by no means bereft of theoretical difficulties, whatever their practical usefulness may turn out to be.

---

24. Cressy and Olofsson (1997) found that some small Swedish firms would rather sell the business altogether rather than give up a share to an outsider! The aversion to outside equity declined with younger firms in the service industries.
25. *Ex post* may be a different story.

Under a loan guarantee scheme the government agrees to indemnify the bank up to a certain proportion of its loan to a borrower without collateral, with the interest rate charged 'on purely commercial grounds', in return for the borrower paying an insurance premium on the loan of 1 or 2 % of its value. The objective is to get the bank to lend to borrowers to whom it would not otherwise lend in view of the borrower's lack of collateral. The theoretical problem with such schemes is that they do not address the issue of adverse selection and moral hazard on which they were predicated. Adverse selection, as we have seen above, under conditions of unobservable borrower quality (talent), is dealt with by the bank by making better quality borrowers place more collateral. Moral hazard, in the context of unobservable borrower effort, is dealt with by the bank by asking for collateral from borrowers. This, as we have seen above, creates an incentive amongst lazy borrowers to put in effort, since by so doing, they are more likely to avoid losing their house!

Unfortunately, neither of these issues is dealt with by the government loan guarantee scheme since by definition the borrower has not been required to place collateral on her loan, and so the bank is unable to charge the good quality applicant differentially from the bad. Likewise, greater effort cannot be engineered by the LGS for the same reason. Of course it is true that some loans are made without collateral; but *ex hypothesi* this is not the case here.

This might seem to be the end of the matter, the last nail in the coffin of the LGS. However, recent empirical research has impugned the oft-quoted maxim of adverse selection in (small) business banking, and whilst the finding was that moral hazard is still with us, the need to use collateral as a sorting device is perhaps no longer quite so compelling (Toivanen and Cressy, 2002). Thus we may need only to provide the incentive to effort otherwise missing in the LGS scheme. Furthermore, several rather competent studies in the UK suggest that LGS performs better than might have been predicted from theoretical considerations alone. Thus the Department of Trade and Industry (DTI) has shown rather convincingly that there is financial and economic additivity[26], at modest levels, in the workings of the LGS: firms are getting money they would not have otherwise got, and producing output that other firms would not have produced, in the absence of the scheme.

17. The Information Regime

Most of the analysis in the theoretical finance literature assumes that (a) asymmetric information regime holds and that (b) this is characterised either by adverse selection and/or by moral hazard. An implication of this theory is that

26. Financial additivity occurs if the funds provided by LGS would not have been provided by other private sector financial institutions. Economic additivity occurs if the output from projects financed by LGS does not 'crowd out' private sector output.

collateral is used only under a regime of *asymmetric* information[27]. This in turn makes the test for the information regime impossible since in practice collateral usage is pervasive. Thus, in order to test for the regime type we need a theory in which collateral can play a role even under *symmetric* information. In Toivanen and Cressy (2000) the first test of the information regime underlying the credit market was made. We allowed for the possibility that collateral might play a role in either a symmetric or an asymmetric regime. We also allowed for the role of market power in determining contract characteristics alongside information asymmetry, a feature of real-world markets largely rejected since the beginning of the information revolution.

So what were the results? Using a critical test for the information regime as to whether the probability of bankruptcy is exogenous (symmetric info) or endogenous (asymmetric info), and a measure of relative bargaining strength to measure monopoly power of firm and bank, we found that (a) the regime is indeed asymmetric information rather than symmetric; but (b) the dominant form is moral hazard rather than adverse selection; and finally that (c) monopoly power plays a significant role in the division of the surplus produced by the project with the bank taking the lion's share. The role of collateral is thus primarily shown to be one of creating incentives amongst borrowers to put in effort to their projects, since collateral is lost in the event of default. By contrast its role as a mechanism to avoid dissembling by the poor quality borrowers was found to be negligible. The conclusion from the analysis is simple: government should pay more attention to the problems of monopoly power in lending relationships rather than to informational asymmetry, particularly to the role of adverse selection a la Stiglitz and Weiss. Government attention was indeed directed to the monopoly power of the banks in the Cruickshank report (HM Treasury, 2000).

18. Conclusion

Are there credit constraints on small businesses in the real world? Is credit rationing an important phenomenon? These questions can only be answered, the above discussion suggests, by a detailed *empirical* examination of the characteristics of firms, the sectors of the economy in which they operate, the specific the time period or part of the macro cycle in question and the nature of the information regime in which all this is embedded. It seems a tall order! Theories of rationing are often abstract constructs based on questionable assumptions and theories that are difficult to test empirically. So we cannot

27. Symmetric information combined with deadweight loss from bankruptcy (deadweight is a loss to both parties to the contract) is enough to ensure that the parties to the credit contract bargain collateral down to zero. This is because the firm values the marginal unit of collateral higher than the bank for all positive levels of collateral. By contrast their valuation of interest payments is the same. In consequence the firm will bribe the bank to substitute interest payments for collateral until the latter is reduced to zero.

always rely on theories to provide the guide to policy. For my own part, the empirical results that seem to me convincing rely less on theory for justification than straightforward questioning of participants together with cross-checks from other sources. By and large, these kinds of studies suggest that credit constraints are not a widespread phenomenon and that effective government intervention in the small minority of cases where it may exist is cheap and effective. Therefore despite the mountain of theoretical literature suggesting the abstract possibility of credit constraints, it does not appear in general to be an important empirical phenomenon. Often the major issue is rather the competitiveness of the banking system and the amount of information on the profitability of small business lending *to banks*. Some personal experience is instructive here. In a recent conference held in Zagreb, former Yugoslavia, which focussed on the role of loan and mutual guarantee schemes in former Eastern Bloc countries, it became clear that in many of the countries present there was a dominant oligopoly in the banking system which preferred to concentrate on large international firms rather than small local ones. The banks therefore had little awareness of the potential market for loans to their entrepreneurial firms – a market long exploited by the Western banks. Part of the problem was clearly the issue of the availability of collateral, and the solution to which as we have seen might have been the introduction of loan or mutual guarantee schemes. But what really lay at the root of the problem was ignorance of the big banks of small firms and the restrictive practices of banking oligopolies that made them complacent about addressing the sme market[28]. Banking information and reform was therefore in my view the first priority and without it these governments would be simply 'rearranging the deckchairs on the Titanic'.

28. Even large Western European banks with many years dealing with the small business sector may be unsure of the profitability of small firms to the bank. To find an answer to this question was one of the objectives of the Startup Tracking Exercise, embarked on in 1990. The conclusion was positive!

Reading: Financial Structure

Brealey, Richard, Stuart Myers, (2003), *Principles of Corporate Finance (7th Edition)*, McGraw-Hill.
Cosh, Andy and Alan Hughes, (1994) "Size, financial structure and profitability", in Hughes and Storey, eds, *Financing small firms*, Routledge, 1994.
Cressy, Robert and Christer Olofsson, (1997) "European SME financing: An overview", *Small Business Economics 9,87-96, 1997.*
Toivanen, Otto and Robert Cressy, (2000), "Lazy firms or dominant banks? An analysis of the UK market for SME loans" (summary version only), *Venture Capital: Special Issue.*

Reading: Financial Constraints

Aston Business School, (1990), *Constraints on the Growth of Small Firms,* Department of Trade and Industry, UK.
Berger A. & Udell G. (1998) The economics of small business finance: The roles of private equity and debt markets in the financial growth cycle; *Journal of Banking and Finance*; 22; pp. 613-673.
Burke, A. E., FitzRoy, F. R. and Nolan, M.A. (2000), When Less is More: Distinguishing between Entrepreneurial Choice and Performance. *Oxford Bulletin of Economics and Statistics*, 62(5): 565-587.
Chan, Yuk-shee, and Anjan V. Thakor, (1987) Collateral and Competitive Equilibria with Moral Hazard and Private Information, *Journal of Finance XLII, No. 2, June.*
Cressy, Robert C., (1993), *The Startup Tracking Exercise: Third Year Report*, prepared for National Westminster Bank of Great Britain, November.
Cressy, Robert and David Storey, (1994), *New firms and their bank*, National Westminster Bank of Great Britain.
Cressy, Robert and Otto Toivanen, (2001), "Lazy firms or dominant banks? An analysis of the UK market for SME loans", *Venture Capital: Special Issue.*
Cressy, Robert (Ed.), (2002), "Funding Gaps: A symposium", *The Economic Journal, February*
Cressy, Robert, (1996), "Are business startups debt-rationed?", *The Economic Journal 106 (September), 1253-1270.*
Cressy, Robert C., (2003a), "Why do most firms die young?", *Small Business Economics* (forthcoming).
Cressy, Robert, (2003b), Upper bounds to random credit rationing frequency from the Startup Tracking Exercise dataset, *Note*, Cass Business School, London.
de Meza, David and David Webb, (1987), Too Much Investment: A Problem of Asymmetric Information, *Quarterly Journal of Economics*, 102, 281-292.
Evans, David and Boyan Jovanovic. (1989). "An Estimated Model of Entrepreneurial Choice Under Liquidity Constraints." *Journal of Political Economy 97,4*: 808-827.
Small Business Research Centre, (1998), *The State of British Enterprise: Growth, Innovation and Competitive Advantage in Small and Medium-sized Firms,* Department of Economics, University of Cambridge.
Stiglitz Joseph E and Andrew Weiss, (1981), Credit Rationing in Markets with Imperfect Information, *American Economic Review* 71,3, 393-410.

Reading: Alternative Explanations

Cressy, Robert, (1995), Borrowing and Control: A Theory of Business Types, *Small Business Economics* 7: 1-10.
Cressy, Robert, (1998), Credit rationing or risk aversion? An alternative explanation for the Evans-Jovanovic finding, *Economics Letters*.
Guiso, Luigi and Monica Paiella, (1999) "Risk aversion, wealth and background risk", *Manuscript*, Birkbeck College, London, 1999.

Reading: Government Intervention

Cowling, Marc and Peter Mitchell, (1996), *A Review of the Loan Guarantee Scheme*, Warwick Business School, Occasional Paper.

National Economic Research Associates (NERA), (1989), *An Evaluation of the Loan Guarantee Scheme*, Research Paper No. 74, Department of Employment, 1990.

Treasury, HM, (2000), Competition in UK Banking: A report to the Chancellor of the Exchequer, by Donald Cruickshank, March (This report can be downloaded from: http://www.hmTreasury.gov.uk/documents/financial_services/banking/bankreview/fin_bank_reviewfinal.cfm) .

10. A Comparative Overview of Venture Capital in Europe and the United States

Andrea Schertler [1]
Kiel Institute for World Economics

Abstract. This paper gives a comparative overview of venture capital in Europe and in the United States. A comparison of aggregated data, which is afflicted with several difficulties, and a comparison of studies using micro data shows a couple of interesting differences and similarities between the European private equity market and the US venture capital market. The two markets are different with respect to the level and specialization of investments. The United States invested more venture capital per capita than Europe. Of each unit invested, Europe spent a larger part in firms' early stages than the United States. The two markets are similar with respect to control mechanisms used, such as incentive-enhancing compensation of fund managers, syndication of investments, and the use of convertible securities albeit the intensities of using these mechanisms differ between the United States and Europe. This paper does not only identify differences and similarities between the two markets but it also discusses several explanations for the existing differences and similarities.

Keywords: venture capital, private equity, market structure, Europe, United States.

1. Introduction

During the 1990s, venture capital activity in Europe experienced an extraordinary increase. In 1993, the investments in young firms amounted to 0.2 billion euros, while in 1999 more than 2.5 billion euros were invested in such firms. This boost raises the question whether the European venture capital market developed along the same lines as the US venture capital market, which is the prototype of venture capital finance. This paper offers a comprehensive description and comparison of the developments in the European and US venture capital markets that is the first step in determining whether the European market is similar to the US market in terms of its efficiency of providing funding for high-technology firms.

Venture capital is often referred to as a prerequisite for productivity and employment growth. In line with the American tradition, venture capital is understood as offering financial means to young high-technology firms in combination with management support for these firms by an experienced

1. Financial support from the European Union, DG Research in the context of the research project *European Integration, Financial Systems and Corporate Performance* is gratefully acknowledged. The author would like to thank an anonymous referee and Andrew Burke for most helpful comments on an earlier version. All errors and inaccuracies are solely in my own responsibility.

This article was originally published in the International Journal of Entrepreneurship Education 1(4): pp. 539-584.

intermediary, the venture capitalist. The role of venture capital in facilitating employment and productivity growth has made venture capital a major target of financial market policies by European governments. European governments have made a variety of attempts to ease the access to equity capital for young high-technology firms by improving the regulatory conditions venture capitalists face and by granting rather generous subsidies.

In order to identify differences and similarities between the US and the European venture capital markets, this paper discusses all parts of the venture capital cycle: fundraising, investment, and divestment. Focusing solely on venture capitalists' investment behaviour would be misleading since the investment behaviour depends in turn on fundraising and divestment opportunities. In particular, venture capitalists may have higher incentives to invest in high-technology firms when they can use liquid stock markets for divestment or when they can use government money for new fundraising. In addition, capital providers, such as banks and pension funds, can substantially affect venture capitalists' investment and divestment behaviour.

A comparison of aggregated data on fundraising, investment, and divestment activities will indicate that the US venture capital market and the European market differ with respect to several characteristics. With respect to fundraising, pension funds were the main capital provider to venture capital funds in the United States, but not in Europe. Only in the middle of the 1990s, did the importance of pension funds as capital provider for venture capital in Europe rise. With respect to investment, US venture capital per capita was much higher than in Europe. But European investments were more specialized in firms' early stages of development than US investments. With respect to divestment, US venture capitalists exit from their participation via stock markets in comparison to trade sales more often than their European counterparts. Differences identified on the basis of aggregated data must be handled with care since statistics are not standardized. In particular, for Europe, only data on general private equity activity are available which covers equity investments in all kinds of firms and not only data on venture capital more narrowly defined. As an approximation of aggregated venture capital activity, private equity investments without buy-outs and private equity investments in firms' earliest development stages can be utilized. However, statements about European fundraising activity are always based on private equity in general.

In order to gain deeper insights into the differences and similarities between the US and the European venture capital markets, I will survey recent studies that analyse the US, the British, the German, and the French markets. While the number of studies analysing the different aspects of the venture capital cycle is large for the United States, it is very small for the European countries. Nevertheless some studies exist that can be used to identify differences and similarities between the US and the European market. These studies indicate that for example US venture capitalists differ from their European counterparts with respect to the intensity of syndication. US venture capitalists more often syndicate their deals and they have more partners when syndicating their investments than their European counterparts. However, US venture capitalists and European private equity investors have several similarities with respect to their age, and the number of firms in their portfolios for example.

The remainder of this paper is divided into five sections. Section two is concerned with venture capitalists' fundraising. In this section, I will not only present aggregated data on fundraising activity in the United States and Europe, but also information on the organizational forms of venture capital companies and compensation systems of venture capitalists, i.e., managers of venture capital companies. Section three deals with venture capitalists' investment behaviour. In this section, I will present aggregated US and European investment figures, I will offer information on the control mechanisms used in the relationship between venture capitalists and the portfolio firms such as convertible securities and the staging of capital infusion, and I will discuss portfolio strategies such as specialization and syndication. Section four discusses venture capital divestment. In this section, I will discuss divestment channels such as trade sales and initial public offerings, and I will offer information on venture capitalists' divestment behaviour and the returns for capital providers. Section five summarizes the main results.

2. Fundraising: the Relationship between Venture Capitalists and Capital Providers

2.1. Aggregated Fundraising Figures

In the United States, venture capital activity has experienced a considerable boom in recent years. In 1990, only 375 venture capital companies were in existence, which managed 734 funds, employed 3,794 professional managers, and financed 1,317 firms. By contrast, in 2000, 693 venture capital companies were in existence, which managed 1,443 funds, employed 8,313 professional managers, and financed 5,412 firms (NVCA 2001). Thus, the average number of firms per professional manager increased from 0.35 in 1990 to 0.65 in 2000.

In Europe, the number of private equity investors has increased in some countries, while in others it has remained constant. In France, 575 venture capital executives that financed 1,654 firms were in existence in 1994. By contrast, in 2001, only 501 private equity executives financed 1,926 firms. In the United Kingdom, the number of private equity executives increased from 693 in 1994 to about 1,722 in 2000. At the same time, the number of private-equity-backed firms increased slightly from 1,954 in 1994 to 2,054 in 2000. In Germany, the number of private equity executives was 340, and the number of private-equity-backed firms was 740 in 1994. In 2001, 1,364 private equity executives financed 1,969 firms. In 2001, German private equity executives had much more time to monitor the progress of the firms in their portfolios than seven years ago. In terms of private equity executives, the German private equity market grew at a higher rate than the British and the French market.

The volume of new funds raised for venture capital and private equity investments increased substantially in the observation period in the United States and in Europe. In the United States, new funds raised for venture capital increased from about three billion euros at the beginning of the 1900s to about 45 billion euros in 2001 (Table 1 opposite). In Europe, new funds raised for private equity increased from about four billion euros at the beginning of the 1990s to about 38 billion euros in 2001. During the 1990s, venture capital markets in the United States and in Europe were affected substantially by the over-valuation of high-technology shares. In the United States, new funds raised for venture capital accounted for more than 55 billion euros in 1999 and even more than 113 billion euros in 2000. In Europe, new funds raised accounted for about 25 billion euros in 1999 and 47 billion euros in 2000. Thus, the increase during the bubble time was stronger in the United States than in Europe.

In order to give an impression of the relative size of the two markets, Table 1 opposite shows US new funds raised for private equity per capita in addition to new funds raised for venture capital per capita. Comparing new funds raised for private equity per capita in the United States with the respective figures in Europe shows that the US market is much larger than the European market for private equity. In particular, in the United States, new funds raised for private equity per capita increased from about 25 euros in 1991 to about 446 euros in 2001, while in Europe new funds raised per capita increased from only 11 euros in 1991 to about 97 euros in 2001.

Table 1: Source of New Funds

	1991	1992	1993	1994	1995	1996	1997	1998	1999	2000	2001
United States											
Billion euros											
Euros per capita											
Venture capital	1.5	3.9	3.2	6.6	7.6	9.8	15.5	27.4	55.2	113.6	45.0
	6	*16*	*13*	*25*	*29*	*37*	*58*	*101*	*202*	*412*	*162*
Private equity	6.3	14.4	19.4	28.4	33.4	44.2	67.2	101.5	132.5	229.1	123.8
	25	*57*	*75*	*109*	*127*	*167*	*251*	*375*	*485*	*832*	*446*
Per cent of new funds raised for venture capital											
Corporations	4.8	3.7	8.2	9.3	4.6	19.9	25.2	11.9	14.2	3.7	2.6
Endowments and foundations	27.4	21.2	11.9	21.9	20.3	11.9	16.6	6.3	17.2	21.1	21.8
Individuals and families	13.4	12.1	7.4	12.2	16.7	6.8	12.5	11.3	9.6	11.8	9.4
Financial and insurance	5.9	17.3	11.6	9.7	20.0	3.1	6.3	10.3	15.5	23.3	24.5
Pension funds	48.4	45.6	60.8	46.9	38.4	58.3	39.5	60.1	43.5	40.1	41.7
Europe											
Billion euros											
Euros per capita											
Private equity	4.2	4.2	3.4	6.7	4.4	8.0	20.0	20.3	25.4	47.2	38.0
	11	*11*	*9*	*18*	*11*	*21*	*52*	*52*	*65*	*121*	*97*
Per cent of new funds raised for private equity											
Corporate investors	5.1	5.1	5.3	10.2	4.9	3.5	11.3	9.8	9.5	10.1	5.5
Private individuals	4.7	4.7	3.1	2.7	3.4	7.4	4.0	7.6	6.2	6.7	6.3
Government agencies	1.6	1.6	6.5	2.7	3.1	2.3	2.2	5.1	4.7	5.1	5.7
Banks	36.2	36.2	30.0	28.4	25.6	29.8	25.8	27.8	29.1	19.4	22.8
Pension funds	14.6	14.6	15.7	19.7	27.3	22.7	25.0	24.0	18.7	22.4	25.8
Insurance companies	11.3	11.3	10.0	12.2	10.8	11.3	16.4	8.9	13.2	11.9	12.2

Note: Europe includes Austria, Belgium, Denmark, Finland, France, Germany, Greece, Iceland, Ireland, Italy, the Netherlands, Norway, Portugal, Spain, Sweden, Switzerland, and the United Kingdom.

Source: European new funds raised and exchange rates are from EVCA 1991-2001, US new funds raised are from NVCA (2002).

The difference in the amounts of new funds raised for private equity between the United States and Europe and the difference in the amounts of venture capital, can be caused by several factors that affect the venture capital demand and/or the venture capital supply. Factors affecting the venture capital demand are discussed in Section 3. Factors affecting the venture capital supply are those that affect the risk-return relationship of venture capital investments in comparison to alternative investments. The risk-return relationship is decisive for capital providers' portfolio decisions. The tax system is expected to have a significant impact on the capital providers' portfolio decisions since it can favour particular forms of investments. For example, outside investors have lower incentives to invest in venture capital funds and higher incentives to invest in bonds when losses made with venture capital investments are not tax deductible. In addition, the risk-return relationship of venture capital investments depends on several pieces of legislation and regulations especially regarding shareholder rights. For example, better anti-director rights, are expected to have a positive effect on returns on equity investments and, thus, on venture capital investments, and a negative effect on risks of these investments since they protect shareholders. Accounting standards are expected to have similar effects than anti-director rights since they reduce transaction costs arising when investors gather information. The better accounting standards are, the easier and cheaper it is to get information about a particular firm.

Differences in venture capital activity may be the result of differences in the financial architecture of the economies. In many European countries, banks are the major players, while, in the United States, shareholders play an important role. Banks seem to have many disadvantages with respect to financing young high-technology firms especially because the control mechanisms of banks do not work well in the case of these firms. High-technology firms that invest a large part of their capital into research and development activities cannot offer collateral. Thus, collateral is not at bank's disposal as a selection mechanism. Additionally, bank managers are less likely to have enough experience to select the most promising high-technology firms.

In addition, only few European countries have large pension funds which seek investment opportunities with a promising risk-return relationship as carried out by US pension funds. Using panel data technique, Jeng and Wells (2000) identify pension funds as a driving factor of new funds raised over time. However, in their analysis, pension fund activity does not explain the differences in new funds raised across countries.

The difference in the importance of large financial players between the United States and Europe is reflected in the structure of capital providers that offered new funds for venture capital and private equity (Table 1). In the United States, pension funds have been the most important capital provider to venture capital funds organized as limited partnerships, while corporations and financial and insurance companies have played a minor role. Pension funds contributed between 38 and 60 per cent of the new funds raised for venture capital between 1991 and 2001. All other types of limited partners, such as financial and insurance corporations, did not contribute more than 20 per cent of the total new funds raised in most years.

The European private equity market differs from the US venture capital market with respect to importance of capital providers. In Europe, banks have contributed large amounts of capital for private equity investments. But, in recent years, the role of pension funds, measured as a percentage of the new funds raised for private equity investments, has increased significantly, while the role of banks has decreased considerably. The significance of other investor groups, such as individuals, corporate investors, and insurance companies varied little during the observation period.

The importance of banks and pension funds as capital providers for private equity differs considerably between the European countries. In Germany, for example, banks contributed as much as 50 per cent of the new funds raised for private equity at the beginning of the 1990s. Only at the end of the 1990s did the share of new funds provided by banks decrease, while the share provided by pension funds increased considerably. The French private equity market is also dominated by banks like the German market. By contrast, the British private equity market is the only European market in which pension funds have continuously provided large amounts of capital.

2.2. Organizational Form

The US and the European market differs with respect to the legal status of venture capital and private equity investors. While the data on the US venture capital market presented in Table 1 mostly cover independent venture capitalists, the data on the European private equity markets also cover dependent equity investors. Independent equity investors have to raise capital in financial markets, while dependent equity investors are legally connected to their capital providers. European independent equity investors comprise investors that invest money without supporting the firms' management teams, and venture capitalists that offer management support in addition to financial means. Dependent equity investors comprise public equity investors, subsidiaries of private banks or savings banks, and corporate equity investors. Public equity investors are controlled mainly by public authorities and are often non-profit oriented. Subsidiaries of private banks rely on funds provided by private banks. Subsidiaries of savings banks can be funded either by savings banks and/or cooperative banks. These private equity investors are distinguished from private banks because they promote firms in the region in which they operate (Kulicke 2001). Corporate equity investors receive their funds from large corporations.

European countries do not show a clear pattern with respect to the importance of dependent and independent private equity investors. Independent private equity investors have dominated the British market: independent private equity investors raised about 77 per cent of new funds in 2000. By contrast, dependent private equity investors have dominated the French market. The share of new funds raised by independent private equity investors was as low as 24 per cent in 1997. However, the share has increased substantially in recent years and reached almost 70 per cent in 2001. For Germany, data on new funds raised by types of private equity investors are only available for the years after 1998. In 1999, independent private equity investors raised about 60 per cent of the new funds. Since German independent private equity investors are comparatively young compared to subsidiaries of banks and subsidiaries of savings banks (Schertler 2001), one can argue that the importance of independent equity investors has not only increased in France but also in Germany.

In Germany, the predominant organizational form of private equity funds has changed from unlimited open funds (so-called evergreens) to limited closed funds in the last years. At the beginning of the 1990s, private equity funds were often organized as funds without specified time frames or volumes, while at the end of the 1990s, more than 60 per cent of the new funds raised were raised by closed funds (BVK 2000). The cause of this is not a change in the behaviour of the private equity investors already acting in the market at the beginning of the 1990s, but a large number of young and independent equity investors that entered the market at the end of the 1990s and refinanced themselves with closed funds (Bascha and Walz 2001b).

In the United States and the United Kingdom, organizations infusing venture capital are typically organized as limited partnerships (Lerner 1995, Barnes and McCarthy 2002). In a limited partnership, the general partner (the venture capitalist) is independent of his limited partners (his capital providers). Institutional investors find these limited partnerships attractive, since taxes are paid only by the (taxable) investors but not by the limited partnership (Gompers and Lerner 1998b). Thus, the organizational form of the relationship between venture capitalists and their capital providers is affected significantly by legal and tax rules. Limited partnerships have to fulfil several legal constraints. They must have a pre-determined, finite lifetime (usually ten years). Participation of limited partners in the active management is forbidden, and the transfer of limited partnerships' shares is restricted (Sahlman 1990). At the end of the lifetime, the general partner (the venture capitalist) typically distributes the shares to his limited partners (his capital providers).

The limited partnerships seem to have some advantages over other organizational forms. One advantage might be the independence of the general partners (venture capitalists) from the limited partners (capital providers). Capital providers of independent venture capitalists do not impose restrictions regarding venture capitalists' investment strategies as their dependent counterparts do. This independence seems to be important to make sure that the market conditions and the profit expectations of venture capitalists are the only driving force for venture capitalists' specialization of investments at particular stages and/or in particular technologies which change when market conditions change. Another advantage might be the limited and pre-specified lifetime of the funds, since it can protect the limited partners from the possibility that the general partner could decide against their interests (Sahlman 1990). In addition, as Brouwer and Hendrix (1998) argue, the limited and pre-specified lifetime of funds seems to make it easier for venture capitalists to invest in start-up firms and to exit from their investments in time.

However, the limited and pre-specified lifetime of the funds may also give venture capitalists incentives to abandon projects too early and to select only firms from which they can exit in time. Furthermore, it must be kept in mind that venture capitalists, when organized in a limited partnership, are not only interested in the performance of the firms in their portfolios but also in raising new funds. Gifford (1997) shows in a theoretical model that venture capitalists spend less time on management support in the firm than would be optimal from the entrepreneurs' point of view, as well as from the capital providers' point of view, since venture capitalists need time to raise new funds. By contrast, dependent venture capitalists can concentrate exclusively on supporting the management of the firms in their portfolios.

The evidence found by Gompers and Lerner (1996) indicates that US limited partnerships are affected by changes in the intensity of competition for funds: the general partners have more negotiation power when the supply of venture capital by limited partners increases. In their regression analysis, the growth rate in the venture pool in the year in which the fund is closed to new limited partners (as an approximation of the change in the venture capital supply) negatively affects the number of covenant classes in the contracts between limited and general partners, since the availability of experienced venture capitalists is fixed in the short-term.

2.3. Compensation System

The compensation system of venture capitalists who are general partners in a limited partnership has two components. Venture capitalists participate in profits of the venture capital funds and they receive a fixed management fee. This compensation system can be interpreted as a mechanism that capital providers utilize to offer venture capitalists strong incentives to carefully monitor and support the portfolio firms after the contract between venture capitalists and the capital providers has been signed. This is necessary because capital providers cannot monitor whether venture capitalists fulfil their management support and monitoring function in the portfolio firms or whether they waste their time.

Venture capitalists who are general partners in a limited partnership receive an annual management fee of usually around 2.5 per cent of the capital committed (Sahlman 1990). Moreover, they receive a part of any realized gains of the fund, the so-called carried interest. 90 per cent of the European private equity funds analysed by Feinendegen et al. (2002) receive 20 per cent of the realized gains of the funds. In the United States, about 80 per cent of the venture capitalists receive 20 per cent of the realized gains, 15 per cent receive 25 per cent of the realized gains, and 5 per cent receive even 30 per cent of the realized gains.

In Germany, professional managers of subsidiaries of private banks often do not receive profit participation in addition to their basic salary. As a consequence, these managers have different incentives to support the management teams and to monitor the development of the firms in which they invest than their independent counterparts (Zemke 1995).

Some evidence exists indicating a learning process in the US venture capital market. This learning process can also be at work in European countries. In particular, the study by Gompers and Lerner (1999) shows that young venture capitalists' compensation depends less strongly on the performance of the funds than the compensation of older venture capitalists. The compensation of young venture capitalists, who have managed few funds and funds with small capital amounts, contains a higher basic fee than the compensation of older venture capitalists. Since Gompers and Lerner (1999) do not find a significant relation between performance and incentive compensation, they argue that the relationship between venture capitalists and capital providers can be explained by a learning model. Young venture capitalists do not need incentive-enhancing compensation because they have sufficient incentives to perform well since they have to build a reputation. The study by Gompers and Lerner (1998b) shows that the age of the venture capital company has a significantly positive impact on the volume of funds raised. Thus, those venture capitalists who have just started their career as active financial intermediaries have comparatively low volumes of funds.

Two explanations for young venture capitalists' low volumes of funds are possible. First, young venture capitalists raise only small volumes even if they can raise more funds at the same price because they find themselves not capable of managing larger funds (one reason for this might be that they do not have experienced staff). In this case, they think they lack or they actually do lack the experience important to finance high-technology firms successfully. Second, they raise only small volumes because they do not receive more funds from capital providers or they receive additional funds only at a much higher price. In this case, young venture capitalists do not lack experience but they lack reputation important to raise new funds from uninformed capital providers at favourable conditions. After some success stories of firms backed by the respective young venture capitalist, capital providers start to believe in the capabilities of the venture capitalist and offer capital at more favourable conditions.

3. Investment: the Relationship between Venture Capitalists and Entrepreneurs

3.1. Aggregated Investment Figures

3.1.1. Investment Levels

In the United States, the recent upswing in venture capital investments started in 1995. As Table 2 below indicates, the venture capital investments accounted for about three billion euros in 1994, while they accounted for more than five billion euros in 1995. However, this increase was rather moderate compared to the increase at the end of the 1990s. In 1998, venture capital investments accounted for more than 19 billion euros, in 1999 venture capital investments exceeded 51 billion euros, and in 2000 they reached about 115 billion euros. This upswing changed the US venture capital model. At the end of the 1990s, there were not only venture capitalists who offered management support in addition to financial means but also 'venture capitalists' who had a get-rich-quick mentality (Evans 2001). As the fundraising activity, venture capital investments dropped sharply after the bursting of the stock market bubble in 2000. In 2001, venture capital investments accounted for 45 billion euros, which is low compared to the investment level of the year 2000 but high compared to the investment levels of the beginning of the 1990s.

The upswing on the European private equity markets took place in a temporally retarded manner when compared to the US venture capital market. As Table 2 indicates, the private equity investments accounted for about five billion euros at the beginning of the 1990s. The European market started to grow between 1996 and 1997, in which the private equity investments increased by more than 40 per cent to about 10 billion euros. After that, investments increased substantially until 2000. However, the growth rate of private equity investments between 1998 and 2000 was lower than the respective rate of US venture capital investments. While European private equity investments grew at a rate of 1.4, US venture capital investments grew at a rate of 5.0. European private equity investments in 2001 are rather low in comparison to the investments in 2000. But they are as high as the private equity investments in 1999.

Table 2: Investment Disbursement by Stages and Technologies

	1991	1992	1993	1994	1995	1996	1997	1998	1999	2000	2001
United States Billion euros *Euros per capita*											
Venture capital	1.8	2.6	3.8	3.3	5.6	9.4	14.2	19.1	51.1	114.7	45.4
	7	*10*	*15*	*13*	*21*	*35*	*53*	*71*	*187*	*417*	*163*
Per cent of venture capital											
Early	35.9	32.2	49.5	41.1	43.1	42.9	30.2	34.0	28.3	27.4	24.9
Expansion	46.8	50.4	38.3	34.8	41.7	42.8	50.9	50.5	55.6	57.6	56.7
Later	17.3	17.4	12.2	24.1	15.2	14.3	18.9	15.5	16.0	15.0	18.5
Information and communication	40.2	36.7	50.6	40.7	40.2	42.1	44.0	47.0	49.0	57.4	59.3
Biotechnology and medical	25.9	34.2	22.7	28.5	25.3	23.3	26.9	16.7	8.0	6.9	14.1
Europe Billion euros *Euros per capita*											
Private equity	4.6	4.7	4.1	5.4	5.5	6.8	9.7	14.5	25.1	34.6	24.0
	12	*12*	*11*	*14*	*14*	*18*	*25*	*37*	*65*	*89*	*61*
Private equity without buy-outs	3.0	3.1	2.4	3.0	3.0	3.6	4.8	7.1	11.8	20.2	12.2
	8	*8*	*6*	*8*	*8*	*9*	*12*	*18*	*30*	*52*	*31*
Per cent of private equity *Per cent of private equity without buy-out*											
Early	6.9	6.9	4.9	5.7	5.8	6.5	7.4	11.4	12.9	19.1	17.2
	10.6	*10.5*	*8.4*	*10.3*	*10.6*	*12.3*	*15.0*	*23.3*	*27.4*	*32.7*	*33.8*
Expansion	52.6	52.6	45.9	42.2	41.4	40.0	35.0	30.0	29.6	36.7	32.9
	80.7	*79.7*	*78.4*	*76.0*	*75.9*	*75.6*	*70.7*	*61.3*	*63.0*	*62.9*	*64.7*
Replacement	5.9	5.9	8.4	8.0	6.4	7.1	7.6	7.5	4.7	2.6	4.8
	9.0	*9.0*	*14.4*	*14.4*	*11.7*	*13.4*	*15.4*	*15.3*	*10.0*	*4.5*	*9.4*
Buy-out	34.6	34.6	40.8	44.1	46.4	46.4	50.1	51.2	52.8	41.6	45.1
	-	-	-	-	-	-	-	-	-	-	-
Information and communication	10.5	10.7	10.8	10.4	16.2	13.6	16.9	20.8	24.5	30.6	28.3
	16.1	*16.2*	*18.5*	*18.7*	*29.7*	*25.7*	*34.2*	*42.5*	*52.1*	*52.4*	*55.7*
Biotechnology and medical	5.7	5.3	5.9	5.0	7.6	6.3	6.9	7.1	6.6	10.9	10.3
	8.7	*8.0*	*10.1*	*9.0*	*13.9*	*11.9*	*13.9*	*14.5*	*14.0*	*18.7*	*20.3*

Note: Europe includes Austria, Belgium, Denmark, Finland, France, Germany, Greece, Iceland, Ireland, Italy, the Netherlands, Norway, Portugal, Spain, Sweden, Switzerland, and the United Kingdom. Early stages contains the seed and start-up stage. Later stage contains investments in the later stage, bridge financing, and open market activities (NVCA 2002). European *Information and communication* contains investments in communications, computer-related, other electronics-related. US *Information and communication* contains communications, computer software, computer hardware and services.

Source: Investment volumes are from EVCA (various issues), exchange rates are from EVCA (various issues), and US investment volumes are from NVCA (2001).

In order to give an impression of the relative size of the two markets, Table 2 reports European private equity investments without buy-outs per capita as a rough measure comparable to US venture capital investments per capita. Comparing these figures indicates that the US venture capital investments per capita were higher than the European private equity investments without buy-outs per capita except in 1991. While the differences between US venture capital investments per capita and European private equity investments without buy-outs per capita were only moderate at the beginning of the 1990s, they were substantial at the end of the 1990s. In particular, per capita, the United States invested only twice as much as Europe in 1993, while the United States invested about 8 times as much than Europe in 2000.

US venture capital has been used traditionally to finance firms' early[2] and expansion stages of development. At the beginning of the 1990s, US venture capitalists invested about one billion euros in firms' early stages, and another billion in firms' expansion stage. In 2001, by contrast, they invested more than 10 billion euros in firms' early stages, and more than 25 billion euros in firms' expansion stage. These stages of firms' development are of special interest because young high-technology firms are believed to be a prerequisite for productivity and employment growth. In their early stages, firms have not yet established their product markets. Firms in the expansion stage require large amounts of external funding because the cash flow often does not yet generate enough liquidity to finance the firm's growth internally.

Between 1991 and 2001, the absolute amounts of European private equity invested in firms' early stages were lower than US amounts, while the absolute amounts of European private equity invested in firms' expansion stage was sometimes higher. With respect to the early stages, European private equity investors invested about 0.3 billion euros in firms' early stages at the beginning of the 1990s. This amount increased up to 6.6 billion euros in 2000. Thus, in absolute terms, US venture capitalists invested three times as much in firms' early stages at the beginning of the 1990s, and even almost five times as much in 2000. With respect to the expansion stage, European private equity investors invested about 2 billion euros at the beginning of the 1990s. This amount increased up to 12.7 billion euros in 2000. Thus, in absolute terms, European private equity investors invested double as much as US venture capitalists in firms' expansion stage at the beginning of the 1990s, while US venture capitalists invested five times as much as the European private equity investors in this stage in 2000.

What about the relative size of early-stage investments in the United States and in Europe? Figure 1 below depicts the early-stage investments for selected European markets and for the US market as per million of GDP for the years

2. The early stages are the seed and start-up stage. In the seed stage, the initial business concept is formed and prototypes of new products are developed and compared with competing products in the market. In the start-up stage, production is set up and an initial marketing campaign is launched, the market reaction to which is carefully analysed.

1991, 1996, and 2001. Figure 1 shows that early-stage investments increased in all European countries. However, the differences between the European markets and the US market in terms of relative investments in firms' early stages are still substantial. In 2001, only Sweden and Finland realized a level of early-stage investments as per million of GDP that is comparable with the level of the United States. While the United States invested about one per million of its GDP as early-stage venture capital, the United Kingdom and Germany invested less then 0.6 and France less than 0.4 million of their GDPs as early-stage venture capital in 2001.

Figure 1: Early-Stage Investments in the United States and Europe (per million of GDP)

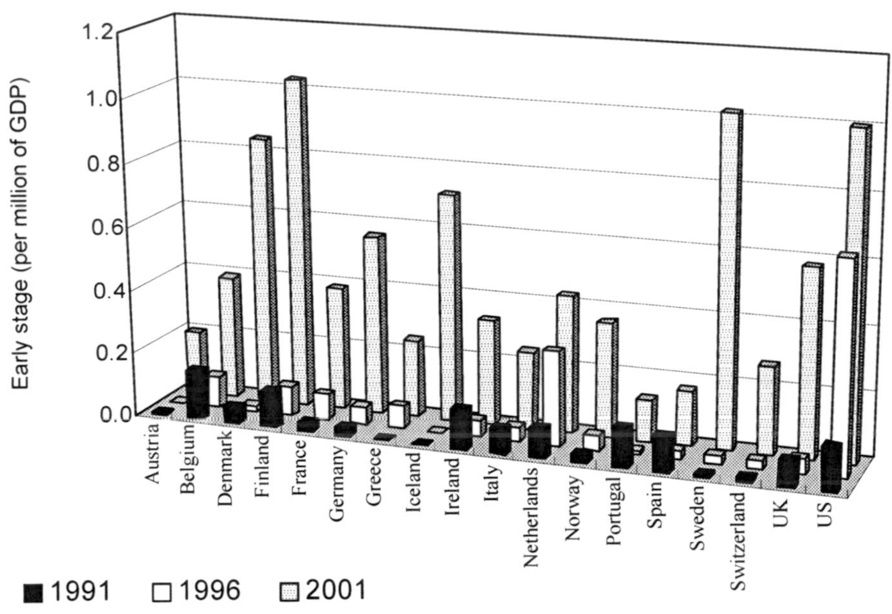

Source: NVCA (2002), EVCA (various issues), and OECD (2002).

3.1.2. Explaining Differences in Investment Levels

How can the difference in venture capital investments be explained? As argued in the last section, differences in private equity and venture capital activity can be caused by factors that affect the venture capital supply, such as individual and corporate taxes and shareholder rights. The difference can also be caused by factors that affect venture capital demand. Venture capital demand by high-technology firms is also affected by individual and corporate taxes, and shareholder rights since they determine individual incentives for entrepreneurship. These incentives also depend on the design of labour markets. The incentives for entrepreneurship are expected to be lower in continental Europe's rigid labour markets than in flexible labour markets. In addition, venture capital demand may depend on human capital endowments of the economies, which determine the number of innovative ideas and, thus, the number of firms that try to realize innovative ideas. Moreover, it may depend on the institutional environment determining the way in which innovative ideas are financed in order to realize them. Unfortunately, no empirical study analyses the impact of the human capital endowments or the innovation system on private equity activity in a cross-country sample. However, one study analyses the impact of the human capital endowments on early-stage investments.

As the study by Schertler (2003) shows, differences in early-stage investments can be explained by the human capital endowments and the availability of liquid stock markets. Using dynamic panel data techniques, she finds evidence that the level of early-stage investments used as a narrow definition of venture capital depends positively on the stock market capitalisation and on the number of research and development employees used as an approximation for the human capital endowments of 14 Western European countries.

The positive impact of the number of research and development employees on early-stage investments can be explained by the specific nature of venture capital. The monitoring and supporting services make venture capital finance expensive compared to other sources of finance. Therefore, demand for venture capital comes only from peculiar firms, such as young high-technology firms, since control mechanisms that can be embedded in standard contracts are not necessarily applicable to these firms. For the development of business ideas in high-technology fields human capital is necessary.

The positive impact of stock markets on venture capital does not only exist for early-stage investments but also for expansion-stage investments as the study by Jeng and Wells (2000) shows. There are three reasons for the positive relationship. First, one can argue that when venture capitalists are exiting from their participations the share price of the respective firm can be determined more efficiently in a stock market sale than in a trade sale to an informed capital provider, such as an established firm in the industry. This is because of the large number of buyers in the case of a stock market sale. Second, as Black and Gilson (1998) argue, stock markets can increase the entrepreneur's incentives since they offer the possibility for venture capitalists and entrepreneurs to enter into an implicit contract over control. Third, stock markets lower the costs for reputation building of venture capitalists and private equity investors. This reputation determines the selling conditions, e.g. the underpricing, of venture-capital-backed firms going public in the future. Reputation in order to determine selling conditions is likewise important for dependent and independent equity investors, while reputation in order to raise new funds at better conditions is mostly important for independent equity investors. In the presence of liquid stock markets, independent equity investors can signal their capabilities and experiences in financing high-technology firms to capital providers at lower costs.

Differences in early-stage investments can also be explained by alternative investment vehicles available. Early-stage investments may differ because of differences in informal venture capital markets, in which the so-called business angels, i.e. wealthy individuals, invest their own financial resources in firms' early stages of development. However, the relationship between formal and informal venture capital markets is not clear from a theoretical point of view. On the one hand, informal venture capital can be a close substitute for formal venture capital investments in firms' early stages. In this case, low levels of early-stage investments may result from high levels of business angel activity. On the other hand, several types of complementarities may exist between informal (business angels) and formal venture capital markets, such as sequential investing and co-investments (Harrison and Mason 2000). In this case, low levels of early-stage investments may result from low levels of business angel activity.

Some of the informal venture capital markets have been analysed in the recent literature. However, estimates can only approximate the volumes of informal venture capital, since official statistics are not available. In the United States, the invested informal venture capital is estimated to be about USD 60 billion annually (Van Osnabrugge and Robinson 2000). In the United Kingdom, the invested informal venture capital is estimated to be of a volume ten times as high as the early-stage investments by formal private equity investors (EBAN 1998). In Germany, 27,000 business angels are thought to be active, with an annual investment volume of about 1.4 billion German marks (Just 2000). Thus, the informal venture capital market in the United States measured in terms of GDP is four times as large as the one in the United Kingdom, which is in turn three times as large as the one in Germany. This is in line with the existence of complementarities between informal and formal venture capital markets so that low levels of business angel activity are associated with low levels of early-stage investments.

Differences in early-stage investments can also be explained by government subsidies. Early-stage investments may differ because national policies in form of subsidies reduce the costs of investments in young high-technology firms. Almost all European governments utilize public policies to improve the capital supply for young, high-technology firms (OECD 1997). European governments try to boost private equity investments in young high-technology firms by utilizing tax incentives for capital providers, by establishing state-owned funds that invest capital in young high-technology firms, and by offering capital at favourable conditions to independent and dependent private equity investors and venture capitalists. When the government refinances private equity investors' participations in high-technology start-ups with loans at favourable interest rates, high-technology start-ups become more attractive for investors compared to other investment possibilities. Therefore, a considerable volume of early-stage investments can be the result of government intervention.

What kinds of public policies have been used in particular countries? The United Kingdom has established tax incentives for private equity investments and has started to offer government equity for small deals (Baygan 2003). In France and Germany, investments are supported using loan and equity guarantees (Dubocage and Rivaud-Danset 2002). Under guarantee schemes, the government covers a share of private equity investors' realized losses. In addition, the French government offers tax incentives for private equity investors who invest a certain percentage of their funds in high-technology start-ups (Dubocage and Rivaud-Danset 2002).

Although European governments have subsidized private equity investments in young high-technology firms, early-stage investments as per million of GDP are lower in European countries than in the United States. This does however not indicate that European subsidies are not successful in promoting early-stage venture capital. In fact, one does not know the US or European equilibrium level of early-stage venture capital given a particular architecture of financial markets, entrepreneurial incentives, individual and corporate taxes, human capital endowments, characteristics of the innovation system and so on. The only thing which can be said is that Europe's subsidies have not been sufficient to catch up with the United States in terms of early-stage investments.

3.1.3. Specialization of Investments

Apart from comparing investment levels, it is interesting to compare the specialization of investments on particular types of firms since this offers information on investments opportunities in venture capital markets. In the United States, investments in firms' expansion stages to total investments increased stronger than the investments in firms' early stages to total investments between 1998 and 2000 (Table 2). The reason for this may be the significant increase in the total capital committed. Greater commitments of capital are in favour of the expansion or later development stages, because firms in these stages are capable of using larger amounts of money than firms in the early stages (Gompers 1998). A boost in the committed capital leads to investments of larger size and not to a larger number of investments. There are two reasons for this. First, individual time constraints lead to a particular number of firms that each venture capitalist can select, monitor and support so that venture capitalists have few incentives to increase the number of firms in their portfolios. Second, the supply of experienced venture capitalists is not very flexible in the short-term (Gompers 1998).

With respect to the share of private equity invested in firms' early stages and expansion stage to total private equity, Europe experienced a different development than the United States. In Europe, the share of private equity invested in firms' early stages increased substantially during the 1990s, while in the United States the share decreased in the second half of the 1990s. In Europe, the share of private equity invested in firms' expansion stage declined between 1991 and 1999, while in the United States the share increased in the second half of the 1990s. To some extent, the decline in Europe's share of expansion-stage investments mirrors the substantial increase of the early-stage investments.

The European and the US shares of early stage investments differed substantially during the 1990s. In 1993, only about 8 per cent of the European private equity without buy-outs was invested in firms' early stages, while the respective number was about 33 (34) per cent in 2000 (2001). By contrast, at the beginning of the 1990s, more than 30 per cent of the US venture capital was invested in firms' early stages, while the respective number was about 27 (25) per cent in 2000 (2001). Thus, at the end of the 1990s, of each unit invested, Europe spent a larger part in firms' early stages than the United States when arguing on the basis of private equity without buy-out activity.

The low European shares of private equity invested in firms' early stages at the beginning of the 1990s are not astonishing because banks were dominant in Europe and banks have several disadvantages with respect to financing young high-technology firms as argued above. But what drove the significant increase in the shares of private equity invested in firms' early stages during the 1990s? The substantial increase in the share can be explained by two developments. First, European governments have started to subsidize early-stage investments more intensively. Thus, early-stage investments have become more profitable in comparison to expansion-stage investments. Second, pension funds as capital providers increased their importance during the 1990s. This may have affected the share of private equity invested in firms' early stages since pension funds provide capital to independent private equity investors who have a higher propensity to invest in firms' early stages than private equity investors who are bank subsidiaries. This explanation holds, however, only if the European private equity market is not a mature market because one expect that higher capital commitments by outside investors in mature markets lead to decreasing early-stage investments and increasing later-stage investments.

Investments are not only specialized in particular stages of development but also in particular technologies. US venture capital investments have been highly specialized in a small number of high-technology industries (Table 2). The share of venture capital invested in firms operating in the information and communication business was always about 40 per cent in the 1990s. After 1996, this share increased significantly and reached about 59 per cent in 2001. Thus, venture capital invested in firms operating in the information and communication business increased in absolute as well as in relative terms. Venture capital investments in biotechnology and medical-related firms, however, increased only in absolute terms but not in relative terms. This investment share decreased from about 27 per cent of the venture capital investments in 1997 to less than seven per cent in 2000.

European private equity investments were not specialized as much in financing information and communication firms as the US venture capital investments were when arguing on the basis of total private equity (Table 2). While the share of venture capital invested in information and communication firms was always at least about 40 per cent in the United States, a share of private equity invested in information and communication firms lower than twenty per cent was not uncommon in Europe. Even at the end of the 1990s, only about 30 per cent of the private equity were invested in information and communication firms.

However, when arguing on the basis of private equity without buy-outs and assuming implicitly that most buy-out investments are not in high-technology industries, then Europe's private equity without buy-outs was as much specialized in financing information and communication firms than US venture capital (Table 2). During the 1990s, the European share of private equity invested in information and communication firms increased from about 16 per cent in 1991 to more than 52 per cent in 1999 and even more than 55 per cent in 2001. Thus, at the beginning of the 1990s, European private equity investments were not specialized as much in particular high-technology industries as the US venture capital investments, while at the end of the 1990s they were when arguing on the basis of private equity without buy-outs.

With respect to the investments in biotechnology and medical-related firms, Europe experienced a different development from the United States at the end of the 1990s. In the United States, venture capital investments in biotechnology and medical-related firms increased only in absolute terms, while the share of investments in these firms to the total investments decreased. In Europe, however, both the absolute volume as well as the share of investments in biotechnology and medical-related firms increased at the end of the 1990s. The increase was so significant that the share of private equity invested in biotechnology and medical-related firms was even larger than the respective share in the United States in 2000.

3.2. Venture Capitalists and Their Portfolio Firms

The relationship between venture capitalists and their portfolio firms has been the focus of many studies. One group of studies examines the value added by venture capitalists, while another group discusses control mechanisms used in the relationship. The question of whether venture capitalists add value to high-technology firms is of particular interest since the answer relates the efficiency of venture capital finance. Discussing control mechanisms, such as soft and contractually specified control mechanisms, is sensible to understand and to explain the differences in venture capital finance across countries.

Although the body of literature addressing soft and contractually specified control mechanisms and the value added by venture capitalists has grown significantly in recent years, studies analysing the European market are still few in number compared to the number of studies for the United States. This is a result of a lack of data availability for European venture capital activity. Because of this, many studies describe only the European market without using large data sets and adequate econometric methods. Table 3 opposite offers some information on these studies using large European or US data sets.

Comparing studies of the US venture capital market and the European private equity market in order to identify similarities and differences is difficult for at least three reasons. First, the number of observations in European data sets is quite often very small and this raises concerns about the robustness of regression results. Second, studies of European markets most often use data from the end of the 1990s, while studies on the US market use different observation periods. This might be a problem because shares of high-technology firms were overvaluated at the end of the 1990s and this over-valuation is expected to have changed the behaviour of US venture capitalists. Third, studies of the European market do not always distinguish between the different types of private equity investors active in Europe. This might lead to non-interpretable results. Let me give an example. Let us assume that control mechanisms such as the staging of capital infusion or entrepreneurs' incentive compensation are not used intensively by private equity investors in a particular country. This observation may be driven by a high proportion of dependent private equity investors in the market. Dependent private equity investors have no incentive to use these control mechanisms if using these mechanisms is costly for them and if they do not participate in the profits of the private equity fund. Thus, observations based on all types of private equity investors are not at all informative and cannot be compared with observations based on particular types of private equity investors.

Table 3: Studies Analysing Soft Control Mechanisms, Contractually Specified Control Mechanisms, and the Value Added by Venture Capitalists

Study	Data Sample	Main Results
Baker and Gompers (1999b)	1,076 IPOs of US firms	♦Insiders' representation on the board of directors decreases with venture-capital-backing and with venture capitalists' reputation. Experienced venture capitalists are more capable of reducing the fraction of insiders on the board of directors than their inexperienced counterparts. ♦The probability of a founder remaining as CEO increases with venture-capital-backing and decreases with venture capitalists' reputation.
Hellmann and Puri (2002)	170 venture-capital- and non-venture-capital-backed Silicon Valley start-ups	♦Venture-capital-backed firms use more often professional contracts to recruit sales and marketing personal and administrative and managerial personnel than their non-venture-capital-backed counterparts. ♦Venture-capital-backing increases the likelihood of adopting stock option plans.
Lerner (1995)	271 venture-capital-backed biotechnology US firms	♦Venture capitalists increase their representation on the board of directors if the CEO is replaced, while other outside investors do not. ♦Venture capitalists' board membership depends on the distance to the firm suggesting significant transaction costs.
Manigart et al. (2002)	73 US, 66 UK, 32 French, 24 Dutch, 14 Belgian venture capital and private equity companies	♦Independent venture capitalists and private equity investors demand significantly higher returns than their dependent counterparts for investments in firms' early and expansion stages. ♦Higher returns are correlated with a higher intensity of venture capitalists' and private equity investors' involvement.
Baker and Gompers (1999a)	1,036 IPOs of US firms	♦CEOs' equity stake and salaries of venture-capital-backed firms are significantly lower than those of their non-venture-capital-backed counterparts. ♦The percentage change in CEOs' wealth for a percentage change in firm value is higher for venture-capital-backed firms than for their non-venture-capital-backed counterparts.
Kaplan and Strömberg (2000)	200 venture capital investments in 118 entrepreneurial firms by 14 venture capital companies	♦Contracts allow venture capitalists to allocate cash-flow rights, voting rights, board rights, liquidation rights separately. ♦Convertible securities are used most frequently. ♦Control rights are often contingent on observable performance measures.
Gompers (1997)	50 US venture capital contracts with convertible preferred equity	♦Convertible securities are converted to common equity if particular milestones are achieved. This is in line with incentive compensation considerations to motivate the entrepreneur. ♦Covenants are used to allocate control rights to venture capitalists that are separated from cash-flow rights.

Study	Data Sample	Main Results
Gompers and Lerner (1998a)	32,364 investments in privately held venture-capital-backed US firms	♦ Corporate venture capitalists tend to invest slightly less frequently in start-up firms compared to their independent counterparts. They prefer investments in the later stages of firms' development and they prefer to invest larger amounts of money per investment deal than independent venture capitalists do. ♦ The group of corporate funds is not homogeneous. Venture capital investments of corporate funds with a strategic focus on a particular technology are significantly more successful than investments of other funds.
Gompers (1995)	794 venture-capital-backed US firms	♦ Firms that go public receive more total financing than other firms and firms in their early stages receive less money per round than firms in their later stages. ♦ An increase in the asset tangibility reduces monitoring intensity and increases financing duration.
Cumming (2002)	179 investment rounds in 132 firms backed by 17 European venture capital companies	♦ Common equity is the financing instrument most often used. ♦ When convertible securities are used as financing instrument, specific contingencies are more likely to be used.
Schwienbacher (2002)	67 US, 19 Dutch and Belgian, 13 French, 23 British, 29 German, and 20 Swedish venture capital companies	♦ European private equity investors use convertible securities three times less often than their US counterparts. ♦ European private equity investors syndicate their investments less often than their US counterparts. ♦ European private equity investors finance less frequently firms' early stages of development than their US counterparts.
Bascha and Walz (2001b)	60 German private equity investor	♦ Germany's private equity investors often use pure equity, and less frequently they use the sort of convertible securities. ♦ 57 per cent of the private equity investors do not use convertible securities at all and 67 per cent do not use debt equity mixes.
Brav and Gompers (1997)	934 US IPOs of venture-capital-backed firms, and 3,407 US IPOs without such backing	♦ Venture-capital-backed firms outperform non-venture-capital-backed ones even after the IPO. Venture-capital-backed firms earned 44.6 per cent after the IPO over five years, while non-venture-capital-backed ones earned only 22.5 per cent on average.
Hellmann and Puri (2000)	173 venture-capital- and non-venture-capital-backed Silicon Valley start-ups	♦ Innovator firms are more likely to obtain venture capital than imitator firms. ♦ High-technology venture-capital-backed firms, especially innovators, bring their products to the market earlier than their non-venture-capital-backed counterparts do.

Study	Data Sample	Main Results
Megginson and Weiss (1991)	320 IPOs of venture-capital-backed US firms are matched with 320 IPOs without such backing	♦ Venture-capital-backing results in lower underpricing and it reduces the underwriting spread charged by the investment banker. ♦ Total costs of going public are lower if venture capitalists are present.
Mull (1990)	340 IPOs of venture-capital-backed US firms are matched with 340 IPOs without such backing	♦ Levels of debt are lower for venture-capital-backed firms than for their non-venture-capital-backed counterparts. ♦ The revenue and total assets of venture-capital-backed firms grow faster than the ones of their non-venture-capital-backed counterparts. ♦ Venture capitalists invest in projects with higher research and development expenses than other investors.
Kortum and Lerner (2000)	US panel data set with industry and time dimension 530 US venture-capital and non-venture-capital-backed firms	♦ Venture-capital-backed firms do patent more than comparable non-venture capital-backed firms. Results suggest that a dollar in form of venture capital stimulates patenting more than a dollar of traditional research and development expenditure. ♦ In order to address measurement problems between patents and innovations, the authors use micro data and find that venture-capital-backed firms do not dilute the economic importance of their patents.
Lerner (1994b)	350 IPOs by venture-capital-backed biotechnology US firms	♦ Experienced venture capitalists are more proficient in timing the IPOs of the firms in their portfolios than less experienced venture capitalists. ♦ Firms backed by experienced venture capitalists are more likely to go public when their valuations are at the maximum than the firms backed by less experienced venture capitalists.
Barry et al (1990)	433 IPOs by venture-capital-backed firms and 1,123 IPOs without such backing in the United States	♦ Venture capitalists' involvement in form of management support affects negatively the degree of underpricing. Proxies for venture capitalists' involvement are: number of calendar months between the IPO and starting date of the lead venture capitalists' board membership, number of calendar years between the IPO and lead venture capitalists' founding year, cumulative number of prior IPOs in which the lead venture capitalist participated.
Franzke (2001)	164 IPOs of venture-capital-backed and non-venture-capital-backed firms on the Neuer Markt	♦ Firms backed by high-ranked private equity investors realized a lower underpricing of their shares than firms backed by low-ranked private equity investors and non-private-equity-backed firms. Underpricing is measured as spread between opening price on the first trading day and initial offering price.
Kraus (2001)	308 firms that went public on the Neuer Markt	♦ When controlling for ex ante uncertainty and underwriter reputation, underpricing does not differ between venture-capital-backed and non-venture-capital-backed firms. ♦ Venture-capital and non-venture capital-backed firms do not differ with respect to risk characteristics and underwriter reputation.

Study	Data Sample	Main Results
Barnes and McCarthy (2002)	85 British firms that went public	♦ Firms backed by young private equity investors are younger at their IPO than those backed by older investors. ♦ Firms backed by young private equity investors do not differ from their counterparts backed by older investors with respect to underpricing and the private equity investors' equity stakes. Young private equity investors do not raise new funds significantly earlier after the date of the IPO than their older counterparts.
Roling (2001)	European panel data with country and time dimension	♦ No significant relationship between the level of private equity investments and the number of patents. ♦ Significant positive relationship between the number of private-equity-backed firms and the number of patents.
Engel (2003)	ZEW panels	♦ Private-equity-backed firms realize higher economic growth than their non-private-equity-backed counterparts. This is the result of the pre-investment screening procedure by private equity investors.
Engel (2002)	ZEW panels	♦ Young private-equity-backed firms realize significantly higher annual growth rates in employment than their non-private-equity-backed counterparts when private-equity and non-private-equity-backed firms are matched.
Audretsch and Lehmann (2002)	341 firms formerly listed on the Neuer Markt	♦ Private-equity-backed firms realized a higher employment growth than their non-private-equity-backed counterparts. ♦ The likelihood and the amount of venture capital is positively related to the board of directors' human capital.

Soft control mechanisms, such as venture capitalists' management support and monitoring, are not only used during the investment process but also when high-technology firms are selected: venture capitalists carefully scrutinize the founders and their business concepts before deciding on an investment (Fried and Hisrich 1994). In order to be actively involved in the firms in their portfolios, venture capitalists need several explicit control rights, such as board and voting rights. With contractually specified control mechanisms, such as incentive compensation of the entrepreneurs, venture capitalists can mitigate several incentive problems after the contract is signed.

With respect to the soft control mechanisms, US venture capitalists provide three critical services to their portfolio firms: venture capitalists build the investor group, review and help to formulate the business strategies, and fill the management teams (Gorman and Sahlman 1989). Lead venture capitalists, who take on the support of the portfolio firms when several venture capitalists invest money, spend on average two hours per week in firms if these firms are in their early stages of development (Gorman and Sahlman 1989). However, the time that the lead venture capitalists spend, on average, in a portfolio firm varies substantially. Elango et al. (1995) report that the most active group in their sample spends more than 35 hours per month per portfolio firm, while the least active group spends less than seven hours. Venture capitalists' active involvement, however, is principally crisis- and project-oriented. They are not involved in the day-to-day management of their portfolio firms.

Soft control mechanisms have an impact on how venture-capital-backed firms are managed. In the United States, venture capital finance results in a reduced number of insiders on the boards of directors (Baker and Gompers 1999b). Thus, the relative importance of venture capitalists on the boards increases since they are classified as outsiders. In addition, stock option plans are more often utilized in venture-capital-backed firms than in non-venture-capital-backed firms (Hellmann and Puri 2002). The view that venture capitalists' active involvement in form of management support is rather crisis-oriented is supported by the empirical study by Lerner (1995), who uses a sample of US biotechnology firms. He finds that the number of venture capitalists on the board of directors increases significantly in situations where monitoring is most important, for example, around the time when the Chief Executive Officer (CEO) leaves the firm.

What about soft control mechanisms used by European private equity investors? In Germany, for example, private equity investors differ with respect to the intensity of management support. Especially, Germany's Mittelständische Beteiligungsgesellschaften (MBGs) often do not offer consulting services that go beyond traditional arm's-length board activity (Wupperfeld 1994). The subsidiaries of the savings banks generally provide limited management support and monitoring (Kulicke 2001). Subsidiaries of financial institutions are often not capable of evaluating the quality of high-technology firms' ideas. Compared to all other groups of private equity investors, the private equity investors that are independent from capital providers offer a high intensity of support to the firms in their portfolios (Kulicke 1997). In addition, Zemke (1995) finds evidence that independent equity investors have a significantly higher intensity in supporting the management teams than their dependent counterparts when strategic decisions must be made in the firms.

Manigart et al. (2002) find evidence that independent venture capitalists and private equity investors, located in the United States, the United Kingdom, the Netherlands, France and Belgium, demand significantly higher returns than their dependent counterparts for investments in firms' early and expansion stages. These higher returns are correlated with a higher intensity of venture capitalists' and private equity investors' involvement. Thus, the intensity of management support by venture capitalists and private equity investors is higher when they are independent from the capital providers.

With respect to the *contractually specified control mechanisms*, several mechanisms can be distinguished. In particular, US venture capitalists compensate entrepreneurs or managers of venture-capital-backed firms with a compensation system, which is usually tied to the firm performance. Second, US venture capitalists almost exclusively use convertible securities when financing high-technology firms. And, third, venture capitalists invest the required capital in stages and not all at once.

The form of entrepreneurs' compensation system with basic salaries and profit participations can be interpreted as a mechanism that offers the entrepreneurs strong incentives to add their specific technological expertise in the development of the firms after the contract has been signed. Moreover, as Weimerskirch (1998) shows, tying the entrepreneurs' compensation to firm value can be interpreted as a mechanism with which venture capitalists can select the most promising firms, since, given this form of compensation, entrepreneurs do not prefer venture capital finance when their firms have dismal growth prospects.

Entrepreneurs of venture-capital-backed firms receive modest salaries in combination with equity stakes that are typically tied to the performance of the firms (Barry 1994). In the United States, the CEOs' equity stakes and salaries of venture-capital-backed firms are significantly lower than the CEOs' stakes and salaries of non-venture-capital-backed firms (Baker and Gompers 1999a). However, the elasticity of a CEOs' wealth to shareholder wealth, which is defined as the percentage change in a CEOs' wealth for a percentage change in firm value, is higher for CEOs of venture-capital-backed firms than for their counterparts of non-venture-capital-backed firms.

Recent theoretical literature has explained the use of convertible securities in terms of incentive problems (Berglöf (1994), Lülfesmann (2000), Bascha and Walz (2001a), Hellmann (2001)). With convertible securities, entrepreneurs have strong incentives to use their knowledge in the development of the firms since they have all residual claims, at least temporarily, so that entrepreneurs substantially participate in increasing profits but do not benefit from increasing risks (Gompers 1997). In addition, convertible securities provide the venture capitalists with incentives to carefully monitor and support the management teams (Schmidt 2003). Thus, convertible securities can be used in such a way that both contracting parties give the opposite party sufficient incentives to add value after the contract has been signed.

US venture capitalists organized as partnerships most often use convertible securities when financing high-technology firms with the automatic conversion of the convertibles when specific milestones are reached. In the sample analysed by Kaplan and Strömberg (2000) consisting of 200 venture capital financing rounds, convertible preferred stocks are used in 189 cases. Only seven of the 200 venture capital financing rounds are without any convertibles. The sample by Gompers (1997), which contains 50 convertible preferred equity contracts, demonstrates the role of automatic conversion. In this sample, 92 per cent of the convertible preferred equity converts automatically at the time of the initial public offering (IPO).

The available evidence suggests that venture capitalists organized as limited partnerships differ significantly from their dependent counterparts with respect to investment behaviour. US limited partnerships use relatively more preferred equity and invest proportionally more in firms' early stages than corporate venture capital funds (Norton 1994). The empirical study by Gompers and Lerner (1998a) likewise confirms that differences exist between corporate and independent venture capital partnerships. According to their study, corporate venture capitalists tend to invest slightly less frequently in start-up firms. They prefer investments in the later stages of firms' development and they prefer to invest larger amounts of money per investment deal than independent venture capitalists do.

The last contractually specified control mechanism to be discussed is the staging of the capital infusion. It can be explained as a consequence of incentive problems arising when information on the firms' characteristics is unequally distributed among venture capitalists and entrepreneurs.[3] The staging of capital offers the entrepreneur the opportunity to use other financial resources after each capital infusion (Smith 1999). Moreover, infusing capital in stages offers the venture capitalist the opportunity to abandon the project after each capital infusion if contractually specified financial or non-financial criteria, so-called milestones, are not met (Sahlman 1990). This sets strong incentives to entrepreneurs to exert high effort and to avoid high risks. On the one hand, the staging of capital mitigates the hold-up behaviour of entrepreneurs (Neher 1999). But, on the other hand, the infusion of capital in stages can also cause several disincentives as well. Cornelli and Yosha (2003) show that an entrepreneur has incentives to manipulate the short-term performance when capital is invested in stages. In the model they use convertible securities to counteract this disincentive.

The staging of the capital infusion for the US venture capital market is analysed in the empirical study by Gompers (1995). According to this study, venture-capital-backed firms differ with respect to the size of each financing round, as well as with respect to the number of financing rounds. The more tangible the assets of the firms are, the higher the amount of money per financing round and the lower the number of financing rounds. Moreover, firms that are in their early stages of development receive less capital per financing round than firms in later stages. And the number of financing rounds is higher for firms that went public than for those which stayed private.

Little is known about the contractually specified control mechanism in Europe. There are only few studies addressing control mechanisms used by European private equity investors. In the sample of European investment rounds analysed by Cumming (2002), common equity is the most often used form of finance. Schwienbacher (2002) compares a sample of private equity funds operating in Europe with a sample of venture capital funds operating in the United States. He finds evidence that convertible securities are more often used in the

3. However, Bergemann and Hege (1998) ascribe the staging of the capital infusion to unknown time profile of future investment needs; staging of the capital infusion has an option value in their model because capital invested is ultimately sunk.

United States than in Europe. Bascha and Walz (2001b) use a data set containing 60 members of the German venture capital association, that is, 49.6 per cent of all members in January 2000. They find that besides using silent partnerships, Germany's private equity investors more often use pure equity, and less frequently use the sort of convertible securities. 33 per cent of the 60 members use silent partnerships, almost 27 per cent use pure equity, while only about eleven per cent use convertible securities.

With respect to the *value created by venture capitalists*, several empirical studies of the US market indicate that venture-capital-backing indeed has a positive impact on the development of firms. Brav and Gompers (1997) find that venture-capital-backed firms outperform non-venture-capital-backed ones even after the IPO. In their sample, venture-capital-backed firms earned 44.6 per cent after the IPO over five years, while non-venture-capital-backed ones earned only 22.5 per cent on average. In the sample of Silicon Valley high-technology start-ups analysed by Hellmann and Puri (2000), high-technology venture-capital-backed firms bring their products to the market earlier than their non-venture-capital-backed counterparts do so that the former can realize first mover advantages. Moreover, evidence found by Megginson and Weiss (1991) suggests that the total costs of going public including the underwriters' fee are lower for venture-capital-backed firms than for their non-venture-capital-backed counterparts. Mull (1990) finds evidence that the revenue and total assets of venture-capital-backed firms grow faster than the ones of their non-venture-capital-backed counterparts. In addition, Kortum and Lerner (2000) show that venture-capital-backed firms take out significantly more patents than other comparable firms.

The effects of venture-capital-backing depend on venture capitalists' experience. In the United States, experienced venture capitalists are more capable of reducing the fraction of insiders on the board of directors than their inexperienced counterparts (Baker and Gompers 1999b). In addition, the empirical analysis by Lerner (1994b) suggests that experienced venture capitalists are more proficient in timing the IPOs of the firms in their portfolios than less experienced venture capitalists. In particular, firms backed by experienced venture capitalists are more likely to go public when their valuations are at the maximum than the firms backed by less experienced venture capitalists. In addition, Barry et al. (1990) find evidence that venture capitalists' experience in supporting the management teams negatively affects the degree of underpricing.

The value created by private-equity-backing has also been analysed for some European markets. Roling (2001) analyses the relationship between patents and private equity for countries of the European Union. He does not find a significant relationship between the level of private equity investments and the number of patents, but he does find a significant impact of the number of private-equity-backed firms on the number of patents. The survey of Bürgel et al. (2000) suggests that there is no significant relationship between a private equity participation and revenue or employment growth among 600 German and British high-technology firms. However, Engel (2003) shows that Germany's private-equity-backed firms realize higher economic growth than their non-private-equity-backed counterparts. But higher economic growth is not the result of private equity investors' active involvement in their portfolio firms. Instead, private equity investors are capable of selecting firms with higher ex ante and ex post growth prospects, i.e., the pre-investment screening procedure by private equity investors is the reason for the higher growth of their portfolio firms (Engel 2003). Moreover, Engel (2002) shows that young private-equity-backed firms realize significantly higher annual growth rates in employment than their non-private-equity-backed counterparts when private-equity and non-private-equity-backed firms are matched. In addition, Audretsch and Lehmann (2002) find evidence that private-equity-backed firms listed on the Neuer Markt realized a higher employment growth than their non-private-equity-backed counterparts.

The effect of private equity investors' experience has also been analysed for two European markets. For private-equity-backed firms that went public on the London Stock Exchange, Barnes and McCarthy (2002) find no differences in the underpricing of firms backed by young and established private equity investors. For private-equity-backed and non-private-equity-backed firms that went public on the Neuer Market, Franzke (2001) finds evidence that high-ranked private equity investors reduce the underpricing of the firms' shares. However, without considering a private equity investor's rank, private-equity-backed firms are not less underpriced than their non-private-equity-backed counterparts (Kraus 2001).

3.3. Portfolio Strategies

At any point in time, venture capitalists and private equity investors have a multitude of firms in their portfolios. This raises the question of whether venture capitalists have particular portfolio strategies such as portfolio diversification over a wide range of firms in different development stages and/or industries, or portfolio specialization in firms at particular development stages and/or on particular industries. Amit et al. (1998) argue that due to specialization, venture capitalists have a comparative advantage in the selection and monitoring of high-technology firms compared to other financial intermediaries. However, this specialization strategy can be expected to lead to portfolios that are not well-diversified, i.e., not all unsystematic risk is diversified away (Norton and Tennenbaum 1993).

In the US venture capital market, two portfolio strategies can be identified: the specialization and syndication of investments. US venture capitalists tend to specialize in firms of particular industries and/or in firms that are at a particular development stage. Venture capitalists that are specialized in early stages demand lower returns for early-stage investments than venture capitalists that are not specialized (Manigart et al. 2002). Moreover, US venture capitalists syndicate their investments, i.e., several venture capitalists finance a single firm and only one of them takes on the monitoring and support of the firm.

In the United States, the degree of venture capitalists' specialization appears to depend on several factors. First, US venture capitalists who focus on the early stages of a firm's development are on average more specialized in particular industries than venture capitalists who focus on the later stages of firm's development (Norton and Tenenbaum 1993, Gupta and Sapienza 1992). Second, venture capitalists managing large funds prefer greater industry diversity than venture capitalists managing small funds (Gupta and Sapienza 1992).

In addition, capital providers can affect the degree of venture capitalists' specialization. In the United States, corporate venture capitalists have a higher degree of specialization in industries than non-corporate venture capitalists, while Small Business Investment Companies seem to have no preference regarding industry diversity (Gupta and Sapienza 1992). In Germany, independent equity investors have a considerably higher degree of specialization than the subsidiaries of private banks, savings banks and public equity investors (Schertler 2001). This holds with respect to industries and the stages of a firm's development, as well as with respect to simultaneous specialization in particular industries and stages.

The degree of syndication seems to depend on the uncertainty of the investment: the higher the uncertainty of an investment, the higher the degree of syndication. For example, US venture capitalists prefer a higher degree of syndication when they finance firms' early stages of development although the investment amount per company is small compared to later-stage deals (Bygrave 1987). Spreading of financial risks does not seem to be the main reason for syndications in the United States (Bygrave 1987, Bygrave and Timmons 1992). Rather, syndication of investments mainly serves to share information, as the empirical study by Lerner (1994a) suggests. Experienced venture capitalists syndicate early-stage investments with venture capitalists that have similar experience. Investments in later stages are also syndicated with less experienced venture capitalists. By contrast, in the United Kingdom, syndication of investments seems to be used to spreading risks and not to sharing information (Lockett and Wright 1999).

European private equity investors and US venture capitalists syndicate their investments with different intensities. Schwienbacher (2002) compares the syndication behaviour in the United States and in Europe. He finds that 54 per cent of the deals by the European private equity investors are syndicated, on average, compared to 80 per cent of the deals by the US venture capitalists. In addition, the number of partners in a syndicate is higher in the United States than in Europe. European private equity investors have 2.7 partners, on average, while US venture capitalists have 4.5 partners on average. Moreover, in twelve per cent of the European syndication a governmental partner was included, while in only two per cent of the US syndications was this the case.

4. Divestment

4.1. Aggregated Divestment Figures

The divestment stage is the last stage in the venture capital cycle. In this stage, venture capitalists and private equity investors who are independent from their capital providers exit from their participations and pay the investment capital and returns to the capital providers. Several exit routes can be distinguished: venture capitalists can sell the shares that they hold in a firm via stock markets, due to an IPO or a sale of already quoted equity, via trade sales or, of course, via write-offs.

Figure 2 opposite depicts the importance of the three exit routes only for the European market since comparable data for the United States are not available. Trade sales were the most important exit route during the observation period. In 2000 and 2001, trade sales accounted for about 33 per cent of all divestments. In all other years, the importance of trade sales measured as a percentage of total divestments was even stronger. Sales via stock markets accounted for only 11 per cent of total divestments in 2001, while they accounted for more than 30 per cent of total divestments in 1995. Write-offs accounted for less than 25 per cent of all divestments. This number understates the risk of venture capital investments because the data on divestment activity include investments in established firms operating in traditional firms that are less risky than investments in young high-technology firms. In 2001, write-offs accounted for more than 22 per cent of all investments, while in 2000 they accounted for less than eight per cent of all divestments. This increase in the importance of write-offs can be attributed to the bursting of the stock market bubble.

A detailed comparison of exit channels between the United States and Europe is impossible due to data limitations. The only data that might offer an impression of exit channels used in the United States and Europe are the number of IPOs and the number of acquisitions (trade sales) presented in Table 4 opposite. The statistic for European countries offers data on private equity investors' exiting, while the statistic for the United States offers data on venture capitalists' exiting. Because of this, the higher number of European trade sales does not seem astonishing. Even if trade sales and acquisitions might not measure the same thing, it seems that US venture capitalists use IPOs relatively more often to exit from their participations than European private equity investors.

Figure 2: Divestment Channels in Europe (million euro)

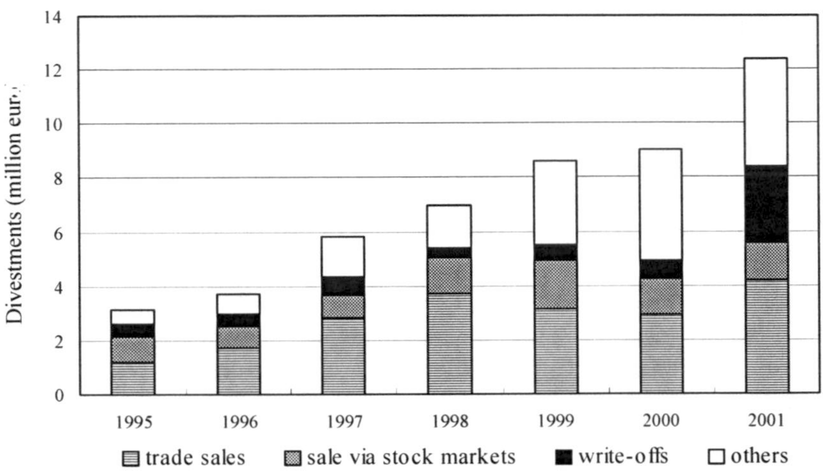

Source: EVCA (various issues).

Table 4: Number of IPOs and Acquisitions

	United States		Europe	
	IPOs	Acquisitions	IPOs	Trade sales
1997	136	161	Na	1,186
1998	77	201	239	965
1999	257	234	149	1,241
2000	226	299	249	1,294
2001	37	322	47	1,215

Note: Europe includes Austria, Belgium, Denmark, Finland, France, Germany, Greece, Iceland, Ireland, Italy, the Netherlands, Norway, Portugal, Spain, Sweden, Switzerland, and the United Kingdom.

Source: EVCA (various issues), and NVCA (2002).

Comparing the absolute number of IPOs suggests that more private-equity-backed firms went public in Europe than venture-capital-backed firms did in the United States. The difference in the number of IPOs of either US venture-capital-backed or European private-equity-backed firms is only moderate in 2000 and 2001. In 1999, the United States had a higher number of IPOs than Europe, while the opposite holds for 1998. Unfortunately the number of private-equity-backed IPOs for 1997 is not available.

Comparison of data on exiting via stock markets is limited for at least three reasons. First, in the second half of the 1990s a multitude of stock markets for shares of fast-growing firms was established in Europe, while a liquid stock market had already been in existence for a long time in the United States (Bottazzi and Da Rin 2002). In the United States, the Nasdaq was established in 1971, while the Nasdaq Europe, formerly Easdaq, a pan-European stock market, was only established in 1996 followed by the Nouveau Marché in Paris in 1996 (Table 5 below). Frankfurt's Neuer Markt was established in March 1997 and the TechMark in London was established in 1999. Because of this, one might argue that the number of IPOs in Europe is above the long-term average, but this might not be the case in the United States.

Table 5: Stock Markets for Fast-Growing Firms in Europe and the United States

	Nasdaq	Nouveau Marché	Neuer Markt	Nasdaq Europe	TechMark
Open since	1971	1996	1997	1996	1999
Number of IPOs	4,876	176	356	62	81
Listed companies	4,109	164	326	49	243
Funds raised	293,364	2,966	21,611	2,300	817.5
Market capitalisation	2,899,000	15,011	49,933	8,000	669,500
Market capitalisation (per cent of GDP)	24.5	1.02	2.41	na	2.61

Note: Listed companies and capitalization at end December 2001, number of IPOs and amount of funds raised from the opening of the market (from 1990 for Nasdaq) through 2001. Funds raised and capitalisation in millions of euros (millions of dollars for Nasdaq).

Source: Bottazzi and Da Rin (2002).

The Neuer Markt was the largest European stock market segment for shares of fast-growing firms in terms of the number of IPOs, listed firms and funds raised but not in terms of capitalisation (Table 5). The largest stock market in terms of capitalisation was the TechMark. While the TechMark had a high capitalisation and a high number of listed firms compared to the Easdaq and the Nouveau Marché, it had a low number of IPOs. Only 81 firms went public on the TechMark, while the respective numbers were 62 on the Easdaq, 176 on the Nouveau Marché, and 356 on the Neuer Markt. The TechMark had a comparatively high number of listed firms and a high capitalisation because it had superseded the Alternative Investment Market that had been founded in 1995.

Second, the comparison of the data is limited since the stock market bubble at the end of the 1990s may have affected the climate on these markets differently. In order to compare the number of IPOs, a longer time period seems necessary since the high number of IPOs in Europe may be mainly driven by the high share prices at the end of the 1990s. In particular, it might be the case that institutional regulations of European stock markets allowed comparatively young and small firms to go public in 1999 and 2000, while the institutional regulations of the Nasdaq did not.

Third, suggestions drawn from a comparison of the number of IPOs may be the result of obscurities in the European statistic, which is especially young with respect to the exit data. In particular, the number of European IPOs seemed to be very high in 1998. A closer look at the country data shows that this high number results from a high number of French IPOs. French private equity investors reported 126 IPOs of private-equity-backed firms. This number is extremely high compared to the 43 firms that went public on the Nouveau Marché in 1998 (Schertler 2001). Thus, comparison of US and European divestment activity is very limited.

From a theoretical point of view, the foundation of a national stock market reduces transactions costs of IPOs compared to trade sales so that European private equity investors should more often favour the IPO of a firm they have chosen to finance. Therefore, I would expect increasing divestments via IPOs after the foundation of the European stock markets in the second half of the 1990s. However, increasing divestments via IPOs are not necessarily attributable to the foundation of stock markets but also to higher share prices at the end of the 1990s. Since the bursting of the stock market bubble increased the transaction costs of IPOs, I expect that trade sales became more favourable for private equity investors.

In Germany, the number of exits via stock markets increased substantially after the foundation of the Neuer Markt (BVK various issues). In 1996, only 18 private-equity-backed firms went public, while in 2000 67 private-equity-backed firms went public (BVK various issues). Of these 67 firms, 60 firms went public on the Neuer Markt. Therefore, the Neuer Markt offered a liquid exit channel for private equity investors until 2000. However, in 2001, the Neuer Markt got into deep trouble and some months later, the Deutsche Börse decided to re-structure this stock market segment.

The bursting of the stock market bubble has affected the German private equity market negatively through several channels. First, most of private equity investors' portfolios were inflated in the course of the stock market bubble, and the bursting of the bubble led to large negative adjustments in the portfolio values. About 70 per cent of all exits were written-off in the second and third quarters of 2001.[4] In the first quarter of 2002, the respective number was only about 50 per cent. Second, the bursting of the stock market bubble affected the solvency of private equity investors listed on a stock exchange that experienced substantial losses in their share prices.

4. http://www.mackewicz.de/venturemall/vc-panel/index.htm.

Aggregated data on German divestments also show a substantial increase and decrease in divestments via IPOs at the end of the 1990s. The divestments via stock markets including IPOs and sale of already quoted equity as a percentage of all divestments reached their peak in 1999. Starting from about three per cent in 1997, divestments via stock markets reached 12.5 per cent of all divestments in 1998, and more than 17 per cent in 1999. In 2000, divestments via stock markets started to decline. They accounted for 12.1 per cent in 2000, and for less than eight per cent in 2001 (EVCA various issues). This decline was even stronger when looking at divestments via IPOs only. Divestments via IPOs accounted for almost 12 (9) per cent in 1999 (2000), while they accounted for less than one per cent in 2001.

In the United Kingdom, the divestments via stock markets as a percentage of all divestments also reached their peak in 1999. In comparison to the German situation, divestments via stock markets were also important in the middle of the 1990s (EVCA various issues). Divestments via stock markets accounted for about 25 per cent in 1996, and 15 per cent in 1997. They accounted for less than 19 per cent in 1998 and reached more than 26 per cent of all divestments in 1999. As German divestments via stock markets, British divestments via stock markets dropped substantially after 1999. In 2000, they accounted for only seven per cent of all divestments. Contrary to the German situation, divestments via stock markets as a percentage of all divestments were slightly higher in 2001 than in 2000. British divestments via IPOs show a similar picture for the divestments via stock markets. Divestments via IPOs accounted for almost 18 per cent of all divestments in 1999. By contrast, in 2000 and 2001 they accounted for less than three per cent.

In France, the divestments via stock markets as a percentage of all divestments reached their peak in 2000. Since the middle of the 1990s, French divestments via stock markets increased almost continuously. In 1995, divestments via stock markets accounted for about eight per cent of all divestments, in 1996 and 1997 they accounted for about 14 per cent, and in 1998 and 1999 they accounted for more than 16 per cent (EVCA various issues). In 2000, divestments via stock markets were almost 25 per cent of all divestments. In 2001, they accounted for almost 17 per cent. Thus, French divestments via stock markets as a percentage of all divestments experienced a different development than the British and German divestments via stock markets as a percentage of all divestments. The latter two experienced a substantial decline between 1999 and 2000, while the former experienced a less strong decline between 2000 and 2001.

As far as the exit channels are concerned, one can conclude that the bursting of the stock market bubble has substantially deteriorated the conditions for IPOs of private-equity-backed firms at least in Germany and the United Kingdom. But also in France the conditions for IPOs of private-equity-backed firms have been deteriorated. Looking at divestments via IPOs of private-equity-backed firms shows a substantial decline between 2000 and 2001. In 2000, divestments via IPOs accounted for more than seven per cent of all divestments, while in 2001 they accounted for less than one per cent (EVCA various issues). This decline was much stronger than the decline in the divestments via stock markets that include divestments via IPOs and sales of already quoted equity.

4.2. Venture Capitalists' Divestment Behaviour

Some aspects of venture capitalists' divestment behaviour have been analysed for some countries: these aspects include the venture capitalists' preference for the various exit channels, and the timing of IPOs of venture-capital-backed firms. The preference of US venture capitalists and European private equity investors for the various exit channels differs. Schwienbacher (2002) reports that eleven per cent of the European private equity investors consider the IPO as the most preferred exit channel compared to 29 per cent of the US venture capitalists. By contrast, 39 per cent of the European private equity investors have a strict preference for trade sales compared to 24 per cent of the US venture capitalists.

Whether young venture capitalists take firms public earlier than older venture capitalists do has been analysed by Gompers (1996) and Barnes and McCarthy (2002). The advantage of taking firms public earlier for young venture capitalists is that they can signal their experience in financing high-technology firms to the market so that they can raise new funds at more favourable conditions. Thus, one can expect that young venture capitalists raise new funds soon after taking firms public. What are the costs of such behaviour? Going public earlier can be associated with greater underpricing because one can expect that the younger the firm is, the larger the asymmetric information is between new and old shareholders. The larger the asymmetric information is, the higher the price reduction demanded by new shareholders.

Gompers (1996) who uses a sample of 433 IPOs in the United States, and Barnes and McCarthy (2002) who use a sample of 85 IPOs in the United Kingdom find evidence that firms backed by young venture capitalists or private equity investors are younger at IPO than those backed by older and thus more established venture capitalists or private equity investors. While young US venture capitalists raise new funds significantly earlier after the date of the IPO than their established counterparts (Gompers 1996), young British private equity investors do not differ from their established counterparts. In addition, in the sample by Gompers (1996), firms backed by young venture capitalists are more underpriced at their IPOs than firms backed by more established venture capitalists. By contrast, in the sample by Barnes and McCarthy (2002), firms backed by young private equity investors do not differ with respect to underpricing from their counterparts backed by more established private equity investors.

4.3. Returns for Capital Providers

After venture capitalists and private equity investors who are independent from the capital providers have exited from their participations, they repay the investment capital and return to capital providers. The return on venture capital determines how much capital is invested in future funds. The return on venture capital investments can be analysed for various aggregation levels with various indicators. With respect to the indicators used, the most common one is the internal rate of return (IRR) that does not offer, however, information on the risk-return profile of venture capital investments or funds.[5] The estimation of a risk-return profile of venture capital investments can be based on the capital asset pricing model. With respect to the aggregation level, the return on venture capital investments for the capital providers can be based either on single venture capital investments, or on venture capital funds including several venture capital investments, or on a venture capital index.

Peng (2001) builds a venture capital index using 12,946 rounds of venture capital investments in 5,643 venture-capital-backed US firms between 1987 and 1999, and controls for missing data, censored data, and sample selection problems. In this sample, the annual returns on the venture capital index are higher than the annual returns of the Nasdaq index between 1987 and 1990 and between 1993 and 1999 except 1997. In 1997, the annual return was lowest with 0.38 per cent, while in 1999 the annual return was extraordinarily high with 681.2 per cent. In all years of the observation period, the venture capital index has a substantially higher volatility than the Nasdaq index. These results indicate that the returns on venture capital investments are highly volatile.

Cochrane (2001) analyses the risk-return profile of a sample of single US venture capital investments from which venture capitalists have already exited. He finds that "an individual VC (venture capital) investment is not particularly attractive, despite the high average returns" (Cochrane 2001). Using maximum likelihood estimates, Cochrane (2001) calculates a mean arithmetic return of almost 57 per cent with a standard deviation of 119 per cent. This risk-return profile seems unfavourable compared with other investment opportunities.

However, if a well-diversified portfolio could be constructed, i.e. if all unsystematic risk could be diversified away, it could yield supernormal returns. But Cochrane (2001) argues that it is probably impossible to construct a portfolio free of unsystematic risks because venture capital investments may have a common component, as indicated by the high business failure rate in the Fall of 2000. Thus, it is rather hard to evaluate whether capital providers receive a part

---

5. The IRR is defined as the discounting rate for which the present value of all future outflows equals the present value of all future inflows that a private equity investor generates over time. Several measurement problems occur when calculating the IRR. For example, as long as the capital of the private equity funds is still being invested, future flows of capital have to be estimated in order to calculate the IRR.

of any surplus created by venture capitalists, especially because the availability of venture capital funds can create diversification gains realized by capital providers that cannot be taken into account. Diversification gains will always be realized except when venture capital investments are strictly dominated by other investment opportunities.

These studies for the United States analyse the risk-return profile of venture capital investments, while studies for European countries concentrate solely on the returns of venture capital investments. *Venture Economics*, for example, has prepared an annual *Pan-European Investment Benchmarks Study* using the IRR technique and funds data. This study provides a comparison of the performance of European private equity with other asset classes on the basis of equivalent net IRR. To calculate equivalent IRRs, the same pattern of private equity investments and divestments over time as in the private equity data set have been utilized to construct a portfolio of an alternative asset class. *Net* means that the often substantial management fees for private equity investors have already been deducted.

According to the Investment Benchmark Study of 2001, net cumulative annualised IRR of all European private equity funds in the sample outperformed alternative asset classes as Table 6 below indicates. European private equity funds had a net cumulative annualised IRR of more than 12 per cent. By contrast, the equivalent IRRs of MSCI Equity was only 8.9 per cent, the equivalent IRR of JP Morgan Bond was lower at 7.0 per cent, and the equivalent IRR of HSBC Small Cap was as low as -1.2 per cent. Only two subgroups, development and generalists, had a slightly lower net cumulative annualised IRR than MSCI Equity.

While the Investment Benchmarks Study of 2001 shows that the return of almost all private equity subgroups outperforms the return of other asset classes, the Investment Benchmark Study of 2000 shows a less clear picture (EVCA 2001a). In particular, in 2000, several subgroups of private equity funds had a lower net cumulative annualised IRR than MSCI Equity, or HSBC Small Cap. Development funds had a lower performance than both HSBC Small Cap and MSCI Equity, while early-stage and all venture capital, including all funds that invest in firms' early and expansion stages, had a lower return than MSCI Equity.

Comparing the returns on private equity reported for 2000 and 2001 shows that the return on private equity has decreased for many groups of private equity. While the Investment Benchmark Study of 2000 reports an IRR on all private equity of 15.6 per cent, the Investment Benchmark Study of 2001 reports an IRR on all private equity of only 12.7 per cent, which is comparatively high given the fall in value on European stock markets. Only Generalists and Development funds show a moderate increase in the IRR.

Table 6: Net Cummulative Annualised IRR (per cent)

	European Private Equity	MSCI Equity	HSBC Small Cap	JP Morgan Bond
Early stage	8.9	8.6	-2.1	6.4
Development	12.3	12.6	6.0	8.0
Balanced venture capital	13.6	10.4	1.3	6.3
All venture capital	12.0	10.7	2.0	6.9
Buy-outs	14.8	6.0	-4.4	7.0
Generalists	11.5	12.0	3.3	7.3
All private equity	12.7	8.9	-1.2	7.0

Note: Morgan Stanley Capital International (MSCI) is an international (originally US) investment bank. HSBC is a British bank. MSCI Equity contains larger and HSBC Small Cap contains smaller companies. When discussing these IRRs, one has to keep in mind that the end of the 1990s was characterised by higher stock prices. Increasing stock prices first have an impact on the larger companies and only thereafter on the shares of smaller companies.

Source: EVCA (2002a).

5. Concluding Remarks

This paper has compared the US venture capital market and the European private equity market in order to identify differences and similarities of these two markets. In the American tradition, venture capital comprises management support and financial means for a subset of young high-technology firms provided by experienced intermediaries, the venture capitalists. The term private equity has been used because data on the European market not only cover venture capital investments but also investments in low-technology areas and investments in already established firms. Private equity investment in firms that are in their early stages of development, or which are classified as high-technology firms, has been used as an approximation of European venture capital activity. Due to data limitations, results based on aggregated data have to be interpreted with caution.

The comparison of aggregated data has shown that Europe's private equity market differ with respect to size and investment specialization from the US venture capital market. In particular, US venture capital investments per capita were higher than European private equity investments without buy-outs during the 1990s. However, the shares of investments in firms that are information- and communication-related to private equity without buy-out activity have suggested that Europe's private equity was as much specialized in particular industries as US venture capital at the end of the 1990s. In addition, the shares of investments in firms' early stages to private equity without buy-out activity have indicated that Europe's investments were even more specialized in firms' early stages than US investments.

The European private equity market also differs from the US venture capital market with respect to the capital providers that invest their money in funds and with respect to the relationship between capital providers and venture capitalists. In the United States, pension funds have been the most important capital provider. By contrast, in Europe, pension funds have been only an important capital provider in the United Kingdom, while banks have been important in Germany and France. However, in the second half of the 1990s, pension funds increased the amounts of capital offered to private equity funds operating in Germany and France. With respect to the relationship between capital providers and venture capitalists, US venture capitalists are most often independent from capital providers and so are private equity investors operating in the United Kingdom. By contrast, private equity investors operating in Germany or France often depend on capital providers.

I have argued that differences between the US and the European venture capital market with respect to the size and depth can be explained by several factors, three of them have been of particular interest. First, the size of the venture capital market may depend on the financial architecture of the economies. Countries in which banks play an important role compared to shareholders may have small venture capital markets because control mechanisms of banks do not work well when financing high-technology firms. Since banks play an important role in many European countries, one can expect that Europe's venture capital market is smaller than the US market. Second, the size of the venture capital market may depend on the availability of informal venture capital. If complementarities exist between informal and formal venture capital markets, the venture capital market would be larger if informal venture capital is available. In Europe, the informal venture capital market is smaller than the respective market in the United States. Thus, one can expect that Europe's formal venture capital market is smaller than the US market. Third, the size of the venture capital market may depend on the possibility of exiting via stock markets since exiting via stock markets can reduce transaction costs between venture capitalists, capital providers and entrepreneurs. Since the United States has an established stock market for shares of fast-growing firms, one can expect that Europe's venture capital market is smaller than the US market. How far the difference in the size of the venture capital markets between the United States and Europe is attributable to other factors such as differences in the human capital endowment, and the style of the innovation system is a still open question.

In addition to presenting aggregated data, the paper has also discussed a multitude of empirical studies based on micro data in order to identify differences and similarities between the US and the European market. These studies most often focus on one part of the venture capital cycle: they either focus on fundraising, or investment, or divestment. With respect to fundraising, evidence suggests that US venture capitalists and European private equity investors who are independent from their capital providers use similar compensation systems. In particular, venture capitalists participate in profits of the venture capital fund and demand a fixed fee for management activities. The levels of profit participations and management fees differ between European private equity investors and US venture capitalists.

With respect to investment, several studies indicate that US venture capitalists create value-added in the firms they finance. For European private equity investors, evidence moves in the same direction but it is much weaker than the evidence for the US market. European private equity investors also use control mechanisms, such as active monitoring and convertible securities, used by US venture capitalists. However, US venture capitalists use convertible securities more often to finance firms' investments than European private equity investors.

With respect to divestment, studies discussed analyse the grandstanding hypotheses for the US and British markets. In particular, these studies ask whether young venture capitalists take firms public earlier than older venture capitalists do. These studies find evidence that firms backed by young US venture capitalists or British private equity investors are younger at IPO than those backed by older and thus more established ones. However, these studies do also show that young US venture capitalists raise new funds significantly earlier after the date of the IPO than their established counterparts, while young British private equity investors do not differ from their established counterparts.

References:

Amit, R., J. Brander and C. Zott (1998). "Why Do Venture Capital Firms Exist? Theory and Canadian Evidence." *Journal of Business Venturing* 13 (6): 441–466.
Audretsch, D.B., and E. Lehmann (2002). "Debt or Equity? The Role of Venture Capital in Financing the New Economy in Germany." CEPR Discussion Paper 3656.
Baker, M., and P.A. Gompers (1999a). "An Analysis of Executive Compensation, Ownership, and Control in Closely Held Firms." Working Paper. Harvard Business School, Boston, MA.
— and — (1999b). "The Determinants of Board Structure and Function in Entrepreneurial Firms." Working Paper. Harvard Business School, Boston, MA.
Barnes, E., and Y. McCarthy (2002). "Grandstanding in the UK Venture Capital Industry." EFMA 2002 London Meetings.
Barry, C. (1994). "New Directions in Research on Venture Capital Finance." *Journal of the Financial Management Association* 23 (3): 3–15.
Barry, C.B., C.J. Muscarella, J.W. Peavy III, and M.R. Vetsuypens (1990). "The Role of Venture Capital in the Creation of Public Companies: Evidence from the Going-Public Process." *Journal of Financial Economics* 27 (2): 447–471.
Bascha, A., and U. Walz (2001a). "Convertible Securities and Optimal Exit Decisions in Venture Capital Finance." *Journal of Corporate Finance* 7 (3): 285–306.
— and — (2001b). "Financing Practices in the German Venture Capital Industry: An Empirical Assessment." Paper presented at the weekly seminar in honour of Erich Schneider, Kiel.
Baygan, G. (2003). "Venture Capital Policy Review: United Kingdom." STI Working Paper 2003/1 Industry Issues.
Bergemann, D., and U. Hege (1998). "Venture Capital Financing, Moral Hazard, and Learning." *Journal of Banking & Finance* 22 (6-8): 703–735.
Berglöf, E. (1994). "A Control Theory of Venture Capital Finance." *Journal of Law, Economics & Organisation* 10 (1): 247–267.
Black, B.S., and R.J. Gilson (1998), "Venture Capital and the Structure of Capital Markets: Banks versus Stock Markets." *Journal of Financial Economics* 47 (3): 243–277.
Bottazzi, L., and M. Da Rin (2002). "Europe's New Stock Markets." CEPR Discussion Paper 3521.
Brav, A., and P. Gompers (1997). "Myth or Reality? The Long-Run Underperformance of Initial Public Offerings: Evidence from Venture and Non Venture Capital-Backed Companies." *The Journal of Finance* 52 (5): 1791–1821.
Brouwer, M., and B. Hendrix (1998). "Two Worlds of Venture Capital: What Happened to US and Dutch Early Stage Investment?" *Small Business Economics* 10 (4): 333–348.
Bürgel, O., A. Fier, G. Licht, and G. Murray (2000). "Internationalisation of High-Tech Start-ups and Fast Growth-Evidence for UK and Germany." ZEW-Discussion Paper 00–35, Mannheim.
BVK (Bundesverband Deutscher Kapitalbeteiligungsgesellschaften) (various issues). *BVK-Statistik*. Berlin.
Bygrave, W.D. (1987). "Syndicated Investments by Venture Capital Firms: A Networking Perspective." *Journal of Business Venturing* 2 (2): 139–154.
Bygrave, W.D., and J.A. Timmons (1992). *Venture Capital at the Crossroads*. Boston, MA: Harvard Business School Press.
Cochrane, J. (2001). "The Risk and Return of Venture Capital." NBER Working Paper 8066. Cambridge, MA.
Cornelli, F., and O. Yosha (2003). "Stage Financing and the Role of Convertible Securities." *The Review of Economic Studies* 70 (1): 1–32.
Cumming, D. (2002). "Contracts and Exits in Venture Capital Finance." Working Paper. University of Alberta, Alberta.
Dubocage, E. and D. Rivaud-Danset (2002). "Government Policy on Venture Capital Support in France." *Venture Capital: An International Journal for Entrepreneurial Finance 4* (1): 25-43.
EBAN (European Business Angels Network) (1998). Dissemination Report on the Potential for Business Angels Investments and Networks in Europe.
Elango, B., V.H. Fried, R.D. Hisrich and A. Polonchek (1995). "How Venture Capital Firms Differ." *Journal of Business Venturing* 10 (2): 157–179.

Engel, D. (2002). "The Impact of Venture Capital on Firm Growth: An Empirical Investigation." ZEW Discussion Paper 02–02. Mannheim.

— (2003). "Höheres Beschäftigungswachstum durch Venture Capital?" *Journal of Economics and Statistics* 223 (1): 1-22.

Evans, D.M. (2001). "Tendenzen in der Venture Capital Finanzierung in den USA." In W. Schmeisser and D. Krimphove (eds.), *Vom Gründungsmanagement zum Neuen Markt: Strategien für technologieorientierte kleine und mittlere Unternehmen.* Wiesbaden: Gabler.

EVCA (European Venture Capital Association) (1991–2002). *Yearbook.* Zaventem, Belgium.

— (2001a). Pan-European Survey of Performance. ENN Supplement, October 2001. Access on March 6th 2002 via: http://www.evca.com/publications.html.

— (2002a). Pan-European Survey of Performance. ENN Supplement, October 2002. Access on December 18th 2002 via: http://www.evca.com/publications.html.

Feinendegen, S., D. Schmidt, and M. Wahrenburg (2002). "Die Vertragsbeziehung zwischen Investoren und Venture Capital-Fonds: Eine empirische Untersuchung des europäischen Venture Capital-Marktes." Center for Financial Studies Working Paper 2002/01.

Franzke, S.A. (2001). "Underpricing of Venture-Backed and Non Venture-Backed IPOS: Germany's Neuer Markt." CFS Working Paper 2001/01. Center for Financial Studies, Frankfurt/a.M.

Fried, V.H., and R.D. Hisrich (1994). "Toward a Model of Venture Capital Investment Devision Making." *Financial Management* 23 (3): 28–37.

Gifford, S. (1997). "Limited Attention and the Role of the Venture Capitalist." *Journal of Business Venturing* 12 (6): 459–482.

Gompers, P.A. (1995). "Optimal Investment, Monitoring, and the Staging of Venture Capital." *The Journal of Finance* 50 (5): 1461–1489.

— (1996). "Grandstanding in the Venture Capital Industry." *Journal of Financial Economics* 42 (1): 133–156.

— (1997). "Ownership and Control in Entrepreneurial Firms: An Examination of Convertible Securities in Venture Capital Investments." Working Paper. Harvard University, Cambridge, MA.

— (1998). "Venture Capital Growing Pains: Should the Market Diet?" *Journal of Banking and Finance* 22: 1089–1104.

Gompers, P.A., and J. Lerner (1996). "The Use of Covenants: An Empirical Analysis of Venture Partnership Agreements." *The Journal of Law and Economics* 39 (2): 443–498.

— and — (1998a). "The Determinants of Corporate Venture Capital Success: Organizational Structure, Incentives, and Complementarities." In: R.K. Morck (ed.), *Concentrated Corporate Ownership.* Chicago: Chicago Press.

— and — (1998b). "What Drives Venture Capital Fundraising?" Working Paper. Harvard University, Cambridge, MA.

— and — (1999). *The Venture Capital Cycle.* Cambridge, MA: MIT Press.

Gorman, M., and W. Sahlman (1989). "What Do Venture Capitalists Do?" *Journal of Business Venturing* 4 (4): 231–248.

Gupta, A.K., and H.J. Sapienza (1992). "Determinants of Venture Capital Firms' Preferences Regarding the Industry Diversity and Geographic Scope of their Investments." *Journal of Business Venturing* 7: 347–362.

Harrison, R.T., and C.M. Mason (2000). "Venture Capital Market Complementarities: The Links Between Business Angels and Venture Capital Funds in the United Kingdom." *Venture Capital: An International Journal of Entrepreneurial Finance* 2 (3): 223–242.

Hellmann, T. (2001). "IPOs, Acquisitions and the Use of Convertible Securities in Venture Capital." Working Paper. Stanford University, Stanford.

Hellmann, T., and M. Puri (2000). "The Interaction between Product Market and Financing Strategy: The Role of Venture Capital." *The Review of Financial Studies* 13 (4): 959–984.

— and — (2002). "Venture Capital and the Professionalization of Start-Up Firms: Empirical Evidence." *The Journal of Finance* 57 (1): 169–197.

Jeng, L.A., and P.C. Wells (2000). "The Determinants of Venture Capital Funding: Evidence Across Countries." *Journal of Corporate Finance* 6 (3): 241–289.

Kaplan, S. N., and P. Strömberg (2000). "Financial Contracting Theory Meets the Real World: An Empirical Analysis of Venture Capital Contracts." NBER Working Paper 7660. Cambridge, MA.Just, C. (2000). *Business Angels und technologieorientierte Unternehmensgründungen-Lösungsansätze zur Behebung von Informationsdefiziten am informellen Beteiligungskapitalmarkt aus Sicht der Kapitalgeber.* Stuttgart: Fraunhofer IRB Verlag.

Kortum, S., and J. Lerner (2000). "Assessing the Contribution of Venture Capital to Innovation." *The Rand Journal of Economics* 31 (4): 674–692.

Kraus, T. (2001). "Underpricing of IPOs and the Certification Role of Venture Capitalists: Evidence from Germany's Neuer Markt." Working Paper. University of Munich, Munich.

Kulicke, M. (1997). "Beratung junger Technologieunternehmen." In K. Koschatzky (ed.), *Technologieunternehmen im Innovationsprozess: Management, Finanzierung und regionale Netzwerke.* Fraunhofer-Institut für Systemtechnik und Innovationsforschung (ISI), Heidelberg.

— (2001). "Innovation Networks and Regional VC Companies in Germany – Experiences for Central and Eastern European Countries." In K. Koschatzky (ed.), *Innovation Networks: Concepts and Challenges in the European Perspective.* Fraunhofer-Institut für Systemtechnik und Innovationsforschung (ISI), Heidelberg.

Lerner, J. (1994a). "The Syndication of Venture Capital Investments." *Journal of the Financial Management Association* 23 (3): 16–27.

— (1994b). "Venture Capitalists and the Decision to Go Public." *Journal of Financial Economics* 35 (3): 293–316.

— (1995a). "Venture Capitalists and Oversight of Privately-Held Firms." *The Journal of Finance* 50 (1): 301–318.

Lockett, A. and M. Wright (1999). "The Syndication of Private Equity: Evidence from the UK." *Venture Capital: An International Journal of Entrepreneurial Finance* 1 (4): 303-324.

Lülfesmann, C. (2000). "Start-Up Firms, Venture Capital Financing and Renegotiation." *Journal of Financial Management and Analysis* 13 (1): 1–15.

Manigart, S., K. DeWaele, M. Wright, K. Robbie, P. Desbrières, H.J. Sapienza and A. Beekman (2002). "Determinants of Required Return in Venture Capital Investments: A Five-Country Study." *Journal of Business Venturing* 17 (4): 291–312.

Megginson, W.L., and K.A. Weiss (1991). "Venture Capitalist Certification in Initial Public Offerings." *The Journal of Finance* 46 (3): 879–903.

Mull, F. (1990). *Towards a Positive Theory of Venture Capital.* Ann Arbor, Mich.: UMI Dissertation Information Service.

Neher, D. (1999). "Staged Financing: An Agency Perspective." *Review of Economic Studies* 66 (2): 255–274.

Norton, E. (1994). "Venture Capitalist Attributes and Investment Vehicles: An Exploratory Analysis." *The Journal of Small Business Finance* 3 (3): 181–198.

Norton, E., and B.H. Tenenbaum (1993). "Specialization versus Diversification as a Venture Capital Investment Strategy." *Journal of Business Venturing* 8 (5): 431–442.

NVCA (National Venture Capital Association) (2001). NVCA Yearbook. Arlington, VA.

NVCA (National Venture Capital Association) (2002). NVCA Yearbook. Arlington, VA.

OECD (Organisation for Economic Co-Operation and Development) (1997). Government Venture Capital for Technology-Based Firms. OECD/GD(97)201, Paris.

Peng, L. (2001). "Building a Venture Capital Index." Yale ICF Working Paper 00–51. Yale University, New Haven, CT.

Roling, J. (2001). *Venture Capital und Innovation: Theoretische Zusammenhänge, empirische Befunde und wirtschaftspolitische Implikationen.* Lohmar: Josef Eul Verlag.

Sahlman, W.A. (1990). "The Structure and Governance of Venture-Capital Organizations." *Journal of Financial Economics* 27 (2): 473–521.

Schertler, A. (2001). "Venture Capital in Europe's Common Market: A Quantitative Description." EIFC Working Paper 01–4, Maastricht.

Schertler, A. (2003). "Driving Forces of Venture Capital Investments in Europe: A Dynamic Panel Data Analysis." EIFC Working Paper 03–27, Maastricht.

Schmidt, K.M. (2003). "Convertible Securities and Venture Capital Finance." *The Journal of Finance* 58 (3): 1139–1166.

Schwienbacher; A. (2002). "An Empirical Analysis of Venture Capital Exits in Europe and in the United States." University of Namur.

Smith, D.G. (1999). "Team Production in Venture Capital Investing." *Journal of Corporation Law 25.*

Van Osnabrugge, M. and R.J. Robinson (2000). *Angel Investing, Matching Start-up Funds with Start-up Companies.* San Francisco: Jossey-Bass.

Weimerskirch, P. (1998). *Finanzierungsdesign bei Venture-Capital-Verträgen.* Wiesbaden: Deutscher Universitäts Verlag.

Wupperfeld, U. (1994). "Die Betreuung junger Technologieunternehmen durch ihre Beteiligungskapitalgeber. Empirische Untersuchung." Working paper. Institut für Systemtechnik und Innovationsforschung (ISI), Karlsruhe.

Zemke, I. (1995). *Die Unternehmensverfassung von Beteiligungskapital-Gesellschaften. Analyse des institutionellen Designs deutscher Venture Capital-Gesellschaften.* Wiesbaden: Gabler.

11. Equivalence of Ten Different Methods for Valuing Companies by Cash Flow Discounting

Pablo Fernández[1]

IESE Business School, University of Navarra.

Abstract. This paper shows that ten methods of company valuation using discounted cash flows (WACC; equity cash flow; capital cash flow; adjusted present value; residual income; EVA; business's risk-adjusted equity cash flow; business's risk-adjusted free cash flow; risk-free-adjusted equity cash flow; and risk-free-adjusted free cash flow) always give the same value when identical assumptions are used. This result is logical, since all the methods analyze the same reality using the same assumptions; they differ only in the cash flows taken as the starting point for the valuation. We present all ten methods, allowing the required return to debt to be different from the cost of debt. Seven methods require an iterative process. Only the APV and business risk-adjusted cash flows methods do not require iteration.

Keywords: company valuation, cash flow discounting, WACC, equity cash flow, free cash flow, adjusted present value, risk-adjusted cash flow.

1. Introduction

To value a company by discounting the expected cash flows at an appropriate discount rate, we may use different expected cash flows, which will have different risks and, therefore, will require different discount rates. As in each case we are valuing the same company, we should get the same valuation, no matter which expected cash flows we use. In this paper we present ten different approaches to valuing companies by discounting cash flows. Although some authors argue that different methods may produce different valuations, we will show that all methods provide the same value under the same assumptions. We were motivated to write this paper because of the question commonly raised by students, faculty and practitioners: "Why do I get different answers from different discounted cash flow valuations and from residual income valuations?"

The most common method for valuing companies is the Free Cash Flow method. In that method, interest tax shields are excluded from the cash flows and the tax deductibility of the interest is treated as a decrease in the weighted average

1. I thank my colleague José Manuel Campa and Charles Porter for their wonderful help revising previous manuscripts of this paper, and two anonymous referees for very helpful comments and suggestions. I also thank Rafael Termes and my colleagues at IESE for their sharp questions that encouraged me to explore valuation problems.

This article was originally published in the International Journal of Finance Education 1(1): pp.141-168.

cost of capital (WACC). As the WACC depends on the capital structure, this method requires an iterative process: to calculate the WACC, we need to know the value of the company, and to calculate the value of the company, we need to know the WACC. Seven out of the ten methods presented require an iterative process, while only three (APV and the two business risk-adjusted cash flows methods) do not. The prime advantage of these three methods is their simplicity. Whenever the debt is forecasted in levels, instead as a percentage of firm value, the APV is much easier to use because the value of the interest tax shields is quite easy to calculate. The two business risk-adjusted cash flows methods are also easy to use because the interest tax shields are included in the cash flows. The discount rate of these three methods is the required return to assets and, therefore, it does not change when capital structure changes.

Section I describes ten commonly used methods for valuing companies by discounting cash flows. We show that all ten methods always give the same value. This result is logical, since all the methods analyze the same reality under the same hypotheses; they differ only in the cash flows taken as the starting point for the valuation. The ten methods are as follows:

1. equity cash flows discounted at the required return to equity;
2. free cash flow discounted at the WACC;
3. capital cash flows discounted at the WACC before tax;
4. APV (Adjusted Present Value);
5. residual income discounted at the required return to equity;
6. EVA discounted at the WACC;
7. the business's risk-adjusted free cash flows discounted at the required return to assets;
8. the business's risk-adjusted equity cash flows discounted at the required return to assets;
9. the risk-free-adjusted free cash flows discounted at the risk-free rate; and
10. the risk-free-adjusted equity cash flows discounted at the risk-free rate.

Section 2 is the application of the ten methods to a specific example.

Section 3 presents four alternative theories about the value of tax shields and discusses their applicability. The four theories are the following:

1) Harris and Pringle (1985) and Ruback (1995, 2002). All of their equations arise from the assumption that the leverage-driven value creation or value of tax shields (VTS) is the present value of the tax shields discounted at the required return to the unlevered equity (Ku).

2) Myers (1974). He assumes that the value of tax shields (VTS) is the present value of the tax shields discounted at the required return to debt (Kd).

3) Miles and Ezzell (1980). They state that the correct rate for discounting the tax shields (D Kd T) is Kd for the first year, and Ku for the following years.

4) Damodaran (1994). He assumes that the beta of the debt is zero.

The appendix presents the derivation of the WACC and WACC before tax formulas; proves that the residual income and equity cash flows methods provide the same value; and proves that valuations using EVA and free cash flow provide the same value.

Table VI contains the formulas used in the paper, and Table VII contains a list of the abbreviations used throughout.

2. Ten Discounted Cash Flow Valuation Methods

Method 1. Using the expected equity cash flow (ECF) and the required return to equity (Ke).

Equation (1) indicates that the value of the equity (E) is the present value of the expected equity cash flows (ECF) discounted at the required return to equity (Ke).

$$E_0 = PV_0[Ke_t; ECF_t] \quad \textbf{(1)}$$

The expected equity cash flow is the sum of all expected cash payments to shareholders, mainly dividends and share repurchases.

Equation (2) indicates that the value of the debt (D) is the present value of the expected debt cash flows (CFd) discounted at the required return to debt (Kd).

$$D_0 = PV_0[Kd_t; CFd_t] \quad \textbf{(2)}$$

The expected debt cash flow in a given period is given by equation (3)

$$CFd_t = N_{t-1}\, r_t - (N_t - N_{t-1}) \quad \textbf{(3)}$$

where N is the book value of the financial debt and r is the cost of debt. $N_{t-1}\, r_t$ is the interest paid by the company in period t. $(N_t - N_{t-1})$ is the increase in the book value of debt in period t. When the required return to debt (Kd) is different than the cost of debt (r), then the value of debt (D) is different than its book value (N). Note that if, for all t, $r_t = Kd_t$, then $N_0 = D_0$. But there are situations in which $r_t > Kd_t$ (i.e. if the company has old fixed-rate debt and interest rates have declined, or if the company can only get expensive bank debt), and situations in which $r_t < Kd_t$ (i.e. if the company has old fixed-rate debt and interest rates have increased).

Method 2. Using the free cash flow and the WACC (weighted average cost of capital)

Equation (4) indicates that the value of the debt (D) plus that of the shareholders' equity (E) is the present value of the free cash flows (FCF) that the company is expected to generate, discounted at the weighted average cost of capital after tax (WACC):

$$E_0 + D_0 = PV_0[WACC_t;\ FCF_t] \tag{4}$$

The free cash flow is the hypothetical equity cash flow when the company has no debt. The expression that relates the FCF with the ECF is:

$$ECF_t = FCF_t + (N_t - N_{t-1}) - N_{t-1}\, r_t (1 - T_t) \tag{5}$$

T_t is the effective tax rate applied to earnings in the levered company in year t.

The WACC is the rate at which the FCF must be discounted so as to ensure that equation (4) gives the same result as that given by the sum of (1) and (2). In the appendix we show that the expression for the WACC is:

$$WACC_t = \frac{E_{t-1}\, Ke_t + D_{t-1}\, Kd_t - N_{t-1}\, r_t T_t}{E_{t-1} + D_{t-1}} \tag{6}$$

$(E_{t-1} + D_{t-1})$ is the value of the firm obtained when the valuation is performed using formula (4). Consequently, the valuation is an iterative process: the free cash flows are discounted at the WACC to calculate the value of the firm (D+E) but, in order to obtain the WACC, we first need to know the value of the firm (D+E).[2]

Some authors, one being Luehrman (1997), argue that equation (4) does not give us the same result as is given by the sum of (1) and (2). That usually happens as a result of an error in calculating equation (6), which requires using the values of equity and debt (E_{t-1} and D_{t-1}) obtained in the valuation. The most common error when calculating the WACC is to use book values of equity and debt, as in

---

2. Obviously, if the required return to debt (Kd) is assumed equal to the cost of debt (r), then the debt value (D) is equal to its book value (N), and equation (6) is transformed into (6a):

$$WACC_t = \frac{E_{t-1}\, Ke_t + D_{t-1}\, Kd_t\, (1 - T_t)}{E_{t-1} + D_{t-1}} \tag{6a}$$

Luehrman (1997) and in Arditti and Levy (1977). Other common errors when calculating $WACC_t$ are:

- Using E_t and D_t instead of E_{t-1} and D_{t-1}.
- Using market values of equity and debt, instead of the values of equity and debt (E_{t-1} and D_{t-1}) obtained in the valuation.
- Using formula (6a) instead of formula (6) when the value of debt is not equal to its book value.

Method 3. Using the capital cash flow (CCF) and the $WACC_{BT}$ (weighted average cost of capital, before tax)

The capital cash flows[3] are the cash flows available for all holders of the company's securities, whether these be debt or shares. They are equivalent to the equity cash flow (ECF) plus the cash flow corresponding to the debt holders (CFd).

Equation (7) indicates that the value of the shareholders' equity (E) today plus that of the debt (D) is equal to the capital cash flow (CCF) discounted at the weighted average cost of debt and shareholders' equity before tax[4] ($WACC_{BT}$).

$$E_0 + D_0 = PV_0[WACC_{BT\,t};\ CCF_t] \tag{7}$$

The $WACC_{BT}$ is the discount rate that ensures that the values obtained using equations (7) and (4) are the same. Ruback (2002) also proves in a different way that the CCF method is equivalent to the FCF method. In the appendix, we show that the expression for the $WACC_{BT}$ is:

$$WACC_{BT\,t} = \frac{E_{t-1}\, Ke_t + D_{t-1}\, Kd_t}{E_{t-1} + D_{t-1}} \tag{8}$$

The expression that relates the CCF with the ECF and the FCF is (9):

$$CCF_t = ECF_t + CFd_t = FCF_t + N_{t-1}\, r_t\, T_t \tag{9}$$

---

3. Arditti and Levy (1977) and Ruback (1995 and 2002) suggest that the firm's value could be calculated by discounting the Capital Cash Flows instead of the Free Cash Flows.
4. Ruback (2002) calls it Pre-Tax WACC.

Method 4. Adjusted present value (APV)

The adjusted present value (APV) equation (10) indicates that the value of the debt (D) plus that of the shareholders' equity (E) is equal to the value of the unlevered equity (Vu) plus the value of the tax shields (VTS):

$$E_0 + D_0 = Vu_0 + VTS_0 \tag{10}$$

Vu is given by (11). Ku is the required return to equity in the debt-free company (also called the required return to assets).

$$Vu_0 = PV_0[Ku_t;\ FCF_t] \tag{11}$$

Most descriptions of the APV suggest calculating the VTS by discounting the interest tax shields using some discount rate. Myers (1974), Taggart (1991) and Luehrman (1997) propose using the cost of debt (based on the theory that tax shields are about as uncertain as principal and interest payments). However, Harris and Pringle (1985), Kaplan and Ruback (1995), Brealey and Myers (2000) and Ruback (2002) propose using the required return to the unlevered equity as the discount rate.[5] Copeland, Koller and Murrin (2000) assert that "the finance literature does not provide a clear answer about which discount rate for the tax benefit of interest is theoretically correct". They further conclude "we leave it to the reader's judgment to decide which approach best fits his or her situation".

Fernández (2004) shows that the value of tax shields is the difference between the present values of two different cash flows, each with its own risk: the present value of taxes for the unlevered company, and the present value of taxes for the levered company. Following Fernández (2004), the value of tax shields without cost of leverage is[6]:

$$VTS_0 = PV_0[Ku_t;\ D_{t-1}\,Ku_t T_t + T_t(N_{t-1}r_t - D_{t-1}Kd_t)] \tag{12}$$

Consequently, (10) may be rewritten as:

$$E_0 + D_0 = PV_0[Ku_t;\ FCF_t + D_{t-1}\,Ku_t T_t + T_t(N_{t-1}r_t - D_{t-1}Kd_t)] \tag{13}$$

In the appendix, we show that the relations between Ke and Ku, and between WACC and Ku are:

$$Ke_t = Ku_t + \frac{D_{t-1}(1-T_t)(Ku_t - Kd_t)}{E_{t-1}} \tag{14}$$

---

5. We will discuss these theories in Section 3.
6. If the cost of debt (r) is equal to the required return to debt, then debt value is equal to its book value, and $VTS_0 = PV_0\ [Ku_t;\ D_{t-1}\ Ku_t\ T_t]$. For no growth perpetuities, equation (12) is VTS = DT. The value of tax shields being DT for no growth perpetuities is quite a standard result. It may be found, for example, in Bodie and Merton (2000), Modigliani and Miller (1963), Myers (1974), Damodaran (2002) and Brealey and Myers (2000).

$$WACC_t = Ku_t - \frac{D_{t-1}\, T_t\, Ku_t}{E_{t-1} + D_{t-1}} - T_t \frac{N_{t-1}\, r_t - D_{t-1}\, Kd_t}{E_{t-1} + D_{t-1}} \quad \textbf{(15)}$$

Equation (15) means that the WACC of a levered company is smaller than Ku, and the difference grows with leverage.

Method 5. Using the residual income[7] and Ke (required return to equity)

Equation (16) indicates that the value of the equity (E) is the equity's book value (Ebv) plus the present value of the expected residual income (RI) discounted at the required return to equity (Ke).

$$E_0 = Ebv_0 + PV_0[Ke_t;\ RI_t] \quad \textbf{(16)}$$

The term residual income (RI) is used to define the accounting net income or profit after tax (PAT) minus the equity's book value (Ebv_{t-1}) multiplied by the required return to equity.[8]

$$RI_t = PAT_t - Ke_t\ Ebv_{t-1} \quad \textbf{(17)}$$

In the appendix, we prove that equations (16) and (1) provide the same valuation even if the financial statement forecasts do not satisfy the clean surplus relation (i.e., net income less dividends does not equal the change in shareholders' equity).

Penman and Sougiannis (1998), Francis, Olsson and Oswald (2000), and Penman (2001) argue that residual income and equity cash flow provide different valuations and that accrual earnings techniques dominate free cash flow and dividend discounting approaches. However, we agree with Lundholm and O'Keefe (2001a), who argue that, properly implemented, both models yield identical valuations for all firms in all years. They identify how prior research has applied inconsistent assumptions to the two models and show how these seemingly minor errors cause surprisingly large differences in the value estimates. Lundholm and O'Keefe (2001b) identify subtle errors in the implementation of the models in prior empirical studies by Penman and Sougiannis (1998) and Francis, Olsson and Oswald (2000).

Method 6. Using the EVA (economic value added) and the WACC (weighted average cost of capital)

---

7. The residual income is also called economic profit, residual earnings, abnormal earnings and excess profit.
8. As $PAT_t = ROE_t\ Ebv_{t-1}$, the residual income can also be expressed as $RI_t = (ROE_t - Ke_t)\ Ebv_{t-1}$

Equation (18) indicates that the value of the debt (D) plus that of the shareholders' equity (E) is the book value of the shareholders' equity and the debt (Ebv_0+ N_0) plus the present value of the expected EVA, discounted at the weighted average cost of capital (WACC):

$$E_0 + D_0 = (Ebv_0 + N_0) + PV_0[WACC_t;\ EVA_t] \qquad \textbf{(18)}$$

The EVA (economic value added) is the NOPAT (Net Operating Profit After Tax) minus the company's book value (N_{t-1} + Ebv_{t-1}) multiplied by the weighted average cost of capital (WACC). The NOPAT (Net Operating Profit After Taxes) is the profit of the unlevered (debt-free) company[9].

$$EVA_t = NOPAT_t - (N_{t-1} + Ebv_{t-1})\ WACC_t \qquad \textbf{(19)}$$

In the Appendix, we prove that equations (18) and (4) provide the same valuation.

***Method** 7.* Using the business risk-adjusted free cash flow and Ku (required return to assets)

Equation (20) indicates that the value of the debt (D) plus that of the shareholders' equity (E) is the present value of the business risk-adjusted free cash flows[10] ($FCF//_{Ku}$) that the company is expected to generate, discounted at the required return to assets (Ku):

$$E_0 + D_0 = PV_0[Ku_t;\ FCF_t\ //_{Ku}] \qquad \textbf{(20)}$$

The definition of the business risk-adjusted free cash flow is obtained by making (20) equal to (4):

$$FCF_t\ //_{Ku} = FCF_t - (E_{t-1} + D_{t-1})(WACC_t - Ku_t) \qquad \textbf{(21)}$$

Method 8. Using the business risk-adjusted equity cash flow and Ku (required return to assets)

Equation (22) indicates that the value of the equity (E) is the present value of the expected business risk-adjusted equity cash flows ($ECF//_{Ku}$) discounted at the required return to assets (Ku):

---

9. As $NOPAT_t = ROA_t\ (Ebv_{t-1} + N_{t-1})$, the economic value added (EVA) can also be expressed as: $EVA_t = (ROA_t - WACC_t)(Ebv_{t-1} + N_{t-1})$.
10. $FCF//_{Ku}$ is the notation for business risk-adjusted free cash flows. Its definition is equation (21). This number is the FCF adjusted in such a way that discounting it at the required return to assets (equation 20) provides the same value than discounting the FCF using the WACC (equation 4). Similarly, $ECF//_{Ku}$ is the notation for business risk-adjusted equity cash flows.

$$E_0 = PV_0[Ku_t;\ ECF_t\ //_{Ku}] \tag{22}$$

The definition of the business risk-adjusted equity cash flows is obtained by making (22) equal to (1):

$$ECF_t\ //_{Ku} = ECF_t - E_{t-1}(Ke_t - Ku_t) \tag{23}$$

Method 9. Using the risk-free-adjusted free cash flows discounted at the risk-free rate

Equation (24) indicates that the value of the debt (D) plus that of the shareholders' equity (E) is the present value of the expected risk-free-adjusted free cash flows ($FCF//_{RF}$) discounted at the risk-free rate (R_F):

$$E_0 + D_0 = PV_0[R_{F\,t};\ FCF_t\ //_{RF}] \tag{24}$$

The definition of the risk-free-adjusted free cash flows is obtained by making (24) equal to (4):

$$FCF_t\ //_{RF} = FCF_t - (E_{t-1} + D_{t-1})(WACC_t - R_{F\,t}) \tag{25}$$

Method 10. Using the risk-free-adjusted equity cash flows discounted at the risk-free rate

Equation (26) indicates that the value of the equity (E) is the present value of the expected risk-free-adjusted equity cash flows ($ECF//_{RF}$) discounted at the risk-free rate (R_F):

$$E_0 = PV_0[R_{F\,t};\ ECF_t\ //\ R_F] \tag{26}$$

The definition of the risk-free-adjusted equity cash flows is obtained by making (26) equal to (1):

$$ECF_t\ //_{RF} = ECF_t - E_{t-1}(Ke_t - R_{F\,t}) \tag{27}$$

We could also talk about an eleventh method: using the business risk-adjusted capital cash flow and Ku (required return to assets). But the business risk-adjusted capital cash flow is identical to the business risk-adjusted free cash flow ($CCF//_{Ku} = FCF//_{Ku}$). Therefore, this method would be identical to Method 7.

And we could talk about a twelfth method: using the risk-free-adjusted capital cash flow and R_F (risk-free rate). But the risk-free-adjusted capital cash flow is identical to the risk-free-adjusted free cash flow ($CCF//_{RF} = FCF//_{RF}$). Therefore, this method would be identical to Method 9.

Table I is an overview of the ten valuation methods.

The formulas relating the betas to the required returns are:

$$Ke = R_F + \beta_L P_M \qquad Ku = R_F + \beta u\, P_M \qquad Kd = R_F + \beta d\, P_M \tag{28}$$

R_F is the risk-free rate and P_M is the market risk premium.

In order to operationalize a valuation, very often one begins with assumptions of βd and β_L, not with βu. βu has to be inferred from βd and β_L. The formula that allows us to calculate βu, may easily be derived by substituting (28) in (14):

$$\beta u = \frac{E\,\beta_L + D\,\beta d\,(1-T)}{E + D\,(1-T)} \tag{29}$$

Once the valuation starts with Ku (or βu), all valuation methods require an iterative process except the APV (method 4) and the methods that use business risk-adjusted cash flows (methods 7 and 8). Therefore, from a computational point of view these three valuation methods are much easier to implement.

3. An Example: Valuation of the Company Tenmethods Inc.

The fictitious company Tenmethods Inc. has the balance sheet and income statement forecasts for the next few years shown in Table II. After year 3, the balance sheet and the income statement are expected to grow at an annual rate of 2%. Although the statutory tax rate is 40%, the effective tax rate will be zero in year 1 because the company is forecasting losses, and 36.36% in year 2 because the company will offset the previous year's losses (see line 16). The cost of debt (the interest rate that the bank will charge) is 9%. Using the balance sheet and income statement forecasts in Table II, we can readily obtain the cash flows given at the bottom of Table II.

Table III contains the valuation of the company Tenmethods Inc. using the ten methods described in Section 2. The unlevered beta (βu) is 1. The risk-free rate is 6%. The cost of debt (r) is 9%, but the company feels that it is too high. The company thinks that the appropriate required return to debt (Kd) is 8%. The market risk premium is 4%. Consequently, using the CAPM, the required return to assets is 10%. As the cost of debt (r) is higher than the required return to debt (Kd), the value of debt (D, line 2) is higher than its nominal value (N, line 6 of Table II). The value of debt also fulfills equation (2i).

The first method used is the APV because it does not require an iterative process and, therefore, is easier to implement. To calculate the value of the unlevered equity (line 3) and the value of tax shields (line 4), we only need to compute two present values using Ku (10%). Line 5 is the enterprise value and line 6 is the equity value. Lines 5 and 6 also fulfill equations (1i) and (13i). Line

7 is the required return to equity according to equation (14). Line 8 is the calculation of the equity value as the present value of the expected equity cash flows (equation (1)). Please note that lines 7 and 8 are calculated through an iterative process because for equation (14) we need to know the result of equation (1), and for equation (1) we need to know the result of equation (14). The equity value in lines 8 and 6 is exactly the same. Line 9 is the WACC according to equations (6) and (15). Line 10 is the calculation of the equity value as the present value of the expected free cash flows minus the debt value (equation (4)). Lines 9 and 10 are calculated through an iterative process because for equations (6) and (15) we need to know the result of equation (4), and for equation (4) we need to know the result of equation (6) or (15). Please note that in year 1 WACC = Ku = 10% because the effective tax rate is zero. The equity value in lines 10 and 6 is exactly the same.

Line 11 is the $WACC_{BT}$ according to equation (8). Line 12 is the calculation of the equity value as the present value of the expected capital cash flows minus the debt value (equation (7)). Lines 11 and 12 are calculated through an iterative process because for calculating the $WACC_{BT}$ we need to know the equity value and viceversa. Note that in year 1 $WACC_{BT}$ – WACC = Ku = 10% because the effective tax rate is zero. The equity values in lines 12 and 6 are exactly the same.

Line 13 is the expected residual income according to equation (17). Line 14 is the calculation of the equity value as the present value of the expected residual income plus the book value of equity (equation (16)). Lines 13 and 14 are calculated through an iterative process because for calculating the residual income we need to know the required return to equity (equation (14)), and for this, we need the equity value. Lines 14 and 6 are equal. Line 15 is the expected economic value added according to equation (19). Line 14 is the calculation of the equity value as the present value of the expected economic value added plus the book value of equity minus the debt value plus the debt book value (equation (18)). Lines 15 and 16 are calculated through an iterative process because for calculating the economic value added, we must know the WACC (equation (6)), and for this, we need the equity value. Lines 16 and 6 are equal.

Line 17 is the expected business's risk-adjusted equity cash flows according to equation (23). Line 18 is the calculation of the equity value as the present value of the expected business's risk-adjusted equity cash flows (equation (22)). As the present value is calculated using Ku (10%), there is no need for an iterative process. Lines 18 and 6 are equal. Line 19 is the expected business's risk-adjusted free cash flows according to equation (21). Line 20 is the calculation of the equity value as the present value of the expected business's risk-adjusted free cash flows minus the value of debt (equation (20)). As the present value is calculated using Ku (10%), there is no need for an iterative process. Lines 20 and 6 are equal.

Line 21 is the expected risk-free-adjusted equity cash flows according to equation (27). Line 22 is the calculation of the equity value as the present value of the risk-free rate-adjusted equity cash flows (equation (26)). Lines 21 and 22 are calculated through an iterative process because for calculating the risk-free-adjusted equity cash flows we need to know the required return to equity (equation (14)), and for that, we need the equity value. Lines 22 and 6 are equal. Line 23 is the expected risk-free-adjusted free cash flows according to equation (25). Line 24 is the calculation of the equity value as the present value of the risk-free rate-adjusted free cash flows minus the debt value (equation (24)). Lines 23 and 24 are calculated through an iterative process because for calculating the risk-free-adjusted free cash flows we need to know the WACC (equation (6)), and for that, we need the equity value. Lines 24 and 6 are equal.

Table IV shows the sensitivity analysis of the valuation of Tenmethods, Inc. as a function of the growth after period 3 (g). As expected, the equity value, the debt value, the value of tax shields and the WACC increase as growth occurs.

4. Comparison to Alternative Valuation Theories

There is a considerable body of literature on the discounted cash flow valuation of firms. The main difference between all of these papers and the approach proposed in sections 2 and 3 is that most previous papers calculate the value of tax shields as the present value of the tax savings due to the payment of interest.

Myers (1974) introduced the APV (adjusted present value) method, but proposed calculating the VTS by discounting the tax savings (N T r) at the required return to debt (Kd). The argument is that the risk of the tax saving arising from the use of debt is the same as the risk of the debt. This approach has also been recommended in later papers in the literature, two being Taggart (1991) and Luehrman (1997). One problem with the Myers (1974) approach is that it does not always give a higher cost of equity than cost of assets and this hardly makes any economic sense.

Harris and Pringle (1985) propose that the present value of the tax saving due to the payment of interest should be calculated by discounting the interest tax savings (N T r) at the required return to unlevered equity (Ku), i.e. VTS = PV [Ku; N T r]. Their argument is that the interest tax shields have the same systematic risk as the firm's underlying cash flows and, therefore, should be discounted at the required return to assets (Ku). Ruback (1995 and 2002), Kaplan and Ruback (1995), Brealey and Myers (2000, page 555), and Tham and Vélez-Pareja (2001), also claim that the appropriate discount rate for tax shields is Ku, the required return to unlevered equity. Ruback (1995 and 2002) presents the Capital Cash Flow (CCF) method and claims that $WACC_{BT}$ = Ku. Based on this assumption, Ruback gets the same valuation as Harris and Pringle (1985).

A large part of the literature argues that the value of tax shields should be calculated in a different manner depending on the debt strategy of the firm. Hence, a firm that wishes to keep a constant D/E ratio must be valued in a different manner from a firm that has a preset level of debt. Miles and Ezzell

(1980) indicate that for a firm with a fixed debt target (i.e. a constant [D/(D+E)] ratio), the correct rate for discounting the interest tax shields is Kd for the first year and Ku for the tax saving in later years.[11] Inselbag and Kaufold (1997) and Ruback (2002) argue that when the amount of debt is fixed, interest tax shields should be discounted at the required return to debt. However, if the firm targets a constant debt/value ratio, the value of tax shields should be calculated according to Miles and Ezzell (1980). Finally, Taggart (1991) suggests using Miles & Ezzell (1980) if the company adjusts to its target debt ratio once a year and Harris & Pringle (1985) if the company adjusts to its target debt ratio continuously.

Damodaran (1994, page 31) argues that if all the business risk is borne by the equity, then the formula relating the levered beta (β_L) to the asset beta (βu) is $\beta_L = \beta u + (D/E)\ \beta u\ (1 - T)$. This formula is exactly formula (29) assuming that $\beta d = 0$. One interpretation of this assumption is (see page 31 of Damodaran, 1994) that "all of the firm's risk is borne by the stockholders (i.e., the beta of the debt is zero)". In some cases, it may be reasonable to assume that the debt has a zero beta, but then the required return to debt (Kd) should also be the risk-free rate. However, in several examples in his books Damodaran (1984 and 2002) considers the required return to debt to be equal to the cost of debt, both of which are higher than the risk-free rate.

Fernández (2004) proves that the value of tax shields without cost of leverage is equation (12). When the cost of debt (r) is equal to the required return to debt, then the debt value is equal to its book value, and $VTS_0 = PV_0\ [Ku_t;\ D_{t-1}\ Ku_t\ T_t]$. This expression does not mean that the appropriate discount for tax shields is the unlevered cost of equity, since the amount being discounted is higher than the tax shields (it is multiplied by the unlevered cost of equity and not the cost of debt). This result arises as the difference of two present values. In the case of no growth perpetuities, equation (12) is VTS = DT. The value of tax shields being DT for no growth perpetuities is quite a standard result. It may be found, for example, in Bodie and Merton (2000), Modigliani and Miller (1958 and 1963), Myers (1974), Damodaran (2002) and Brealey and Myers (2000).

Table V contains the most striking results of the valuation performed on the company Tenmethods, Inc. according to Fernández (2004), Damodaran (1994), Ruback (2002) and Myers (1974). It may be seen that:

- Equity value (E) grows with residual growth (g), except according to Damodaran (1994).

---

11. Lewellen and Emery (1986) also claim that this is the most logically consistent method. Although Miles and Ezzell do not mention what the value of tax shields should be, this may be inferred from their equation relating the required return to equity to the required return for the unlevered company (equation 22 in their paper). This relation implies that

- Required return to equity (Ke) decreases with growth (g), except according to Damodaran (1994) and Ruback (2002).

- Required return to equity (Ke) is higher than the required return to assets (Ku), except for Myers (1974) when $g > 5\%$.

Please note that these exceptions are counterintuitive.

5. Conclusion

The paper shows that ten commonly used discounted cash flow valuation methods always give the same value. This result is logical, since all the methods analyze the same reality under the same hypotheses; they differ only in the cash flows taken as the starting point for the valuation.

We present all ten methods, allowing the required return to debt to be different from the cost of debt. Seven methods require an iterative process. Only APV and the business risk-adjusted cash flows methods do not require iteration; that makes them the easiest methods to use.

The relevant tax rate is not the statutory tax rate, but the effective tax rate applied to earnings in the levered company on each year.

The value of tax shields is not the present value of tax shields using either the cost of equity or debt to discount the tax write-offs. It is the difference between the present values of two different cash flows, each with its own risk: the present value of taxes for the unlevered company and the present value of taxes for the levered company. The paper also compares the valuation result with three alternative theories on the calculation of the VTS: Myers (1974), Ruback (2002), and Damodaran (1994).

References:

Arditti, F. and Levy, H. (1977), "The Weighted Average Cost of Capital as a Cutoff Rate: A Critical Examination of the Classical Textbook Weighted Average", *Financial Management* (Fall): 24-34.

Bodie, Z. and Merton, R. (2000), *Finance*. (Prentice Hall, Upper Saddle River, New Jersey).

Brealey, R. and Myers, S. (2000), *Principles of Corporate Finance*. (McGraw-Hill, New York, sixth edition).

Copeland, T., Koller, T. and Murrin, J. (2000), *Valuation: Measuring and Managing the Value of Companies*. (Wiley, New York, third edition).

Damodaran, A. (1994), *Damodaran on Valuation*. (John Wilcy and Sons, New York).

Damodaran, A. (2002), *Investment Valuation*. (John Wiley and Sons, New York, second edition).

Fernández, P. (2002), *Valuation Methods and Shareholder Value Creation*. (Academic Press, San Diego, CA.).

Fernández, P. (2004), "The Value of Tax Shields is not Equal to the Present Value of Tax Shields", *Journal of Financial Economics* 73/1: 145-165.

Francis, J., Olsson, P. and Oswald, D. (2000), "Comparing the accuracy and explainability of dividend, free cash flow, and abnormal earnings equity value estimates", *Journal of Accounting Research* 38 (Spring): 45-70.

Harris, R. and Pringle, J. (1985), "Risk-adjusted discount rates extensions form the average-risk case", *Journal of Financial Research* (Fall): 237-244.

Inselbag, I. and Kaufold, H. (1997), "Two DCF approaches for valuing companies under alternative financing strategies (and how to choose between them)", *Journal of Applied Corporate Finance* (Spring): 114-122.

Kaplan, S. and Ruback, R. (1995), "The Valuation of Cash Flow Forecast: An Empirical Analysis", *Journal of Finance* 50: 1059-1093.

Lewellen, W. and Emery, D. (1986), "Corporate debt management and the value of the firm", *Journal of Financial Quantitative Analysis* (December): 415-426.

Luehrman, T. (1997), "What's it worth: A general manager's guide to valuation", and "Using APV: A better tool for valuing operations", *Harvard Business Review* (May-June):132-154.

Lundholm, R. and O'Keefe, T. (2001a), "Reconciling value estimates from the discounted cash flow model and the residual income model", *Contemporary Accounting Research* 18 (Summer): 311-335.

Lundholm, R. and O'Keefe, T. (2001b), "On comparing residual income and discounted cash flow models of equity valuation: A response to Penman 2001", *Contemporary Accounting Research* 18 (Winter): 215-220.

Miles, J. and Ezzell, J. (1980), "The weighted average cost of capital, perfect capital markets and project life: a clarification", *Journal of Financial and Quantitative Analysis* (September): 719-730.

Miles, J. and Ezzell, J. (1985), "Reformulating tax shield valuation: A note", *Journal of Finance* Vol. XL, 5: 1485-1492.

Modigliani, F. and Miller, M. (1958), "The cost of capital, corporation finance and the theory of investment", *American Economic Review* 48: 261-297.

Modigliani, F. and Miller, M. (1963), "Corporate income taxes and the cost of capital: A correction", *American Economic Review* (June): 433-443.

Myers, S. (1974), "Interactions of corporate financing and investment decisions – Implications for capital budgeting", *Journal of Finance* (March): 1-25.

Penman, S. (2001), "On comparing cash flow and accrual accounting models for use in equity valuation", *Contemporary Accounting Research* 18 (Winter): 203-214.

Penman, S. and Sougiannis, T. (1998), "A comparison of dividend, cash flow, and earnings approaches to equity valuation", *Contemporary Accounting Research* 15 (Fall): 343-383.

Ruback, R. (1995), "A note on capital cash flow valuation", Harvard Business School Note, 9-295-069.

Ruback, R. (2002), "Capital cash flows: a simple approach to valuing risky cash flows", *Financial Management* 31: 85-103.

Taggart, R. (1991), "Consistent valuation and cost of capital. Expressions with corporate and personal taxes", *Financial Management* 20: 8-20.

Tham, J. and Vélez-Pareja, I. (2001), "The correct discount rate for the tax shield: the N-period case", SSRN Working Paper.

Appendix: Proofs

Derivation of the expression of WACC

The intertemporal form of equations (1), (2) and (4) is:

$$E_t = E_{t-1}(1 + Ke_t) - ECF_t \tag{1i}$$

$$D_t = D_{t-1}(1 + Kd_t) - CFd_t \tag{2i}$$

$$E_t + D_t = (E_{t-1} + D_{t-1})(1 + WACC_t) - FCF_t \tag{4i}$$

Substracting equation (4i) from the sum of (1i) and (2i), we get:

$$0 = E_{t-1} Ke_t + D_{t-1} Kd_t - (E_{t-1} + D_{t-1}) WACC_t + (FCF_t - ECF_t - CFd_t)$$

From (3) and (5), we know that $FCF_t - ECF_t - CFd_t = - N_{t-1} r_t T_t$. Therefore,

$$WACC_t = \frac{E_{t-1} Ke_t + D_{t-1} Kd_t - N_{t-1} r_t T_t}{E_{t-1} + D_{t-1}} \tag{6}$$

Derivation of the expression of $WACC_{BT}$

The intertemporal form of equation (7) is:

$$E_t + D_t = (E_{t-1} + D_{t-1})(1 + WACC_{BT_t}) - CCF_t \tag{7i}$$

Substracting equation (7i) from (4i), we get:

$$0 = (E_{t-1} + D_{t-1})(WACC_t - WACC_{BTt}) + (CCF_t - FCF_t)$$

From (9), we know that $CCF_t - FCF_t = N_{t-1} r_t T_t$. Therefore,

$$WACC_{BT_t} = WACC_t + \frac{N_{t-1} r_t T_t}{E_{t-1} + D_{t-1}} = \frac{E_{t-1} Ke_t + D_{t-1} Kd_t}{E_{t-1} + D_{t-1}} \tag{8}$$

Relation between Ke and Ku

Equation (13) may be rewritten in its interemporal form as:

$$E_t + D_t = (E_{t-1} + D_{t-1})(1 + Ku_t) - [FCF_t + D_{t-1} Ku_t T_t + T_t(N_{t-1} r_t - D_{t-1} Kd_t)] \tag{13i}$$

Subtracting equation (13i) from the sum of (1i) and (2i), we get:

$$0 = E_{t-1}\,Ke_t + D_{t-1}Kd_t - (E_{t-1} + D_{t-1})Ku_t + \left[FCF_t + D_{t-1}\,Ku_t\,T_t + T_t(N_{t-1}\,r_t - D_{t-1}\,Kd_t)\right] - ECF_t - CFd_t$$

From (3) and (5) we know that $FCF_t - ECF_t - CFd_t = - N_{t-1}\,r_t\,T_t$. Therefore,

$$0 = E_{t-1}\,Ke_t + D_{t-1}Kd_t - (E_{t-1} + D_{t-1})Ku_t + D_{t-1}\,Ku_t\,T_t - D_{t-1}\,Kd_t T_t$$

Therefore, the relation between Ke and Ku is:

$$Ke_t = Ku_t + \frac{D_{t-1}(1 - T_t)(Ku_t - Kd_t)}{E_{t-1}} \quad \textbf{(14)}$$

Relation between WACC and Ku

Substituting (14) in (6), we get:

$$WACC_t(E_{t-1} + D_{t-1}) = E_{t-1}\,Ku_t + D_{t-1}(1 - T_t)(Ku_t - Kd_t) + D_{t-1}\,Kd_t - N_{t-1}\,r_t T_t$$

Therefore, the relation between WACC and Ku is:

$$WACC_t = Ku_t - \frac{D_{t-1}\,T_t\,Ku_t}{E_{t-1} + D_{t-1}} - T_t\,\frac{N_{t-1}\,r_t - D_{t-1}\,Kd_t}{E_{t-1} + D_{t-1}} \quad \textbf{(15)}$$

Valuations using residual income and cash flow to equity provide the same value

The expected equity cash flow is the sum of all cash payments to shareholders, mainly dividends and share repurchases.

Consequently[12]:

$$ECF_t = PAT_t - (Ebv_t - Ebv_{t-1}) \quad \textbf{(30)}$$

By substituting (30) in (1i) we get:

$$E_t = E_{t-1}(1+Ke_t) - PAT_t + (Ebv_t - Ebv_{t-1})$$

Rearranging terms, we get:

$$E_t - Ebv_t = (E_{t-1} - Ebv_{t-1})(1+Ke_t) - (PAT_t - Ke_t\,Ebv_{t-1}) = (E_{t-1} - Ebv_{t-1})(1+Ke_t) - RI_t$$

---

12. If the clean surplus relation does not hold (i.e. $ECF_t\ \ PAT_t - Ebv_t$), for example, because the company allocates a quantity Π directly to retained earnings, then Profit After Tax should be adjusted as follows:
$PAT_t = PATbv_t - \Pi$, where $PATbv_t$ is the Profit After Tax shown in the income statement.

Valuations using EVA and free cash flow provide the same value

From (30) and (9), the relationship between the FCF and net income or profit after tax (PAT) is:

$$FCF_t = PAT_t - (Ebv_t - Ebv_{t-1}) + N_{t-1}\, r_t\, (1-T_t) - (N_t - N_{t-1}) \quad \textbf{(31)}$$

As $PAT_t = NOPAT_t - N_{t-1}\, r_t\, (1-T_t)$, equation (31) may be expresed as:

$$FCF_t = NOPAT_t - (Ebv_t - Ebv_{t-1} + N_t - N_{t-1}) \quad \textbf{(32)}$$

Substituting (32) in (4i), we get:

$$E_t + D_t = (E_{t-1} + D_{t-1})\,(1 + WACC_t) - NOPAT_t + (Ebv_t - Ebv_{t-1} + N_t - N_{t-1})$$

Rearranging terms, we get:

$$E_t + D_t - (Ebv_t + N_t) = [E_{t-1} + D_{t-1} - (Ebv_{t-1} + N_{t-1})]\,(1+WACC_t) - [NOPAT_t - (N_{t-1} + Ebv_{t-1})WACC_t]$$

EVA calculated using WACC with book values of debt and equity is economic profit

The WACC calculated using book values of equity and debt is:

$$WACCbv_t = \frac{Ebv_{t-1}\, Ke_t + N_{t-1}\, r_t\,(1-T_t)}{Ebv_{t-1} + N_{t-1}} \quad \textbf{(33)}$$

Consequently:

$$Ebv_{t-1}\, Ke_t + N_{t-1}\, r_t\,(1-T_t) = WACCbv_t\,(Ebv_{t-1} + N_{t-1}) \quad \textbf{(34)}$$

As $PAT_t = NOPAT_t - N_{t-1}\, r_t\,(1-T_t)$, the residual income can also be expressed as:

$$RI_t = NOPAT_t - N_{t-1}\, r_t\,(1-T_t) - Ke_t\, Ebv_{t-1} \quad \textbf{(35)}$$

Taking into consideration that $NOPAT_t = ROA_t\,(Ebv_{t-1} + N_{t-1})$ and replacing (33) and (34) in (35), we get the definition of EVA using a WACCbv (WACC calculated with book values of debt and equity):

$$RI_t = (N_{t-1} + Ebv_{t-1})\,(ROA_t - WACCbv_t) \quad \textbf{(36)}$$

Consequently, another way of expressing (16) is[13]:

$$E_0 = Ebv_0 + PV_0\,[Ke;\, (N_{t-1} + Ebv_{t-1})\,(ROA_t - WACCbv_t)]$$

The difference between residual income and EVA is:

$$RI_t - EVA_t = (N_{t-1} + Ebv_{t-1})\,(WACC_t - WACCbv_t) \quad \textbf{(37)}$$

13. ROA *(return on assets)* is also called ROI *(return on investments)*, ROCE *(return on capital employed)*, *ROC (return on capital)* and RONA *(return on net assets)*. ROA = ROI = ROCE = ROC = RONA. ROA is equal to ROE in the unlevered company.

Table I: Ten valuation methods

Method	Cash flow	Discount rate	Value
1	ECF (Equity cash flow)	Ke (cost of levered equity)	E (Equity)
	CFd (debt cash flow)	Kd (required return to debt)	D (Debt)
2	FCF (free cash flow)	WACC (weighted average cost of capital)	E + D
3	CCF (capital cash flow)	$WACC_{BT}$ (weighted average cost of capital before taxes)	E + D
4	FCF (free cash flow)	Ku (cost of unlevered equity)	Vu (Unlevered equity)
	D T Ku	Ku (cost of unlevered equity)	VTS (Value of tax shields)
5	RI (Residual income)	Ke	E - Ebv
6	EVA (Economic value added)	WACC	E + D – Ebv - N
7	$FCF//_{Ku}$ (Business risk-adjusted free cash flow)	Ku	E + D
8	$ECF//_{Ku}$ (Business risk-adjusted equity cash flow)	Ku	E
9	$FCF//_{RF}$ (Risk-free-adjusted free cash flow)	R_F (Risk-free-rate)	E + D
10	$ECF//_{RF}$ (Risk-free-adjusted equity cash flow)	R_F	E

Table II: Balance sheet, income statement and cash flows of Tenmethods, Inc.
Growth of income statement and balance sheet after period 3 = 2%. Cost of debt (r) = 9%

line	***Balance sheet***	**0**	**1**	**2**	**3**	**4**	**5**
1	Working capital requirements (WCR)	800	890	1,000	1,100	1,122.00	1,144.44
2	Gross fixed assets	1,200	1,300	1,450	1,660	1,895.10	2,134.90
3	- accumulated depreciation		200	405	615	829.20	1,047.68
4	Net fixed assets	1,200	1,100	1,045	1,045	1,065.90	1,087.22
5	TOTAL ASSETS	2,000	1,990	2,045	2,145	2,187.90	2,231.66
6	Debt (N)	1,500	1,500	1,500	1,550	1,581.00	1,612.62
7	Equity (book value)	500	490	545	595	606.90	619.04
8	TOTAL LIABILITIES	2,000	1,990	2,045	2,145	2,187.90	2,231.66

	Income statement	**1**	**2**	**3**	**4**	**5**
9	EBITDA	325.0	450.0	500.0	510.00	520.20
10	Depreciation	200.0	205.0	210.0	214.20	218.48
11	Interest payments	135.0	135.0	135.0	139.50	142.29
12	PBT (profit before tax)	-10.0	110.0	155.0	156.30	159.43
13	Taxes	0.0	40.0	62.0	62.52	63.77
14	PAT (profit after tax = net income)	**-10.0**	**70.0**	**93.0**	**93.78**	**95.66**
15	NOPAT (Net operating profit after taxes)	125.00	155.91	174.00	177.48	181.03
16	**Tax rate** = line 13 / line 12	**0.0%**	**36.36%**	**40.0%**	**40.0%**	**40.0%**

	Cash Flows	**1**	**2**	**3**	**4**	**5**
14	**PAT** (profit after tax)	**-10.00**	**70.00**	**93.00**	**93.78**	**95.66**
17	+ depreciation	200.00	205.00	210.00	214.20	218.48
18	+ increase of debt	0.00	0.00	50.00	31.00	31.62
19	- increase of working capital requirements	-90.00	-110.00	-100.00	-22.00	-22.44
20	- investment in fixed assets	-100.00	-150.00	-210.00	-235.10	-239.80
21	**ECF** (equity cash flow)	**0.00**	**15.00**	**43.00**	**81.88**	**83.52**
22	**FCF** (free cash flow)	**135.00**	**100.91**	**74.00**	**134.58**	**137.27**
23	**CFd** (debt cash flow)	**135.00**	**135.00**	**85.00**	**108.50**	**110.67**
24	**CCF** (capital cash flow)	**135.00**	**150.00**	**128.00**	**190.38**	**194.19**
25	ROE (Return on Equity)	-2.00%	14.29%	17.06%	15.76%	15.76%
26	ROA (Return on Assets)	6.25%	7.83%	8.51%	8.27%	8.27%

Table III: Valuation of Tenmethods, Inc.

This table presents the valuation of the firm in Table I using ten different methods of discounted cash flow valuation: Adjusted present value (lines 3-6); equity cash flows discounted at the required return to equity (lines 7 and 8); free cash flow discounted at the WACC (lines 9 and 10); capital cash flows discounted at the WACC before tax (lines 11 and 12); residual income discounted at the required return to equity (lines 13 and 14); EVA discounted at the WACC (lines 15 and 16); the business's risk-adjusted equity cash flows discounted at the required return to assets (lines 17 and 18); the business's risk-adjusted free cash flows discounted at the required return to assets (lines 19 and 20); the risk-free-adjusted equity cash flows discounted at the risk-free rate (lines 21 and 22); and the risk-free-adjusted free cash flows discounted at the risk-free rate (lines 23 and 24). All ten methods provide the same valuation.

Valuation parameters: R_F = 6%; P_M (market risk premium) = 4%; Kd = 8%; βd = 0.5; βu = 1.0;

line	Formula		0	1	2	3	4	5
1		Ku		10.00%	10.00%	10.00%	10.00%	10.00%
2	(2)	D = PV(Kd; CFd)	1,743.73	1,748.23	1,753.09	1,808.33	1,844.50	1,881.39
3	(11)	Vu = PV (Ku; FCF)	1,525.62	1,543.18	1,596.59	1,682.25	1,715.90	1,750.21
4	(12)	VTS = PV[Ku; D T Ku + T (Nr - DKd)]	762.09	838.30	860.33	878.33	895.90	913.82
5	(10)	E + D = VTS + Vu	2,287.71	2,381.48	2,456.92	2,560.58	2,611.80	2,664.03
6		E = VTS + Vu - D	543.98	633.25	703.83	752.25	767.29	782.64
7	(14)	Ke		16.41%	13.51%	12.99%	12.88%	12.88%
8	(1)	E = PV(Ke; ECF)	543.98	633.25	703.83	752.25	767.29	782.64
9	(6) (15)	WACC		10.000%	7.405%	7.231%	7.256%	7.256%
10	(4)	E = PV(WACC; FCF) - D	543.98	633.25	703.83	752.25	767.29	782.64
11	(8)	$WACC_{BT}$		10.000%	9.466%	9.429%	9.435%	9.435%
12	(7)	E = PV($WACC_{BT}$; CCF) - D	543.98	633.25	703.83	752.25	767.29	782.64
13	(17)	RI (Residual income)		-92.05	3.78	22.21	17.12	17.46
14	(16)	E = PV(Ke; RI) + Ebv	543.98	633.25	703.83	752.25	767.29	782.64
15	(19)	EVA		-75.00	8.55	26.12	21.84	22.28
16	(18)	E = Ebv - (D-N) + PV(WACC; EVA)	543.98	633.25	703.83	752.25	767.29	782.64
17	(23)	$ECF//_{Ku}$		-34.87	-7.25	21.96	60.18	61.38
18	(22)	E = PV(Ku; $ECF//_{Ku}$)	543.98	633.25	703.83	752.25	767.29	782.64
19	(21)	$FCF//_{Ku}$		135.00	162.71	142.02	204.85	208.94
20	(20)	E = PV(Ku; $FCF//_{Ku}$) - D	543.98	633.25	703.83	752.25	767.29	782.64
21	(27)	$ECF//_{RF}$		-56.63	-32.58	-6.19	30.09	30.69
22	(26)	E = PV(R_F; $ECF//_{RF}$)	543.98	633.25	703.83	752.25	767.29	782.64
23	(25)	$FCF//_{RF}$		43.49	67.46	43.75	102.42	104.47
24	(24)	E = PV(R_F; $FCF//_{RF}$) - D	543.98	633.25	703.83	752.25	767.29	782.64

Table IV: Sensitivity analysis of the Valuation of Tenmethods, Inc.
Changes in the valuation as a function of the growth after period 3 (g)

g	Equity value(E)	Debt value(D)	Enterprise value (E+D)	Value of tax shields (VTS)	WACC t=1	WACC t=4	Ke t=1	Ke t=4	$WACC_{BT}$ t=1	$WACC_{BT}$ t=4
0.0%	502.08	1692.46	2194.54	625.54	10.00%	7.14%	16.74%	13.02%	10.00%	9.43%
1.0%	521.20	1714.43	2235.63	685.91	10.00%	7.19%	16.58%	12.95%	10.00%	9.43%
2.0%	543.98	1743.73	2287.71	762.09	10.00%	7.26%	16.41%	12.88%	10.00%	9.44%
3.0%	571.24	1784.74	2355.98	861.35	10.00%	7.33%	16.25%	12.82%	10.00%	9.44%
4.0%	603.42	1846.27	2449.69	996.38	10.00%	7.43%	16.12%	12.78%	10.00%	9.44%

Table V: Sensitivity analysis of the Valuation of Tenmethods, Inc. according to Damodaran (1994), Harris and Pringle (1985), and Myers (1974)
Changes in the valuation as a function of the growth after period 3 (g)

	E				**VTS**			
g	Fernández (2004)	Damodaran (1994)	Ruback (2002)	Myers (1974)	Fernández (2004)	Damodaran (1994)	Ruback (2002)	Myers (1974)
0 %	502.08	281.03	376.92	515.20	625.54	404.48	500.38	638.65
1%	521.20	279.02	382.25	553.04	685.91	443.73	546.96	717.75
2%	**543.98**	**274.29**	**387.07**	**605.11**	**762.09**	**492.40**	**605.18**	**823.22**
3%	571.24	264.13	389.93	680.75	861.35	554.25	680.05	970.87
4%	603.42	242.28	386.90	799.39	996.38	635.24	779.86	1192.35
5%	638.51	191.74	366.26	1008.13	1191.86	745.09	919.61	1561.48
6%	659.97	53.60	284.03	1454.55	1505.17	898.80	1129.23	2299.75

	WACC, t=4				**Ke, t=4**			
g	Fernández (2004)	Damodaran (1994)	Ruback (2002)	Myers (1974)	Fernández (2004)	Damodaran (1994)	Ruback (2002)	Myers (1974)
0%	7.14%	7.81%	7.57%	7.14%	13.02%	18.64%	16.29%	13.02%
1%	7.19%	7.84%	7.61%	7.14%	12.95%	18.78%	16.29%	12.63%
2%	**7.26%**	**7.88%**	**7.66%**	**7.15%**	**12.88%**	**19.02%**	**16.33%**	**12.19%**
3%	7.33%	7.93%	7.71%	7.17%	12.82%	19.46%	16.43%	11.66%
4%	7.43%	7.99%	7.78%	7.19%	12.78%	20.35%	16.70%	11.04%
5%	7.55%	8.07%	7.87%	7.24%	12.79%	22.62%	17.40%	10.32%
6%	7.71%	8.18%	8.00%	7.33%	13.00%	34.16%	20.03%	9.50%

Table VI: Main formulas used in the paper

$$E_0 = PV_0\left[Ke_t ; ECF_t\right] \tag{1}$$

$$D_0 = PV_0\left[Kd_t ; CFd_t\right] \tag{2}$$

$$CFd_t = N_{t-1}\, r_t - (N_t - N_{t-1}) \tag{3}$$

$$E_0 + D_0 = PV_0\left[WACC_t ;\ FCF_t\right] \tag{4}$$

$$ECF_t = FCF_t + (N_t - N_{t-1}) - N_{t-1}\, r_t (1 - T_t) \tag{5}$$

$$WACC_t = \frac{E_{t-1}\, Ke_t + D_{t-1}\, Kd_t - N_{t-1}\, r_t T_t}{E_{t-1} + D_{t-1}} \tag{6}$$

$$E_0 + D_0 = PV_0\left[WACC_{BT\,t} ;\ CCF_t\right] \tag{7}$$

$$WACC_{BT\,t} = \frac{E_{t-1}\, Ke_t + D_{t-1}\, Kd_t}{E_{t-1} + D_{t-1}} \tag{8}$$

$$CCF_t = ECF_t + CFd_t = ECF_t - (N_t - N_{t-1}) + N_{t-1}\, r_t = FCF_t + N_{t-1}\, r_t\, T_t \tag{9}$$

$$E_0 + D_0 = Vu_0 + VTS_0 \tag{10}$$

$$Vu_0 = PV_0\left[Ku_t ;\ FCF_t\right] \tag{11}$$

$$VTS_0 = PV_0\left[Ku_t ;\ D_{t-1}\, Ku_t T_t + T_t (N_{t-1} r_t - D_{t-1} Kd_t)\right] \tag{12}$$

$$E_0 + D_0 = PV_0\left[Ku_t ;\ FCF_t + D_{t-1}\, Ku_t T_t + T_t (N_{t-1} r_t - D_{t-1} Kd_t)\right] \tag{13}$$

$$Ke_t = Ku_t + \frac{D_{t-1}(1 - T_t)(Ku_t - Kd_t)}{E_{t-1}} \tag{14}$$

$$WACC_t = Ku_t - \frac{D_{t-1}\, T_t\, Ku_t}{E_{t-1} + D_{t-1}} - T_t \frac{N_{t-1}\, r_t - D_{t-1}\, Kd_t}{E_{t-1} + D_{t-1}} \tag{15}$$

$$E_0 = Ebv_0 + PV_0\left[Ke_t ;\ RI_t\right] \tag{16}$$

$$RI_t = PAT_t - Ke_t\, Ebv_{t-1} \tag{17}$$

$$E_0 + D_0 = (Ebv_0 + N_0) + PV_0\left[WACC_t ;\ EVA_t\right] \tag{18}$$

$$EVA_t = NOPAT_t - (N_{t-1} + Ebv_{t-1})\, WACC_t \tag{19}$$

$$E_0 + D_0 = PV_0\left[Ku_t;\ FCF_t\ //_{Ku}\right] \tag{20}$$

$$FCF_t\ //_{Ku} = FCF_t - (E_{t-1} + D_{t-1})(WACC_t - Ku_t) = FCF_t - D_{t-1}(1 - T_t)(Ku_t - Kd_t) - N_{t-1} r_t T_t \tag{21}$$

$$E_0 = PV_0\left[Ku_t;\ ECF_t\ //_{Ku}\right] \tag{22}$$

$$ECF_t\ //_{Ku} = ECF_t - E_{t-1}(Ke_t - Ku_t) = ECF_t - D_{t-1}(1 - T_t)(Ku_t - Kd_t) \tag{23}$$

$$E_0 + D_0 = PV_0\left[R_{Ft};\ FCF_t\ //_{RF}\right] \tag{24}$$

$$FCF_t\ //_{RF} = FCF_t - (E_{t-1} + D_{t-1})(WACC_t - R_{Ft}) \tag{25}$$

$$E_0 = PV_0\left[R_{Ft};\ ECF_t\ //_{RF}\right] \tag{26}$$

$$ECF_t\ //_{RF} = ECF_t - E_{t-1}(Ke_t - R_{Ft}) \tag{27}$$

$$Ke = R_F + \beta_L\ P_M \qquad Ku = R_F + \beta u\ P_M \qquad Kd = R_F + \beta d\ P_M \tag{28}$$

$$\beta u = \frac{E\,\beta_L + D\,\beta d\,(1-T)}{E + D\ (1-T)} \tag{29}$$

$$E_t = E_{t-1}\ (1 + Ke_t)\ -\ ECF_t \tag{1i}$$

$$D_t = D_{t-1}\ (1 + Kd_t)\ -\ CFd_t \tag{2i}$$

$$E_t + D_t = (E_{t-1} + D_{t-1})(1 + WACC_t)\ -\ FCF_t \tag{4i}$$

$$E_t + D_t = (E_{t-1} + D_{t-1})(1 + WACC_{BT\,t})\ -\ CCF_t \tag{7i}$$

$$E_t + D_t = (E_{t-1} + D_{t-1})(1 + Ku_t) - \left[FCF_t + D_{t-1}\, Ku_t\, T_t + T_t(N_{t-1}\, r_t - D_{t-1}\, Kd_t)\right] \tag{13i}$$

$$E_t - Ebv_t = (E_{t-1} - Ebv_{t-1})(1 + Ke_t) - (PAT_t - Ebv_{t-1}\, Ke_t) = (E_{t-1} - Ebv_{t-1})(1 + Ke_t) - RI_t \tag{16i}$$

Table VII: Dictionary

βd = Beta of debt
β_L = Beta of levered equity
βu = Beta of unlevered equity = beta of assets
D = Value of debt
E = Value of equity
Ebv = Book value of equity
ECF = Equity cash flow
$ECF//_{Ku}$ = business risk-adjusted equity cash flows
$ECF//_{RF}$ = expected risk-free-adjusted equity cash flows
RI = Residual income
EVA = Economic value added
FCF = Free cash flow
$FCF//_{Ku}$ = business risk-adjusted free cash flows
$FCF//_{RF}$ = risk-free-adjusted free cash flows
g = Growth rate of the constant growth case
I = Interest paid
Ku = Cost of unlevered equity (required return to unlevered equity)
Ke = Cost of levered equity (required return to levered equity)
Kd = Required return to debt
N = Book value of the debt
NOPAT = Net Operating Profit After Tax = profit after tax of the unlevered company
PAT = Profit after tax
PBT = Profit before tax
P_M = Market premium = $E(R_M - R_F)$
PV = Present value
r = Cost of debt
R_F = Risk-free rate
R_M = Market return
ROA = Return on Assets = $NOPAT_t / (N_{t-1}+Ebv_{t-1})$
ROE = Return on Equity = PAT_t / Ebv_{t-1}
T = Corporate tax rate
VTS = Value of the tax shields
Vu = Value of shares in the unlevered company
WACC = Weighted average cost of capital
$WACC_{BT}$ = Weighted average cost of capital before taxes
WCR = Working capital requirements = net current assets

12. Spin-outs from Universities: Strategy, Financing, Monitoring and Incubation Models

Mike Wright and Andy Lockett[1]
Nottingham University Business School

Abstract. Spin-outs of ventures from universities are growing in importance yet their process is little understood. This paper reviews evidence from the spin-out and university level relating to four key research questions: What mechanisms are in place to facilitate the spinning-out of new technologies into companies? What financial resources are made available by universities and outsiders to facilitate spin-out companies and at what stage? What mechanisms and processes are in place to monitor spin-out companies once they have been established? How effective are these systems and processes from the viewpoint of the participants and in terms of spin-out company success. Implications for practice and areas for further research are identified.

Keywords: universities, technology transfer, entrepreneurship, venture capital, spin-offs, and incubators.

1. Introduction

There is increasing policy focus on universities' ability to exploit their science base and transferring their scientific knowledge to the private sector. The majority of existing research on the performance of university technology transfer has emphasized the licensing activities of US universities (see, for example, Thursby and Thursby, 2002; Thursby and Kemp, 2002; Siegel, Waldman and Link, 2003; Sine, Shane and DiGregorio, forthcoming). However, the focus of attention is increasingly being directed towards the creation of new ventures (Siegel *et al.*, 1999). Through spin-outs (USOs), universities may be able to capture the full value of their technology (Franklin, Wright and Lockett, 2001). The more active universities in this respect, in the UK at least, tend to be more willing to cede significant amounts of equity to academic inventors (Lockett, Wright and Franklin, 2003).

This increased interest in USOs is being observed in North America, the UK, Australia and Continental Europe (DiGregorio and Shane, 2003; Shane and Stuart, 2002; Wright, Vohora and Lockett, 2002). Small sample survey evidence indicates that taking equity in a USO company produces a greater average return in the long run compared to the average return available from the average license (Bray and Lee, 2000). Some research attention has been addressed towards the

1. Financial support for this research from the ESRC is gratefully acknowledged.

This article was originally published in the International Journal of Entrepreneurship Education 2(3): pp. 309-328.

inputs associated with the number of USOs created by US universities (DiGregorio and Shane, 2003) and the survivability of start-ups that exploit academic knowledge (Nerkar and Shane, 2003). However, there is concern, expressed for example in the Lambert Review, that many USOs that are created may not generate significant wealth that greater focus should be placed on identifying whether a USO was the most appropriate means to exploit technological inventions produced in universities (Lambert, 2003). A central issue, therefore, is the need to examine the factors influencing the generation of wealth in spin-outs.

Although universities are being encouraged by a number of government pronouncements and initiatives to commercialise their intellectual property by launching entrepreneurial spin-outs companies, this mode of technology transfer is not well-understood. Their ability to create wealth from spin-outs has, therefore, important implications for how well universities are equipped to respond to this new agenda.

Strictly defined USOs involve ventures created on the basis of innovative, and typically patentable intellectual property in which the university and the academic entrepreneur are the main equity holders, possibly together with outside investors such as surrogate entrepreneurs, business angels and venture capitalists. However, ventures may also be created by university academics which do not depend on such intellectual property but which may nevertheless have wealth generating possibilities (we return to these differences in our discussion of the different spin-out development models that universities may adopt). The academic may either remain in full-time employment with the university or leave to concentrate effort on the spin-out (Nicalaou and Birley, 2003a). In other cases, the venture may be a joint one with an existing corporation. Druilhe and Garnsey (2004) distinguish between spin-outs in terms of development companies based on a novel scientific breakthrough, product companies involving opportunity recognition that builds on the scientist's knowledge, and software companies.

The process of spinning-out companies is – arguably – much more complex than licensing. DiGregorio and Shane (2003), in their examination of why some universities generate more start-ups than others, focus on university level factors, including a university's propensity to undertake industry sponsored research, intellectual eminence and policy towards IP commercialization; and external factors such as the availability of venture capital in a region. However, a number of key issues are raised concerning the processes involved in the development of successful spin-out strategies. Opportunity recognition is a key first step in enterprise creation and there is a need, therefore, to consider how this is achieved in universities. The realisation of university aims to recognise and exploit commercial opportunities may be influenced by the expertise and approaches adopted by university technology transfer officers to screen and prepare potential ventures. Similarly, there are questions concerning the feasibility and desirability of academic inventors becoming heavily involved in the commercialisation process. Franklin, Wright and Lockett (2001) show that those universities that were more active in spinning-out companies made greater use of external [surrogate] entrepreneurs with commercial experience, who would enter the firm and take the lead in developing it. These points, in turn, raise questions concerning the feasibility and desirability of developing external commercial links. The problems for new start-ups in accessing finance are well-recognised and are expected to be particularly pertinent with regard to university spin-outs (USOs) because of the restricted resources available to universities for funding this kind of venture and attitudes and access to external finance. Close monitoring is a key aspect of early stage venture capital investment. This raises questions concerning the expertise of university personnel and the nature of the monitoring they undertake to enable a new technology to become commercially viable.

A common link between these issues concerns the availability of resources within universities. In the traditional non-commercial environment of universities, the development of spin-outs may be constrained by major deficiencies in resource endowments and capabilities (West and De Castro, 2001). Our approach builds on the general resource based view of the firm and capabilities framework (Barney, 1991; Teece, et al., 1997; Eisenhardt and Martin, 2000) and specifically on the work of Brush, Green and Hart (2001) who adapt this perspective to new ventures.

In this paper we examine four key research questions:

1. What mechanisms are in place to facilitate the spinning-out of new technologies into companies?

2. What financial resources are made available by universities and outsiders to facilitate spin-out companies and at what stage?

3. What mechanisms and processes are in place to monitor spin-out companies once they have been established?

4. How effective are these systems and processes from the viewpoint of the participants and in terms of spin-out company success?

In answering these research questions we consider both the spin-out firm level and the university level of analysis.

2. Method

The evidence reviewed in this paper is based on data gathered in two stages:

1. Qualitative

Data were collected using in-depth face-to-face and telephone interviews with representatives from twelve USOs, as well as each of their financial investors and seven associated universities over the period July 2001 to July 2002. These universities were selected on the basis that they are among the top ten research elite universities in the UK and that they are actively pursuing a programme of university technology transfer. In each case we obtained considerable cooperation from the relevant parties in the spin-out process. Each university had a different orientation towards the commercialisation of research, which is reflected in their idiosyncratic cultures and institutional norms. Therefore, each university was at a different point in transforming its policies, routines and incentive mechanisms towards commercialisation through USOs. To assist in theory generation we also selected a range of different ventures in terms of their technology and stage of development. We found it more difficult to obtain detailed access to spin-out companies than universities.

For each case, interviews were carried out with the head of the university technology transfer office (UTTO) or equivalent, business development managers (BDMs) and the members of a spinout company who had taken the venture through the process including both the academic entrepreneur and the "surrogate" entrepreneur where applicable. We also gained access to the seed stage investors in each of the USOs. In addition, we interviewed the head of each department from which the USO originated. The interviews lasted from one to two hours and were openly recorded and afterwards transcribed. By using a number of key actors from each university we ensured that we elicited views on the universities' role in the spinout process to cross-check our interpretation of events.

2. Quantitative

It was recognised that it would be crucial to obtain support and cooperation in advance from potential respondents who might otherwise be reluctant to complete another questionnaire. We established a collaborative link with the University Companies Association (UNICO) who agreed to circulate their members to alert them to the survey and to lend their support in designing the questionnaire and encouraging responses. We also subsequently had a meeting with HEFCE who expressed a view that they would be interested in the findings; this was useful in helping us to encourage responses.

A complete listing of 167 institutions was obtained from the funding bodies. In total, 122 universities were contacted, the remaining 45 universities accounting for just 0.2% of total research grants and contract expenditures by UK universities in financial year 2001. In February 2002, a joint letter from the principal researcher and the Chair of UNICO requesting cooperation and the nomination of a respondent was sent to the vice-chancellors. In most cases the nominee was either the head of the technology transfer office (TTO), the research office, or the commercial office. As it was recognised that various information requests would need inputs from different departments or units, two questionnaires were developed: one seeking quantitative responses (number of spin-outs, licences, etc.) and one asking for qualitative information concerning the technology transfer process (Likert scales). The quantitative metrics were harmonised with the US Association of University Technology Managers (AUTM) Licensing Survey to enable international comparisons to be made at a later date. The draft questionnaires were sent to a selected sample of UNICO members to obtain comments.

In late March 2002, hard copies and electronic versions of both questionnaires were sent to the nominated respondent. Versions of the survey were available to be completed on the Internet and submitted electronically. The nominated respondents were contacted to confirm receipt of the questionnaires and a dialogue was maintained to ensure progress was being made in completing the questionnaires. These procedures enabled us to identify more accurately the appropriate respondents and to reduce delays in obtaining information.

In total, 98 institutions responded to the survey, accounting for 84.9% of the total amount spent on research in UK universities during financial year 2001. We obtained responses from 18 of the top 20 institutions. Among the 98 responses, we received 81 completed numerical data questionnaires and 77 completed process questionnaires. In addition, we received 17 nil responses (i.e. the data was unavailable) to the numerical data questionnaire and 21 nil responses to the process questionnaire.

Considerable effort was involved in collecting the data because often they did not exist in a collated form in a number of institutions, while in others they were located in several places requiring the questionnaire to be circulated around the relevant departments. As a result, we feel we have now obtained a unique, novel and very rich dataset. We identified that 175 spinouts had been created in universities in 2001, compared to an average of 95 per year during the period 1997-2000. However, experience is highly skewed. A quarter of responding institutions did not create any spinouts during the period 1997-2001 while 27% created 10 or more spinouts each during the same period.

3. Results

3.1. Mechanisms for Spinning-out Companies

To examine the systems and mechanisms for spinning-out companies we developed an approach that linked a resource-based view of the process with a dynamic perspective based on the phases in the life-cycle of the development of the spin-out company. The resources required to facilitate the spin-out process can be categorised into human capital, financial, physical, technological and organizational. Our analysis of the process identified five phases (see Figure 1 below) in the development of a spin-out company: research phase, opportunity phase, pre-organization phase, re-orientation phase and sustainable high-growth phase. It was evident that each venture needs to pass through the previous phase in order to progress to the next stage of development. Importantly, this is not a linear activity but rather involves a non-linear, iterative process. Druilhe and Garnsey (2004) see the development of spin-out phases as a continuous process of adjustment but observe that the phases that the spin-out passes through depends on the maturity of the entrepreneurs initial resources and the business model selected.

Figure 1: The Critical Junctures in USO Development (adapted from Vohora, Wright and Lockett, 2004)

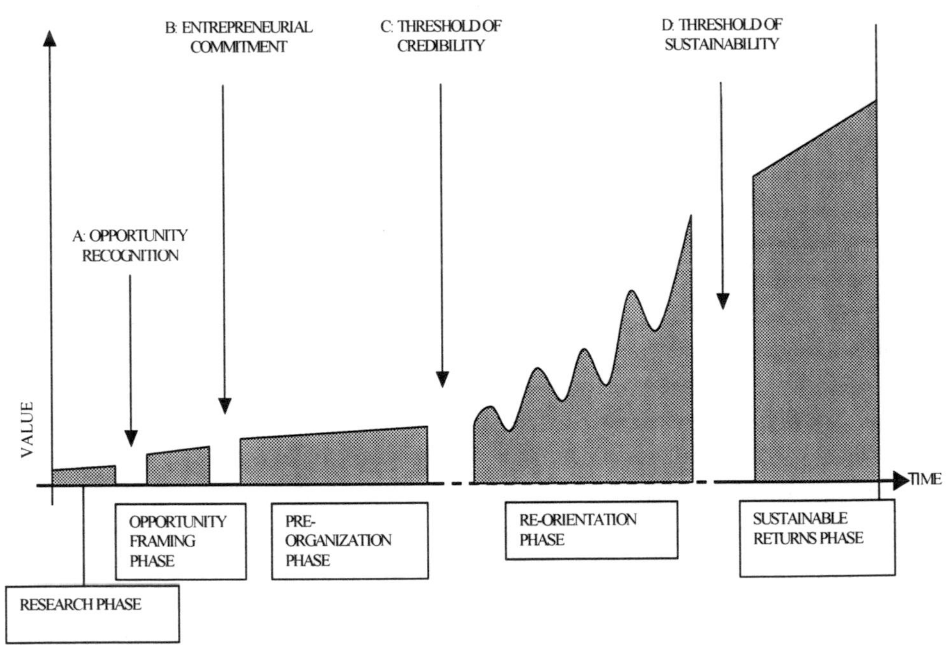

At the four interstices between the five phases of development, we found that ventures face ‘critical junctures’ which must be overcome to enable progress to the next stage to occur. However, such progress was not automatic. The critical junctures were identified as opportunity recognition, entrepreneurial commitment, credibility and sustainability and were found to arise due to deficiencies in social capital, other resource weaknesses and inadequate internal capabilities. The main features and implications of each critical junctures are as follows (see Vohora, Wright and Lockett, 2004 for detailed discussion).

Opportunity Recognition: Universities and academic entrepreneurs involved in creating USOs were found to lack the necessary human entrepreneurial capital and social capital synonymous with commercial awareness and prior business experience. As a result, there is an inability to conceptualise how a technological discovery can be best applied to satisfy a market need. It was also common in all but one USO case for the parent universities to provide little incentive for their scientists to think and behave entrepreneurially. In the case of Biomedical Co. [a pseudonym], during studies to investigate how a particular technology could be applied to new areas of science the research team recognized a new application that presented a real commercial opportunity. In contrast, in the case of 3G Wireless Co [also a pseudonym], the scientist had been working for nearly 10 years on science that did not have an obvious market application. The technology provided a solution to a market need that was only recognised by a surrogate entrepreneur.

Our interviews suggested it was important for universities to devote more resources to increasing their social capital (networks) through developing and exploiting existing external partnerships, links and interactions with industry, venture capital firms and surrogate entrepreneurs so that academics and UTTOs may become better positioned to recognise entrepreneurial opportunities. In a related study, Niclaou and Birley (2003b) examine the networks of academic entrepreneurs and note the importance of non-redundant ties, that is the links that academic scientists have with the external commercial world.

Entrepreneurial Commitment: For a venture to succeed, there is a need for a 'champion' committed to the entrepreneurial development of the spin-out. These champions may be academics or entrepreneurs from outside with commercial expertise, so-called surrogate entrepreneurs (Franklin, Wright and Lockett, 2001). Primarily as a result of universities: allocating insufficient resources to encourage and facilitate the spin-out process, failing to realign institutional incentives, an institutional culture that discriminates against those with an entrepreneurial orientation, neglecting to devise clear policies and guidelines, and not developing a deep network of external relationships with key actors, academic scientists and surrogate entrepreneurs did not become sufficiently emotionally and financially committed to championing the commercialisation of university scientific discoveries. These factors appear different from those present in a normal start-up in holding back initial progress towards exploiting the value that has been recognised in an opportunity. In Biomedical, early test results encouraged one member of the academic team to carry out market research and to develop a business plan in order to assess the potential in commercializing the research. The academic formed a company and initially ran the business in his spare time, in order to test the market. In 3G Wireless the scientist's biggest weakness was that he did not have the business experience or the managerial expertise to grow a business. He did not want to give up his research post at the university because it provided him with the infrastructure to create new technologies.

Credibility: Credibility is a general problem for new ventures (Birley and Norburn, 1985). While similar issues arise for USOs, lack of credibility of USOs with respect to potential trading partners and financiers particularly arises from their intangible initial resources, the typical lack of commercial track record of the founding entrepreneur, the effect of the academic culture and values, and the absence of clear policies on the commercialisation of scientific discoveries, despite the rhetoric of senior university management (Lockett, Murray and Wright, 2002). Universities can demonstrate the credibility of their USOs by presenting intellectual property as a potential portfolio of products, demonstrating proof of concept of technological assets, clarifying the route to market and profitability, being able to locate the venture off the university campus, and implement mechanisms to attract surrogate entrepreneurs. However, in order to attract a potential surrogate entrepreneur it may first be necessary for the nascent pre-organisation stage USO to develop some credibility with the surrogate. We noted differences in the existence and quality of formalised systems and mechanisms through which USOs were formed and created in the seven universities we examined, as well as the level of social capital that had been developed with external sources of expertise and resources. In Biomedical, the team realized it needed quickly to assemble resources to create a professional image for the firm in order to attract customers and more revenue. In 3G Wireless, the credibility of the entrepreneurial team and the potential of the technology were excellent. The entrepreneurial team was able to package and sell itself as a business with all the necessary resources ready to be put in place in order to attract venture capital investment.

Sustainability: Sustainability depended on a USO's social capital for identifying opportunities and accessing resources, as well as integrating them with existing resources to create organisational capabilities that enables the USO to cope with the challenges of growth. There was a need to move from entrepreneurial individuals in the early phases to the development of entrepreneurial teams. In Biomedical, the team struggled to maintain its high rate of growth and become a market leader, whilst continuing to develop and commercialize new innovations. It became more difficult to co-ordinate and control activities as the venture became more successful. In 3G Wireles, although a team was developed, unfortunately they raised too little seed finance to support their growth plans and the venture stagnated in a period when the venture capital market for high-tech investments had gone flat.

From the quantitative survey, it was evident that the areas where universities had greater involvement than the founders of a spin-out were confined to carrying out intellectual property due diligence, serving as a sounding board, developing a professional support group, obtaining alternative sources of financing and interfacing with financiers. Somewhat surprisingly, universities had less involvement in formulating strategy and monitoring financial performance than the founders. Universities' involvement in the spin-out process was generally confined to the pre-start-up and start-up phases rather than the later stages and had its greatest influence in carrying out intellectual property due diligence at the pre-start up phase. Notably, given the importance of recruiting commercial management and in gaining credibility with trading partners identified from the qualitative interviews, in a substantial proportion of cases, universities were not involved in these activities. Evidence from our interviews suggests that joint ventures with industrial partners may be an effective means by which universities can overcome some of their skills and resources shortcomings that may create difficulties in developing spin-outs to the point where they are ready to receive investment from external financial investors (Wright, Vohora and Lockett, 2004).

3.2. Financial Resources

Of the total 554 spinouts reported to have been created in the five years from 1996 to 2001, 339 (61.2%) were formed using external equity finance. An average of 4.2 spinouts per institution received external equity finance in this period. Experience was highly skewed, with 32 universities (41% of respondents) having no spinouts that were formed using external sources of finance. Almost a quarter of ventures were formed using finance supplied by venture capital firms, the most common source of external finance. This was followed by business angels (17% of spinouts formed in the last five years), other university sources of finance (15%), university challenge funds (12%), and equity joint ventures with industrial partners (6%).

The responses to the attitudinal/perceptions part of the quantitative survey supported these figures (Wright, Vohora and Lockett, 2002). We compared the perceptions of those universities that had created 6 or more spinout companies since 1996 using some form of external equity finance ("Top Performers") with the remaining institutions that had created spinout companies during this period. Initial analysis using Mann-Whitney tests showed that venture capital sources of finance and University Challenge Funds were significantly more important to the top performers. The significantly greater importance of University Challenge Fund finance to Top Performers reflects the fact that they were more likely to have access to this source of finance. Both top performers and non-top performers groups rated business angel finance as an "important" source of finance. Joint-ventures were also rated as "important" by all respondents.

3.3. Mechanisms and Processes to Monitor Spin-outs

We identified that the top-performing institutions, as defined above, operated a number of procedures and policies that were significantly different from the non-top performing institutions, as follows.

Management of Portfolio: A significantly greater proportion of the top-performers said that they managed the portfolio of equity in their spinouts closely. Both top-performers and non-top performers require board membership of the university at the USO, to a similar important degree. A greater proportion of non-top performers compared to top-performers agreed that they allowed spinout management teams a great deal of freedom and only became involved when there was a problem. The lower score for non-top performers is consistent with them having fewer skills and resources to engage in close monitoring. These findings suggest that the top performers on average are approaching the kind of degree of involvement of venture capital firms but that this is not the case for those universities that are less active in creating spinouts.

Reporting: Both top performers and non-top performers had a policy that required each spinout company to provide a set of audited accounts, and this item received the highest score for any item regarding the mechanisms for monitoring investments. While top performers showed a slightly higher agreement that they required spinouts to provide monthly management accounts, this was not significantly greater than for non-top performers. There was little difference between the approaches of both groups to using a stage system for monitoring spinouts at appropriate milestones. These findings suggest that universities in general obtain lower levels and frequencies of information for monitoring purposes than venture capital firms (Mitchell, Reid and Terry, 1995).

Valuation: Generally, least importance was attached to valuation aspects of monitoring. However, the top performers were significantly more likely than the non-top performers to report regularly on the valuation of their institutions' portfolios and to use the British Venture Capital Association (BVCA) guidelines for valuing their investment portfolios. Institutions did not regularly use a Discounted Cash Flow (DCF) or similar valuation approach. These findings are in line with other research regarding the use of such techniques by venture capital firms (Wright and Robbie, 1996).

3.4. Factors Impeding or Promoting Commercialisation Activities

Only one clear factor *promoting* spin-outs was identified: the commitment of the originating academic to commercialising the technology. The other factors presented to respondents acted as either an impediment or had "No Effect". Below, we summarise the main aspects of impediments to spinout company development based on mean scores and Mann-Whitney tests for differences between top performers and non-top performers as identified above.

Availability of Finance: Lack of seed funding from the university was seen to be the greatest impediment to the creation of spinout companies. A lack of pre-seed funds for conducting market research was significantly more of an impediment for the non-top performers than the top performers. Difficulties in attracting funding from venture capital firms and business angels were rated higher by non-top performers than top performers. The differences between the two groups were, however, not significant in respect of these two source of finance variables.

People: The amount of time university staff have available to help spinout companies was a highly important inhibitor to the creation of spinout companies. For academics to be able to commit themselves to developing a spin-out, they may need space from other activities such as administration and academic research. The demands of the Research Assessment Exercise may pose problems in diverting academics from their research and, indeed, continuing to research may be important in generating follow-on products for the venture. But expecting a potential academic entrepreneur to also be a head of department and/or dean of a faculty, for example, may be counter-productive to the university's aims to generate income from spin-outs. The second most important people issue was related to the clash of commercial and academic cultures as all respondents rated the lack of understanding regarding university, corporate or scientific norms and environments as an impediment. Manifestations of this problem are the need to appreciate the amount of effort required to take an invention from the laboratory to a marketable product, and the need to appreciate the skills needed to make that shift. These problems give rise to the role of surrogate entrepreneurs who have the expertise to develop the spin-out commercially, leaving the academic to continue with their university responsibilities and to become technical director of the spin-out with a role to provide the research skills necessary to adapt the product to perceived market needs.

Infrastructure: The most important infrastructure related impediment was the availability of suitable space on a science park for spinout companies. A lack of suitable space outside the university to accommodate spinouts may impact how quickly these firms are recognised as credible business entities by suppliers, customers and investors.

Incentives and Rewards: The availability of incentives and rewards for university staff to spend time on spinouts was ranked as the fourth most important impediment towards the creation of spinouts. This barrier was significantly more important for non-top performers. Negotiations over the ownership of intellectual property rights impeded the creation of spinouts for both top performers and non-top performers. Closely related to this factor was the impediment of deciding on the distribution of equity in the spinout company. The availability of incentives and rewards to attract commercial management into spinouts was a significantly greater impediment to the creation of spinouts for non-top performers. Those universities that were more active in spinning out were more willing to provide larger equity stakes. Jealousies in relation to the prospect of some staff earning significant capital gains may lead some universities to be reluctant to provide significant equity stakes, and some universities also want potential academic entrepreneurs to carry heavy administrative and other burdens that distract their attention from focusing on developing the spin-out.

Process Related Impediments: The availability of a clear process for spinning out companies was highly significant in distinguishing between the impediments to spinout development cited by top performing and non-top performing institutions. Top performing institutions found that the procedures, and processes that they had in place promoted their efforts.

4. Typology of Approaches to Spinning-out Companies

At the university and research institute level, different approaches may be adopted to create viable spin-outs (Clarysse, et al., 2004). Adopting a resource-based approach and cross-case analysis involving 56 university case studies in the UK and Continental Europe, Clarysse et al. identify three main approaches: Low selectivity; Supportive and Incubator.

Low selectivity organisations have low selection criteria and are rather passive in their support. They are typically public organisations linked to universities, with small spin-out teams with public sector experience, no technological focus or specialism, offering office space and infrastructure in universities, basing their financial support on public money and fostering an entrepreneurial climate within the university. The University of Twente in the Netherlands is an example of this model. The region surrounding the University of Twente was confronted in the mid 1980s with relatively high levels of unemployment and the university deliberately chose to play a major role in the rejuvenation of the region by engendering an entrepreneurial climate and promoting itself as the "entrepreneurial" university.

The Supportive model also involves a relatively passive approach to identifying potential ventures but growth is an important selection criterion. Support is provided in terms of patent and licence negotiation with industry, specialized incubation space at market prices, helping start-up companies become viable. They are typically private organizations linked with universities (e.g. a university owned company) with a larger multidisciplinary team with commercial experience and links to financial community, focusing on the best performing applied science departments in universities, having public/private financial partners and an important entrepreneurial context. The Leuven R&D case represents an example of this model. The Leuven R&D spin-out service was formally created in the early 1970s, but was only professionalized in the mid-

1990s. The nearby university and the presence of IMEC (see below) had resulted in several high tech spin-outs and had attracted several technology intensive companies in the science park, some of which were highly successful. In order to support spin-outs that were struggling in the early years and to enhance the creation of spin-outs in a more consistent way, the interface service was restructured and further professionalized.

The Incubator model is based on centres of excellence with close links with industry. Opportunity seeking is proactive with selection criteria close to those of venture capital firms. IPR platforms may be acquired at an early stage with significant in-house support being provided at all stages of the spin-out process. Human resources comprise experienced in-house specialists in a relatively narrowly defined area with commercial experience. The technology transfer activity may have its own significant venture capital fund and the funds invested are private sector. Internal research space and infrastructure are offered for free. Scientific Generics, located in the Cambridge (UK) region is an example of this model. Generics was founded in 1986 with four main objectives: top level technology consulting; creating and licensing out IP; investing in the creation of spin-outs; investing in other high tech start-ups. Being located in a known high tech pole, it is able to attract top researchers to its base in Cambridge. The motivation of creating spin-offs is purely a financial one.

Clarysse et al. (2004) also identify two other problematical categories where universities face difficulties in achieving their objectives for spinning-out: the resource deficient and the competence deficient cases. The resource deficient model has similar features at a superficial level to the Supportive model but the human capital involved in the technology transfer officers is largely derived from a public sector context with limited (mainly public) funds being available. Hence, while the model is attempting to be supportive in a commercial manner it does not possess the necessary resources to enable significant wealth creation to be achieved from the spin-outs created, except by accident. The competence deficient model involves cases where universities have committed resources but have not developed sufficient specialist capabilities, especially in terms in human capital skills to develop the spin-outs to meet the institution's objectives.

5. Implications and Effectiveness of Spin-out Processes

The case and quantitative analysis reviewed here suggests a number of areas where the effectiveness of the spin-out process might be enhanced. First, findings indicate that more focus should be applied to how universities can overcome their existing culture, values and incentives that primarily reward academics for their research efforts. Those universities that had attempted to address this issue, had managed to create a more accommodating culture for those academics that were entrepreneurially oriented, resulting in more technologies being commercialised.

Second, evidence shows a clear difference between universities in their ability to commercialise technologies due to the existence and quality of internal capabilities and organizational routines as well as clearly communicated policies and guidelines. This includes resources of expertise and pre-seed finance. It also emerges that to enhance the effectiveness of the process there is a need to address the role of academic entrepreneurs' head of department in the context of universities' overall strategies. Third, the process could be enhanced where UTTOs devoted more attention to identifying how ventures would achieve proof of market and proof of technology and to carrying out effective IP due diligence prior to submitting proposals to external financiers.

Fourth, the process might be enhanced by the provision of greater career support and entrepreneurial training to those academics who wish to participate in the commercialisation of their academic research in order to gain their commitment to the commercialisation process in some form, otherwise the tacit knowledge necessary to make the technology function in the marketplace is likely to be missing. A key role in the provision of training and support for the development may be provided by business schools. Wright et al. (2004) find that much of the involvement of business schools in the development of entrepreneurship for spin-outs relates to courses for Masters and Undergraduate students as well as for academics. There are some specific schemes designed to build capabilities among scientists to effect academic entrepreneurship, such as the Medici scheme where science-based fellows are trained by business school & others to be able to bridge networks between scientists and external commercial networks. In contrast, direct involvement of business school academics on boards of spin-outs is unusual. The role of MBA/MSC students was found to be important in preparing business plans and MBA alumni databases may be a useful source of recruitment of managers for spin-outs.

Wright et al. (2004) identify a number of barriers to the involvement of business school academics in spin-outs. First, the scope of BS academic skills is typically too 'late stage' for spin-outs. Second, there may be a mismatch of language and codes. Third, business schools, spin-outs and TTOs may have different goals and incentives. Fourth, the large corporation based skills of BS academics may mean that they fail to understand entrepreneurs. They suggest there is a need to build university processes & policies that help develop links between the networks of business schools, TTOs and scientists.

6. Conclusions

This paper has reviewed the evidence on USOs, with particular emphasis on the European context. It is evident that this topic is an emerging one. Existing research is limited and there is scope for further research in this area. A first priority is to continue to develop quantitative analysis at the university level in a multivariate framework that establishes links between the extent of spin-out activity, university characteristics and perceived impediments to the development of spin-outs. Initial evidence by Lockett and Wright (2004) indicates that the number of spin-out companies created is significantly positively associated with total research expenditure, the number of employees engaged in spin-out activities, expenditure on IP protection and the business development capabilities of technology transfer offices. They also find that equity investments in spin-out companies are positively associated with a university's investment in IP protection, the experience of the university and its business development capabilities. These results highlight the importance not just of resources but also the skills of the TTOs in spinning-out companies. Further research is required to examine the nature of the skills of TTOs and how these are being developed over time.

Second, there is a need to develop longitudinal datasets at the university level which will enable the analysis of the development of spin-out activity over time including its extent and nature as well as changes in the factors restricting or facilitating such development.

Third, there is a need for international comparative analysis at the university level with a view to identifying the influence of institutional differences between the efficiency of the spin-out process between countries and to obtain insights that may be useful for development of spin-outs in the different contexts.

Fourth, as spin-out activity is developing across Europe, where there are differences in local contexts, there is a need for further analysis of the impact of internal and external university environments on the development of spin-out activity.

Fifth, there is a need to examine the specificities involved in developing spin-outs in different sectors and disciplines. Research to date has typically suggested that the processes involved and problems encountered are generic. However, there may be important differences, for example, between spin-outs in bio-technology sectors and those involved in computer software. Software firms may be able more easily to use a service business model to test the market whereas biotechnology firms may find this more difficult. Different sectors may require considerably different amounts of external funding for R&D and also have significantly longer lead times to development. There is, therefore, a need to understand the different business models and support processes that may be necessary to achieve success in these areas.

Sixth, at the spin-out firm level, there is a need for quantitative analysis of the development of the spin-out companies themselves, and in particular of the factors determining the performance of these firms.

Finally, at the individual level, there is limited research on the nature of the entrepreneurs involved in spin-outs. Further research might usefully examine the roles played by academic entrepreneurs, surrogate entrepreneurs and TTOs. In particular, there is a need to consider the nature of the entrepreneurial team formation in spin-outs – e.g. what is the mix of skills? To what extent is there overlap or complementarity in these skills? (Clarysse and Moray, 2004). Importantly, there is growing recognition that entrepreneurial teams may be quite dynamic, with entry and exit occurring over the development cycle of the venture (Ucbasaran, Lockett, Wright and Westhead, 2003). Such changes in the ventures' teams seems to be especially important in the case of USOs, where gaps in the requisite commercial skills would appear to be more likely. Preliminary evidence suggests that some researchers that are actively involved in the first phase of the spin-out process, where the market opportunity is identified, do not show the entrepreneurial commitment to create the spin-out and leave this spin-out process before the formal creation of the spin-out (Vanaelst, et al., 2004). Alternatively, researchers may leave the spin-out during the phase in which the spin-out has to prove its viability since they found it was taking too long. Once the spin-out has survived this phase, the researchers stay and take the spin-out to maturity. While new team members bring in different kinds of experience but in contrast to existing literature reinforce shared cognition.

While this paper has focused on issues in the successful development of spin-outs, a number of issues need to be recognised in respect of the development of policy in this area. As we have noted, spin-out activity is highly skewed, reflecting the skewed nature of university research in the UK. Hence, it is unrealistic to expect all universities to develop spin-outs. Indeed, such signals lead to the creation of many spin-outs with no possibility of creating wealth. We have identified different models for universities to create spin-outs and have shown that the scope for high growth, high financial return spin-outs is likely to be limited to a few specialist research universities. Policies to promote these kinds of spin-outs, therefore, need to be focused on those universities with the appropriate science base. Policy to promote spin-outs may also have other objectives, in which case, as we have shown, other models may be appropriate. Whichever model is chosen, universities need to recognise that ventures such as spin-outs are likely to have high failure rates.

We would also emphasize, however, two further points. First, spin-outs may not be the appropriate mode of development of a new invention in all cases. Licensing agreements may be appropriate in many cases where the invention is likely to be viable as an independent entity. Second, in assessing the contribution of universities to so-called Third Stream activities [the others being research and teaching] there is a need for policy to recognise that some universities, while not having the science base to generate high wealth creating spin-outs, may have other significant contributions to make in the general reach-out area. More fine-grained policy, therefore, may need to be developed that recognises these other dimensions. One approach to addressing this issue is being developed by the Higher Education Funding Council for Wales, which aims to take account of social and cultural contributions as well as broadly defined economic returns, in assessing third stream activities conducted by Welsh universities.

We have provided some indication of the extent of spin-out activity. Obtaining data on the performance of spin-outs is difficult and is an area for further research. An indicator of the relatively low level of returns is provided by the finding in the 2001 survey that only nine universities reported to us that they had realised any money from selling all or part of an equity stake in a spin-out company. A few spin-outs are sold for significant sums but the issues we have identified above suggest that without further enhancement to the technology transfer process, opportunities for significant gains may be being missed. A further returns issue arises concerning the distribution of gains between the academic entrepreneurs and the universities. We have noted above the need for adequate incentives for academics and at the same time universities also need to ensure they are receiving a fair return. As the spin-out process develops, universities need to be more aware of negotiating an appropriate balance of risks and returns between the parties involved.

References:

Barney, J., 1991. "Firm resources and sustained competitive advantage". *Journal of Management* 17, 99-120.

Birley, S., Norburn, D., 1985. "Small versus large companies: the entrepreneurial conundrum". *Journal of Business Strategy* 6(1), 81-87.

Bray, M.J. and Lee, J.N. 2000. "University revenues from technology transfer: Licensing Fees vs Equity Positions". *Journal of Business Venturing*, 15(5/6), 385-392.

Brush, C., Greene, P., Hart, M., Haller, H. 2001. "From initial idea to unique advantage: The entrepreneurial challenge of constructing a resource base". *Academy of Management Executive* 15(1), 64-78.

Clarysse B, and Moray N. 2004. "A process study of entrepreneurial team formation : the case of a research based spin off". *Journal of Business Venturing*, 19(1), 55-79.

Clarysse, B., Wright, M., Lockett, A., van de Elde, E. and Vohora, A. 2004. "Spinning out new ventures: A typology of incubation strategies from European research institutions". *Journal of Business Venturing*, forthcoming.

DiGregorio, D. and Shane, S. 2003. "Why do some universities generate more start-ups than others?" *Research Policy*, 32(2), 209-227.

Druilhe, C. and Garnsey, E. 2004. "Do academic spin-outs differ and does it matter?" *Journal of Technology Transfer*, 29, 269-285.

Eisenhardt, K. M., Martin J. A., 2000. "Dynamic capabilities: What are they?" *Strategic Management Journal* 21, 1105-1121.

Franklin, S., M. Wright and A.Lockett. 2001. "Academic and Surrogate Entrepreneurs in University Spin-out Companies". *Journal of Technology Transfer*, 26,127-141.

Lambert, R. 2003. *Lambert Review of Business-University Collaboration*, London:HMSO.

Lockett, A., Murray, G. and Wright, M. 2002. "Do UK venture capitalists still have a bias against technology investments?" *Research Policy*, 31, 1009-1030.

Lockett, A., Wright, M., Franklin, S., 2003. "Technology transfer and universities' spin-out strategies". *Small Business Economics*, 20, 185-2000.

Lockett, A. and Wright, M. 2004. "Resources, capabilities, risk capital and the creation of spin-out companies", working paper, Centre for Management Buy-out Research, Nottingham University Business School.

Mitchell, F., Reid, G. and Terry, N. 1995. "Post investment demand for accounting information by venture capitalists", *Accounting and Business Research*, 25, 186-196.

Nicolaou, N. and Birley, S. 2003a. "Academic networks in a trichotomous categorizatioon of university spinouts". *Journal of Business Venturing*, 18,333-359.

Nicolaou N. and Birley S. 2003b. "Social networks in organizational emergence : the university spin-out phenomenon". *Management Science*, 49(12), 1702-1725.

Shane, S. and Stuart, T. 2002. "Organizational endowments and the performance of university start-ups". *Management Science*, 48(1), 154-170.

Siegel, D., Waldman, D., Link, A., 2002. "Improving the effectiveness of commercial knowledge transfers from universities to firms". *Journal of High Technology Management Research,* 14, 111-133.

Siegel, D., Waldman, D., Link, A., 2003. "Assessing the impact of organizational practices on the relative productivity of university technology transfer offices: an exploratory study". *Research Policy,*32(1), 13-27.

Sine, S., Shane, S. and DiGregorio, D. 2003. "The halo effect and technology licensing: the infleunce of institutional prestige on the licensing of university inventions". *Management Science*, 49(4), 478-497.

Thursby, J. and Kemp, S. 2002. "Growth and productive efficiency of university intellectual property licensing". *Research Policy*, 31, 109-124.

Thursby, J. and Thursby, M. 2002. "Who is selling the Ivory Tower? Sources of growth in university licensing". *Management Science*, 48, 90-104.

Ucbasaran, D., Lockett A., Wright, M., and Westhead, P. (2003). "Entrepreneurial Founder Teams : Factors associated with Members Entry and Exit". *Entrepreneurship Theory and Practice*, 28(2), 107-128.

Vanaelst, I., Clarysse, B., Wright, M., Lockett, A., Moray, N. and S'Jegers, R. 2004. "Entrepreneurial team development in academic spin-outs: an examination of team heterogeneity", working paper, University of Ghent.

Vohora A., Wright M. & Lockett A. 2004. "Critical junctures in the development of university high-tech spin out companies". *Research Policy*, 33(1), 147-176.

West, G. and DeCastro, J., 2001. "The Achilles Heel of Firm Strategy: Resource Weaknesses and Distinctive Inadequacies". *Journal of Management Studies* 38 (3), 417-442.

Wright, M. & Robbie, K. 1996. "Venture Capitalists, Unquoted Equity Investment Appraisal and the Role of Accounting Information". *Accounting & Business Research,* 26,153-170.

Wright, M., Vohora, A. and Lockett, A. 2002. *UNICO-NUBS Survey on University Commercialisation: Financial Year 2001.* Nottingham University Business School.

Wright, M., Birley, S. and Mosey, S. 2004. "Entrepreneurship and University Technology Transfer". *Journal of Technology Transfer*, 29, 235-246.

Wright, M., Vohora, A. and Lockett, A. 2004. "The Formation of High-Tech University Spinouts Through Joint Ventures". *Journal of Technology Transfer*, 29, 287-310.

Wright, M., Lockett, A., Tiratsoo, N., Alferoff, C. and Mosey, S. 2004. "Academic Entrepreneurship, Knowledge Gaps & the Role of Business Schools". Paper presented at the Academy of Management Conference, New Orleans, August.

13. Bringing Technology to Market: a Macro View of Technology Transfer and Commercialization

Kathleen Allen
University of Southern California

Abstract. In the past decade, a number of diverse factors converged to propel the issue of technology commercialization and the role of innovation in stimulating economic growth to the forefront of attention in both industry and academe. Universities, in partnership with industry, are playing an increasingly important role in the innovation and commercialization process. This article, which is written in chapter format, examines at a macro level the issues related to technology commercialization, the issue of complexity, the commercialization process, and the challenges associated with commercialization of technology.

Keywords: intellectual property, technology commercialization, technology transfer, technological change, economic growth, disequilibrium, disruptive technology, complexity, technology diffusion, Bayh-Dole Act, fuzzy front end.

1. Introduction

In the past decade, a number of diverse factors converged to propel the issue of technology commercialization and the role of innovation in stimulating economic growth to the forefront of attention in both industry and academe. For industry, companies seeking to commercialize the technologies they develop now face a dynamic set of challenges, attitudes, and values. The marketplace demands better, faster, and cheaper technology products, a product development nightmare for companies trying to survive while staying ahead of their competitors.

Intellectual property has taken on a new and more vital position. Once a cost center for a corporation, intellectual property (IP) has now become a revenue center and essential competitive advantage for those firms that possess valuable IP portfolios. Consequently, firms must now find ways to create value from archived patents to justify the ever increasing expense of new product development. Moreover, companies can no longer survive simply on incremental innovation - improving existing technology. Today companies must seek ways to add radical innovation to their product development mix to stimulate future opportunities before their existing technologies become obsolete. Although thousands of new products reach the market every year, the vast majority of these products fail to make a profit for the companies that created them. Therefore, it is not surprising that 40 percent of major corporations in business in 1975 are not in business today (Foster, 2000). A critical reason for this dismal record is

This article was originally published in the International Journal of Entrepreneurship Education 3(1): pp. 321-358. © 2005, Senate Hall Academic Publishing.

ineffective commercialization processes that attempt to link emerging technologies with existing markets rather than with emerging markets (Stevens and Burley, 1997). Satisfying customer needs today is like trying to hit a moving target.

Universities are playing an increasingly important role in the innovation and commercialization process. They rely heavily on research grants to support their R&D function, but, more and more, government and foundation funders are stipulating that the results of research must have a commercial application, that is, return something of value to society. As a result, universities are faced with the dilemma of how to stay true to their primary mission - to educate, conduct independent research, and provide service to their communities - while simultaneously responding to demands to commercialize their research findings. Although arriving late to the game of technology commercialization, university licensing activity has had a significant impact on the economy. For example, in 1999, commercialized academic research produced more than $40 billion in economic activity, including over $5 billion in federal, state, and local tax revenues; more than 340 new companies started; and more than 270,000 jobs (AUTM, 1999).

Despite more effective tools and knowledge about commercialization, new technology adoption is still a very slow and incremental process with only a mere fraction of all new technologies ever achieving mass adoption. Those technologies that do achieve mass adoption do so only after significant delays (Farzin, Huisman, and Kort, 1997). The Technology Marketing Group (TMG) of Acton Massachusetts worked with a new firm in the chemical industry to develop a technology for use in pharmaceutical research, development, and production (Hruby & Lutz, 2002). The firm assumed that since it was a pharmaceutical company, its initial customers would definitely fall into the early adopter category. After much research, TMG discovered that the lag time for adoption of the company's new technology was five years; however, since innovators in the industry had not yet adopted the technology, TMG estimated that it would be 10 years before the new firm could sell sufficient volumes of the product. Calculating the return on investment over that length of time resulted in a decision not to pursue the technology. The slow pace of technology adoption is due in large part to the uncertainties inherent in the commercialization process. The more rapidly an invention gets to market, the more likely it is that it meets market needs defined during the development process. Yet, there are no guarantees and perhaps one of the major uncertainties of the process is that so much of the process is out of the control of the entrepreneur or firm.

Given the environment described above, it is no wonder that interest in understanding, refining, and perfecting the commercialization process has quickened. Yet an understanding of the commercialization process and its outcomes at a macro level is still in the early stages.

2. Technology Commercialization from a Macro Perspective

Technological change and its impact on the economy were nowhere to be found in economic growth models until the work of Paul Romer and others in the 1980s (Romer, 1986). Traditional growth models relied solely on inputs of labor and capital. Entrepreneurship was also not found in the neoclassically dominated economic theory of the twentieth and early twenty-first centuries. In neoclassical economic theory, good management is needed to maintain equilibrium. That equilibrium is disrupted by entrepreneurs who recognize previously unrecognized profit opportunities. Traditional economic models considered productivity growth as essential to maintaining economic growth, but several research studies have identified an unexplained, yet substantial residual in the calculation of growth in output of workers. Two studies in particular, the work of Robert Solow and Edward Denison, succeeded in estimating the contribution of traditional inputs (labor and capital) to increases in traditional outputs (productivity). Their conclusions, which were arrived at by different methods, found that more than a quarter of productivity growth can be explained by R&D activity. (Solow, 1957; and Cohen & Noll, 1991). Early economic research also made a link between the pace of technological change and the magnitude of resources devoted to R&D (Baily & Chakrabarti, 1988).

As depicted in Figure 1 (page 325), technological change results from an entrepreneur identifying new, emerging customer segments, new customer needs, existing customer needs left unsatisfied, and new ways of manufacturing and distributing products and services (Allen, 2003). Therefore, R&D alone does not produce opportunity, but it does create an environment that allows profit opportunities to exist (Holcombe, 2001). For example, the former Soviet Union invested heavily in research and development, physical assets, and human capital, which are the inputs required for economic growth. Despite this enormous investment, R&D in the Soviet Union did not lead to economic growth because the economic environment did not support exploitation by entrepreneurs. Therefore, simple investment in R&D will not always lead to growth; growth requires the combination of innovation and entrepreneurship.

Since entrepreneurial opportunity is a critical factor in economic growth, it would be important to understand where these opportunities come from. Holcombe divides entrepreneurial opportunities into two categories: those that derive from the innovative activity of the entrepreneur and those that arise from recognizing a need or gap in the market. In the first case, the entrepreneur as innovator, the entrepreneur is by definition the only one who has the ability to see the opportunity because it derives directly from his or her expertise, knowledge, and innovative activity. The second type of entrepreneurial opportunity is available to anyone with an opportunistic mindset who can spot a gap in the market (Holcombe, 2001, 301). But it requires a market or environment that produces profit opportunities. Three broad categories of factors seem to create profit opportunities for potential entrepreneurs (Holcombe, 2001, 303):

1. *Factors that disequilibrate the market.* Market equilibrium is disrupted when customer preferences change, requiring the reallocation of resources, or when environmental forces deplete natural resources or normal weather patterns are disrupted. For example, as landfills reach capacity, new sites must be found, which provides a new entrepreneurial opportunity. The Internet certainly served to disequilibrate the economy providing new business opportunities that had not previously existed.

2. *Factors that enhance production possibilities.* The increase in production possibilities creates entrepreneurial opportunities by increasing inputs and allowing them to be combined in new ways to expand markets. For example, improvements in highways and the lowering of air freight costs extended the market for firms like Federal Express that were able to increase their division of labor and their productivity. Another example is the wider variety of specialized business services that are now available outside of big cities due to reductions in transportation and communications costs. Nationwide financial services firms now can serve customers at a distance through telephone communication and the Internet. These same services cost too much to be feasible in the 1950s.

3. *Entrepreneurial activity that creates new possibilities.* One of the most important outcomes of entrepreneurial activity is to produce more entrepreneurial activity. The act of one entrepreneur opens up new opportunities for other entrepreneurs to act. One example is the microcomputer industry. Xerox developed the mouse, but Apple Computer recognized the commercial potential of this input device and brought it to market. Microsoft, appreciating how effectively the device worked, built an operating system that leveraged that technology. Had the mouse not been developed as an input device, no one would have had the opportunity to develop the infrared mouse, touch pad, pointing stick, and trackball. So the original idea for the mouse led to new entrepreneurial opportunities.

Figure 1: Technological Change

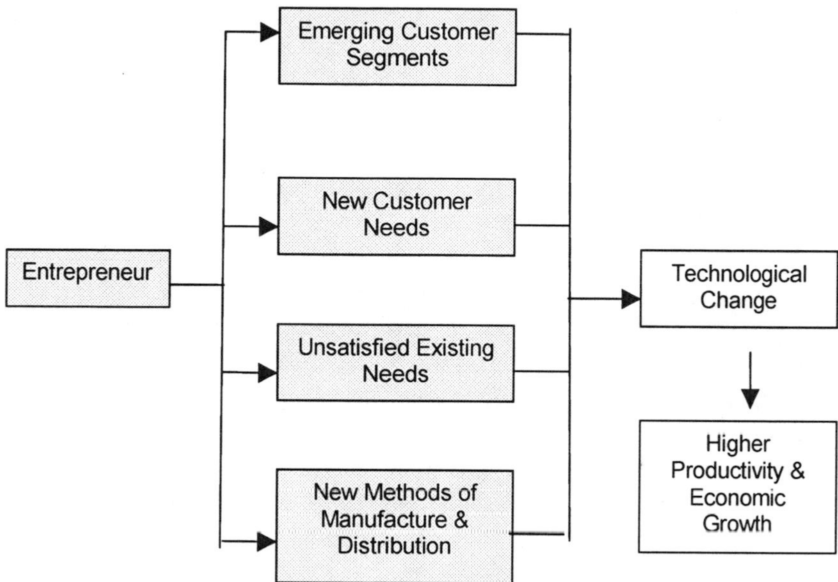

2.1. Definitions

Since terms related to the concept of technology commercialization are defined in a variety of ways, it would be important to begin by defining some key terms that will be used throughout the chapter.

- *Technology.* For our purposes, Burgelman's, Madique's, and Wheelwright's definition will be employed; that is, technology is "the theoretical and practical knowledge, skills, and artifacts that can be used to develop products and services as well as their production and delivery systems. Technology can be embodied in people, materials, cognitive and implementing a new idea" (Burgelman, Madique, & Wheelwright, 1996).

- *Invention.* The creation of a novel and new idea.

- *Innovation.* Refers to improvements on existing technology or to the exploitation of an invention (Van de Ven & Angle, 1989). Whereas invention is usually a random and unpredictable process, innovation is a manageable process that turns an invention into something with commercial value (Miller & Morris, 1999).

- *Sustaining technology.* These technologies foster improved product performance of established products and comprise the vast majority of technological advances (Christensen, 1997).

- *Disruptive or radical technology.* These technologies bring about a paradigm shift, that is, they obsolete technologies that precede them. Initially they result in poorer product performance, but a cheaper, simpler, smaller, and more convenient application (Christensen, 1997).

- *Technology transfer v. technology commercialization.* These two terms have frequently been used interchangeably; however, it is important to note that technology commercialization has a broader meaning. In general, technology transfer deals with disclosure of inventions, record keeping and management of inventions, evaluation and marketing, patent prosecution, negotiation and drafting of license agreements, and management of active licenses (Allan, 2001). It typically refers to the means by which technologies are transferred from the inventor to the market. Technology commercialization involves a lengthy and complex process that begins with discovery, moves through product development and all its associated issues such as prototyping and intellectual property development, involves business concept development, market feasibility analysis, and business plan development, and takes the concept to a license agreement, acquisition or the start-up of a spin-off venture. In both the university and in large companies, the focus tends to be more on licensing than the start-up of new ventures. Whereas market research is a critical and ongoing component of technology commercialization, the technology transfer practices of most universities and many companies consist of posting intellectual properties on a web site. Many universities, large and small, lack the resources to conduct a full-scale market research or marketing effort (Allan, 2001).

- *Spin-off Company.* A spin-off is a new company formed by former employees of a parent organization and based on a technology that originated in the parent organization and then was transferred to the new company (Carayannis, Rogers, Kurlhara & Allbritton, 1998). In the case of a university spin-off, the technology is licensed from the university.

- *R&D.* R&D is more than simply an inquiry process in the hard sciences; it is a "fundamental process for generating knowledge" (Link, 1999). The National Science Foundation refers to R&D as the "advancement of the discovery of scientific knowledge and development is the systematic use of such knowledge" (Link, 1996).

2.2. Determinants of Technology Commercialization

Many factors work to determine whether a technology moves from laboratory to market and how smooth or bumpy that path might be. Here we look at some of the precipitators of technology commercialization, how the nature of the technology affects the process, how the screening process determines which concepts move forward, and how the ability of the technology to be transferred can affect the commercialization process.

2.2.1. Precipitators of Technology Commercialization

The commercialization process is more creative than scientific. The creative process literature, which dominates the research in creativity, asserts that the purpose of creativity is the production of unique and useful ideas (Deazin, 1999). Another research stream holds the view that creativity is about the generation of valuable and useful products, services, procedures, and processes, which is similar to the purpose of the commercialization process.

In general the commercialization process is precipitated by a discovery or recognition of a market need. The two are quite distinct. The discovery process is about making a connection between two or more disparate ideas to elicit something new. Once that connection is made, a period of exploration and experimentation begins that can result in an invention. By contrast, recognition of a market need or customer pain produces a problem that must be solved. The solution results in a new technology or the enhancement of an existing technology.

We are learning more about opportunity recognition from a growing body of research. While not all of the variables that affect opportunity recognition have been identified or their impact determined, we do know that most people find opportunities in industries with which they are familiar or in which they have experience (Zietsma, 1999). There is also a positive correlation between the number of weak ties (those outside family and friends) an entrepreneur has and the number of opportunities recognized (Singh et al., 1999). Some research has suggested that opportunity recognition involves active, well-planned searches in addition to serendipity (Herron & Sapienza, 1992). Other research has suggested a five-step framework that describes an iterative process with many feedback loops (Hill, Schrader, and Lumpkin, 1999).

1. *Preparation.* Because entrepreneurs bring prior knowledge and experience to the opportunity recognition process, it is idiosyncratic to each entrepreneur.

2. *Incubation.* Incubation is a period of time where the entrepreneur contemplates the solution to a problem.

3. *Insight.* This can be described as the "eureka" moment, when the solution becomes apparent.

4. *Evaluation.* Insight is followed by a process of defining a business concept and testing in the marketplace to determine its feasibility.

5. *Elaboration.* With a feasible concept comes the planning and creation of a company to execute the concept.

Despite research findings, it appears that opportunity recognition is a fairly unique journey for an individual; that is, each individual finds his or her own path to it. Nevertheless, entrepreneurs increase their probability of finding opportunity by 1) increasing their knowledge and experience in an industry in which they are interested; 2) building a diverse network of strong and weak professional ties; 3) developing an opportunistic mindset; and 4) exercising patience as the incubation period may take a long time (Allen, 2003, p.35).

2.2.2. Sustaining Versus Disruptive Technologies as Commercialization Determinants

The type of technology being developed will have an important impact on the commercialization process. Disruptive technologies are those that fundamentally change the way things are done and obsolete previous technology. Some examples are the PC, the fax machine, and the birth control pill. Disruptive technologies are not a simple change from one technology to another, but a radical change at a systemic level with far-reaching implications (Allen, 2003). They are borne from needs that can no longer be met inside current technology parameters. Historically, we saw these cataclysmic changes only once a decade, but today they are occurring almost annually. It is a curious phenomenon that disruptive technologies don't achieve their full value until they reach mass-market acceptance, which for most is several years. This fact has important implications for the commercialization process.

Disruptive technologies have been placed into three categories (Leifer et al, 2000):

1. *Innovation within the markets of existing business units.* These types of disruptive technologies completely replace existing technologies in the same market and with the same customers.

2. *Innovation in the white spaces.* Here the disruptive technology targets the gap between a company's existing businesses and often borrows knowledge, experience, and technology from two or three business units to create a new technology.

3. *Innovation outside a company's current strategic objectives.* These types of disruptive technologies open up new markets that are substantially different from current markets and therefore incur the highest level of risk for the company.

If is often believed that large companies have the highest probability of successfully developing and introducing a disruptive technology, but the reality is that large companies are plagued by the "incumbent's curse" (Chandy & Tellis, 2000). The theory of the incumbent's curse has been studied to a great extent in the research literature. The notion is that because incumbents have invested heavily in the development of their technology, they face inertia and resist investing in any technology concept that might cannibalize or obsolete the existing technology (Scherer, 1980). As a result, most disruptive or radical technology comes from small firms with no sunk costs and no turf to protect.

1. There is no incentive to take on the development of disruptive technologies because they typically don't produce an income for years. By contrast, incremental or sustaining technologies produce a relatively quick return on investment (Conner, 1988).

2. Large firms tend to focus on their core competencies and therefore filter out unrelated information, which may include a potential threat from a small, innovative company.

3. Large firms tend to rely on existing routines and are reluctant to change what has worked previously to support a disruptive technology.

Sustaining technologies, by contrast, are major improvements on existing technologies, generally in the area of performance. Consequently, their adoption rate is almost immediate, and they are profitable much earlier. Most firms rely on sustaining or incremental innovation, often to their detriment, because over time incremental innovations experience diminishing returns and eventually are overcome by a new technology on a different platform.

2.2.3. Technology Screening

Ideas usually come easily, but opportunities - those ideas that have commercial potential - are often more difficult to identify. Successful technology commercialization relies on a screening process to sift through potential opportunities and settle on the most appropriate one. Figure 2 (page 332) presents a screening framework to assist in determining which of many ideas might actually go through the commercialization process.

Development of a new technology opportunity is normally undertaken when it is compatible with the entrepreneur's personal goals and/or the company's strategic direction. It must be demonstrably worth the investment in time, money, and other resources. At this early screening it is critical to view a new technology from the customer's point of view, whether that customer is a potential licensee or a buyer of a finished product.

In doing an initial screen of a potential new technology, consideration of its future economic value will be an important determinant of the decision to go forward with commercialization.

Intellectual property has a legal life, but it also has an economic life; that is, the length of time a patent can generate revenue for its owner. That length of time and the amount of revenue generated is a function of several factors (Allen, 2003, p.40):

- *The probability that competitors design around the patent* and develop a competing product.

- *The probability that the patent is challenged.* This is often done by competitors as a strategy to tie the company up in patent litigation and divert its attention from developing the market.

- *The probability that development costs exceed estimates.* The cost of developing a new technology is difficult to estimate with any degree of accuracy. Frequently, developers will estimate on the high side to such a degree that the project never happens because it is judged to be financially infeasible.

- *The impact of new laws on the development of the technology.* A new law can shorten or cut off a new technology's economic life. Regulations on stem cell research have threatened to end many promising opportunities to cure many diseases. By contrast, environmental protection regulations have spawned many new businesses in the areas of diagnostics and compliance.

- *The escalation of supply pricing or loss of source of supply.* Supply prices are rarely stable, but rather change fairly frequently, sometimes significantly. When that happens, the higher prices can effectively reduce the economic life of the technology by forcing companies to find alternative sources of supply or get out of the business entirely if it no longer makes financial sense. The loss of a key supplier to a catastrophe such as fire or to bankruptcy can also start a chain reaction that could put the company out of business. Understanding the volatility of the industry is important in estimating future economic value. Having a back-up supplier would help in situations where a supplier is lost.

Figure 2: Technology Screening Framework

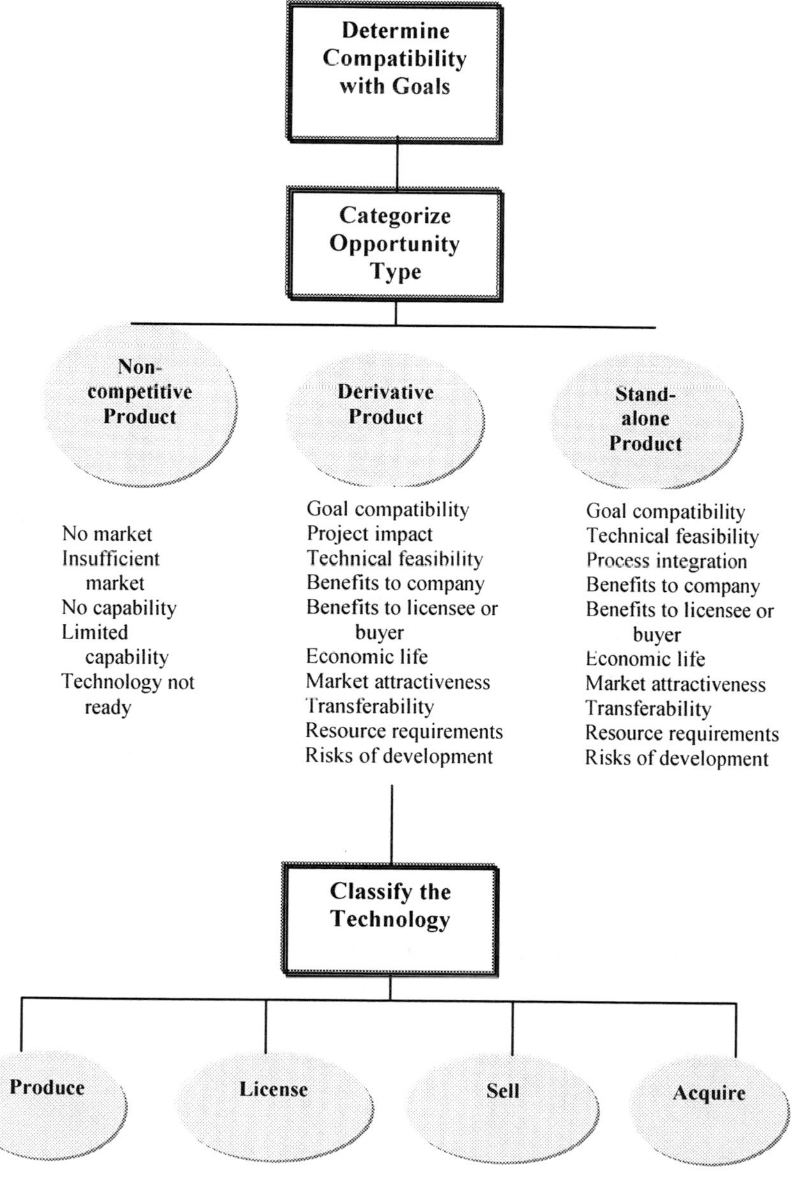

2.2.4. Determine the Ability of the Technology to be Transferred and the Resource Requirements to Transfer the Technology

It has been suggested that transaction cost economics research might provide the appropriate framework to identify the conditions under which a technology might be successfully transferred (Shane, 2002). The most effective commercialization of university technologies is conducted by entrepreneurs and other economic players who have a comparative advantage in terms of market research, product development, manufacturing, and distribution capabilities and resources. In general, licensing is a way to identify the best players to commercialize a specific technology where markets are free of problems (Teece, 1980). But the market for inventions is imperfect and is characterized by problems of adverse selection, moral hazard, and hold-up. We find adverse selection in markets where low-quality inventions are misrepresented as high quality and potential buyers are unable to discern the difference (Anton and Yao, 1994). This is due principally to problems of disclosure. Buyers will not purchase without sufficient information about the invention, but often once that information is revealed, the invention no longer holds any value for the buyer.

Moral hazard occurs where, for instance, the buyer refuses to pay for knowledge transferred and that knowledge cannot be unlearned once it is transferred (Arora, 1996). Alternatively the seller may not fully disclose all relevant knowledge in an effort to reduce his or her costs.

Hold-up occurs because of the high degree of uncertainty in the commercialization process. Often, the parties involved in technology transfer must agree to resolve some issues at a future date, because not enough information is available at the time of negotiation.

It is important to note that patents tend to overcome the problems of adverse selection, moral hazard, and hold-up by forcing the buyer to purchase the invention to use it (Anton and Yao, 1994). Patents are also used as a negotiating tool to prevent the parties from taking part in moral hazard and they minimize the problem of hold-up by permitting full disclosure. But, there are many instances where patent strength varies by industry. For example,

- In some industries like software, it is relatively easy to design around a patent (Teece, 1986).

- Some patents cannot stand up to challenge, particularly when their owners cannot defend them.

- In some industries, competitors can legally invent around a patent, particularly if technology is changing so rapidly that patents may be considered irrelevant (Levin et al. 1987).

It is also important to identify the risks associated with the development of the technology. Every project endures two types of risk: technical and market (Smith, 1999). Technical risks come about when developers are unable to produce a product that meets the technical specifications they have designed. Market risks come from misreading the market or failing to meet customer needs. Most product failures are actually due to market risks. The work of Robert Cooper over 25 years and more than 2,000 products has led to six factors that predict new product success (Cooper, 2001).

- A superior and unique product
- A clearly defined product at the earliest stages of development
- Thorough technical and market feasibility analyses
- A well-executed marketing plan
- A well-executed technology plan
- A cross-functional team with expertise in all critical areas

Note that only one of these factors is related to product development; the rest are clearly within the domain of market research. Successfully managing risk (it cannot be completely eliminated) during product development is critical certainly for achieving rapid time-to-market, but also for increasing the odds of securing funding. The amount of equity a company must give up to investors is a function of how much of the inherent risk in the technology it has reduced. Investors will provide funding where they perceive that the inventing team has reduced the technical and market risk to their level of comfort.

Once the initial screen is complete, a technology is typically classified in terms of how it is to be transferred or commercialized. In general there are four categories of commercialization opportunities.

- *Start a company and produce the product.* This route works when the inventor has the expertise and access to required resources to start a company and do an effective job of marketing and distributing the product. These functions may be outsourced and the new company may choose to focus on what it does best, product development, for example. Where it is important to retain complete control of intellectual property (ie. know-how), the inventor may choose to start a company so that the technology can be held captive as a trade secret.

- *License the technology.* Licensing the right to make and distribute a technology is a common route of technology transfer, certainly for universities. This option gives the inventor an opportunity to benefit from reaching more markets than he or she could have achieved alone. Getting to many markets quickly is critical to achieving mainstream adoption of a radically new technology.

- *Sell the technology.* In some cases, an inventor may choose to sell the technology outright, often to a larger company. This is particularly true where the technology is not captive and has no relationship to other technologies the company produces. Another reason to sell is when the buyer has better access to raw materials than the inventor.

- *Acquisition.* Merging with or partnering with another company to share technologies is another choice available to the entrepreneur.

3. The Issue of Complexity in the Commercialization Process

While the entire commercialization process is highly complex, prototype development and manufacturing of a market-ready product involve perhaps the highest degree of complexity. Complexity is a concept that has been studied in fields ranging from biological and physical to manmade systems and organizational structures. In general, there are four categories of complexity: logistical, organizational, technological, and environmental (Khurana, 1999).

3.1. Logistical Complexity

Logistical complexity arises where there are a high number of tasks and/or products. The more inputs and outputs required to manufacture and distribute a product, the higher the degree of logistical complexity. Those inputs and outputs include suppliers, raw materials, distributors, distribution channels, and so forth.

3.2. Organizational Complexity

Organizational complexity can arise from the number of inputs and outputs required by the organization's policies and procedures as well as from layers of management - the hierarchy. Often a high degree of complexity in an organizational structure will actually slow the product development and manufacturing process, creating a competitive disadvantage for the company. By contrast, the generally flatter organizational structures of entrepreneurial companies often give them a competitive advantage in reducing time to market. Where a company outsources many of its product development and manufacturing tasks to other companies, organizational complexity actually increases because of the need to coordinate tasks across companies whose policies and procedures may not be compatible.

3.3. Environmental Complexity

Environmental complexity includes all those things outside the commercialization process that have an impact on it. The nature of the industry in which a company operates can add complexity to the product development and manufacturing process by requiring the company to deal with multiple suppliers, access complex distribution channels, and satisfy diverse customers.

The work of Michael Porter is often used as a reliable framework for analyzing industry complexity and its impact on the firm. Porter describes five forces that affect every industry and also the profit potential and competitive strategy of businesses in that industry (Porter, 1980): barriers to entry, threat of substitute products, buyer power, supplier power, and degree of competitor rivalry. This author has added technology to the framework to reflect the dynamic rather than static nature of industries over time.

Barriers to entry make it difficult for new entrants to enter an industry. Some of these barriers include economies of scale in marketing, production, and distribution. Another common barrier is brand loyalty, which means that the loyal customer base perceives high switching costs to move to another technology. Overcoming this barrier may mean introducing a superior technology or partnering with a major player to gain entry.

Competition from substitute products, products that perform the same basic function but in a different way or for a different price, can also be a significant entry barrier to new firms. The *purchasing power of the major players* in an industry gives them the ability to force down prices from their suppliers and thus incur costs that are much less than the new entrants must pay. *Suppliers* also have the power to control prices or change quality, particularly if they control necessary raw materials.

Highly competitive industries drive down prices and return on investment. In this situation, price wars and advertising skirmishes are common. To enter such an industry, a new venture needs to define a niche that will give it a temporary monopoly serving a gap in the market. Finally, technology enables business goals and also drives change. Where *technology* is critical to an industry, the industry tends to be more volatile, more virtual than physical, and more intuitive than analytical.

3.4. Technological Complexity

Technological complexity refers to the system and its various technologies. Research proposes the existence of two dimensions of technological complexity: interaction complexity and nondecomposability. Interaction complexity is the result of many interactions among the product components or subsystems. One change in any component or subsystem of the product generally requires redesign and reengineering of the whole product. In some cases, a product cannot be reduced to its individual components without suffering a loss of performance. In other words, the synergy created by the interaction of the components is essential to the performance of the product itself. A similar situation exists with processes. The various steps in a process may have complex interactions such that they cannot take place independently (Weick, 1990; Buchanan & Bessant, 1985). This inability to disconnect processes is known as nondecomposability. For example, the manufacture of picture tubes for televisions is a complex process involving more than 200 production steps and employing more than 24 interacting process technologies including electrical, optical, chemical, and mechanical (Khurana, 1999). Changing any one of these processes will affect the entire system and the ultimate performance of the product.

An inherent problem with complex systems and processes is how often specifications in an engineered design do not match what actually happens when the product is built. Specifications that work in theory or in a computer simulation may still run into problems when the physical prototyping stage is reached because complex processes are, by their very nature, unpredictable. They display episodes of punctuated equilibrium and path dependence. With punctuated equilibrium, the system is relatively stable for periods of time and then experiences a dramatic change. One can ever be certain when a dramatic change will occur. Even smaller, more random changes can frequently lead to radically different outcomes in the future (Bak, 1996). Therefore, to ensure a sound and consistently reliable product, it is necessary to conduct numerous experiments that test all the potential variables that might affect the final outcome. A more sinister problem is that having identified punctuated equilibrium and path dependence in the past does not provide a reliable guide to future events. The commercialization process is not linear, so the future cannot be predicted from either the present or the past.

Some research has suggested that adopting an adaptive strategy provides a variety of options which optimizes outcomes over many different circumstances. More flexibility increases the probability of success (Beinhocker, 1999).

4. The Commercialization Decision - Technology Diffusion and Gap Theory

The market system does not allow for the natural diffusion of technologies to the marketplace. One of the primary reasons for this is that the investment community does not invest sufficiently in basic research largely because there are no reliable methods for accurately assessing risk at such an early stage (Cohen & Noll, 1991, 18). A further problem is that of appropriability, which is the gap between private and social rates of return on R&D; that is, it is unlikely that the rates of return to the investor will match or even come near to matching the returns to society (Jamison & Jansen, 2000). Because most of the benefit of technological advances is passed on to consumers and is not part of profitability calculations, the profit to the inventing company is generally too small to justify a private investment (Mansfield, 1980 & Scherer, 1982). It has been estimated that the private rate of return on investment in R&D is about 25 percent and the social rate of return on R&D is 56 percent (Mansfield, 1986). The appropriability problem often extends to applied research as well where the application does not have a specific value to a particular company.

The "technological gap theory" applies in the U.S. where defined mechanisms for supporting applied research don't exist; consequently, a gap exists between scientific advances arising from academic research and technologies commercialized in the market (National Academy of Sciences, 1992). The Bayh-Dole Act of 1980 has gone a long way toward narrowing this gap by making it easier for industry to participate in the development of federally funded basic research. The Bayh-Dole Act, the popular name for the Patent and Trademark Act Amendments of 1980, radically changed the incentive structure for non-government organizations performing federally funded research. Prior to the act, the federal government retained title to patents generated from its grants. Since it then gave non-exclusive licenses to develop technologies, there was no incentive by companies to do the development because their competitors could also obtain a license on the same technology. With the increase in global competition, however, the government became concerned that most of the technologies developed under its grants were not being commercialized. So Congress pushed through the Bayh-Dole Act, which provides for ownership by universities and others of patentable inventions resulting from federally-funded research. In addition, a series of federal judicial decisions that followed the passage of the act significantly broadened the definition of patentable inventions and strengthened the legal protections of holders of intellectual property rights (Newberg and Dunn, 2002).

4.1. The Role of Intellectual Property in Technology Diffusion

Securing intellectual property protection is a critical element of the commercialization process where licensing and outside funding are being considered. Since the Bayh-Dole Act, the number of invention disclosures and patents filed at universities has been increasing, which has stimulated interest from the investment community (Santoro & Betts, 2002). In fiscal year 2000, 13,032 invention disclosures at universities were reported, up 6 percent from 1999. 6,375 new U.S. patent applications were filed, up 15 percent from FY 1999. In FY 2000, 4,362 new licenses and options were executed, up 11 percent from FY 1999. Ninety percent of these licenses and options to start-ups were exclusive (Pressman, 2002), which is surprising because universities tend to be reluctant to grant exclusive licenses to industry partners. The opportunity cost of revenue streams from other segments of that company's industry or other industries is lost with an exclusive license. Moreover, exclusivity can impede the university's ability to disseminate knowledge - it's primary mission.

4.1.1. Incentives to Invent

Several economic theories form the basis for the rationale behind intellectual property protections. Under the incentive-to-invent theory, without the temporary monopoly created by intellectual property protections, the original inventor would be left open to having his or her invention stolen and produced, often at a lower price, before the inventor could recoup the costs of research and development. With patent protection and the quiet period it provides, inventors, theoretically, will be induced to invent. Some research has not found a relationship between patents and the incentive to invent, but today in more volatile industries like pharmaceuticals, software, and telecommunications, a greater interest in protecting inventions is taking place (Baumol, 1999).

4.1.2. Incentives to Disclose

With formal legal protections in place, inventors are incentivized to disclose their inventions without fear of their proprietary information being revealed until the patent is issued. Disclosure is important to the diffusion of knowledge in a field of study because it prevents the duplication of research effort and moves the field forward more quickly. Without these protections, inventors might retain their inventions as trade secrets to maintain their value. Given that trade secrets are difficult to sell or license because once the secret is disclosed, it loses its proprietary value, new inventions would not be disseminated to the public and technological change would not occur.

4.1.3. Incentives to Commercialize

Most inventors need to work with strategic partners such as manufacturers who incur the expense of setting up for manufacture. The temporary monopoly granted by a patent provides the manufacturer with a quiet period to produce and distribute at a fair price before it needs to find a way to lower costs to compete with other manufacturers who have entered the market (Allen, 2003).

4.1.4. Disincentives to Securing Intellectual Property

Many arguments have countered the notion that intellectual property protections are incentivising to the inventor. One claim is that these protections hurt consumers and end users because they must pay higher prices for patented products than for non-patented products. Another argument posits that if the patent holder does not permit other companies to develop improvements and derivative innovations of the original patent, the patent will never realize its full profit potential (Allen, 2003). The reality is that rarely does a single inventor recognize all the potential applications for a particular technology. A third argument is that typically the initial inventor never realizes a profit from the invention. In general, the second or third mover, who improves on the invention and learns from the mistakes of the pioneer, generally sees more financial rewards from the commercialization process. Finally, patents commonly affect the direction of research. In one study it was found that 60 percent of patented innovations were imitated within four years of their patents and at two-thirds the original innovation's cost (Mansfield, Schwartz and Wagner, 1981).

4.2. The Role of University-Industry Collaborations in Technology Diffusion

Private industry has played an increasing significant role in university research by encouraging and financially underwriting the costs of research, and this collaboration has increased competitiveness of U.S. firms and improved technological capacity (Newberg & Dunn, 2002). The 1996 Council on Competitiveness, a nonprofit forum of chief executives from industry and academe, established the position that "R&D partnerships hold the key to meeting the challenge of transition that our nation now faces" (Council on Competitiveness, 1996, p.3). These public/private partnerships increasingly require the participation of universities in the R&D function.

The climate for university-industry collaboration is far more encouraging than in the past. For industry, global competition has forced businesses to turn to universities to find ways to make their organizational processes more effective (Abrahamson, 1996, Micklethwait & Wooldridge, 1996, Pfeffer & Sutton, 2000).

Moreover, many companies, in an effort to reduce overhead, have decreased the size of their R&D staff and are using universities to fulfill that function (Cohen, Florida, Randazzese, & Walsh, 1998). An additional benefit is that public policy provides tax breaks for corporate funding of university research and requires university/industry partnerships as a condition of funding.

In the past, collaborations were essentially sponsorships by industry of university research to solve industry-specific problems. Today industry views the university as a source of complementary expertise, knowledge, and resources that are frequently not easily available in the industry environment (Starbuck, 2001). Moreover, university partnerships usually don't carry with them the conflicts of interest so prevalent in industry partnerships. At the same time, industry-university collaborations have also sparked serious criticism that they compromise and weaken the academic mission (Cohen, 1998). One of the main dilemmas is the conflict between the open inquiry principle at universities and industry's desire to restrict the diffusion of information to maintain a competitive advantage. Despite some of the negatives, industry's and the university's share of R&D is increasing while government's share is decreasing (National Science Foundation, 1996).

Four basic models of industry-university collaboration exist (Newburg & Dunn, 2002). They will be reviewed briefly here.

4.2.1. University to Industry Technology Licensing

Licensing university technology is generally the most common form of collaboration where the university grants certain rights of use to its knowledge, generally in the form of a patented invention. In return, the university receives royalty payments. University technology transfer is a result of the Bayh-Dole Act (P.L. 96-517, later amended by PL. 98-620), which incentivized universities to transfer the results of their research. By creating a uniform federal patent policy that allowed universities to retain title to inventions developed with government funding, universities became partners with government and industry to raise the level of innovation and commercialization. Since the Bayh-Dole Act, invention disclosures at universities have increased dramatically. Between 1991 and 1998, invention disclosures increased by 59 percent and new patent applications increased by 164 percent in the same period. The number of licenses executed increased by 120 percent (Pressman et al, 1999). Research by Rogers, Yin, and Hoffmann (2000) determined that the most effective universities in technology transfer are large research universities with more resources, higher faculty pay, and an office of technology licensing that was established early.

4.2.2. Industry-Sponsored University Research

In this model, the university trades its expertise and resources in exchange for industry funding to solve a particular research problem. The funding company may be entitled to right of first refusal to license the technology resulting from the research. In this situation, the university must carefully weigh the risks and advantages of being essentially in a work-for-hire situation.

4.2.3. Spin-off Companies

Some technologies are more appropriate for a start-up company that is spun-off out of the university. In this scenario, the inventor may take a leave of absence from the university to work full-time in the new company for a year or two, then return full-time to his or her research position at the university. Some universities offer incubator facilities on or off campus where researchers can locate their spin-off ventures for a period of time before taking spinning out of the university.

4.2.4. Idea Laboratories

The Massachusetts Institute of Technology's (MIT) Media Laboratory and the University of Southern California's (USC) Integrated Media Systems Center (IMSC) are unique structures that permit multiple projects to coexist as a single research center. Under this model, private companies support the laboratory financially in return for the ability to follow a stream of research and have first right to license any technologies coming out of the lab. Projects within the lab are usually synergistically related; that is, they have value as individual technologies, but integrated, they create many more opportunities for new applications. For example, USC's IMSC focuses on media systems: sound, panoramic video, haptics, streaming, and compression technologies. Together these technologies form an immersive technology platform that permits the development of such diverse applications as the treatment of social phobias and learning disorders, immersive music and video environments, and interactive simulations. The mutual benefit of the idea lab structure is that it provides unrestricted industry support for academic research while at the same time giving private industry access to university talent.

5. Commercialization as a Process

Considering technology commercialization as a process is a way to study individual tasks as part of an integrated whole. A process is a linked chain of interdependent activities that cross many functions to develop, produce, and distribute or transfer a technology from concept to market (Garvin, D.A., 1998). In addition to the engineering and market analysis processes, the overall commercialization process is comprised of research, strategy, decision-making, communication, political, negotiating and selling processes. Perhaps the most studied of these processes has been decision-making beginning with the work of Barnard and Simon that described decision-making as a distributed activity, extending over a period of time and involving several people (Barnard, 1938 and Simon, 1975). Early research attempted to model, without much success the decision process as a sequence of events. Later research concluded that decision-making involves simultaneous activities that occur in different stages rather than sequenced (Witte, 1972). But even a stages approach cannot capture the intricacies of the commercialization process: the scope of interrelated activities, the impact on the whole process of one change at one point, the numbers of people that move in and out of the process at various points, and the impact on resource allocation.

The commercialization process is also a learning process that involves knowledge acquisition, explanation, diffusion, and retention. How knowledge is acquired determines the activities, behaviors, and sub-processes that affect the overall commercialization process from creation through market research, intellectual property protections, product development, and business planning. How that knowledge is interpreted and diffused throughout the process affects everything from time to market to launch decisions. Furthermore, the combination of scientific and technical knowledge with tacit manufacturing and sales knowledge can create a significant competitive advantage for a company. When know-how represents a relatively high portion of overall investment, it is typical to find correspondingly high R&D expenditures (John, Weiss, and Dutta, 1999). Yet another advantageous characteristic of know-how is that it cannot be used up; it is regenerative (Glazer, 1991). The result is that once the cost of producing the first unit is recouped, the cost of replication declines precipitously.

Another aspect of commercialization processes that is often overlooked when discussing how an invention moves from idea to market is the political processes that can derail a project at any point and certainly contribute to making commercialization more art than science. The ability to move successfully through the commercialization process, particularly in a large organization, is often a function of how effective the project champion is in aligning and harmonizing competing interests while simultaneously motivating and securing commitment from everyone involved (Garvin, 1998). This is no easy task, particularly in the development of radical technologies because typically costs are high, outcomes are uncertain, and economically the development of radical technologies makes no sense because the return on investment is many years out if ever.

Some research has found that most technology projects have more than one champion (Leifer et al, 2000). In fact they were able to identify technical champions, project champions, business unit champions, and executive champions. Technical champions are typically the inventors or discoverers who drive the idea forward in its earliest stages. Project champions, by contrast, are the interface between the project, the rest of the organization, and external partners. Business unit champions are those who have the ability to see that the project transitions from project status to an operating unit or start-up venture. The executive champion is the senior executive who can cut through all the barriers and smooth the path to completion. Many a technology has successfully made it through product development only to fail to complete the commercialization process because it didn't have the right champion at the right time to break down the barriers.

In Figure 3 opposite, I offer a framework for studying and explaining the technology commercialization process. It is based on the work of Cooper, 1999, and others and highlights the key issues developed throughout this chapter. While the major components of the framework will be discussed in more detail in later sections, it is appropriate to provide an explanatory overview at this point.

Figure 3: Framework for the Innovation and Commercialization Process

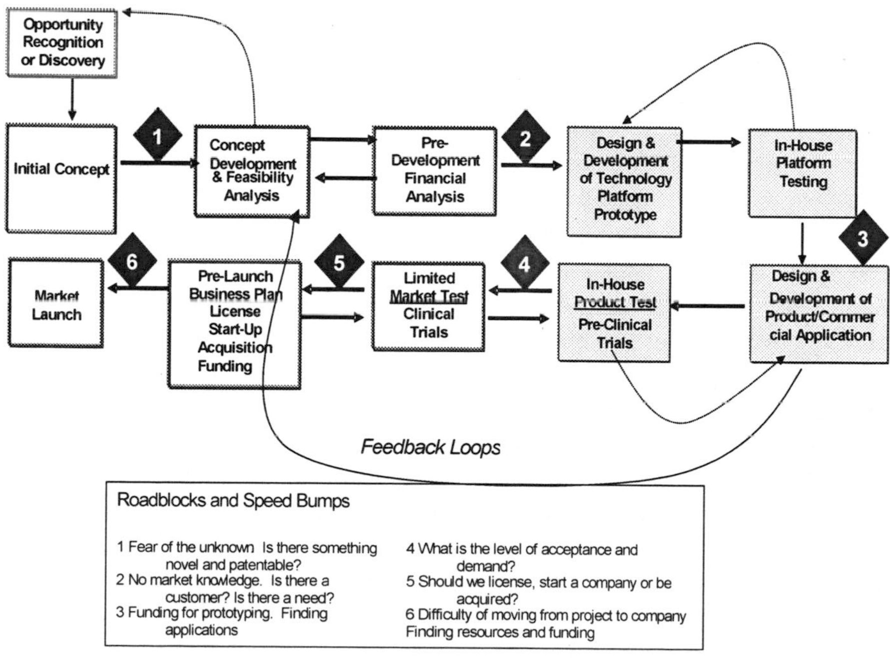

Although the framework depicts what appears to be a linear process, the technology commercialization process is, in fact, iterative with many feedback loops and tasks that may occur in parallel. Throughout the process, one finds several challenges in the form of speed bumps that slow down the process and roadblocks that may send a project in a new direction or stall it indefinitely. In fact, the period between discovery or invention and reaching the market is often called the "valley of death." The valley of death is characterized by a lack of structure, resources, and expertise (Markham, 2002). One of the principal explanations for this period with a high potential for failure is that the technical people often do not understand the motivations and focus of the business members of the team. They tend to have different goals. The primary challenges (there are many more) are listed below the diagram in Figure 3.

5.1. Discovery and Opportunity Recognition - the Fuzzy Front End

The innovation and commercialization process is precipitated by a discovery or recognition of a need. This discovery usually results from exploratory research that originally had no specific goal or outcome as its purpose. In fact, radical new technologies depend on exploratory research that may have preceded their development by years. The challenge at the discovery stage is to determine if the invention is truly novel and capable of being patented. Whether or not the invention has commercial potential is often not apparent early on, particularly in the case of a radical or disruptive technology for which there is no precedent.

While any technology that ultimately reaches the market is born of either a discovery or a recognized customer need, many invented technologies never go beyond these early stages because no commercial application can be found. Alternatively, one core technology may produce many possible applications, each with a different value proposition and a different customer. The challenge then is to determine which application should be pursued first. The Valley of Death exists because of the difficulty of making connections between technology in the laboratory and customer needs in the marketplace.

Most new projects fail at the beginning rather than at the end of the process (Khurana and Rosenthal, 1998). The discovery stage is part of what is frequently referred to as "the fuzzy front end," those activities that take place prior to the more formalized processes of feasibility analysis and product development. While much research has focused on the more formal aspects of the technology commercialization process, little has been done about looking at the most effective practices in the fuzzy front end of the process. The FFE is characterized by experimentation, bootstrap funding, and a high degree of uncertainty. It is generally comprised of five elements (Koen, Ajamian, Burkart, Clamen, 2001):

1. *Opportunity Recognition.* Here the firm (alternatively the entrepreneur) identifies opportunities that it wishes to pursue that are in alignment with its business goals. Opportunity recognition may entail a formal process or a more ad hoc, informal process.

2. *Opportunity Analysis.* Here the opportunity is held to the first level of scrutiny, which may be more or less intense depending on the attractiveness of the opportunity.

3. *Idea Genesis.* Here the idea is worked into something much more concrete. At this point, potential customers (if markets exist) may be brought in to provide input. Again, this may be a formal process or more informal.

4. *Idea Selection.* Since ideas are generally ubiquitous in creative environments, a screening process needs to be in place to select those ideas worth of continued study and application of resources. Screening at this point in the process is far less rigorous than in the more structure part of the commercialization process.

5. *Concept and Technology Development.* At this point, a business case is developed for the technology concept that includes some initial and broad estimates of market potential, customer needs, funding required, competitor analysis, technology risks, and so forth.

Some research has found that the proficiency of the FFE is directly correlated to a high level of innovation and not to a high level of proficiency in the product development process. That is, companies that have effective processes in the FFE tend to experience higher levels of innovation (Koen, Ajamian, Burkart & Clamen, 2001). It is difficult to go forward with a project or secure the necessary resources and commitment where market, technological, and competitive uncertainties exist. Uncertainties in the commercialization environment include emerging technologies, changing customer needs, shortened product life cycles and the impact of outsourcing and partnering with external organizations. To succeed at this stage in developing a robust product definition requires accessing information and feedback from potential customers and others in the value chain as well as internal sources of feedback in the form of engineering, R&D, manufacturing, and marketing. One of the key goals of the FFE is to reduce the level of uncertainty so that the new technology can move into the more formalized new product development (NPD) phase.

It is important to note here that radically new or disruptive technologies follow a different path in the FFE as they generally do not have identified markets in the early stages. Their market opportunities are usually unpredictable or emerging so conventional strategies for market identification and research are not appropriate. As a consequence, the FFE for radical technologies is especially fuzzy.

5.2. Feasibility Activities

Invention and innovation are followed by a period of general feasibility analysis, both technical feasibility of the invention and market feasibility. These tasks typically proceed simultaneously and result in a well-developed and compelling business concept and business model. In addition, the first estimates of the cost to produce a prototypical design are developed as well as an initial plan for pricing. The decisions made at this stage in the process are critical because from this point forward the costs increase exponentially and the project becomes more focused, so fewer changes are permitted. The roadblocks at this stage typically revolve around lack of market knowledge and ability to identify and test a particular market, an unforeseen technical problem, or the ability to fund the development of the prototype. Feasibility analysis is part of the whole design process. The design process then is both intentional and evolutionary, coming about from a series of refinements and iterations. Design "grounds a particular innovation in its particular time and place" by defining it with specific meanings and values (Hargadon, 2001). The design is robust when it can immediately and effectively position an innovation into a world that is familiar to the customer while maintaining sufficient flexibility to allow for future evolution (Eccles, Nohria, & Berkley, 1992).

Effective design strategy calls for a combination of familiar features, new features, and some features that are kept hidden. Achieving a robust design is more difficult with a radical innovation where the benefits are usually not yet recognized or appreciated. For example, in 1999, TiVo launched the digital video recorder in the United States, which allows the user to program, record, and replay television programs in a digital format. TiVo's developers faced many challenges because for the company to survive in the short term, there had to be rapid adoption of the technology so the company could recoup the enormous development costs. To achieve rapid adoption, TiVo had to show customers that TiVo exploits the very familiar television and VCR. So the product was introduced as an advanced generation of VCRs. Over the long term, however, TiVo believes that its technology will replace existing technologies while leaving customer habits unchanged so it must be able to evolve beyond current familiarity with the VCR (Hargadon, 2001). TiVo intends to change the way television is broadcast and viewed. Because it contains a modem and a computer, TiVo, which runs on an open-source Linux operating system, can evolve far beyond the capabilities and scope of a VCR. In an effort to avoid confusing customers and to keep some capabilities hidden, TiVo minimized the ability to record TV shows without commercials. Of course, it also did this to pacify the networks that it needed to provide scheduling (Lewis, 2001). The bottom line is that TiVo walks a fine line between relying on familiar functionality and distinguishing itself from existing technology, so its adoption rate has been slow.

5.3. Product Development Activities

The next stage in the process focuses on prototype design and development and in-house product testing. In the case of a radically new technology, the platform or base technology is developed and tested; it then serves as the foundation for a family of products based on the core technology. Each of the derivative applications of the core technology will also need to be developed, tested for technical and market feasibility, and refined. The challenges at this stage center on determining if there is sufficient market demand and who the first customer is likely to be.

Once the product passes in-house testing and is suitably market ready, it is usually tested in a limited market to check for final bugs and to ensure that the correct first customer has been identified.

5.4. Commercialization Activities

In preparing to launch the new technology, the main speed bump is the critical decision of whether to license, start a company, or be acquired by a larger firm. In any case, a business plan needs to be developed that will detail the launch strategy and transition the project to a fully operational company. The biggest stumbling block at this stage is the transition because starting and running a company requires a very different set of skills than running an R&D project.

Successfully crossing the Valley of Death requires a champion, whether that be the entrepreneur, the inventor, or the corporate venturing champion. Someone must take the lead in driving the technology and its associated business concept forward in a timely fashion.

6. The Challenges Associated with Commercialization

There are many challenges associated with the commercialization process. At the University of Southern California, we did a study to determine the key challenges that face researchers as they attempt to make their way through the process. We found that these challenges are 1) fear of the unknown, 2) lack of market knowledge, 3) funding the prototype, 4) determining how to commercialize, 5) transitioning from project to operations, and 6) the role of failure.

6.1. Fear of the Unknown

In the discovery stage and the fuzzy front end of the commercialization process, it is difficult, if not impossible, to determine economic impacts from a fundamental discovery like quantum theory, wave mechanics, or magnetic resonance. Yet universities and industry alike employ the yardstick of economic impact to make decisions about intellectual property protections, funding development, and so forth to reduce risk and ensure their funders that their investment is well placed.

University researchers in particular, and industry researchers to some degree, tend to be so focused on their work that they often fail to disclose their discoveries to the university's office of technology licensing (OTL) or even to their departments until they are about to publish in a research journal and or present at a conference (Allen, Maya, and Valencia, 2002). At that time, they realize that they have not yet protected the IP and seek last-minute help. Along the way they have been open to discussing their discoveries with colleagues and others without the protection of non-disclosure agreements or provisional patents because of their naturally collegial relationships. However, this desire to share information leaves them vulnerable to having their research commercialized by someone else. Moreover, researchers often do not know how to disclose their inventions in a manner that makes the market potential and benefit to the university clear to the OTL, which must typically make a rapid decision whether to file a provisional patent application or not. Furthermore, researchers are often not familiar with the OTL's decision-making process and criteria for submitting a patent application. Consequently, they grow angry and discouraged when they are denied the university's services for filing a patent.

Working on the patent application, even with the aid of a patent attorney, is a daunting and time-consuming task for which most researchers have no patience. They variously perceive the patent process as long, arduous, arbitrary, and capricious, and are frustrated by the detail and attention to wording that is associated with a patent application. They also face having to educate the patent attorney in their technology so that the attorney understands the invention enough to prepare the patent application, leading to comments such as "I should have written it myself." They are also unaware of the importance of thinking ahead to potential applications of the technology in areas outside their area of expertise. As a result, they make it easy for someone to take their technology and patent it for a new use, thereby potentially denying the inventor and the university their rightful royalties.

6.2. Lack of Market Knowledge

Researchers, in general, have had no experience researching markets and testing potential customers. They tend to focus on the technological challenge without consideration of its need in the market. Consequently, there is a significant gap between science and technology requirements and market-level requirements. Industry solves this problem by bringing potential customers into the product development process at the earliest stages, even as early as the fuzzy front end. Universities often tap the expertise of their business schools employing qualified students to undertake market feasibility analyses.

6.3. Funding the Prototype

It is not uncommon for researchers to come to the end of a grant period with no strategy in place for funding the commercialization portion of the product development process. This lack of follow-on funding leaves them vulnerable to pressured decisions and to undervaluing their technology to secure quick financing. Furthermore, a researcher's idea of an effective funding presentation generally focuses too much on details of the technology, which the researcher understands, and pays little attention to the customer, the value proposition, or the business model, which is of primary interest to the funding source. The result is an inability to secure funding.

6.4. Determining How to Commercialize: Start-up, License, Acquisition

Researchers generally do not have sufficient business exposure to allow them to see the breadth of potential options for commercializing their technology. In general, they will identify applications in industries with which they are familiar, but usually not any applications outside that industry. They typically do not have the time or the interest to network outside their areas of specialization. They also tend to assume that letting the OTL license their technology is their only option, so they often don't consider finding their own licensee or strategic partner, or starting a new venture to commercialize the technology.

6.5. Transitioning from Project to Operations

It is only in an ideal world that new technologies move from project status to operations easily with a product ready for manufacture and manufacturing ready to produce the product. Part of the problem stems from the fact that most development projects go through several iterations, changes based on feedback from the test market. Having satisfied the early adopters, the team is often faced with a completely new set of challenges from the mass market customer (O'Connor, Hendricks, and Rice, 2002). These modifications often affect manufacturing procedures and slow the manufacturing launch.

To improve the ability of a project team to move successfully to an operations status, the Industrial Research Institute, in conjunction with a group of academic scholars devised a tool, the Transition Readiness Assessment Form (TRAF), for assisting transition teams in assessing what remains to be done to prepare for full operations and who is accountable for what. Those filling out the form consider two issues: (1) whether or not any work to address a particular section of the TRAF is required and (2) the extent to which that section is relevant or important to the project's success (O'Connor, Hendricks, and Rice, 2002). Key findings from companies using the tool were lack of manufacturing and sales readiness, lack of resources for the launch phase, and lack of partner and human resource readiness.

6.6. The Role of Failure

Much of the research literature has looked at which factors are essential for new-product success. It is generally believed that five factors contribute to effective new-product development as depicted in Figure 4 (Connell, Edgar, Olex, Scholl, 2001).

Figure 4: Essential Factors for Product Deveopment Success

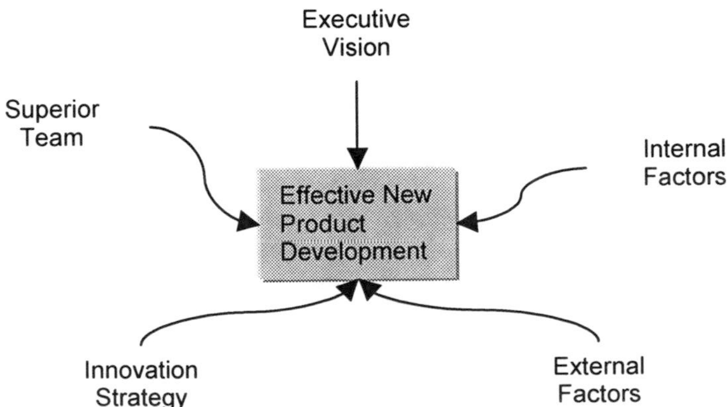

Executive vision suggests that top management support and commitment to the new product development process will facilitate its success. An appropriate innovation strategy will match activities to goals. With radical technologies, a learning-based strategy is appropriate, while for incremental innovation, a stage-gate approach with milestones is important (Lynn and Akgun, 1998). In addition, putting together a superior, cross-functional project team will ensure the execution of the innovation strategy. The correct organizational structure is also critical to facilitating communication, knowledge-sharing, and reporting functions. External factors that affect successful NPD are economic, regulatory, environmental, political, and social in addition to industry forces such as the supply chain, competition, and customers. Absent these factors, failure would seem to be the outcome, but some research has found that this is not always true (Connell, Edgar, Olex and Scholl, 2001). Sometimes the critical factors can work against a project, but through the exceptional efforts of a superior team, the project can still succeed. At other times, a single factor can be the downfall of a project that otherwise would have been successful.

Today, it is common for companies to claim that they are market driven, that their research and development match corporate strategic interests. Unfortunately, this attitude frequently leads to new product failure because there has been no prior exploratory research that would position the technology ahead of the competition (Beall, 2002). In general, exploratory research takes place in new or novel arenas. For example such well-known inventions as glass light bulbs, heat-resistant Pyrex glass, and ultrapure glass-based optical fibers are the result of exploratory research. In fact, Hyde's discoveries of silicones and chemical vapor deposition in the 1930s and Stookey's discovery of ceramics in the 1950s contributed to the development of many products that we take for granted today. Important discoveries are typically random and unexpected; if they are not embraced for their potential value, a new technological opportunity may be lost until someone else chances upon the discovery. That is why the FFE is so important; the willingness to take advantage of a laboratory surprise can lead a team in a whole new direction. Unfortunately, exploratory research is often discouraged by holding such scientists to short-term return-on-investment criteria and by a premature focus on applications.

7. Conclusions and Implications

The process of taking an invention from idea to business concept and then to market is embedded with a unique set of challenges and opportunities that occur in an uncertain, volatile, and demanding environment. Products today must be developed faster, prototyped earlier, and brought to market in record time. In many respects, it is easier for small entrepreneurial companies to accomplish these daunting feats than it is for large companies to break away from their inertia to do it. But in all cases, a thorough knowledge of the commercialization process and the challenges that might derail a project along the way are critical to commercialization success.

In a new environment where industry and academe are both being pressured to improve their ability to bring the results of government-funded research to market, it is important to identify, analyze, and improve on the commercialization processes that currently exist, particularly with respect to those processes in the fuzzy front end. Most private companies and all colleges and universities are faced with limited resources to direct toward these efforts, so it is critical that any choices made be the right ones. The emphasis on innovation and technology commercialization is not a fad that will go away in a relatively short period of time. Rather it is a vital component of economic growth. Investment in R&D and the support of an environment that encourages entrepreneurship will fuel economic growth for a long time to come.

References:

Abrahamson, E., 1996, "Management fashion", *Academy of Management Review,* 21, 254-285.

Allan, M.F., 2001, "A review of best practices in university technology licensing offices", *The Journal of the Association of University Technology Managers,* XIII, www.autm.net/pubs/journal/01/bestpractices.html.

Allen, K., 2003, *Bringing New Technology to Market.* Upper Saddle River, NJ: Prentice-Hall; 2.

Allen, K., I. Maya, and P. Valencia, 2002, *Technology Commercialization Alliance Business Plan,* Unpublished results of primary research on the campus of the University of Southern California.

Anton, J., D. Yao. 1994. "Expropriation and inventions: Appropriable rents in the absence of property rights". *American Economic Review*, 84, 190-209.

Arora, A. 1995. "Licensing tacit knowledge: Intellectual property rights and the market for knowhow". *Economic Innovation New Tech.* 4:41-59.

Association of University Technology Managers, Inc., 1999, AUTM Licensing Survey.

Baily, M. & A.K. Chakrabarti, 1988, *Innovation and the Productivity Crisis,* Washington D.C.: The Brookings Institution, 35.

P. Bak, 1996, *How Nature Works,* New York: Springer-Verlag.

Barnard, C.I. 1938, *The Functions of the Executive* (Cambridge: Harvard University Press), pp. 185-189, 205-206.

Baumol, W.J., 1999, Licensing proprietary technology is a profit opportunity, not a threat, *Research-Technology Management* 42, (6), 10-11.

Beall, G.H., 2002, "Exploratory research remains essential for industry", *Research Technology Management,* Nov/Dec, 45 (6), 26-30.

Beinhocker, E.D., 1999, "Robust adaptive strategies", *Sloan Management Review,* Spring.

C.I. Barnard, 1938, The Functions of the Executive, Cambridge, MA: *Harvard University Press,* 185-189, 205-206; and H.A. Simon, *Administrative Behavior*, third edition (New York: Free Press, 96-109, 220-228.

Buchanan, D.A. and Bessant, J., 1985, "Failure, uncertainty, and control: The role of operators in a computer-integrated production system", *Journal of Management Studies*, 22:3, 292-308.

Burgelman, R.A., M.A. Madique, and S.C. Wheelwright (eds), 1996, *Strategic Management of Technology and Innovation* (2nd ed.) New York: McGraw-Hill, p.2.

Carayannis, E.G., E.M. rogers, K. Kurihara & M.M. Allbritton, 1998, "High-technology spin-offs from government R&D laboratories and research universities", *Technovation,* 18(1), 1-11.

Chandy, R.K. & G,.J. Tellis, 2000, "The incumbent's curse? Incumbency, size, and radical product innovation", *Journal of Marketing* 64, no.3, 1-17.

Christensen, C., 1997, *The Innovator's Dilemma,* Boston, MA: Harvard Business School Press, xv.

Cohen, W.M. et al., 1998, "Industry and the academy: uneasy partners in the cause of technological advance", In *Challenges to Research Universities,* 171, 193-94 (Roger G. Noll ed.)

Cohen, L.R. & R.G. Noll, 1991, *The Technology Pork Barrel,* Washington D.C.: The Brookings Institution, 8.

Cohen, W.M., Florida, R., & Randazzese, L. & Walsh, J., 1998, "Industry and the academy: uneasy partners in the cause of technological advance". In R.G. Noll (Ed.), *Challenges to Research Universities,* Washington DC: Brookings Institution Press, 171-199.

Conner, K., 1988, "Strategies for product cannibalism", *Strategic Management Journal* 9, 9-27.

Connell, J. G,.C. Edgar, B. Olex, R. Scholl, 2001, "Troubling successes and good failures: Successful new product development requires five critical factors", *Engineering Management Journal,* 13 (4), 35-39.

Cooper, R.G., 1999, *Winning at New Products,* 3rd ed. Cambridge, MA: Perseus Publishing, 53-57.

Council on Competitiveness, 1996, *Endless Frontiers, Limited Resources: U.S. R&D Policy for Competitiveness,* Washington D.C.

Deazin, R.D., "Multilevel theorizing about creativity in organizations: A sensemaking perspective", *Academy of Management Review;* Also, Deazin, R., 1990, "Professionals and innovation: structural-functional versus radical-structural perspectives", *Journal of Management Studies* 27, 245-263; Amabile, T.M., "A Model of creativity and innovation in organizations", In B.M. Staw and L.L. Cummings, eds, *Research in Organizational Behavior*, 10, Greenwich, CT: JAI Press, 123-167.

Eccles, R.G., N. Nohria, and J.D. Berkley, 1992, *Beyond the Hype: Rediscovering the Essence of Management*, Boston: Harvard Business School Press.

Ettlie, J.E., 2000, *Managing Technological Innovation,* New York: John Wiley & Sons, 31.

Farzin, Y.H., K.J. M. Huisman, & P.M. Kort, 1997, "Optimal timing of technology adoption", *Journal of Economic Dynamics and Control,* 22: 779-799.

Foster, R.N.,2000, "Managing technological innovation for the next 25 years", *Research Technology Management* 43,1(January-February 2000):29.

Garvin, D.A., 1998, "The processes of organization and management", *Sloan Management Review,* Summer.

Glazer, R., 1991, "Marketing in an information-intensive environment: Strategic implications of knowledge as an asset", *Journal of Marketing,* 55, 1-19.

Hargadon, 2001, "When innovations meeting institutions: Edison and the design of the electric light", *Administrative Science Quarterly,* September.

Herron, C. & H.J. Sapienza, 1992, "The entrepreneur and the initiation of new venture launch activities", *Entrepreneurship: Theory & Practice,* 17, no.1, 49.

Hills, G.E., R.G. Shrader, & G.T. Lumpkin, 1999, "Opportunity recognition as a creative process", *Frontiers of Entrepreneurship Research,* www.babson.edu/entrep/fer/papers99/X/X_C/X_C.html.

Holcombe, R.G., 2001, "The invisible hand and economic progress", *Entrepreneurial Inputs and outcomes,* Vol.13, 281-326.

Hruby, M. and M. Lutz, 2002, *Valuing technology in new applications*, Acton, MA: Technology Marketing Group Inc. www,.technology-marketing.com/index.html.

Jamison, D.W. & Jansen, C., 2000, "Technology transfer and economic growth", *The Journal of the Association of University Technology Managers,* XII, www,.autm.net/pubs/journal/00/techtransfer.html.

John, G. A.M. Weiss, and S. Dutta, 1999, "Marketing in technology-intensive markets: Towared a conceptual framework", *Journal of Marketing* 63:78-91.

Koen, P. G. Ajamian, R. Burkart, A. Clamen, 2001, "Providing clarity and a common language to the 'fuzzy front end'," *Research Technology Management,* 44 (2), 46-55.

Khurana, A., 1999, "Managing complex production processes", *Sloan Management Review,* Winter.

Khurana, A. and Rosenthal, S.R., 1997, "Integrating the fuzzy front end of new product development", *Sloan Management Review*, Vol. 38 No. 2, 103-20.

Leifer et al., 2000, *Radical Innovation: How Mature Companies Can Outsmart Upstarts,* Boston: Harvard Business School Press, 6-7.

Levin, R., W. Cohen, D. Mowery. 1985. "R&D appropriability, opportunity and market structure: New evidence on some Schumpeterian hypotheses". *American Economic Review,* 75, 20-24.

Lewis, M., 2001, *Next: The Future Just Happened,* New York: W.W. Norton, 172.

Link, A.N., 1999, "A suggested method for assessing the economic impacts of university R&D: Including identifying roles for technology transfer officers", *The Journal of the Association of University Technology Managers,* XI, www.autm.net/pubs/journal/99/methods.html.

Link, A.N., 1996, On the classification of R&D, *Research Policy,* May, 379-401.

Lynn, Gary S., and Ali E. Akgun, 1998, "Innovation strategies under uncertainty: A contingency approach for new product development", *Engineering Management Journal,* 10:3 (September 1998), 11-16.

Mansfield, E., 1986, "Microeconomics of technological innovation", In R.Landau & N. Rosenbert, eds. *The Positive Sum Strategy: Harnessing Technology for Economic Growth,* Washington, D.C.: National Academy Press, 307-325.

Mansfield, E., M. Schwartz, & S.Wagner, 1981, "Imitation costs and patents: An empirical study", *The Economic Journal* 91, 908-918.

Mansfield, E, 1980, "Basic research and productivity increase in manufacturing", *American Economic Review,* 70, 863-873.

Markham, S.K., 2002, "Moving technologies from lab to market," *Research Technology Management,* November/December.

Micklethwait, J. & Wooldridge, A., 1996, *The Witch Doctors,* New York: Times Books.

Miller, W.L. & L. Morris, 1999, *4th Generation R&D,* New York: John Wiley & Sons, 1-4. "The government role in civilian technology: Building a new alliance", *National Academy of Sciences,* Washington D.C.: National Academy Press 1992.

National Science Foundation, 1996, Survey of research and development expenditures at universities and colleges, Fiscal Year 1996.

Newberg, J.A. and R.L. Dunn, 2002, "Keeping secrets in the campus lab: Law, values and rules of engagement for industry-university R&D partnerships", *American Business Law Journal,* 39,2, 187-240.

O'Connor, G.C., R. Hendricks, & M.P. Rice, 2002, "Assessing transition readiness for radical innovation", *Research Technology Management* 45, 6, 50-56.

Pfeffer, J. & Sutton, R.I., 2000, *The Knowing-Doing Gap: how Smart Companies Turn Knowledge Into Action,* Boston: Harvard Business School Press.

Porter, M. E., 1980, *Competitive Strategy: Techniques for Analyzing Industries and Competitors,* New York: The Free Press: 3.

Pressman, L. (ed.), 2002, AUTM licensing Survey: FY 2000, *The Association of University Technology Managers, Inc.*

Pressman, L. et al., 1999, "Summary estimated sales on licensed technologies, pre-production investment, and jobs projection (FY98 and FY97)", *Journal of the Association of University Technology Managers.*

Rogers, E.M., J. Yin, & J. Hoffmann, 2000, "Assessing the effectiveness of technology transfer offices at U.S. research universities", *The Journal of the Association of University Technology Managers,* XII, www.autm.net/pubs/journal/00/assessing.html

Romer, P., 1986, "Increasing returns and long-run growth", *Journal of Political Economy* 94:1,002-1,037.

Santoro, M.D. & S.C. Betts, 2002, "Making industry-university partnerships work", *Research-Technology Management,* 45, 3, 42-46.

Scherer, F.M., 1982, "Inter-industry technology flows and productivity growth", *The Review of Economics and Statistics,* 64, 627-634.

Scherer, F.M., 1980, "Historical research in marketing", *Journal of Marketing* 44, 52-58.

Shane, S. 2002, "Selling university technology: Patterns from MIT", *Management Science,* 48:1, 122-137.

H.A. Simon, *Administrative Behavior*, 3rd Ed. (New York: Free Press), pp. 96-109, 220-228.

Singh, R.P. et al., 1999, "Opportunity recognition through social network characteristics of entrepreneurs", *Frontiers of Entrepreneurship Research,* Wellesley, MA: Babson College, www.babson.edu/entrep/fer/papers99/X/X_C/X_C.html.

Smith, P.G., 1999, "Managing risk as product development schedules shrink", *Industrial Research Institute, Inc.*, September/October, 25-32.

Solow, R.M., 1957, "Technological change and the aggregate production function", *The Review of Economics and Statistics,* 39, 312-320.

Starbuck, E. "Optimizing university research collaborations", *Research - Technology Management,* 40-44.

Stevens, G.A. and J. Burley, 1997, "3,000 raw ideas = 1 commercial success", *Research-Technology Management* (May-June 1997).

Teece, D. 1980. "Economies of scope and the scope of the enterprise", *J. Econom. Behavior Organ.* 1223-247. 1981. "The market for know-how and the efficient international transfer of technology", Ann. Amer. Acad. 458 81-96.

G. Taguchi and D. Clausing, 1990, "Robust quality", *Harvard Business Review,* 68, January-February, 65-72.

Van de Ven, A.H. & H.L. Angle, 1989, "An introduction to the Minnesota Innovation Research Program", in Van de Ven, H and M. Poole (eds), *Research on the Management of Innovation, New York: Ballinger Publishing Company,* p. 12.

Weick, K.E., 1990, "Technology as equivoque: sense-making in new technologies", in P.S. Goodman and L.S. Sproull, eds., *Technology and Organizations*, San Francisco: Jossey-Bass Publishers,pp. 1-44.

E. Witte, 1972, "Field research on complex decision-making processes - the phase theorem", *International Studies of Management and Organization,* Volume 2, Summer, 1972, 179.

Zietsma, C., 2999, "Opportunity Knocks—or does it hide? An examination of the role of opportunity recognition in entrepreneurship", in *Frontiers of Entrepreneurship Research*, Wellesley, MA: Babson College, www.babson.edu/entrep/fer/papers99/X/X_C/X_C.html.

14. Universities, Academics, and Spinout Companies: Lessons from Imperial

Sue Birley
Imperial College of Science, Technology and Medicine

Abstract. This paper explores the issues faced by organisations when attempting to commercialise their Intellectual Property. It draws upon the particular experiences of Imperial College of Science, Technology and Medicine, the largest university in the UK in terms of research revenue and with the largest medical school. Because of the nature of the academic system, and the concept of academic freedom, these issues are more complicated and more difficult to solve in a university than anywhere else. Nevertheless, the lessons are common to all types of organisation. The paper argues that there are three types of spinout, which are called orthodox, hybrid and technology, with the hybrid being the most common and most complicated within the university context. The issues explored include establishing proof of both technology and market concept, the potential roles of the inventor, the multiple stakeholders, the various conflicts of interest, the allocation of equity, the assigning of Intellectual Property, and the resultant need to provide warranties.

Key words: spinouts, universities, intellectual property, entrepreneurship.

1. Introduction

By their nature, scientific and technological inventions rarely happen in a vacuum. They usually evolve from a body of research conducted in a variety of research laboratories over many years, sometimes with teams of researchers working on parallel projects. Witness the current genome project. In other words, they work within an organisational context – not in the shed at the end of the garden. These organisations may be independent research laboratories, companies, national defence agencies, or universities. All have their individual norms, policies, and rules about the relationship between their employees and their ideas, their Intellectual Property, and about the commercialisation of these ideas whether through licensing or through spinout companies. However, whatever the specific organisational environment may be, the underlying issues are common. In this paper, I will explore these issues within the context of the university.

Why have I chosen the university context? The simple answer is because that is where I work, because I am a director of my university technology transfer company, and because we have spent considerable time over the past few years exploring and debating these issues. This has not been a trivial exercise. Imperial College of Science, Technology and Medicine is one of the largest universities in the UK in terms of research revenue. It also has the largest medical school.

This article was originally published in the International Journal of Entrepreneurship Education 1(1): pp. 133-153.

But my reason goes beyond my personal experience. Because of the nature of the academic system, and the concept of academic freedom, the issues are more complicated and more difficult to solve in a university than anywhere else. As a result, there are bound to be lessons for others, whatever their situation. The universities stand in stark relief.

My aim is not to produce a technology transfer template. I do not believe that is possible or desirable. But rather my aim is to inform the debate, to help researchers to understand their organisation and to help organisations understand the many black holes that we face in the entrepreneurial world. Beyond this, there is a wider debate and that is the role of the universities in commercialising their inventions. Any managed technology transfer activity is likely to be both costly and peripheral to the main purpose of the university, which is to develop and disseminate knowledge. It will also require a different form of managerial structure and style than the rest of the institution. In other words, it is akin to a corporate venture.

2. Technology Transfer and Universities

The growth of new technology-based firms around university incubators such as Stanford University and MIT (Roberts, 1991) and Cambridge (Segal, 1986) has provided exemplars for other universities both in the United States and elsewhere. Indeed, in the United Kingdom, universities are now being exhorted by Government to reap the harvest of their intellectual investment through the creation of Technology Transfer Offices (TTO) which are charged both with licensing the university technology to industry and through the creation of new businesses (Auril, CBI and DTI, 1997; HM Treasury and DTI, 1998).

Whilst a number of these universities have been actively involved in licensing for many years, in the UK the focus upon spinout companies is relatively new. However, recent research in the United States by Bray and Lee (2000) found that the average value of equity held by universities in spinout companies is greater than the average annual license income. Moreover, Mustar (1997) found that in France spinouts constituted 40% of the high technology firms founded between 1987 and 1997, and AUTM[1] (1999) found that approximately 12% of university-assigned inventions are transferred to the private sector through the founding of new organisations. In other words, spinout companies have the potential to be a significant contributor both to the national economy as well as to university revenues.

Despite their apparent importance, very few studies have examined the phenomenon of university spinout companies (Lindholm, 1997). Of those that have been conducted it is clear that the culture and strategy of the university is

1. Association of University Technology Managers, USA.

central to the level of activity (Segal, 1986; Smilor et al., 1990). For example, Roberts (1991) notes "MIT's tacit approval of entrepreneurs, to some extent even making it the norm, was in my judgement a dramatic contribution to the Greater Boston culture" (p.45). By contrast, Bok (1982) suggests that a focus upon the commercial imperative may corrupt academic research, a point echoed by Rosenberg and Nelson (1994). This issue of culture also translates to the departmental level where departmental norms and the attitudes of peer group to commercial activity may be critical factors in the individual's decision to consider a spinout (Doutriaux, 1991; Peters and Etzkowitz, 1990, Louis et al., 1989). Beyond this, there is the issue of academic reward systems and the possible conflict between the institutional rewards for research publication and the commercial rewards of ownership (Butler and Birley, 1998; Downs and Eadie, 1998; Franklin, Wright, and Lockett, 2000; Lissenburgh and Harding, 2000).

These issues of culture and reward systems, the "rules of the game" (Baumol, 1990) have resulted in some academics operating outside the system and creating companies without the knowledge of the university. This black market activity has, in turn, resulted in an unquantifiable level of technology leakage (Birley 1992, 1993) and very little reliable data about the level of entrepreneurial activity amongst academics, although there have been some studies of the characteristics of the academic entrepreneur (Louis et al., 1989; Chrisman et al., 1995).

The research described above allows some insight to the potential importance of spinout companies to some of the cultural issues faced by the university when deciding to actively pursue a spinout strategy. However, it does not help in understanding the detailed issues that need to be resolved when creating these new companies.

This paper explores the issues that we faced at Imperial College of Science, Technology, and Medicine as we moved from a technology transfer strategy that focused upon licensing technologies to large organisations and positively discouraged faculty entrepreneurial activity to one that focuses upon actively encouraging the creation of new ventures from faculty research; from the occasional spinout each year to a current rate of more than a company a month formed from faculty research.

3. What is a Spinout?

It is relevant at this point to introduce a definition of the term "spinout" since there is certainly confusion in the literature and, more particularly, in the UK. For example, a recent Government consultation paper defined a spinout as a company wholly owned by the university. How can this be? Surely, that is a subsidiary such as, in our case, the university technology transfer company!

In my view a spinout is a company that is created using the intellectual assets of the university but which is neither wholly owned nor managed by the university.

My colleague, Nicos Nicolaou, and I have been looking at spinouts from Imperial College (Nicolau and Birley, 2001), and they fall into three distinct types that we have named:

The Orthodox Spinout is the one to which most people usually refer. It is a company formed by one or more academics, all of whom have contributed to the IP. They leave the university to form the company and the break is clean. It is a kind of Management Buyout (MBO) and the founders are often called academic entrepreneurs.

The Technology Spinout is more akin to a Management Buy-In (MBI). An outside investor/manager buys or leases the IP from the university and forms a new company. The inventor academics continue with their research and have nothing to do with the day-to-day management of the company, although they may hold equity and/or act as consultants.

The Hybrid Spinout is the most complicated for reasons which will be explored later in this paper. It arises where one or all of the following apply:

- Only a subset of those who have contributed to the IP (the inventors) become shareholders of the company (the founders).
- Some of the founders of the company may stay in the university and have a role in the company, whilst others may spin out with the company (the academic entrepreneurs). Those who stay in the university may be a director of the company, sit on a Scientific Advisory Board, or act as a part-time, paid consultant.
- One or more of the founders take a sabbatical from the university to start the company for, say, a year.

Not only is the hybrid the most complicated, but it is also the model that predominates at Imperial College. Figure 1 shows our analysis of the current distribution of spinouts at the College. It is clear from this that the majority of our spinout companies retain relationships with the College through their founders, and it is this set of relationships that give rise to a number of the managerial issues that I will explore later in the paper. First, however, it is important to be clear about the start-up process and the ways in which the academic entrepreneur maps onto this process.

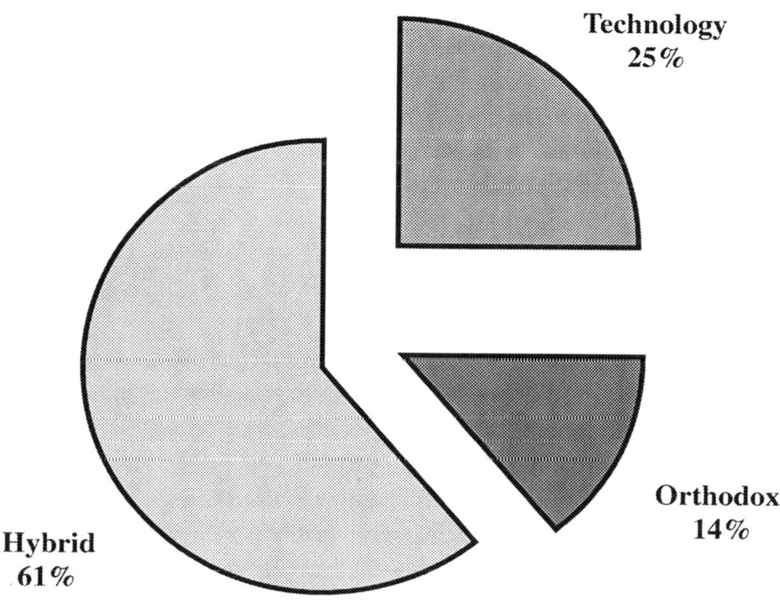

Figure 1

4. Translating the Vision into a Plan

Academics love problems to solve and the more complicated the better. Depending upon their inclination, these problems can be either immediately practical, such as stopping the Tower of Pisa from falling over, or theoretical such as finding the Higgs boson or "God's particle"[2]. Whichever is the case, at some time along the path, they will need to persuade others to buy in to their vision and their route to the solution. For the theoretician, this will be through discussion with colleagues, working with doctoral students, and publishing academic papers; for the practitioner, it will be through convincing those who hold the purse strings to release resources. Of course, the better the track record, the more the chances improve each time. Successfully shoring up the Tower of Pisa is likely to increase the chances of winning the next difficult, high profile, engineering project.

---

2. This is the particle that is thought to give matter its mass. First proposed by Peter Higgs in the early 1960s, an estimated £6 billion has been spent on experiments to no avail ... until 2000!

In other words, the successful academic has some of the skills and attributes of the successful entrepreneur such as vision, creativity, ability to think laterally, understanding of how to translate the vision into reality, self-belief, and dogged determination. They also understand how to manage risk. These attributes are particularly critical during the start-up process. I do not mean how to create a company or set up a research laboratory. I mean the process prior to this. The process by which the vision, the idea in your head, the feeling in the gut that this one *will* work begins to move forward. How does the entrepreneur take the intangible and create the tangible. What do they have to do? Quite simply, they have to persuade others to invest resources.

5. Translating the Dream into a Business Plan

Take the following simple, but very common, story. Peter is a producer of television programmes working for one of the major companies. He has a vision for a series about the development of the brain that he *knows* will work and is convinced that it could command major international sales. But he is tired of working for others and wants to use this as the foundation for a new, independent production company. He also knows that he will need £3m because that is how much the series will cost to make. He has heard that there is no point in approaching venture capitalists since they are not interested in project financing and, anyway, he is not asking for enough money for them to be interested. So, he goes along to his bank manager and broaches the possibility of a loan. Of course, he is laughed "out of court". Thc bank manager says….."That is much more than I can lend on the security of your house (assuming that your wife would agree)…and, anyway, who else is involved in this,….and, most important, your business plan is just a dream….where is the order?"

Undeterred, Peter approaches a couple of producers in other companies with his "concept". They express interest. They usually do. It is a way of keeping their options open! But they are not able to commit without a more detailed "Proof of Concept", and a fully resourced plan. In other words, what is the evidence that this will syndicate worldwide, what is the technical team that Peter plans to use, who is going to "front it", and who will provide the scientific support.

So, he approaches the acknowledged world expert on the brain, the best animators, technicians and camera crew. To a person, they ask (or imply) "What is in it for me, how do I know you can make this work, and where do you plan to set up the studio?"

Still undeterred, he scours the available studio facilities, but the landlords are not interested in talking until Peter is prepared to sign a lease, produce guarantees, and pay a deposit. He also talks to camera and computer manufacturers that he has dealt with previously about the arrangements for leasing or buying equipment, but finds a very different reaction when they realise that this is a new venture. No longer can he negotiate special discounts and credit. Now they want full price and cash up front.

The Credibility Carousel. What are all these people saying? It is simple. Peter is asking them to invest in his business idea by taking a risk. For example, the bank manager has credit limits and is evaluated on his bad debt record. He is worried about his job. The brain expert does not want to waste time in working on something that will not get off the ground. He also does not want to be associated with a second rate product, which could be the case if the best animators are not involved. The salesman for the equipment manufacturer is not able to alter company credit regulations.

So what to do? How does anyone manage to start a business? Basically, Peter is caught in the Credibility Carousel illustrated in Figure 2 (Birley and Norburn, 1985). All are protecting their jobs or their reputations and are unwilling to "invest" in just an idea.

In order to have a chance of moving forward, he needs to persuade someone to believe in him and to break the credibility carousel. For example, the world expert on the brain commits to the idea and begins to persuade others, his previous employers to agree to let him use an old studio, or a rich maiden aunt agrees to provide bank guarantees. Slowly, people begin to believe in him and the project gains credibility. It also gains more reliable data.

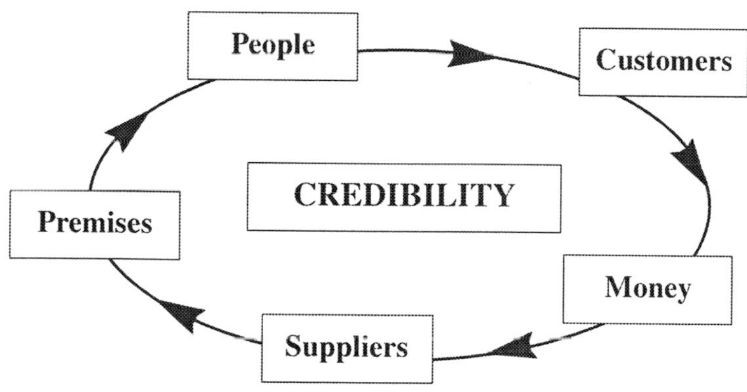

Figure 2

How did he do it? Almost certainly through his personal network, the people who know him personally or have been introduced to him by someone they trust. For example, the world brain expert just happens to play golf with his father!

Now the dream is becoming a reality. More importantly, the business concept is becoming a business plan, with increasingly credible assumptions and costs.

6. What Has This to Do with Academics and Researchers?

A great deal. Increasingly, all organisations are asking their employees to produce the "business case" for new projects, and academics are not excluded. If they wish to raise research funds, they have to explain why. They need to explain what is the likely output of their research in the future and what is the likely demand? For example, if they do find a cure for hepatitis C, is the incidence of the disease great enough to support both the research costs and the costs to market, as well as providing a significant income stream to give an acceptable return on the investment. In other words, what is the business case? What is the "Proof of Market Concept?"

Consider Sandra, a post-doctoral biochemist who is fascinated by tropical diseases. She and a colleague in the medical field are convinced that if they pool their experience and skills, they can produce a cure for a particularly debilitating skin disease found in tropical climates. But, they need money to fund a major research project.

There are three possible sources – the drug companies, the government funded research councils, or independent funding organisations such as the Wellcome Trust or the Kellogg Foundation. Each will expect a different arrangement or "deal", should the project be successful, and Sandra and her colleague need to think about that at the beginning. But first, they need to write a proposal.

Let us assume that they are targeting a medical research council. There will be standard forms that Sandra and her colleague must complete and a suggestion that corporate sponsorship and support would add weight to their case. After all, the council receives many more applications than they can fund. So, Sandra writes to the marketing directors of all the major drug companies asking for an endorsement but is either ignored or told that they only deal with a select group of universities or senior academics.

Returning to the application form, Sandra is in more familiar territory. She is asked to produce a research proposal that outlines prior research and indicates how her proposed research will contribute to knowledge. The first part is relatively easy, but she is nervous about the second part, about giving away too much of her intellectual property. After all, her proposal will be evaluated by other academics working in the field.

The forms also require a detailed explanation of how the research will be conducted and the resources that will be used – a timescaled and costed plan. Sandra knows that she will need two research assistants to do the experiments. She also knows that the application will be greatly strengthened if she has the support, and involvement, of a senior member of her department, who happens to be an expert in the field. So, she needs to convince her Professor to agree to allocate, say, half a day a week to the project if she raises the funds. However, she is currently on a one-year contract, and this is a three-year project. Her Professor will want to see the research proposal and some of her written papers since she has to decide if she wants to continue to employ Sandra. In other words, she needs to decide if Sandra is likely to develop into an academic who will enhance the reputation of the department. Her Professor will also need to decide if this project is sufficiently interesting to justify asking the Head of Department for extra laboratory space.

7. The Research Credibility Carousel

What is happening here? Much the same as for Peter but this time, Sandra has to break the Research Credibility Carousel. She has to convince others to invest their reputation and their resources in her idea. How does any junior academic raise funds? Like Peter, by using their network. Indeed, it could be argued that your personal network is the only real asset that you have at this stage. However, for Sandra, her professional network is likely to be narrow and to include mainly other academics. So, like many entrepreneurs, she must also draw upon her social network. For example, her cousin is a doctor and knows someone in one of the major drug companies who is prepared to talk to her or Sandra is working in the department where she gained her doctorate and her supervisor is encouraging her to make the application. She is riding the Research Credibility Carousel (Figure 3).

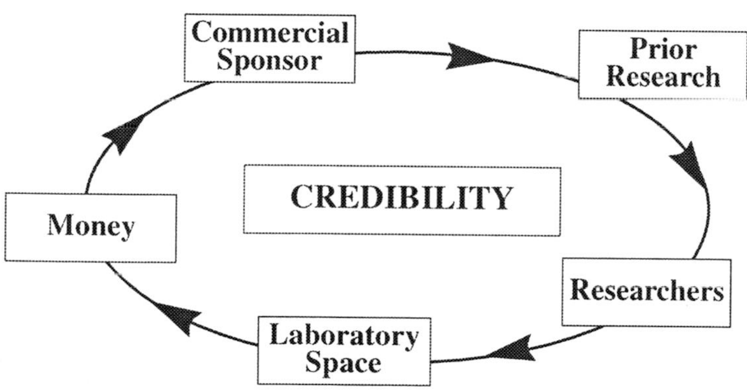

Figure 3

8. Proof of Concept

What does the story of Sandra tell us? That even in the development stage of a research idea, the academic will increase their chances of raising resources if they are able to establish both their research credibility and their understanding of potential market opportunities.

However, should the academic wish to go a step further and build a company from intellectual property that has a scientific, technological, or biomedical base they will require two proofs (Figure 4).

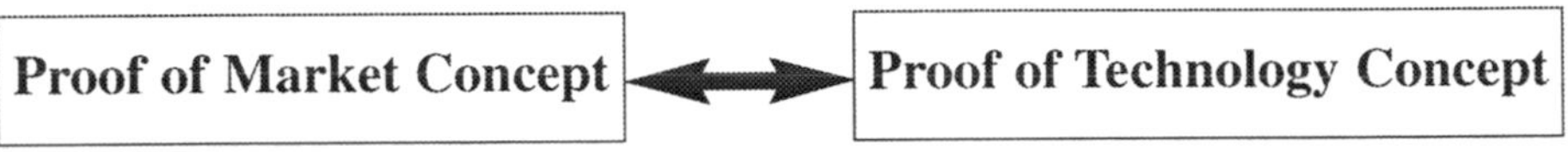

Figure 4

Platform Technologies: All of the above depends upon identifying the target market space and that is fine if the market opportunity is clear. It is more difficult if the academic is developing a platform technology, one that could be used in many industries or for many products. On the surface, this would seem to be a greater market opportunity and, indeed, it would be if the research is successful and the technology is developed. At this stage, however, the academic is faced with presenting an argument for support from a variety of possible sponsors.

So, selecting the particular market opportunity and matching that to particular sponsors interests may be critical. Often, the market chosen depends upon serendipity or personal interest. For example, a colleague from the Mathematics department developed an algorithm that allows a computer to produce music scores when it is attached to an instrument. Wonderful for composers. So, he talked to piano manufacturers because he plays the piano. What he hadn't realised, and why should he, is that he has created a product that can recognise pitch in sound – and this could be useful in a range of manufacturing industries for stress testing.

9. The Credibility Loop

What do the combined stories tell us? They tell us that academic entrepreneurs will have to establish their credibility both scientifically and in their understanding of the business concept by riding the *Credibility Loop* (Figure 5) if they are to have a chance of creating a business from their technology.

From my conversations with colleagues over the past few years, most understand this and make clear choices as to their involvement in the business.

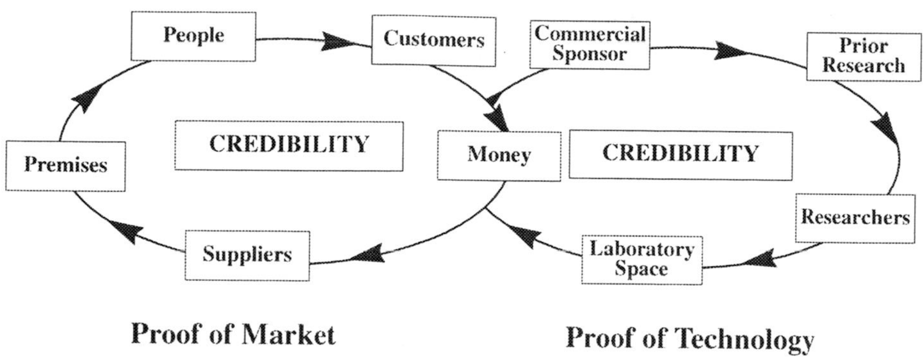

Figure 5

10. Intellectual Property

Dr. Chris Evans, Founder and Chairman, Merlin Ventures and Visiting Professor at Imperial College, is of the view that "Academics and universities....have no management, no muscle, no vision, and no business plan and that is 90% of the task of exploiting science and taking it to the marketplace" (Times Higher, March 1998). This may be true, and yet these same scientists manage to run large research laboratories, international collaborative research projects, and create science that, for example, allows Professor Ara Darzi at Imperial to conduct heart bypass surgery remotely. In other words, it is not necessarily a question of skill but of experience and inclination. Quite simply, most academics did not join the university to become business people, though some eventually change their mind, but, rather, to be researchers and teachers.

Continuing the quote, Dr Evans notes that "There is a tendency for universities to think we invented the thing so we are already 50% there. The fact is they are 50% to nowhere." Quite true, but the reverse is also the case. Without the idea, the customers and investors cannot benefit. So, we arrive at the critical issue of *Who Owns the Intellectual Property (IP).* For companies, it is usually straightforward and, in the UK, is embedded in company law and the employment contract. Any IP developed whilst in the pursuance of the job is owned by the company unless, of course, the company waives the right.

For university research, however, it is neither simple nor obvious although it is central to the governance in the organisation, a point that is often forgotten or ignored. After all, the IP of the university is its prime asset. Therefore, as effective directors of the organisation, it is the responsibility of the Chairman and Board of Governors to manage these assets prudently on behalf of the stakeholders.

So, the university must have a policy on the ownership of IP and this should be clear, simple, and evident to all concerned. Nice idea, but I am afraid that the reality is more complicated. Let me start by assuming that the university owns the IP of all its employees. Some have waived this right, but I am afraid that this doesn't mean that the problem goes away, as will become evident.

The Organisational Stakeholders: The first step is to determine the stakeholders in the process. They are the people who have contributed to the development of the IP by providing resource and support. They are also the people who will facilitate the commercialisation process (or not) and who, therefore, will expect a stake in the proceeds. In other words, the stakeholder group is wider than simply the inventors. There will usually be three levels (Figure 6).

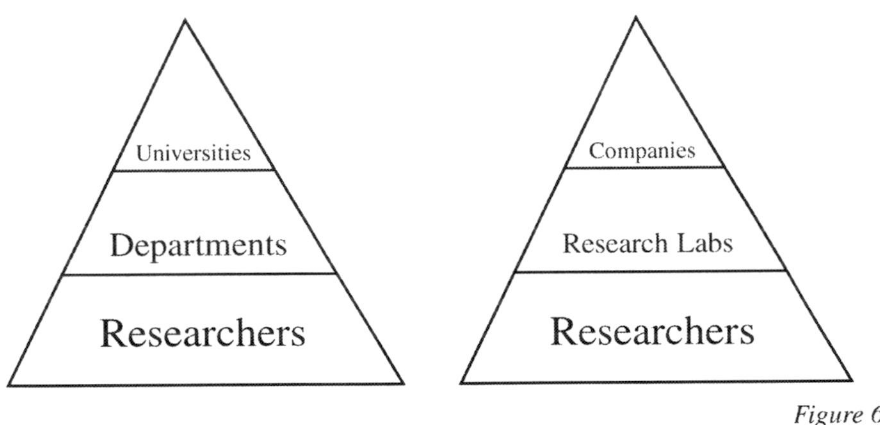

Figure 6

Notice that I have used the plural in each case. At Imperial, we have a number of research projects that include more than one researcher, from more than one department, and more than one university. And to make it even more complicated the partner university(ies) does not necessarily have the same IPR policy as do we. Even worse, they may not be in the UK and so will operate under different norms and legal structures. Yet, at some stage, the rewards of any commercialisation activity must be divided equitably.

Moreover, there is the issue of student IP. What is the university policy on this? After all, students are customers and, in my view, are entitled to retain their IP. Certainly, that is the policy that we have at Imperial after debate with both faculty and students. So the problem is solved. Students own the IP that they develop whilst at university and the university has neither liabilities nor responsibilities.

Well, not quite. There is, for example, the issue of how we deal with students who are sponsored by a company, or students who use IP developed in joint projects with other students or with faculty to start a business. This issue is particularly keen when doctoral students are working on developing new solutions to problems in a sponsoring organisation, or on ideas developed from the IP of their supervisor.

11. The Sponsor Stakeholders

The majority of research in universities is funded by outside bodies, whether they are Government Research Councils, Charitable Trusts, or Companies. Increasingly, these organisations are seeking, as part of the research contract, a lien on any IP developed as a result of their funding. After all, they have governance responsibilities too! To make it more complicated, imagine what you might be dealing with if the product to be commercialised is a result of bundling platform technologies! Why does this all matter? For two reasons. First, because the venture is unlikely to succeed in reaching first base without the positive, or at least neutral, support of all the stakeholders. This is particularly the case if the department is positively against such activities, even though the university may be positively for it (Samson and Gurdon, 1993). Second, the owners of, and stakeholders in, the IP have liabilities and responsibilities should they choose to commercialise.

12. Transferring the IP to the New Company

Assume that the chosen route to market is through a spinout, whatever the type. Seems simple. All we have to do is to form a company that owns the IP and off we go. Not quite. The IP may not be self-contained. It may be a piece of software that has been developed as part of an on-going research project and it is essential that the researchers continue to have use of it. So, it could be licensed back to the university for research purposes. This is certainly possible, but what if the company was acquired or failed and the IP is lost? Perhaps the solution is for the Department to retain ownership of the IP and to assign it to the company for a fixed period of time. Of course, this will almost certainly need legal agreements and long-term management. The need for university procedures and for lawyers is clearly looming!

There is another issue that needs to be dealt with at this point. The founders of the company will almost certainly want first call on future associated research developments. Indeed, their potential investors may wish to make this a condition of any deal. But how will the researchers who are not part of the company, and may even have joined the department after the company was started, feel about the university mortgaging their future research? This is a particularly sensitive issue in hybrid spinouts should such arrangements be put in place and where, as a result, some members of the department may be seen as unfairly benefiting from the research of others through their ownership of the company.

13. The Equity Issue or the Question of Greed

When the company is founded, it is relatively simple if there are just two or three founders sharing the equity with the university. However, in many of our spinouts, and certainly the hybrids, the list of eventual stakeholders may be long. Beyond those shown in Figure 6, and the sponsoring stakeholders listed above, there may be venture capitalists, angel investors, and employees, all expecting a real and substantive "piece of the action". There is also the question of where the university technology transfer company or office and its employees fit. After all, they may have been pivotal in identifying and bundling technologies from across the campus, and in steering the deal to a conclusion. They may also feel that they ought to have a "carried interest"[3].

Sadly, there are no rules for the sharing of equity, except one. Add up the shares that each stakeholder believes that they are due and the total will almost certainly be greater than 100%. If nobody is prepared to compromise, this can be a deal-breaker. Indeed, some 60% of projects that venture capitalists are prepared to invest in never happen because the parties cannot come to an agreement on the deal.

This division of the equity is a very real issue for the university. Academics are usually fair-minded people, recognise that the university has contributed to the genesis of the business, and believe that this entitles the university to a **fair** share in the equity. The question is – what is fair? If the university is not perceived to behave fairly, either the business will have no chance of starting or the academic inventors will go underground and start anyway (Birley 1992, 1993). Clearly, therefore, the task for the university is one of developing transparent policies and procedures that are accepted by the faculty.

14. Providing Warranties

Venture capitalists may take more risks than most investors, but they are calculated risks. Therefore, one of the things that they are almost always clear about when investing in technology-based companies is that the patent, copyright and IP portfolio is clean – ownership is clear, and warranties as to ownership have been provided. This makes sense from their perspective but look at it from the university point of view. A warranty as to ownership implies that the university is able to state that they know all the inventors who have contributed to the IP and that, as a result, they can warrant ownership. But what if one of the researchers has left or been forgotten? For example, what if a doctoral student was working on a particular element of the project for her thesis some five years ago? When she graduated, she moved to another country and has continued to work on it

3. A mechanism whereby Venture Capitalists carry a shadow equity interest on the capital gains made on realisation of a fund or portfolio.

unbeknown to her supervisor, and later emerges with a competing product. The company sues the university. Alternatively, what if the company is spectacularly successful and she suddenly realises that her work is being used, and sues the university? Either way, it is the university that may be liable, not the inventors, since it is the university that signs the warranty.

What recourse does the university have? Take a simple example from our experience. The company asks the university to warrant ownership of the IP. The university asks the team leader of the research project to list those who have contributed in order that the university can be confident in agreeing to the warrant. However, the team leader is also the person spinning out the company and, as such, the one who has asked for the warrant. Without entering into any probable legal technicalities, it is clear that the university is taking a risk. The question is whether the university should accept such liabilities and insure against them. Indeed, is this the business they are in? In truth, it has no choice if it wishes to promote spinouts. So, it is obviously extremely important for universities, departments and academics to keep clean research records and laboratory files, just in case. Of course, in reality these problems only arise when a spinout company is very successful, the virus of envy takes hold, and the "greedometer" begins to rise.

15. Wearing Many Hats

This is a particular issue in hybrid spinouts and stems from the various roles that academics may hold. It is an issue not only for the individual founders concerned but also for their department, the university, and the company. Let me give an example of a particular situation at Imperial. PSE Ltd was a spinout from the Centre for Process Systems Engineering. In this hybrid spinout, equity was divided between five inventor-founder shareholders and the university. Table 1 shows the roles played by the various involved parties.

Sandro was seconded to the company for the first 18 months, after which he returned to run the research centre, but continued as Chairman of the company. Sue (me) is the College nominated Director of the Company since Imperial has a significant equity holding. In 2000, Costas took a sabbatical from the department to join the company as Technical Director to develop a new business opportunity. Mark joined the company as Managing Director when Sandro returned to Imperial. Nilay, John, and Stratos act as consultants to the company but are not directors. However, their close involvement in strategic issues and their regular attendance at board meetings in the early days made them Shadow Directors at the time.

As the table shows, all except Mark are full-time faculty at the university. This can create tensions as the academics have a language and a common experience not shared by Mark. Yet he has to manage them, and to manage the relationship with the university. This is not always an easy task!

Table 1

	Sandro	Sue	Costas	Mark	Nilay	John	Stratos
IC Faculty	*	*	*		*	*	*
Inventor	*		*		*	*	*
Shareholder	*		*		*	*	*
Chairman	*						
Director	*	*	*	*			
Shadow Director					*	*	*
Manager			*		*		
FT Employee			*	*			
Consultant	*				*	*	*

16. What has this meant for the academics?

16.1. Learning New Skills

Negotiating legal agreements and financial deals are not new to senior academics, who will almost certainly have been involved in negotiating major research contracts. However, the terminology and the "rules of the game" will certainly be different, as it is for most entrepreneurs who will not have seen a Shareholders Agreement or Articles of Association before, much less negotiated the fine detail. Yet these documents are critical since, for example, the former embodies the rules by which the equity is managed. So, it might outline pre-emption procedures with regard to equity if a shareholder wishes to sell. Certainly, the university may wish to include veto arrangements in the event that the directors wish to sell the company.

Beyond this, there is the need to research and understand the market, prepare cash flow forecasts, and to understand balance sheets. More important is the need for both founder directors and university nominated directors to understand their roles and responsibilities as company directors. Indeed, it is for this reason that at Imperial we now run regular seminars on this issue for founder shareholders and nominated directors.

16.2. Managing the Conflicts of Interest

Even a glance at Table 1 will make it clear that there are likely to be potential conflicts of interest for the academics (including myself) between their role in the company and that in the university. Take three simple examples:

1. There is a need to monitor the involvement of university staff in the company since there is a possibility that they could end up being paid twice for the same work! This is a particularly difficult issue if the spinout company is, in effect, the development arm of its research incubator department.

2. In a number of cases the research leader within the incubator department is also a shareholder of a company, which may be looking to place research contracts in the department.

3. In Imperial, we frequently nominate directors[4] of our spinout companies from the faculty or staff of the College. This means that the director may be faced with a situation where a decision that is right for the company is against the interests of the university. Of course, they must act on behalf of the company since they hold the company in trust for all the shareholders, not just the university but what, if anything, should they tell the university? The answer is that they should treat all shareholders equally. This is easy to say but not always clearly understood by the various parties, either within the company or within the university, where the nominated director may be seen as a "spy" for the university.

Each of these examples is drawn from our experience at Imperial. They are difficult issues that demonstrate the clear potential for conflicts of interest to arise and an evident need for the creation and management of a variety of Chinese Walls within the university.

17. Managing the Business

All that I have said so far implies that academics will manage the business in both the hybrid and the orthodox spinout; and that an outside investor-manager will have initiated the technology spinout. In reality, this is often not the case. Despite Government enthusiasm for "Academic Entrepreneurs", the majority of academics wish to stay associated with the university system. The research bug is what drives them. I am relieved that this is so. Indeed, this is why the majority of our spinouts are hybrid. The academic inventors are the very ones that I believe we need to keep in the university continuing to develop yet more

4. Like the policy adopted by some venture capitalists, the university may wish to retain the right to nominate a director of the company.

commercialisable ideas and so becoming *habitual spinout inventors*. As Ronstadt (1988) states when developing his corridor principle "the mere act of starting a venture enables entrepreneurs to see other venture opportunities they could neither see nor take advantage of until they had started their initial venture" (p. 31). Beyond this, these resident spinout entrepreneurs provide important role models for colleagues throughout the university.

In such cases, what is needed is a businessperson to launch and manage the company, a professional manager or surrogate entrepreneur (Radosevich, 1995). Of course, this is a start-up and so they will want equity. This is not the only reason for seeking professional management. Investors are wary of academics and will be concerned to see a strong, experienced, and focused management team in place. However, these surrogate entrepreneurs will need to understand and manage the academic's strong sense of ownership of their research, which can often manifest itself in attitudes of scientific purity and of commercial meddling. They will also need to understand the scientific base of the products that they will be marketing. In other words, they will need a particular set of skills that are not easy to find, and one of the roles of the Technology Transfer Office will be to build a network of contacts who may be interested in investing in, and managing, technology-based spinouts. Interestingly, these can often be found within the alumnus base. For example, we currently have a team of three MBA students who are running a technology spinout.

18. Dividing the Spoils

There are three types of potential revenue that flow from the university investment in spinout companies – royalties, dividends, and capital gain – and it is important to have clear policies for each.

Most universities are used to dealing with licensing arrangements that involve royalties flowing from the assignment of IPR. However, there is one difference for a spinout. In a licensing deal, the only possible reward for individual academics is through the license fee and the royalty stream. Therefore, all can be treated equally. In a spinout where a portion of the IP from a department or research centre has been assigned to the company, the shareholder academics could benefit from dividend and capital gain through ownership of the company, and a share in the university royalties as an inventor. In other words, they could "feed at the trough" three times. Clearly the university needs a policy to deal with such circumstances if it is to avoid anger, envy and conflict within the department.

So, we come to the question of capital gain. In a recent study of American universities, Bray and Lee (2000) concluded that *"...even if none of the start-ups produces a million dollar equity sale, the financial return of equity will be within the range normally received as a license issue fee. Taking equity leaves the door open for the occasional jackpot, which will bring in significantly more money than a standard license"* (p.386). Government policy is vindicated! Encourage more academic entrepreneurs to spinout and then sit back and wait for the rewards to roll in. Well, not quite. There are a couple of other issues to take into account.

- Remember portfolio theory? Capital gain from an individual investment in a start-up company is unreliable. That is why venture capitalists have a portfolio of investments. Certainly, regular, annual capital gain cannot be assumed. Therefore, it must not be assumed for university revenue purposes. In short, it is no substitute for student fees.

- Most start-up companies are cash hungry and require more than one round of funding to finance their growth. Universities are not venture capitalists. Usually, they do not invest cash but Intellectual Property. Therefore, they are unlikely to participate in any further funding rounds and so, inevitably, they will be diluted. For example, in a recent case from Imperial, one of our spinouts, Turbogenset, was floated at a market capitalisation of around £540m which rose rapidly to over £1bn. By the time of the float, Imperial had just less than 10%. However, in this case as in many IPOs the founder shareholders were constrained by a "lock in"[5] clause whereby gains can only be realised over a period of time after which there is the question of when to realise - another committee for the university! And, of course, not all the capital gain will stay with the university. There may be academic inventors who were not founders that the university may wish to reward. Moreover, any capital gain must be set against the cost of making the investment in the first place not least the cost of the technology transfer office.

19. Conclusion

As I said at the beginning, it is complicated. There are major managerial issues that need to be resolved. However, the fact that it is complicated is not a reason not to do it. Academics should never be under-estimated. They may be commercially naïve but they know how to seek knowledge, can speed read and digest complicated documents, and they learn very fast. They also enjoy seeing their ideas used. The university simply needs to have clear and fair policies and procedures, and to communicate them positively and enthusiastically. I do not believe that we really want our finest scientific brains to become CEOs of companies but rather they should do what they are best at – researching.

5. Whereby at the float there are conditions as to when founder shareholders are allowed to sell.

References:

Auril, CBI, and DTI (1997*) Research partnerships between industry and Universities* CBI.

AUTM (1998) *Licensing Survey* AUTM: Norwalk, CT.

Baumol, W.J. (1990) "Entrepreneurship: Productive, unproductive, and destructive". *Journal of Political Economy* 98 (5), 893-921.

Birley, S. (1992) The Venture Phenomenon, Part 1, *IC Engineer* Autumn, 12-13.

Birley, S. (1993) The Venture Phenomenon, Part 2, *IC Engineer* Spring, 10-11.

Birley, S. and Norburn, D. (1985) "Small versus large companies: the entrepreneurial conundrum". *Journal of Business Strategy* 6(1), Summer, 81-87.

Bulter, S. and Birley, S. (1998) "Scientists and their attitudes to industry links". *International Journal of Innovation Management* 2(1), 79-106.

Bok, D. (1982) *Beyond the ivory tower: Social responsibilities for the modern university* Cambridge, MA: Harvard University Press.

Bray, M.J. and Lee, J.N. (2000) "University revenues from technology transfer: licensing fees versus equity positions". *Journal of Business Venturing* (15): 5/6, 385-392.

Chrisman, J.J., Hynes, T. and Fraser, S. (1995) "Faculty entrepreneurship and economic development: the case on the University of Calgary". *Journal of Business Venturing* 10, 267-281.

Doutriaux, J. (1991) "University culture, spin-off strategy and success of academic entrepreneurs at Canadian universities". In *Frontiers of Entrepreneurship Research* Wellesley, MA: Babson College.

Downs, R. and Eadie, G. (1998) "Knowledge creation and social networks in corporate entrepreneurship; The renewal of organisational capability". In Oakey, R. and During, W.E. (Eds) *New Technology-based Firms in the 1990s Volume 5,* London: Paul Chapman Publishing Ltd.

Franklin, S.J., Wright, N. and Lockett, A. (2000) "*Academic and surrogate entrepreneurship in university spinout companies*". Working Paper, University of Nottingham.

HM Treasury and DTI (1998) *Innovating for the future: investing in R&D.*

Lindholm, A.D. (1997) "Growth and inventiveness in technology-based spin-off Firms". *Research Policy* 26, 331-344.

Lissenburgh, S. and Harding, R. (2000) *Knowledge links: Innovation in university-business partnerships* London: IPPR.

Louis, K.S., Blumenthal, D., Gluck, M.E., and Stoto, M.A. (1989) "Entrepreneurs in academe: An exploration of behaviours among life scientists". *Administrative Science Quarterly* 34(1), 110-131.

Mustar, P. (1997) "Spinoff entreprises. How French academics create high-tech companies; the conditions for success or failure". *Science and Public Policy* 24(1), 37-43.

Nicolaou, N. and Birley, S. (2000) Academic networks in a trichotomous categorisation of university spinouts *10th Annual Global Entrepreneurship Research Conference* Imperial College: London.

Peters, L.S. and H. Etzkowitz (1990) "University-industry connections and academic values". *Technology in Society,* 12, 427-440.

Radosevich, R. (1995) "A model for entrepreneurial spin-offs from public technology sources". *International Journal of Technology Management* 10(7/8), 879-893.

Roberts, E. (1991*) Entrepreneurs in High Technology: Lessons from MIT and Beyond* Oxford University Press; Oxford.

Ronstadt. R., (1988) "The Corridor Principle". *Journal of Business Venturing 3, 31-* 40.

Rosenberg, N. and Nelson, R.R. (1994) "American universities and technical advance in industry". *Research Policy* 23, 323-348.

Samson, K.J and Gurdon, M.A. (1993) "University scientists as entrepreneurs: a special case of technology transfer and high technology venturing". *Technovation* 13(2), 63-71.

Segal, N.S. (1986) "Universities and technological entrepreneurship in Britain: some implications of the Cambridge Phenomenon". *Technovation* 4(3), 189- 205.

Smilor, R.W., Gibson, D.V., and Dietrich, G.B. (1990) "Research co-optation via social contracting: resource acquisition strategies for new ventures". *Strategic Management Journal* 5(1), 63-76.

15. Methods of Evaluating the Impact of Public Policies to Support Small Businesses: the Six Steps to Heaven

David J. Storey
Centre for Small and Medium Sized Enterprises
University of Warwick

Acknowledgements. This paper was first formulated as a result of the authors participation in the evaluation group convened by Anders Lundstrom from the Swedish Foundation for Small Business Research (FSF). The paper inevitably reflects the contributions made by other key members of the group such as Dennis De, William Dennis, Lois Stevenson and Jane Wickman as well as Anders himself, Christer Öhman and Hakan Boter. However a key influence on the ideas has been the author's involvement with the Best Practice Working Party on SMEs at the OECD. Early versions of the paper were also presented to the I.G. Conference "Processes of Enterprise Creation and Consolidation" in Rome 12 December 1997, in Mikkeli, Finland on "Growth and Job Creation in SMEs", January 7-9, 1998, and then at the ICSB Conference in Singapore 8-10 June 1998. Helpful feedback was provided in all instances, particularly from Frank Hoy who pointed me towards U.S. literature of which I was unaware. I also appreciated comments received from Marc Cowling.

Abstract. Virtually all developed economies utilize taxpayer's money to provide either free or subsidized assistance to small businesses, the self-employed or to potential small business owners. This paper provides an outline methodology for evaluating the impact of these policies. It identifies six approaches, beginning with the most simple and ending up with the most sophisticated. These are referred to as the 'Six Steps', with step Six being viewed as 'best practice' or 'heaven' in this area.

Keywords: small businesses, public policy, evaluation.

1. Introduction

Virtually all developed economies utilise taxpayers money to provide either free or subsidised assistance to small businesss, the self employed or to potential small business owners. Sometimes this assistance is direct financial payments in the form of subsidies to encourage investment in human or physical capital. In other cases subsidies are in the form of free or subsidised advisory services in starting or developing small business or in specialist areas such as exporting or the use of new technology.

Taxpayers money may also be used to bribe individuals or organisations to behave in a way which is perceived to benefit both small businesses and the economy as a whole. These bribes often take the form of tax relief. For example, wealthy individuals may be given 'tax breaks' to become equity participants in small or young businesses. Finally, some government procurement programmes focus upon small businesses, and taxpayers money is used to offset any efficiency

This article was originally published in the International Journal of Entrepreneurship Education 1(2): pp. 181-202.

losses to government by its having to contract with small businesses where these are not optimal suppliers. The wide range of public support programmes to small firms in developed economies and their appraisal is best reviewed in OECD [1995, 1996, 1997].

Given the huge variety of schemes, the diversity of countries in which the schemes are found, and the often inflated claims on the part of those administering the schemes for their effectiveness, it is disappointing that the academic community has been rather slow in seeking to address this area. Perhaps even more seriously, even where the issues have been addressed by small business academics, the methods of evaluation employed have rarely been at the intellectual frontier.

This paper seeks to provide an outline methodology for evaluating the impact of public policies to assist the small business sector. It begins, however, by emphasising the impossibility of conducting an evaluation in the absence of clearly specified objectives for the policy concerned. Ideally, in fact, these objectives should be specified in a quantitative manner in the form of targets.

The paper then moves on to provide a review of the various methodological approaches to evaluation of small business support policies found in developed countries. It does not seek to present a comprehensive review of the area. Instead it provides an analytical framework within which a wide variety of types of analyses can be classified. In total it identifies six approaches, beginning with the most simple and ending up with the most sophisticated. These are referred to as the 'Six Steps' with Step 6 being viewed as 'best practice' or 'Heaven' in this area. The paper also makes a distinction between 'monitoring' and 'evaluation'. Monitoring is viewed as Steps 1-3, with the more sophisticated approaches being classified as 'evaluation' in Steps 4-6.

2. Specification of Objectives

It is a fundamental principle of evaluation that its prerequisite is the specification of the objectives of policy. Unfortunately it appears to be a characteristic of governments in all developed countries to be, at best, opaque about the objectives of small business policy. Many phrases characterise this area. Governments talk about 'creating an enterprising society', or 'maximising SMEs contribution to economic development', or 'enhancing competitiveness', or even 'creating jobs'. So far as this author is aware, however, no developed country produces a clear set of objectives for each component of small business policy. Analysts therefore are required to infer the objectives of policy, rather than having these clearly defined. Only then is it possible to determine whether or not the target is achieved and hence be able to judge whether or not policy is successful.

Instead, what governments favour are lists of policies. Lists of the various measures which have been introduced to help the small business sector, such as taxation exemptions, late payment, administrative burdens, finance and information provision. Typical of these lists are those presented in ENSR (1997) at a European level or DTI (1998) for a national level.

Analysts such as de Koning and Snijders (1992) have made attempts to compare SME policies in countries. Their work, on EU countries, was only able to compare, using such lists, the number of policy measures focused upon SMEs in policy fields such as Fiscal policies, Export policies, Information and Counselling etc. This is clearly not the same, and indeed is significantly inferior to, specifying objectives.

Not only is there a conspicuous absence of clear objectives for SME policy, but the implied objectives can often be conflicting. The United Kingdom can be taken as illustrative. Table 1 reproduces my earlier (Storey 1994) effort to seek to identify the appropriate objectives for UK small business policy. Note the table only defines the objectives and not the numerical values of the objectives (i.e. targets) themselves.

Table 1: Intermediate and Final Objective

Intermediate	**Final**
1. Increase Employment	– Increase Employment – Reduce Unemployment
2. Increase Number of Start Ups	– Increase Number of Start Ups – Increase Stock of Firms
3. Promote Use of Consultants	– Promote Use of Consultants – Faster Growth of Firms
4. Increase Competition	– Increase Competition – Increase Wealth
5. Promote "Efficient" Markets	– Promote "Efficient" Markets – Increase Wealth
6. Promote Technology Diffusion	– Promote Technology Diffusion – Increase Wealth
7. Increase Wealth	– Votes

Source: Storey (1994)

The table distinguishes between intermediate and final objectives. Taking the top line as illustrative, we can identify 'increasing employment' as an objective, with a target being where this objective was given a particular measure – such as increasing employment by 5% over a five year period.

Taking now the objectives, politicians in most developed countries have SME policies because they believe, rightly or wrongly, that SMEs are both currently a major source of employment and likely to be an increasing source of new jobs in the future [Hughes (1997)]. Failure to address/encourage the SME sector may lead to slower rates of job creation and hence unemployment being higher than otherwise.

Whilst political leaders frequently couch their rhetoric in terms of employment creation, their prime concern is, in fact, to seek to reduce unemployment, rather than to increase employment. Increases in employment therefore can be considered as an intermediate objective, with the final objective being that of reducing unemployment.[1] Utilising the vehicle of SMEs to create jobs can however have a mixed effect upon reducing the numbers of individuals registered as unemployed. From the positive side, SMEs are more likely to employ individuals who are comparatively heavily represented amongst the unemployed – unskilled, very young and very old (Brown, Hamilton and Medoff 1990). Yet, in other respects, job creation in SMEs is likely to have only a modest effect upon reducing registered unemployment. This is because SMEs are disproportionately likely to provide part time work and these part time workers (often females) are less likely to be registered as unemployed. There is therefore immediately a question as to whether the real objective of policy in row 1 is the creation of employment or the reduction in unemployment. This is rarely made explicit in policy pronouncements.

A second area of possible conflict between job creation and reduction in unemployment is that the latter can often be reduced by out-migration from a country or region. Policies of job creation, if they are successful, can lead to lower rates of out-migration because workers feel there is a prospect of getting a job in the locality. Success at creating jobs can even, perversely, lead to increased unemployment. Those specifying objectives have to be clear where their priorities lie.

In row 2 of Table 1 an alternative objective of SME policy is articulated. Many countries have policies to encourage individuals to start businesses. This may be related to aspects of objective 1 – such as a view that more people starting businesses leads directly to additional jobs or to reducing the numbers of unemployed. Alternatively, policies to increase the number of start ups may merely reflect (be a result of) a more dynamic economy and one likely to exhibit prosperity in the longer term. However it is widely recognised that policies to assist the start up of new enterprises are most likely to be targeted upon individuals who are unemployed, since these individuals are the most 'susceptible'. Experience, both in the UK and the United States (Storey and Strange, 1992, Bendick and Egan, 1988), shows these individuals often enter trades with low entry barriers – such as vehicle repairers, window cleaners, taxi

1. Here targets are sometimes specified. For example the Swedish government is committed to halving unemployment over a five year period to the year 2002.

drivers, etc. for which there is a finite and highly localised demand. The net effect of such policies is that public money is used to encourage unemployed individuals to start a business in these sectors, but this serves primarily to displace other unsubsidised traders in the locality with no obvious benefit either to the local consumer or to the economy in general. The effect then is to increase the number of start ups i.e. satisfy intermediate objective 2, but also to increase the number of businesses which cease to trade, with little net change in the stock of firms and so not satisfy final objective 2. Even where there is an increase in the stock of firms, there may well be a compensating fall in average firm size without any apparent increase in employment (Storey and Strange 1992). A choice therefore has to be made between Intermediate objective 1 and Intermediate objective 2.

The remainder of table 1 identifies several other objectives which are apparent from observing the characteristics of public support for SMEs in the United Kingdom. The interested reader can consult Storey (1994) for a fuller discussion of other potential conflicts. Perhaps the only objective requiring further comment at this point is that in row 7, where the final objective is 'Votes'. This clearly is a fundamentally different objective, since it is explicitly political, rather than being one of the other more 'economic' objectives specified elsewhere. As noted in Storey (1994), there is nothing undesirable in public policies being focused on the achievement of economic objectives and, as a reward for achieving good economic performance, politicians being re-elected. Indeed such logic is at the cornerstone of democracy. What is more questionable is where policies, using taxpayers money, are couched in terms of economic objectives but are really a mechanism for persuading a numerically significant group (in this case small business owners) to vote for the government through the provision of 'sweeteners'. In many countries there is an overtly political element to small business policies, and failure by analysts to take it into account, would be to underestimate the role which it plays in politician's calculations.

Governments, then, should be required to specify their objective in the provision of small business support. Identifying a wide range of sketchy objectives may serve the government's purpose of being able to point to success if there is an improvement in that objective area, but this is clearly unsatisfactory from the viewpoint of the taxpayer. Paraphrasing Harrison and Leitch (1996) "It is clearly unsatisfactory for the government to claim that the target is anything it happens to hit". Instead governments should set objectives, with an indication of which, if there is more than one, takes priority. Once the objectives are set, then numerical targets need to be specified. Only then can evaluation take place.

It is interesting to note that, whilst this paper was in preparation, the issue received 'heavyweight' support in the UK from the House of Commons Select Committee (1998). It said:

> The Government has yet to state clearly what its policy objectives are with regard to SME policy; how the achievement of these broad objectives can be assessed, or how existing policy measures fit within a broader context . . . the

means by which competitiveness can be measured and the reasons for targeting competitiveness, in terms of its impact on employment, unemployment, GDP and other indicators can only be guessed at . . . we are not convinced that the Government's SME policy is characterised by sufficient structure and focus. We recommend that, as a matter of urgency, the government define the objectives of SME policy. The objectives chosen must be accompanied by measurable targets, with a timetable for their attainment. Clearly such a development would be highly desirable and ought to be implemented with all speed.

3. The Six Steps

This section makes the unrealistic assumption that objectives, either of small business policy as a whole, or of the particular programme under consideration, are specified. The remainder of the paper seeks to review how, in practice, appraisal is undertaken. Table 2 identifies the six steps and these are ranked in terms of sophistication, with Step 1 being the least sophisticated and Step 6 being the most sophisticated.

Table 2: The Six Steps

Monitoring	
STEP I	* Take up of schemes
STEP II	* Recipient's opinions
STEP III	* Recipient's views of the difference made by the assistance
Evaluation	
STEP IV	* Comparison of the performance of 'Assisted' with 'Typical' firms
STEP V	* Comparison with 'Match' firms
STEP VI	* Taking account of selection bias

Although all six steps are often referred to as 'evaluations' in the literature, Steps 1-3 can be considered as merely monitoring, with only Steps 4-6 being evaluation.[2] The difference between monitoring and evaluation is that the latter are attempts, demonstrating analytical rigour, to determine the impact of the policy initiatives. Monitoring, on the other hand, merely either documents activity

2. Monitoring has narrower objectives than evaluation. It is limited to observing and recording practical indicators of inputs and outputs .... Evaluation has two prime aims: – An improving and learning aim, and A proving aim" Bridge et al (1998)

under the programme or reports participant's perception of the value of the scheme. In short, the difference between monitoring and evaluation is that monitoring relies exclusively upon the views of the recipients of the policy. Evaluation however seeks, by some means, to contrast these with non-recipients, in order to present a 'counter-factual'. The difference between actual changes and the 'counter-factual' is viewed as the impact of the policy – or its 'additionality'.

3.1. Monitoring

Step 1: Take up of Schemes

Table 3 describes Step 1. This monitoring procedure identifies the characteristics and nature of the take up of the scheme. For example, it might quantify the

Table 3: Take Up of Schemes

Questions

* How many firms participated?
* What sectors were they in?
* What locations were they in?
* How big were these firms?
* How much money was spent?

Problems

* Tells you almost nothing about policy effectiveness
* Tells you almost nothing about satisfying objectives

Examples

Author:	Date:	Topic:	Country:
USA Delegation to OECD	1997	Small Business Investment Co.	USA

number of firms which participated in a particular scheme, their sectoral distribution, the size of such enterprises and possibly their regional distribution. Step 1 reviews also frequently include public expenditure on the schemes, so that it is possible, for example, to identify expenditure by firm size or the proportion of expenditure 'consumed' by particular regions. What is much less frequently available is information on the money received by individual firms, since this is thought to contravene a confidentiality relationship between government and the enterprise.

The data used in Step 1 are primarily collected by the public sector for accounting purposes. In many instances they appear as Appendices to government documents but, because they are collected simply for accounting purposes, they do not even seek to evaluate whether the monies have been effectively spent. Their sole concern is to document expenditure, making it clear that expenditure is compatible with the purpose for which is was intended. In short, Step 1 serves an accounting and legal function, but plays no economic role.

The second section of Table 3 makes it clear that, whilst Step 1 appraisals are the most frequently conducted, the results obtained provide no insight whatsoever into policy effectiveness. They do not even seek to answer the question 'To what extent did the policy achieve the types of objectives outlined in Table 1?

Despite their ubiquity, Step 1 appraisals can only be considered as the 'building blocks' for evaluation. Whilst they provide data on the numbers of firms participating, and on expenditure, these items are not linked.

Step 2: Recipient's Opinions

In Step 2 those firms who participated in the schemes are asked for their opinions. For example, those participating in subsidised training activities are asked about whether they felt there was value in the training provided; firms in receipt of subsidised loans are asked about whether they thought the loan to be valuable; those who participated in export counselling services are asked whether they felt the advice was helpful and whether it led to new orders. Firms participating in Loan Guarantee Schemes are asked about whether they would have received funding for a project without the availability of the scheme.

Firms are also normally asked about the application procedures to participate in the Scheme to determine whether these can be streamlined. For example, firms are asked about how they became aware of the service, about the complexity of the application procedure and whether the application was speedily and fairly handled by the bureaucrat. Step 1 data is therefore 'objective' financial accounting data, whereas Step 2 seeks to obtain the viewpoint of the firms both on the effectiveness of the scheme and on its accessibility.

The 'Problems' section of Table 4 however shows that, despite the frequency of such studies, Step 2 information does not help determine whether objectives are achieved. Take for example participants upon training courses: here participants are often asked to express an opinion as to whether they felt the training to be of use to them and whether it was professionally delivered - the so-called 'happy sheets'. It is however a strong leap of faith to believe that satisfaction with the course delivered relates to enhanced firm performance; yet it is only enhanced firm performance which will be related to the objectives of policy[3].

Table 4: Recipient's Opinions

Questions

* Course Participants: Did they like it?
* Firms : Were there problems in applying?
  : Were procedures too slow?
  : Cumbersome?
* How much money was spent?

Problems

* Even if they like it, it does not tell you if it is effective
* All it can do is offer insights into policy delivery – but that is not they key question

Examples

Author:	Date:	Topic:	Country:
Moint	1998	Export Assistance	USA
Rogoff and M-S Lee	1996	Small business support services, in general	USA
Ernst & Young	1996	Business Links	USA

In short, whilst such assistance may make the recipients happier - and conceivably more likely to vote for the politicians - it does not necessarily relate to the economic objectives of the policy, such as increasing the competitiveness of the firm or job creation.

If the objective of the investigation is, in part, to identify the problems with accessing aid then only addressing these questions to those firms which were successful in overcoming any barriers leads to biases. In particular it is likely that those who have surmounted the barriers will have a more 'positive' view than those who were discouraged. Questioning only participant firms fails to estimate the extent to which firms are discouraged from participating in a scheme by the real or imagined barriers which exist. It is therefore of paramount importance that

3. Despite this, the link is frequently made. For example, the Barclays 1998 small business review on training reports high levels of satisfaction reported by owner-managers on training courses (91% felt that quality was good or very good), but no attempt was made to link this to formal performance measures. Despite this Barclays asserted that they believe it to be a critical element to a successful small business. However where such links have been sought through careful work [Hughes et al (1998)] associations are very weak or non-existent.

the views are sought of all relevant businesses - whether or not they applied. From this, a list of applicants. but who did not access the aid, must also be drawn. Only in this way is it possible to obtain an accurate measure of the extent of any application barriers.

Overall, Step 2 appraisals can offer some insight into policy delivery (especially when combined with the views of non recipients), but they remain almost irrelevant to determining the effectiveness of policy. This is because there may be no link between the views of the firm on the value of the policy and the ability of the policy to achieve the objectives specified in Table 1. For example, the privately rationed firms will prefer public subsidies with high dead-weight elements and might be tempted to speak positively about such policies if they felt this was likely to influence government provision of such subsidies. On the other hand some firms may be more truthful, yet the evaluator has no means of distinguishing the truthful from the selfish firms.

Step 3: Recipients Views of the Difference Made by the Assistance

In Step 3 recipients of policy are asked, not simply whether they liked the policy – the happy sheets – but also whether they thought this made any difference to the performance of their firm. Normally quantitative estimates are sought, to determine whether the initiative provided additionality in terms of additional jobs, sales, or profits.

Table 5 shows that, in the more ‘sophisticated’ Step 3 appraisals, firms may also be asked questions as to what would have happened to them if they had not been in receipt of the policy initiative. Perhaps, most difficult of all, firms may be asked to estimate the extent to which, if there is any enhanced performance on their part, this is at the expense of other firms. Such questions are designed to estimate the extent of any ‘displacement’.

The ‘Problems’ section of Table 5 shows there are several fundamental problems with this approach in addition to those referred to in Step 2. The most important of these is the extent to which businesses are capable, even if they choose to be truthful, of conducting the mental gymnastics required to answer such questions. To ask a small manufacturer to estimate the extent to which the

Table 5: Recipient's view of the difference made by the assistance

Questions

* Did firms think it prvided 'additionality'?
* Would firms have done it anyway?
* Does it cause 'displacement'?

Problems

* Even if they like it, it does not tell you if it is effective
* All it can do is offer insights into policy delivery – but that is not they key question

Examples

Author:	Date:	Topic:	Country:
Moint	1998	Export Assistance	USA
Rogoff and M-S Lee	1996	Small business support services, in general	USA
Ernst & Young	1996	Business Links	USA

provision of a loan or subsidised advisory service received two or three years previously influenced the subsequent profitability of his/her firms merely encourages guessing. There are so many influences upon the performance of small enterprises that being able to attribute precisely a number, or even a range, is an unreasonable question.

In many instances it is a perfectly understandable reaction of businesses to provide answers which they think the questioner wishes to hear in order to be able to continue untroubled with the running of their business. If they do adopt this response there is, yet again, no way of checking.

Whilst some entrepreneurs will provide the answer which they think the questioner wishes to hear in order to get them out of the door - and by implication therefore overestimate the impact of the initiative - others may adopt the reverse strategy. Many entrepreneurs are fiercely proud of their business and are very reluctant to admit to receiving any assistance whatsoever. Such individuals are therefore likely to underestimate the contribution of policy by claiming that any improvements in their business reflected their entrepreneurial skills, rather than public money. Faced with these extreme groups the analyst has no basis for judging which of the two are numerically dominant in any group.

There is also the issue of when such questions should be asked, and of whom. Clearly they cannot be asked at the time of the loan since any effects (on profitability/sales etc.) will not have had an effect. On the other hand a period of more than three years after the loan will mean that too many other influences will have affected firm performance. A balance therefore has to be struck between not waiting long enough for effects to appear and waiting so long that recall deteriorates.

Finally, it is the case for both Step 2 and Step 3 appraisals that interviews can only be conducted for firms which continue to trade. It is very difficult to contact enterprises which are no longer trading and yet all firms are the target for policy. To have responses only from surviving firms will clearly bias the interpretations placed upon the effectiveness of the policy, serving to make the outcomes more positive than would be the case by the inclusion of both survivors and non-survivors..

Overall, therefore, monitoring alone is incapable of offering policy relevant insights into policy effectiveness, where the objective of policy is to enhance the performance of SMEs. This is because the effect of policy cannot be estimated simply by seeking the views of recipient firms, even if these views were honestly provided. It is only capable of soliciting views from operational businesses so, if one objective of policy is to raise survival rates of firms, then this procedure is precluded. To overcome these problems it is necessary to compare the assisted firms with groups of firms not assisted by the policy. This is defined as evaluation. Its challenge is to isolate the appropriate group of firms with which to make the comparison, and to hold constant all other influences.

3.2. Evaluation

Step 4: Comparison of the Performance of 'Assisted' and 'Typical' Firms

The earlier discussion of Table 2 emphasised that a key distinction between monitoring and evaluation was that monitoring focused exclusively upon firms which have been assisted by policy. Yet to evaluate the impact of the policy it is necessary to decide what would have happened to businesses in the absence of policy - the so-called 'counter-factual'. The effect of policy is therefore defined to be the difference between what actually happened and what would have happened in the absence of policy.

Step 4 estimates this impact by comparing the performance in firms assisted by the policy with those which have not been assisted. The inference is that any difference in the performance of the two groups can be attributed to the impact of the policy.

In Table 6 assisted firms are compared with typical firms in the population. For example, employment or sales growth in assisted firms is compared with typical firms; alternatively the differences in survival rate of assisted firms may be compared with the survival rates of firms more generally in the economy.

Table 6: Comparison of the performances of 'Assisted' with 'Typical' firms

Approach

* Employment/Sales growth of assisted firms compared with 'typical' firms?

* Survival of assisted firms compared with 'typical firms'

Problems

* Assisted firms are not typical

Examples

Author:	Date:	Topic:	Country:
Chrisman et al	1985	Subsidised Consultancy	USA
Deschoolmeester I et al	1998	Management Training	Belgium

The advantage of this approach is that, for the first time, a 'control' group of enterprises is identified. This enables comparisons between the 'assisted' and the 'control' group to be made; it also enables comparisons, in principle, to be made between the survival and non-survival of firms in both groups.

The problem, as noted in the second half of Table 6, is that firms in receipt of assistance may not be typical of firms in the economy as a whole. For example those firms where the entrepreneur seeks training, even where this is subsidised by the state, may be more likely to be growth orientated than firms more generally throughout the economy. Those seeking training from a premier University Business School are more likely to have graduates in the business than 'typical' firms. As Deschoolmeester et al (1998) show, those seeking training are generally younger and have significantly better educated owners than the population of firms as a whole. Given this, they may also be starting businesses in different sectors. Equally, firms seeking advisory services may be more 'aware' businesses and therefore more likely to be better performing businesses. Thirdly there may be sectoral or geographical characteristics of recipients, which distinguish them from the population of firms overall. These effects can be either positive or negative.

For example some SME policies are focused upon the unemployed or 'at risk' groups. A classic example is Law 44 in Italy, described in detail in OECD (1995, 1997). This is a scheme which targets young unemployed individuals in Southern Italy; it provides financial and mentoring support to these people in starting up and developing, during their early years, their businesses. It would clearly be inappropriate to compare these businesses with typical Italian small firms for at least two reasons. The first is that these businesses are founded by young people, the survival rate of whose businesses is known to be markedly lower than those of other age groups [Cressy and Storey (1994)]. The second difference is that the economic and trading environment of Southern Italy is significantly more difficult than in other parts of that country, making it more difficult for new businesses to flourish. For these two reasons, to compare Law 44 firms directly with 'typical' Italian firms and attribute any difference in performance to the Law would be to risk seriously underestimating impact.

The study by Deschoolmeester et al (1998), comparing start-ups of businesses from 'graduates' of the Vlerick school finds marked differences in age, sector and education between the graduates and the population of firms. All these factors will influence the subsequent performance of the firm. To attribute performance differences to the provision of the training requires explicit account to be taken of these factors.

It is therefore necessary to more explicitly take into account the factors likely to influence the performance of the assisted and non-assisted firms and to seek to hold these constant. This process is called matching.

Step 5: Matching

In Step 5 researchers identify a specific 'control group' with which to compare the assisted businesses. For example, if a policy were implemented to enhance the survival rates of new businesses then it would clearly be inappropriate to compare survival rates of assisted new businesses with that of typical small firms because it has been consistently shown that young businesses have lower survival rates than longer-established businesses (Storey 1994). It is also consistently shown that larger firms have higher survival rates than smaller firms (Storey 1994). Failure to take account of these elements would clearly bias the picture. Equally, if the scheme were focused upon high-tech businesses, then these types of businesses generally have faster growth rates than the SME population as a whole. Hence it would be unreasonable to compare the performance of the two groups of firms and infer that the difference in performance is attributable to the policy.

For these reasons Table 7 shows that Step 5 appraisals formally identify a 'control group' of firms. These are called 'match' firms, and matching generally takes place on four factors known to influence, to different extents, the performance of firms. In principle the 'assisted' and the 'match' firms would be expected to be identical on the basis of age, sector, ownership and geography.

Given such controls it is then possible to compare the performance of both groups over the same time period. The inference drawn is that any differences in performance between the two groups are attributable to the policy.

However Table 7 shows that, even here, there are both technical and inferential problems. The technical problem is that perfect matching upon all four criteria simultaneously can be difficult. Ideally such matching should take place

Table 7: Comparison with 'Match' firms

Approach

* Compare assisted with 'Match' firms on the basis of:
  - age
  - sector
  - ownership
  - geography

* Compare performance of both groups over same time period

Problems

* Perfect matching on four criteri can be very difficult
* Sample selection bias
  - More 'motivated' firms apply
  - Attribute differential performance to scheme and not to motivation

Examples

Author:	Year:	Topic:	Country:
Storey & Westhead	1994	Science Park Evaluation	UK
Lerner	1997	Small Business Investment Companies	USA
Hart & Scott	1994	Financial assistance	UK

immediately prior to the time at which the policy is implemented so that the performance of the two cohorts can be monitored over time. In practice this rarely happens. Instead information may be available for the assisted firms over a period of time, but then the control group is constructed as part of the evaluation procedure after the policy has been in operation. This means that it can be difficult to accurately estimate the survival/non-survival impact of policy - and yet this is a crucial element of SME policy initiatives in most countries.[4]

Whilst there are technical problems in constructing the sample, there are also major inferential problems. In particular, even if the four matching characteristics are held constant there may be other factors, which are not, where the two groups differ. In the terminology of labour economics, whilst it is possible to take account of 'observables', it is much more difficult to take account of ''unobservables' (Lalonde 1986, O'Higgins 1994). The 'observables' can be

4. A classic example of this are the attempts which began to be made in 1997 to evaluate the impact of Business Links in the UK. These seek to provide 'soft' assistance to small firms but Business Links had been in operation for three years before any Step 5 type evaluations were contemplated under the Inter-Departmental Working Group on Impact Assessment of Business Support.

considered to be age, sector, etc., as discussed above. The key 'unobservables' in this context can be considered to be the possibly linked issues of motivation and selection.

Taking motivation first; it may be that although firms do not differ in terms of 'observables', those who seek assistance are more dynamic and growth orientated. They may be run by individuals who are more aware, better networked and more open to new ideas. If we compare the performance of assisted and non-assisted firms and find the former outperform the latter, it may be tempting to infer the difference is attributable to the policy. But, if the two groups also differ in terms of motivation, any performance differences may reflect motivation rather than policy impact. In technical terms the motivated firms are self-selecting and this has to be taken into account. This is subsequently referred to as 'self selection'.

A second source of selection bias occurs where the scheme providers choose some applicants and not others; this is called administrative selection. Illustrations of administrative selection include the SBIR programme in the United States (Lerner 1997), Law 44 in Italy or the Prince's Youth Business Trust in the United Kingdom. In all three schemes an individual or a business applies to participate. A judgement is made as to whether that individual is suitable (we assume all individuals are eligible but that resources are deemed insufficient to fully satisfy all eligible applicants). Under this selection procedure it is reasonably assumed that the selectors will seek to identify the 'best' cases, or at least seek to avoid the 'worst' cases. Otherwise there would be no value in a selection procedure.

We have to assume the selectors are capable of making informed judgements – otherwise there would be no point in having selectors. In this case the performance of the selected group will, even if the policy yielded no benefits whatever to the firms, be superior to that of the 'match' group since the better cases are being selected. It therefore cannot be inferred that the whole of the observed difference between the assisted group and the non-assisted group in terms of performance is attributable exclusively to the policy.

Two factors are likely to enhance this bias. The first is the extent of competition for the funds. If 99 out of 100 applicants are successful, sample selection bias is likely to be less than where only 10 applicants in every 100 are successful. Secondly the ability of the selectors to make good decisions is also of considerable importance. Our judgement is that, since so many small business support policies are selective, and substantial resources are devoted to the selection procedure, it must be believed, at least by policy makers, that selection makes a difference. Quite simply, the bigger the difference which the selection makes, the bigger the deflation component required from the use of control groups, which only take account of 'observables'.

Step 6: Taking Account of Selection Bias

How then do we seek to overcome these problems? Table 7 shows that Step 6 procedures seek to compare assisted with matched firms, taking account of sample selection. Two procedures can be employed. The first is the use of statistical techniques which seek to explicitly take account of sample selection bias. These have become standard practice within the labour economics literature dealing with assessing the impact of training upon subsequent employment prospects of individuals. (Dolton et al 1989, O'Higgins 1994). The analysis utilises the technique originally formulated by Heckman (1977). In non-technical terms the Heckman 2-step adjustment procedure formulates a single equation to explain the selection procedure and then, taking of the selection procedure factors, formulates a second equation to explain performance change, taking account of factors included in the selection equation.

The value of the procedure is that the extent, if any, of selection can be taken into account. Thus the selection equation generates a coefficient (inverse Mills ratio) which is significant where selection is present. Where it is not, then a Stage 5 procedure is perfectly valid.

Where selection is shown to be present the impact deflation can be considerable. For example, the Wren and Storey (1998) analysis of the impact of the United Kingdom's subsidised consultancy services showed that, taking no account of selection, the policy appeared to raise the survival rate of firms by up to 16% over an eight year period and raised it up to 3% over a two year period. However, when account was taken of selection, these fell to 5% over the long term and 2% in the short run. Failure to take account of selection can therefore lead to serious overestimates of the impact of policy and whilst this can be favoured by some policy makers, it clearly is not in the public interest.

Many policy makers, however, are not happy with these statistical methods because the procedures are so complicated and technical that they feel uncomfortable. Their discomfort is supported by the findings of LaLonde (1986) who compared the use of random panels with the econometric analysis and found the former to yield superior results. Random panels are particularly valuable if the object is to take account of 'committee selection' but they are of only limited value when taking account of 'self selection'. If we take, as an example, individuals or entrepreneurs who seek to obtain an award either of finance or advice - an example might be SBIR or Law 44 - then it would be appropriate to make a selection in the normal way, but, as a control, to allow a random sample of applicants access to the award without selection. The performance of the random access group would then be monitored over the same time as that of the selected applicants. If the selected applicants differ significantly in terms of observables from the random applicants then this would also have to be taken into account in the analysis.

Table 8: Compare assisted with 'Match' firms taking account of sample selection

Approach

* Use of Statistical Techniques: Heckman 2 Step Estimator for testing and adjustment
* Use of Random Panels

Problems

* Policy makers (and some academics) feel uneasy about statistical 'adjustment'
* Use of random panels could mean public money is given to firms/people who we know will not benefit

Examples

Author:	Year:	Topic:	Country:
Wren & Storey	1998	Subsidised Marketing Consultancy	UK
Westhead & Storey	1998	Undergraduate placement programme (STEP)	UK

Nevertheless the prime purpose of the random access group is to seek to take account of the 'administrative selection' influence.

The effect of the impact of the policy would be the difference in performance between the assisted and the control group, after also eliminating the influence of selection.

The second part of Table 8 however shows problems remain even with these two approaches. Many analysts feel that the fairly complex statistical analysis in the Heckman 2-step procedure[5] is difficult to communicate in simple language. Even if they understand it themselves, politicians, faced with having to explain the Heckman 2-step to taxpayers and the small business community, would risk being branded as indulging in 'statistical hocus pocus'. It is therefore unattractive on these grounds.

In principle, the use of random panels is more attractive because it is more easily understood. But, if it is known with some degree of certainty that only a small proportion of firms will significantly benefit from the scheme, and it is also known, in advance, the characteristics of those who will benefit - i.e. selection is accurate - then public money is being wasted in providing assistance to businesses which are unlikely to succeed. The business community itself could therefore justifiably complain that money which otherwise could be usefully used on the

5. Despite the fact that Heckman is now a standard procedure in mid-range statistical analysis packages such as STATA or LIMDEP. It is not available on basic packages such as SPSS.

scheme is being wasted upon businesses with little prospects, in order merely to evaluate the impact of the scheme.

Overall, however, the key message is that selection, both in the form of 'self-selection; and 'administrative selection' is an important issue. Failure to take it into account seriously risks overestimating the impact of policy. Where administrative selection, in particular, is clearly prevalent there is a strong case for the limited use of random panels. Where self selection is likely then the more sophisticated statistical analysis has to be conducted - even if explaining the outcome to politicians could be tricky!

4. Conclusions

If public money is spent on SME support then it is vital that evaluation of the impact of these initiatives takes place. Unfortunately evaluation is not possible unless objectives, which are clear and, in principle, measurable are specified. Too often objectives are either not specified, or specified in a way which is overly vague and incapable of being used as the basis for deciding whether or not the policies are successful. In our judgement these objectives should be quantified and become explicit targets.

This paper has also argued that evaluation and monitoring are not identical. We view monitoring as collecting information about the firms in receipt of the scheme, together with financial information of monies expended. We also view monitoring as seeking only the opinions of recipients of the scheme. On the other hand evaluation seeks to compare performance of recipients with other groups of individuals or enterprises. Unfortunately most policy initiatives in OECD countries currently are merely monitored, rather than evaluated. In the terminology of this paper, such appraisals as are conducted rarely pass beyond Step 3, and in many instances do not pass beyond Step 1.

There are problems with all stages in the evaluation procedure, but currently best practice is Step 6. In our judgement new SME policies should ensure that, prior to their implementation, a budget is set aside to ensure that an evaluation plan is established to achieve at least a stage 5 level of evaluation. Governments are failing in their responsibilities to their taxpayers if they continue to finance 'evaluations' which are below those of Stage 5.

From the viewpoint of the research community it is important for the most sophisticated analysis possible to be undertaken. Almost all small business policies involve an element of selection - either 'administrative selection' or 'self selection'. The challenge to researchers is to seek to address the issue of selection. The problem, however, is the payoff to researchers is likely to be negative. This is because the experience chronicled in this paper suggests that, the more sophisticated and careful the analysis, the weaker the apparent impact of 'policy'. This is because the sophisticated analyst does not attribute to the policy, effects which are actually attributable to other influences such as selection, or firm characteristics.

Unfortunately the realpolitik of the situation is that policy makers generally (but not always) wish to demonstrate the effectiveness of their policies. They are therefore likely to favour sloppy analysts who are capable of "demonstrating" major policy impacts and disfavour careful analysts.

This has potentially serious consequences for the serious research community; it means we risk exclusion from the policy arena because we do not have access to data. Even where access is granted, the data will almost certainly have not been collected in an ideal way, i.e. not collected prior to the policy being implemented; no data on 'control' firms included; data on 'administrative selection' not collected.

The challenge then for the research community is to persuade policy makers that it is in their long term interests to carefully appraise policy, and to be involved with that appraisal prior to policies being introduced. Unfortunately such ideas may be somewhat naive since policy makers with apparently often very limited budgets prefer 'cheap and cheerful' research which will yield them 'positive' findings, rather than accurate and careful research where policy impact is likely to be less. The emphasis which most governments have upon competitive tendering for research contracts only serves to reinforce these competitive advantages of the 'cheap and cheerful' brigade.

References:

Barclays Bank (1998), *Small Business Review*, London.

Bendick, M. Jr., and Egan, M.L. (1987), "Transfer Payment Diversion for Small Business Development: British and French Experience". *Industrial and Labor Relations Review*, 40, pp.528-42

Bridge, S. O'Neill, K. and Cromie, S. (1998), *Understanding Enterprise, Entrepreneurship and Small Business.* MacMillan, London

Brown, C., Hamilton, J., and Medoff, J. (1990), *Employers Large and Small.* Harvard University Press, Cambridge, Mass.

Christman, J.J., Nelson, R.R. Hoy, F. and Robinson, R.B. (1985), "The Impact of SBDC Consulting Activities". *Journal of Small Business Management*, July, pp.1-11.

Cosh, A. Duncan, J. and Hughes, A. (1998), "Investment in Training and Small Firm Growth and Survival: An Empirical Analysis for the UK 1987-95". *DfEE Report* No.36

Deschoolmeester, D. Schamp, T. and Vandenbroucke, A.M. (1998), *The Influence of Management Training on Entrepreneurial Attitudes and Managerial Techniques of SMEs.* deVlerick School of Management, Ghent.

Dolton, P.J., Makepeace, G.H. and van der Klaaw, W. (1989), *Occupational Choice and Earnings Determination: The Role of Sample Selection and Non-Pecuniary Factors.* Oxford Economic Papers 41: 573-94.

DTI (1998), *Small Business Action Update*, Department of Trade and Industry, London, June.

Elstrot, J.B. (1987), "Procedures for Improving the Evaluation of SBDC Consulting Activities". *Journal of Small Business Management*, January, pp.67-75.

ENSR (1997). *The European Observatory for SMEs*, EIM, Zoetermeer, Netherlands.

Ernst & Young (1996), *Evaluation of Business Links.* Department of Trade and Industry, London.

Harrison, R.T. and Leitch, C.M. (1996), "Whatever You Hit Call the Target: An Alternative Approach to Small Business Policy", in *Small Firm Formation and Regional Economic Development*, M.W. Danson (ed), Routledge, London and New York.

Hart, M. and Scott, R. (1994), "Measuring the Effectiveness of Small Firm Policy: Some Lessons from Northern Ireland". *Regional Studies*, Vol.28, No.8, pp.849-858.

House of Commons, Trade and Industry Committee (1998). "Small and Medium Sized Enterprises", *Sixth Report*, The Stationary Office, London.

Hughes, A. (1997), *Small Firms and Employment*, ESRC Centre for Business Research WP 71, September, University of Cambridge.

de Koning, A. and Snijders, J. (1992). "Policy on Small and Medium Sized Enterprises in Countries of the European Community", *International Small Business Journal*, Vol.10, No.3, pp.25-39.

LaLonde, R.J. (1986), "Evaluating the Econometric Evaluations of Training Programs with Experimental Data". *American Economic Review*, Vol.76, No.4, pp.604-620.

Lerner, J. (1997), *The Government as Venture Capitalist: The Long Run Impact of the SBIR Programme.* Harvard Business School.

Moint, A.H. (1998), "Small Firms Exporting: How Effective are Government Export Assistance Programs". *Journal of Small Business Management,* January, pp.1-15.

O.E.C.D. (1995, 1996, 1997), "Best Practice Policies for Small and Medium Sized Enterprises" Paris.

O'Higgins, N. (1994), "YTS, Employment and Sample Selection Bias". *Oxford Economic Papers* 46: 605-28.

Rogoff, E.G. and Lee, M.S. (1996), "Putting Government's Role in Perspective: The Impact of Government Programmes on Entrepreneurs and Small Business Owners". *Journal of Developmental Entrepreneurship*, Vol.1, No.1, Spring, pp.57-73.

Sardar, J.H., Ghosh, D. and Rosa, P. (1997), "The Importance of Support Services to Small Enterprise in Bangladesh". *Journal of Small Business Management*, Vol.35, No.2, April, pp.26-36.

Segal Quince Wicksteed (1991b), *Evaluation of the Consultancy Initiatives - Third Stage.* Department of Trade and Industry, HMSO, London.

Storey, D.J. (1994), *Understanding the Small Business Sector.* Routledge/ITP, London.

Storey, D.J. and Strange, A. (1992), "Entrepreneurship in Cleveland 1979-1989: A Study of the Effects of the Enterprise Culture". Employment Department, *Research Series* No.3.

Westhead, P. and Storey, D.J. (1994), *An Assessment of Firms Located on and off Science Parks in the UK*. London, HMSO.

Wren, C. and Storey, D.J. (1998), "Estimating the Impact of Publicly Subsidised Advisory Services upon Small Firm Performance: The Case of the DTI Marketing Initiative". *SME Working Paper* No.58.

Printed in the United Kingdom
by Lightning Source UK Ltd.
130542UK00002BA/16-30/A

9 780954 667313